THE
PATH
FINDERS

THE ELITE RAF FORCE THAT
TURNED THE TIDE OF WWII

WILL IREDALE

WH ALLEN

1

WH Allen, an imprint of Ebury Publishing,
20 Vauxhall Bridge Road,
London SW1V 2SA

WH Allen is part of the Penguin Random House group of companies
whose addresses can be found at global.penguinrandomhouse.com

Penguin
Random House
UK

First published in the United Kingdom by WH Allen in 2021
This edition published in the United Kingdom by WH Allen in 2022

www.penguin.co.uk

A CIP catalogue record for this book is available from the British Library

ISBN 9780753557822

Printed and bound in Great Britain by Clays Ltd, Elcograf S.p.A.

The authorised representative in the EEA is Penguin Random House Ireland,
Morrison Chambers, 32 Nassau Street, Dublin D02 YH68

For Polly

Contents

Part Four – The Rapier and the Sledgehammer
(June 1943–February 1944)

Part Five – Relentless Skies
(March 1944–May 1945)

Cast of Characters

Sir Arthur Harris: Air Officer Commanding-in-Chief (AOC-in-C), RAF Bomber Command

Sydney Bufton: Deputy Director (later Director) of Bomber Operations, Air Ministry

Don Bennett: Air Officer Commanding (AOC) RAF Bomber Command Pathfinder Force (8 Group)

Ralph Cochrane: AOC RAF Bomber Command 5 Group

Hamish Mahaddie: pilot and Pathfinder training inspector

John 'Doc' Macgown: Pathfinder medical officer

Dr Wilfred Coxon: Technical Officer, Directorate of Armament Development, and inventor of the target indicator

Dr Alec Reeves: inventor of Oboe

Dr Bernard O'Kane: co-inventor of H2S

Allan Ball: wireless operator, 35 Squadron

Colin Bell: pilot, 608 Squadron

Ian Bazalgette: pilot, 635 Squadron

Max Bryant: navigator, 156 Squadron

John Christie: pilot, 35 Squadron

Alec Cranswick: pilot, 35 Squadron

Ulric Cross: navigator, 139 Squadron

Ernie Holmes: pilot, 35 Squadron

John Kelly: pilot, 83 Squadron

John Ottewell: navigator, 7 Squadron

Dick Raymond: flight engineer, 83 Squadron

Gwen Thomas: Pathfinder signals' teleprinter operator

Prologue

TUESDAY, 19 MAY 1942. The bubbly song of the nightingale drifted on the warm air as the technicians finished setting up their recording equipment in the fading light of the early summer evening.

Two decades before, the BBC had made its first ever live outside broadcast as the renowned cellist Beatrice Harrison played to a nightingale singing in the woods around her Surrey home. It had gone down a storm with the public listening on the radio, and live performances of Harrison and the nightingales had been broadcast most years since.[1]

Now, once again, millions of people across Britain were preparing to tune in to the wireless and enjoy a few minutes of magical escape from the grim reality of war. As the technicians started recording, all that could be heard was the proud song of the little bird and the single distant whistle of a steam train.

However, another sound soon emerged. The soft hum of a solitary aeroplane high above, its tone changing as it flew overhead. Within minutes more planes followed. The hum became a drone until the sky all around throbbed with hundreds of engines.

Guessing the aircraft were from the RAF's Bomber Command on a mission to Germany, the BBC pulled the live feed, fearing the broadcast could potentially alert the Germans to an impending raid. But they kept the recording running, capturing the poignancy of the moment as the passing bombers failed to silence the plucky nightingale.

Two miles above, 29-year-old Hector Pilling focused on the controls of his Stirling bomber. The 6,380 horsepower from its four Bristol Hercules engines steadily pulled the 27-ton aircraft through the black sky towards the English coastline. An hour earlier, Pilling and his six RAF 7 Squadron crewmates had taken off from RAF Oakington in Cambridgeshire. After joining up in the air with almost 200 other aircraft from Bomber Command bases around eastern England, they headed towards mainland Europe.[2]

More than 1,000 men – most in their teens or early twenties – flew alongside Pilling in their cramped bombers, focused on the mission ahead. Their objective was to attack Mannheim, an industrial town straddling the River Rhine in south-west Germany.

Fresh-faced and good-looking, Pilling was a popular figure in his squadron. He took pride in helping new crews learn the ropes. 'He flopped, he sprawled, and he walked or rather shuffled along, with a rolling gait. He spoke in a jerky manner, clipping and gobbling his words,' said one friend. 'But behind all this was a decisive, forceful personality . . . full of fun and enthusiasm.'[3]

The son of a diplomat, Pilling was born in Fiji, grew up in New Zealand and read law at Brasenose College, Oxford. Like many who went on to fly in wartime Bomber Command, he had joined a university air squadron, which promised the chance to fly and meet well-connected types in the RAF. A keen oarsman, Pilling prepared for a 1933 regatta by giving up alcohol and living on a milk diet. He fell off the wagon for the boozy university air squadron summer dinner and ended the evening over-enthusiastically bear-hugging the chief instructor – who happened to be Keith Park, the First World War flying ace and future Fighter Command commander during the Battle of Britain.

No lasting harm was done, however, and by 1941 Pilling had volunteered for the RAF. He wanted to be a fighter pilot. 'Bombers don't much interest me,' he'd written home. But it was not to be. He excelled as a pilot and Bomber Command was desperate for decent 'drivers'.

Five months later he'd started operations over Germany: '"Ops" themselves are not too bad, though they have their shaking moments . . .

Started with a rather warm visit to Cologne where alternately I chewed gum hard or held my breath'.

In another bombing raid, on the French port of Brest, Pilling's crew came under attack from three German fighters. His crew shot down one, peppered a second with gunfire, and the third broke off its attack, '. . . at which Hector became so furious that he turned round and chased it all the way back to Brest. I can picture him sitting at the controls getting very red in the face and muttering "imprecations",' his navigator said later.

Now, as they headed towards Mannheim, Pilling drew on the experience of 26 successful operations under his belt – many against the heavily defended German industrial heartland in the Ruhr Valley. But he badly needed a rest from operational flying. 'The Ruhr grows less attractive every day,' he wrote a few days before. 'I have had rather a bellyful of it relieved, occasionally by visits to hospitable Hamburg and the like.'

Despite their relative familiarity with the route, as the bomber force approached Mannheim in the early hours of 20 May, without decent navigational aids many of the crews struggled to locate their targets – even though the glow of fires started by the initial bombs could be seen 100 miles away.

Worse still, they had woken up the *Nachtjäger* – the feared German night fighters – which began plucking off the lumbering British bombers as they began their return journey across the Low Countries towards England.

They included German Luftwaffe pilot Friedrich Gutezeit, a 27-year-old Oberleutnant nicknamed 'Fritz' by his squadron mates. Targeting the British aircraft gave him the chance to bag his third kill of the war. It had been a long time coming. Almost three years before, on 1 September 1939, he had become one of the first Luftwaffe pilots to claim a victory in the war by shooting down a Polish P-24 fighter aircraft. In April 1941 he claimed an RAF Wellington bomber. Another British kill now would be a major achievement.

Piloting a Messerschmitt Bf 110 – a twin-engine heavy fighter armed with two 20mm cannons and four 7.92mm machine guns – Gutezeit patrolled a 30-mile square box of sky through which the

returning British bombers flew. Via radio, German ground controllers directed him using radar towards a British Stirling flying at
14,000 feet.

Pilling and his crew had found Mannheim, but the relief at dropping their 96 incendiary bombs and heading for home was short-lived.
Cannon fire from Gutezeit's aircraft ripped through the soft skin of
the Stirling and ruptured the fuel tank, causing a massive explosion.

Gutezeit had scored another aerial victory at last.

But his satisfaction lasted seconds. Red-hot metal spewed out from
the Stirling and sliced through Gutezeit's plane as he tried to fly clear.
In his hunger to claim another kill, Gutezeit paid the ultimate price.
He and a crewmate were killed, along with Pilling and his six young
crewmates. The twisted, charred wreckage of metal, bone and flesh
from both aircraft was strewn across a Belgian field.[4]

The returning British bombers touched down on airfields across
England at around 4am. As the airmen were debriefed over cigarettes
and rum-laced cups of coffee, it became clear the mission to Mannheim had been a complete failure. Eleven RAF bombers had been lost,
killing 46 men, with another 23 captured.

However, just as concerning for Bomber Command was that while
155 of the 200 aircraft that took off had reported hitting Mannheim,
the bombing photographs from their onboard cameras revealed most
had dropped their bombs on forests or open countryside.

Bombs from just ten aircraft had actually landed on the town, hitting a blanket factory, a mineral-water factory, a chemical wholesaler
and a timber merchant. The only fatal casualties on the ground were
two German firemen.[5] It wouldn't exactly cause the German high
command to panic.

'Station and squadron commanders must endeavour to impress
upon all their crews the great extent to which our present effort is
being rendered abortive by indiscriminate bombing,' said an angry
commanding officer of one RAF bomber group three days later.[6]

This sorry state of affairs could hardly be blamed solely on the men
who crewed the aircraft. After horrific losses in the first two years of
the war, Bomber Command realised obsolete aircraft could not defend
themselves in the clear light of day. They had been forced to abandon

daylight bombing and turn to the concealment of night raids, for which their crews were neither adequately trained nor given the tools they needed to operate effectively.

Flying through the pitch black to find a target hundreds of miles away was hard enough. But combined with the foul weather, enemy night fighters and hundreds of anti-aircraft guns, the efforts of the brave crews were all the more commendable. And despite a change in strategy to chip away at the morale of the German people by attacking towns and cities, the failures of the Mannheim raid proved this was still a feat too far for many bomber crews.

The RAF's own evidence from the previous year showed that of those crews who claimed to have made a successful attack on a target, only one in three had been within five miles of it. On moonless nights this ratio fell to a measly 1 in 15.[7]

'I foresee a never-ending struggle to circumvent the law that we cannot see in the dark,' one senior RAF figure observed wearily.[8]

In a memo written a month before the Mannheim raid, the RAF's Director of Intelligence had warned that 'powerful agents' were at work in the British Government to dismantle Bomber Command. He forecast that unless results improved, there was a 'very grave risk of our striking force being subjected to a constitutional change which disregards the accepted principles of the role of a bomber force. This might prove calamitous in spite of an apparent justification for the disintegration of Bomber Command'.[9]

This was a life or death moment for Bomber Command. It was the only part of the Allied war effort with the potential to strike at the heart of Nazi Germany, but it was failing to accurately hit its targets at night – the most essential part of its job. For Britain's Prime Minister Winston Churchill and his Chiefs of Staff, something radical needed to be done – and fast.

Introduction

T HE PATHFINDERS WERE THE *corps d'élite* of Britain's air bombing campaign over mainland Europe. A secret air force of 20,000 teenagers and men in their early twenties which transformed Bomber Command from the brink of extinction in 1942 to a weapon capable of razing whole cities to the ground in a single night or hitting targets just a few hundred feet wide.

The secret of its success was an unlikely combination of characters, including a humble university chemistry lecturer and fireworks boffin, a clairvoyant Scottish scientist who invented the world's first bombing device that could see in the dark, and an abrasive Australian cowboy considered to be one of the most talented airmen of the war.

At the very heart of the Pathfinders' formation, evolution and ongoing survival lay a battle of alpha-male personalities, giant egos and entrenched rivalries. This book will reveal the fascinating story of how the Pathfinder force was created and how it became a pawn in a bitter power struggle between senior commanders which threatened to tear Bomber Command apart.

It will also tell the tales of the brave effort by thousands of ordinary young men thrust into extraordinary circumstances as Pathfinders, who didn't know or really care about the political machinations of their bosses. Their fight was for survival and their job was clear: to fly over enemy territory to locate and 'mark' targets in the dark so that the main force of Bomber Command's aircraft following behind could bomb accurately – or at least try to.

Pathfinder airmen took to the skies in iconic British aircraft such as the Lancaster and the Mosquito, facing hours of often monotonous existence punctuated by fearful periods of unimaginable violence from enemy fighter planes, anti-aircraft flak and foul weather. To be a bomber boy operating inside an aircraft was to experience a life of extremes. One minute they might be enduring temperatures 20 times colder than a fridge freezer, the next fighting a blazing inferno of over 500°C.

In its quest to achieve more effective bombing, the Pathfinder force turned to cutting-edge devices such as radio and radar, in a scientific game of cat and mouse with the Nazis – pitting British and German scientists against each other in a race to develop the airborne technology that would win the war.

The Pathfinder force was also supplied with specially designed 'target indicators' built with the help of Britain's fireworks industry. Vivid yellow, red and green flares, each burning as bright as a hundred street lamps, were dropped onto a target so the bombers thousands of feet above had an aiming point shining through cloud, smoke or haze. Young airmen who as children had gawped in wide-eyed awe at pre-war fireworks displays were now using the same materials to wreak death and destruction on the enemy.

Combined with daring new flight tactics, the Pathfinders turned Britain's air bombing force from an impotent and increasingly obsolete unit to a slick operation where 900 aircraft could pass over a target in just 20 minutes, repeatedly pounding an area just a few miles wide.[1] In a series of Pathfinder-led attacks on the German city of Hamburg during the summer of 1943, two thirds as many Germans were killed in a single week as the Luftwaffe had managed in its combined raids across Britain throughout the entire war.[2]

In the RAF's push to bomb Germany into submission, the raw power and destruction for those on the receiving end was truly grim. One British newspaper reported in December 1943 that since the introduction of the Pathfinder Force 'many of our recent attacks on Germany have reached a rate of 120 tons per square mile per hour, or eighty times the intensity of the heaviest air raid on London.'[3]

Central to the RAF approach was the divisive concept of area bombing – the widespread and sometimes undiscerning destruction of mostly German cities under the cover of darkness. In terms of the raw statistics, the figures are horrific. Combined with the daylight bombing of Germany by the American Eighth Air Force, Allied bombing killed 600,000 Germans – overwhelmingly civilians. Between 1939 and 1945, Bomber Command lost at least 55,573 young airmen. Incredibly, an RAF crewman in Bomber Command had a higher chance of dying than a junior infantry officer on the Western Front in 1916.[4]

Were these sacrifices justified? As one British historian has observed: 'This is the ugly reality of Total War that our wartime generation had to carry out. War isn't about winning, but about who loses the least.'[4]

At the time, in the heat of war, the morality of area bombing was not paramount. Airmen and their commanders had little time for abstract theories of right or wrong, or the nuances of international law. In one rare political statement, a Pathfinder navigator carried a brick wrapped in a copy of the *Jewish Chronicle*, which he threw out of the cockpit window over Germany in the hope it would 'drop on some Nazi bastard's head'.[6] But by and large, most men didn't dwell on such matters – their aim was simply to survive another operation.

The effective bombing of Germany was driven by inter-service rivalry, operational possibilities, strategic intentions, a hatred for the enemy and a desire for revenge. In other words – the RAF would do whatever it took to make Bomber Command the most lethal and effective bombing force possible in order to destroy German industry, demoralise its civilians and bring about victory over Hitler.

Thanks to the Pathfinders, the numbers of Bomber Command crews reaching within three miles of their targets rose from as low as 25 per cent in August 1942 to 95 per cent in some operations in April 1945.[7] This increasing accuracy played a critical role in the bombing ahead of the Allied D-Day invasion in June 1944 and the advance across Europe.

I have sought to capture the vivid recollections of those who were there. Most Pathfinder airmen were volunteers, often – but not always – hand-picked from the cream of the regular crews and specially trained for the role, who knew the odds were stacked against them.

Later in the war, as losses grew, the most promising students were plucked straight from operational training units.

The Pathfinders led some of the most nerve-wracking and important operations in the war, targeting the feared Ruhr Valley – grimly nicknamed 'Happy Valley' by the bomber crews – and the 'Big City' of Berlin, protected by the thin fingers of myriad searchlights and a ring of guns pumping thousands of shells into the air. But even against the hellish backdrop of a large bombing raid, there were moments of eerie beauty. After one mission to Hanover on 27 September 1943, a young bomb aimer on just his second sortie scribbled down in his diary how he watched the target indicators spill out from a Pathfinder aircraft:

> As we came nearer to the target there came an ethereal vision of a heavy attack under cloudless conditions. The searchlights stood around and formed a vast area of light as bright as day . . . Above the smoke and fires of the target within the circle of light I could see one vast pyramid of little brown clouds. There were thousands of them and they seemed to float so quietly there just like a colossal shoal of fish in a clear water tank lit by coloured lights from the bottom . . . Occasionally strings of tracer crawled slowly across the great cone and then suddenly there was something else. Shower after shower of green target indicators fell downwards like loose broken spheres of emerald snow. Now red ones like rubies and yellow ones like gold and then more green. And across the leeward rolled the smoke clouds glowing, below brown and black above.[8]

Pathfinders were required to open a raid, braving the flak and fighters before the main force arrived and swamped the defences. They were often exposed to dangers for longer than regular crews, required to repeatedly circle an area under attack to direct the main force or re-mark the target.

At the height of Britain's bombing campaign against the German capital between August 1943 and March 1944 – which became known as 'the 'Battle of Berlin' – the Pathfinders lost at least 210 crews on operations or in accidents and crashes.[9] In one horrific six-week period, 87 Pathfinder crews – more than 600 men – became casualties in missing or crashed aircraft. The two heaviest hit squadrons in Bomber Command during the Battle of Berlin were Pathfinders.[10]

The pressure and responsibility on Pathfinder aircrews leading the raids were immense. If they failed to accurately find, identify and mark the right target, as many as 6,000 airmen manning bombers in the skies behind would be risking their necks for nothing. Timings needed to be precise. On a mission to Berlin, for example, Pathfinder crews were expected to be at the target within a minute of their designated time – a margin of error of ten seconds for every 100 miles flown – despite enemy flak, German night fighters and bad weather.

And while a regular Bomber Command crew was expected to complete a tour of 30 consecutive missions, Pathfinders accepted a tour of duty of at least 45 missions – each mission lasting up to ten hours. They were attracted by an automatic rise in rank and pay, and the hope of earning the coveted golden eagle Pathfinder badge.

Little wonder the Pathfinders' commander Don Bennett claimed – albeit with some degree of bias – that the contribution of a Pathfinder 'in the same terms of intensity and duration of danger – and indeed of responsibility – was at least twice that of other Bomber Command crews'.[11]

Largely unknown too is the role played by the Pathfinders' Light Night Striking Force, flying the mostly wooden Mosquito – a plane so agile and quick it could outrun most enemy aircraft. It had no guns, yet carried the same bomb load as the American B-17 Flying Fortress – made famous by the battle-hardy *Memphis Belle* – and often flew two missions in a single night over Berlin.

More than 20,000 men were recruited as Pathfinders and over 3,600 were killed in action between 1942 and 1945. On average, a Pathfinder crew member could expect to die after 12 sorties. At one point of the war this figure stood at only eight sorties.[12]

However, despite these odds, some Pathfinder aircrew flew 100 missions in a row, in the full knowledge that if they were shot down and captured, they could be lynched by angry civilians, executed by the feared Gestapo or sent to a prisoner-of-war camp.

United in spirit by a 'press on' attitude, the Pathfinders were nevertheless an eclectic mix in background and origin. Coal miners rubbed shoulders with school teachers, accountants with farm labourers.

Crews were rich with different accents – Cockneys, Geordies, Scousers, or perhaps a soft West Country burr. More than half of the Pathfinder airmen came from Commonwealth countries, including Australia, New Zealand, South Africa and Canada. Others hailed from America, Norway and Hong Kong. Ulric Cross, a Trinidadian Mosquito-bomber navigator whose colleagues nicknamed the 'Black Hornet', became the most decorated West Indian of the war.

Pathfinder aircrew experienced rapid changes in fortunes. Just a few hours after facing a terrifying life or death fight for survival at 18,000 feet over a target, the Bomber Boys could be back in their warm beds on some quiet leafy aerodrome in Eastern England. And supporting them were thousands of ground crew. The armourers fusing the bombs. The fitters and riggers keeping *their* 'kites' airworthy. The young women of the Women's Auxiliary Air Force (WAAF) staffing the operations rooms. And when they weren't on 'ops', they drank in local pubs or headed to the nearest town for a night out.

Operating at such close proximity under high pressure with death so near provided a heady mixture. Airmen and airwomen flirted. Some married. Others had casual sex. WAAFs were exhorted to avoid sex because of the stigma of unwanted pregnancy, but it happened, of course. One medical officer from the Pathfinders suggested a scheme to provide accommodation, medical care and 'mothercraft' to support unmarried pregnant airwomen who could not, or would not, be looked after by their families.[13] This was contrary to Air Ministry policy of immediate expulsion from the service. The Pathfinders, it seems, were not just ahead of their peers in the technology they used.

But a story can only be fully told through the prism of all involved. The Pathfinder crews came to fear the German Luftwaffe night fighters, who specifically targeted the *Pfadfinder* before they had a chance to drop their brightly coloured target indicators. For the young Luftwaffe airmen flying the night fighters, the experiences were often equally violent and terrifying. German civilians braced themselves for nightly raids. Some were tasked with trying to extinguish the flares dropped by the Pathfinders – which the children nicknamed 'Christmas trees' – before they attracted the bombers of the RAF's main force.

It was the powerful BBC recording of the nightingale and the bombers on that fateful day in 1942 – which can be heard in full online 80 years later – that drew me to tell this story. I wanted to find out more about the raid the broadcast had unwittingly recorded. What happened, and why was it a failure? More importantly, how was Bomber Command transformed afterwards?

Pathfinders often feel their efforts have been overlooked. Many diaries and letters written at the time revealing their stories have remained untouched and unread for eight decades. Meanwhile, for many of those who survived – now all in their late nineties or older – this is the first time they have publicly spoken about their experience. For all, it will most probably be the last.

And with the last living link to the handful of surviving veterans just a few years from being broken for ever, their stories must be revealed now, so future generations never forget the sacrifices that were made for their benefit.

PART ONE

We Cannot See
in the Dark

NOVEMBER 1940 – JUNE 1942

CHAPTER ONE

X Marks the Spot

THURSDAY, 14 NOVEMBER 1940. Early evening. The moon was already shining brightly over Coventry as the pink glow from the winter sun faded in the west. It was going to be a beautiful crisp night. But many knew what a full moon meant. It was a bombers' sky.

The cobbled streets of the Midlands city thronged with people making their way home from work. Coventry wasn't an especially big place, but its population had swelled to around 260,000 over the previous decade, driven by the growth in heavy industry as war approached. Factories and warehouses fringed its medieval centre of timbered shops and houses, dominated by a magnificent Gothic cathedral. Dozens of companies, including Daimler, Armstrong Siddeley and Humber, manufactured military aircraft components on the outskirts of the city. Other firms made gear boxes for tanks, radios and guns.[1] One in every seven bombers produced during the war for the RAF came from a factory based in Coventry.[2]

This made it a legitimate target for enemy bombing. The people of Coventry had become used to trekking to the shelters on hearing the howl of the air-raid sirens, or decamping to the safety of the surrounding Warwickshire countryside by car, bus or even on foot. The city was supposedly protected from attack by at least 40 anti-aircraft (AA) guns and 64 barrage balloons.[3] But they'd been of little use in stopping the bombers so far. Since September, Luftwaffe bombers had pounded Britain's cities in what had become known as the Blitz.

Coventry had already endured 17 small raids. Yet nothing could have prepared its residents for the hell that was about to be unleashed.

As the moon rose over Coventry, 330 miles to the south at a grass airfield in Maucon, near the town of Vannes in Brittany, 52 young German airmen climbed into their bombers. To a casual observer, the thirteen Heinkel 111s – a workhorse plane of the Luftwaffe – looked like pretty standard aircraft. But two additional aerials on the rear fuselage gave an indication of their real intention. Each was packed with sophisticated electronic navigation equipment which would change the course of the bombing war in Europe. This was the home of the Kampfgruppe 100 – a special unit tasked with dropping fire-bombs onto British cities, with the resultant flames then used as a guide for the rest of the force to drop high-explosive bombs.

The Kampfgruppe 100 was established before the German invasion of Poland in September 1939. Directly under the control of Göring, it was a vital part of the Nazis' armoury in successfully softening British morale and destroying its war industry through aerial bombing. It only accepted the most elite crews, and the unit's emblem depicted a Viking longboat with a black hull and a red and white striped sail, painted on the noses of every aircraft.[4]

The airfield at Maucon was basic, with one small open-ended hangar and an old barn for a workshop. But aircrews stationed there lived a good life in comfortable local hotels, where they enjoyed fine food and wine. Later, as the pressure and strain of missions increased, an *Erholungsheim* – or convalescent home – was set up in the hotel of a local town, where men could recover from the strain of operational flying. Brittany's unspoilt beaches were only a few miles away. Morale in the unit was high.

The Kampfgruppe 100 also had the best equipment.[5] Throughout the 1930s German scientists designed and built a range of sophisticated electronic navigation aids. These had originally been developed as blind-landing devices to guide civil and military aircraft back to an airfield at night or in bad weather. But with war clouds looming, the boffins were tasked with converting them into tools of terror to help aircraft find their targets and bomb more accurately.

One system, called *Knickebein* (German for 'crooked leg') used two beams of radio pulses sent from separate transmitters on the ground.

The first sent Morse code dashes, the second dots. When they merged, the pilot heard a steady note through his headphones and knew he was on the right track to the target. The technology had been used to successfully destroy bridges in Warsaw when Germany invaded Poland in September 1939.[6] Knickebein soon became standard in most Luftwaffe aircraft.[7]

A second, more complex and accurate triangulation system called X–Verfahren[8] used an approach beam pointed at the target from a transmitter in Normandy, with three separate beams intersecting it from transmitters in the Pas de Calais. The first crossbeam was 30 miles from the target, the second 12 miles away and the third just before the target itself. Listening through headphones, the attacking German bomber crew knew by a change in the tenor of the beams if they were correctly on the approach beam, while the cross beams indicated how far they were from the target. When the aircraft met the final crossbeam at precisely the pre-calculated distance, a timer onboard automatically released the bombs.

It was state-of-the-art technology at the time, and on that chilly November evening it was about to be used by the Kampfgruppe 100 with devastating effect.

At around 6.15pm, the aldis lamp at the end of the runway flashed green. The pilot of the Heinkel 111 pushed the throttle forward until the little dial on his dashboard read 2,400 rpm, released the brake and felt a jerk as the two 1,200hp Junkers engines pulled the black four-man aircraft down the bumpy grass runway. Within minutes, 13 aircraft had taken off from Maucon and were heading north from the Brest peninsula over the English Channel. *Unternehmen Mondschein-sonate*, or Operation Moonlight Sonata – so named because it coincided with the full moon – had begun.

Soon after 7pm the leading Heinkel bomber crossed over the upper reaches of the River Thames west of Oxford and moved into the centre of the main approach beam targeting Coventry. The pilot concentrated on flying straight and level, maintaining a constant speed. Six minutes later – three miles south of the spa town of Leamington – the plane flew through the second crossbeam. In the gloom of the Heinkel's cabin, the young navigator pressed a button on the bomb release clock and the first of two black hands started ticking round a white analogue face, a bit like the sweeping hands of a stopwatch. About three miles south of Coventry the wireless operator next to him heard a steady note in his ear as the plane crossed the third beam and the observer pressed the button on his special bombing clock a second time. The first hand on the clock stopped and a second hand started rotating to catch it up. The bomb doors underneath the fuselage opened. When the clock hands coincided fifty seconds later, a pair of electrical contacts closed. They were over the target.

In the bomb rack below, 32 cylindrical canisters tumbled into the sky from the belly of the aircraft. After a few seconds, a tiny electro-magnet activated a clockwork mechanism inside each canister which released a rod linking two end plates. The canister split open, shedding 36 2.2lb incendiaries. The 14-inch long bombs had green tail fins designed to speed up their descent and punch a hole through tiled roofs when they landed. Each one was packed with highly flammable thermite – a mixture of ferrous oxide and powdered aluminium – that burst into flames on impact and burnt for up to 15 minutes. The raid on Coventry had started. The time was 7.20pm.[9]

In the streets below, the air-raid sirens had been whining for ten minutes. The planes rumbled overhead and the first incendiaries fell through the sky with a swishing noise, bursting into flames when they hit buildings and streets. To start with, dealing with the small incendiaries was manageable. ARP wardens and civilians knew what to do and most households had access to a stirrup pump which sucked water from a bucket into a jet to douse the flames. The incendiaries could also be popped into a bucket of sand or water using a long-handled shovel. Other more unusual methods included scooping them up with a dustpan and brush and chucking them in a galvanised dustbin.

One of the youngest ARP wardens in the city – 16-year-old Alan Hartley – lived with his parents in a 1930s semi-detached house in Grayswood Avenue, to the east of the city. As the sirens sounded he walked to the hall, donned his black steel helmet marked with a white 'M' that denoted he was a messenger, opened the front door and ran to the ARP post at the top of his road. When one of his colleagues was splattered with red-hot metal from an explosive device, Hartley rode on his bike to the city centre to fetch an ambulance. 'I will never, ever forget that ride. There was shrapnel from all the guns firing and I was heading to all the flames. The city was on fire,' he recalled.[10]

Later, with the raid intensifying, Hartley and a group of other messengers came across a number of small fires in a field. With no access to water or sand they heaved fresh cow pats onto the incendiaries and watched with satisfaction as the flames died away.

Others had less luck. Some incendiaries dropped by the German pathfinders had been fitted with a small explosive charge which detonated as the bomb was burning. William Wilson – the future MP for Coventry – was shovelling sand onto a fire when it exploded in his face, ripping the shovel from his grasp. He staggered away dazed and partially blinded and spent the rest of the night in a public shelter, before seeking treatment in hospital the following morning.[11]

Despite heroic efforts, the firefighters were soon overwhelmed as hundreds of incendiaries showered down. Everyone began to realise that this was unlike any other raid they'd experienced. Another stream of German bombers carrying high-explosive bombs and parachute mines approached Coventry from the east and more waves barrelled towards the city from the south.[12] One German pilot flying north-east over the English Channel caught sight of a small pinpoint of white light which looked like a torch. 'My crew and I speculated as to what it might be – some form of beacon to guide the British night fighters, perhaps. As we drew closer to our target the light gradually became larger until suddenly it dawned on us: we were looking at the burning city of Coventry.'[13] The pathfinders of the Kampfgruppe 100 had done their job, and German bombers were easily finding their target in their droves. Coventry's fate was sealed.

Over the next eleven hours 500 tons of high explosives and oil bombs 'rained in torrents' from 400 German aircraft, ripping apart Coventry's cathedral and streets.[14] The heat was so severe the lead from the cathedral melted down its drainpipes. Emergency services fought in vain. By 3am 200 fires had been reported. Fire hydrants were buried under debris and smaller fires had to be left to burn themselves out. Death was random and indiscriminate. Four police constables who had spent two hours trying to rescue trapped people were killed when a high-explosive bomb fell on them. 'I saw a van filled with bodies,' said one observer. 'Two men were carrying a stretcher with a body on it and a little girl was running after them screaming "Mother!" I shall never forget that all my life.'[15]

In another part of the city, Albert Bawien, a 36-year-old builder and a police special constable, seemed immune to the bombs falling all around as he repeatedly dodged blasts. He cheerfully reassured his colleagues, 'There's no bomb big enough for me', as he ran out yet again into the street from the police station to help rescue survivors.[16] He was killed moments later. Almost three quarters of Coventry's police force were killed or injured during the raid. A desperate plea saw 200 reinforcements arrive from surrounding forces.

The medical services struggled too. Two local hospitals continued taking in casualties despite being badly damaged. Some people had horrific injuries more usually seen in a battlefield hospital. Others were unmarked. A mother was wheeled in clutching a baby in her arms. At first the doctor treating them assumed they were asleep or had fainted. But to his horror, he realised they had been killed by massive internal injuries caused by the force of a bomb blast.[17] At the leading first-aid post, a single female doctor worked alone treating 180 casualties.

The anti-aircraft fire was intense but largely useless, as many German aircraft bombed above their range at heights of 20,000 feet or more. RAF air cover also proved impotent. Over 120 fighters were scrambled, but not one enemy aircraft was intercepted, despite the full moon and the glare of the fires which should have made it easier to spot the silhouettes of the attacking bombers.

At dawn the following morning, the full extent of the carnage was revealed. Swathes of the city's old town were totally destroyed. Hundreds of shops, ten pubs, six theatres and three churches lay in smoking ruins. The historic cathedral was no more. Once thriving streets were simply charred skeletons. Dozens of factories made useless. The air stank of burning flesh. A dog was seen running down the street with a child's severed arm in its mouth. One policeman leant down over a line of bodies stretched out on blankets, making a sign of the cross while gently weeping. A weary observer looked on: 'An earthquake could not have rendered the scene more desolate or distressing.'

At least 2,369 people had been made homeless and over 33,000 houses had been destroyed or damaged. Water, gas and electricity were knocked out. With an estimated 15,000 electric cookers installed in Coventry, many people could not cook food. The authorities quickly set up 50 field kitchens while another canteen provided 1,000 meals an hour. But fresh food was in short supply – 40,000 loaves of bread and 60,000lb of canned meat were ferried in. More than 400 unexploded bombs and others with delayed fuses continued to hamper rescue and salvage efforts. Simple, everyday tasks became deadly. A man was killed by a delayed-action bomb as he tried to get back into his house to retrieve some money.

But life went on and the clear-up began. When arrangements for free transport to evacuate 10,000 people out of the city were advertised, only 300 people turned up. A visit from the King two days later 'sealed the steadiness of the citizens' despite his weeping when he surveyed the damage. Some locals were even accused of becoming 'choosy' by rejecting the offer of free corned beef for their usual meat rations. 'If we can't roast it, we'll boil it or find some other way of cooking it,' they said. Efforts started to restore crucial utilities so the war factories could function again. Barclays Bank, which had taken a direct hit from a bomb in the central banking hall, was open for business 48 hours later. Coventry had 'taken it'.

But the 'Blitz spirit' was not universal. There was widespread anxiety for many weeks. Twenty-four people – including three soldiers and six children – were prosecuted for looting damaged houses and stealing coins from gas meters. Police had to disperse inquisitive onlookers who gathered in large groups to rubber-neck at the most damaged sites.

And the human cost of the accurate German bombing on Coventry was grim. The air-raid had killed 554 people and seriously injured 865. At one stage more than 60 bodies an hour arrived at the local mortuary. Half could not be identified because they were so mutilated. Timber for coffins ran out and people were buried in communal graves. The officiating clergy at one mass funeral looked back at the long line of mourners. 'At last the great crowd was gathered around the graves . . . in the distance against a grey, scudding sky, a Spitfire wheeled and twisted; the sound of its engine came fitfully to us down the wind.'[18]

The raid was all the more brutal because of the comparatively small size of the target. Unlike the sprawling miles of London, the death and destruction in Coventry seemed more intimate. Nearly everyone knew someone who had died. Entire families were killed, sheltering together under stairs and kitchen tables and in cellars. A local civil defence inspector surveying the scene on the ground reckoned Coventry had suffered 'the most terrible onslaught yet inflicted on a single town in this country'.

While the full moon had made the use of high-tech navigation almost superfluous, it laid bare the success of the Kampfgruppe 100 and opened the eyes of the RAF to the devastating potential of using aircraft as pathfinders to lead other crews. Air power had been used against a small city with the aim of obliterating it. 'The advantages to the attacker of good pathfinding were all too obvious,' noted an RAF intelligence report.[19] The raid on Coventry was not the first time the X–Verfahren system had been used by the Luftwaffe. But it was certainly one of the most effective, with an estimated 47 per cent of the aircraft despatched finding the target – more than any other raid in that period.[20]

Back in Berlin, the attack on Coventry was a propaganda win for the Nazis and the state-owned Deutschlandsender radio station milked it for all its worth, broadcasting numerous graphic accounts of the damage. 'Coventry is the first place to be attacked this way outside London and Liverpool, but we are bloody sure it's not going to be the last,' announced one broadcast. 'There is none of Coventry left . . . all night long the bombs fell . . . the loss of life is just appalling.' British intelligence monitoring German media reports wryly noted that the German commentators 'ransacked the dictionary for adjectives' to describe the devastation.[21] The Germans created a new verb, *coventrieren* – to Coventrate – to illustrate their awareness of the unprecedented damage the raid had achieved.

The British capital didn't escape the German pathfinders either. On 29 December 1940, the Kampfgruppe 100 led a devastating night-time raid on London. Ten aircraft opened the attack by dropping more than 11,000 incendiaries in the space of 33 minutes, followed by wave after wave of bombers which dropped almost 30,000 firebombs.[22] Soon, vast swathes of the city were in flames.

As he looked up at the sky, one London firefighter became 'absolutely fascinated' by the clouds of sparks: 'they were really very pretty.

We looked up and saw them, and they felt exactly like snowflakes. When they hit you in the face it was exactly the same reaction, of course, since the nerve centres which register heat and cold are very much the same.'[23]

A US war reporter based in the city cabled his office: 'The second Great Fire of London has begun'.[24] In the light created by the fires, confused flocks of pigeons flew around in circles thinking it was daytime. Christopher Wren's masterpiece, St Paul's Cathedral, was soon surrounded by fires and seemed doomed. Less than a mile away, 37-year-old photographer Herbert Mason climbed onto the roof of the *Daily Mail* newspaper's headquarters, just off Fleet Street, and snapped away on his camera. Mason's picture of the great cathedral standing proud amongst the smoke and flames was published around the world and quickly became an iconic symbol of London's defiance of the Blitz.

Once again, the German pathfinders had done their job. If left unchecked, they would continue guiding the German air force to yet more devastating raids. But unbeknown to the public, another secret and intensive air war was taking place in a battle to stop them, between the finest scientific brains in Britain and Germany.

CHAPTER TWO

Ruffians

O N 21 JUNE 1940, five months before the brutal raid on Coventry, the tension in the Cabinet Room of 10 Downing Street was decidedly frosty as a young, rather nervous-looking young man called Reginald Victor Jones walked in and quietly sat on a chair near the door.

Since the spring, the British had been aware of rumours that the Germans were using beams to direct their planes over Britain and locate targets, and had learnt as much as they could from interrogating Luftwaffe pilots who had been shot down. A team of Air Ministry boffins, led by Jones – an enthusiastic Oxford University physics graduate – were trying to crack how the German technology worked and the best ways to stop them. It became known as the 'Battle of the Beams'.

Jones – a tall man with lean, striking features who was known as RV – was obsessed with what he called 'chasing' scientific intelligence to help him uncover the secrets of the German beams. Every morning he would kiss his wife Vera goodbye and set off from their flat overlooking Kew Gardens in south-west London to catch the train from Richmond station, arriving at his Victoria Street office in Westminster around 10am.

Jones had seen first-hand just how effective the beams were in laying the path for German pathfinders to follow. One night he was having supper in his flat during an air raid when an incendiary dropped from a German bomber rattled across the roof, 'sounding rather like ghosts in hollow chains'. Looking out of the window, Jones saw the entire neighbourhood silhouetted in the pale bluish light from dozens of incendiaries. He quickly ushered his dinner guests to the window to marvel at the sight before shouting 'now run downstairs like hell!' a few seconds before bombs shook the building.[1]

Much of the intelligence provided to Jones came from experts at Bletchley Park in Buckinghamshire, who were busy decoding German radio signals from its Enigma machine. Tantalising snippets of what the Germans were doing also emerged through covert recordings of Luftwaffe aircrew who had been shot down and sent to the Prisoner of War Interrogation Centre in Trent Park – a large red-brick country house in Cockfosters, north London. Although most POWs were reluctant to give away secrets under interrogation, little did they realise their private conversations were being secretly monitored by hidden microphones.

This combined intelligence allowed Jones and his team to piece together vital information. Other 'gen' about the location of the beam transmitters in France was gleaned from sources such as notebooks found on German airmen shot down over England.

Jones reported to Churchill's friend and trusted scientific adviser, Professor Frederick Lindemann – 'Prof' was an important influence on much of the Prime Minister's wartime thinking – who subsequently warned Churchill about Jones's hunch that the Germans had developed a device which could bomb day or night whatever the weather, using a radio beam 'like an invisible search light' that could 'certainly hit a city or town'.[2]

Churchill needed to know more. On that warm, sunny morning of 21 June, Jones was summoned to Downing Street. Arriving 25 minutes late after thinking his secretary had been pulling his leg about the meeting, the brown-haired, fresh-faced Jones was ushered into the Cabinet Room. Sitting in front of him along a narrow, cloth-covered table were some of Britain's most senior military and scientific leaders – including Hugh Dowding, head of RAF Fighter Command, and Sir Henry Tizard, the chief scientific adviser and personal adviser to the Minister of Aircraft Production – and Churchill himself. The meeting was so secret even staff and secretaries had been forbidden from joining.

When Jones arrived, the dozen or so men were already in deep dis-
cussion about whether aircraft could in fact be guided by long-range
radio beams. Lindemann and Tizard had clashed – the latter insist-
ing that bending beams was not possible. Given the imposing
reception, Jones would have been forgiven for feeling nervous. He sat
down in a chair at the end of the table in the 'no man's land' between
the two sides, feeling rather isolated but wanting to appear impartial.
But as he listened to comments around the table, it quickly became
clear most of those gathered had little comprehension of what was at
stake.

'Although I was only 28,' Jones recalled later, 'and everyone else
round the table much my senior in every conventional way, the threat
of the beams was too serious for our response to be spoilt by any nerv-
ousness on my part.' Jones felt increasingly confident as the minutes
ticked by. He could see he would need to start from scratch and capture the imagination of the one man in the room who really mattered.
When, finally, Churchill asked him a direct question about the detail,
Jones ignored the question and replied: 'Would it help, sir, if I told you
the story right from the start?'[3]

Churchill was surprised. After a moment, he replied 'Well, yes. It
would!' He lit a cigar, sat back and listened as the young scientist's
calm, crucial words poured into the room. For Churchill, hearing the
drama unfold was enthralling. 'For twenty minutes or more he spoke
in quiet tones,' Churchill later recounted, 'unrolling his chain of cir-
cumstantial evidence the like of which for its convincing fascination
was never surpassed by the tales of Sherlock Holmes or Monsieur
Lecoq.'[4]

Jones had set Churchill's imagination alight, and was quietly exhil-
arated that he'd stood up to the PM's questioning and convinced him
of the need to act quickly. More importantly, he now had the ear of the
most powerful man in Britain.

Churchill was stunned by the 'painful shock' of what Jones and his
team had uncovered.[5] 'Being master, and not having to argue too
much,' Churchill later said, 'once I was convinced about the principles
of this queer and deadly game I gave all the necessary orders that very
day in June for the existence of the beam to be assumed, and for all
countermeasures to receive absolute priority.'[6]

It was, Churchill later said, 'one of the bleakest moments in the war'.[7] For him, despite the battle between the British and German air forces and the 'fortitude' of the British people, this was a secret war involving small scientific circles. 'No such warfare had ever been waged by mortal men. The terms in which it could be recorded or talked about were unintelligible to ordinary folk.'[8]

There was no time to lose. That night, spurred on by Churchill's support, Jones sent up a solitary Anson aeroplane which intercepted and confirmed the existence of the Knickebein beam – 400 yards wide, over Lincolnshire. It originated from Kleve, in Germany. This meant only one thing – the Germans intended to use the beam as a blind-bombing aid to attack Britain. A highly secret operation to try and destroy or distort the beams was launched. It was codenamed 'Headache', and by October 1940, the path of the other beams had been identified. Innocuous-looking wooden sheds and transmitters sprung up at 15 rural sites across the south and east of England. Little did locals realise that inside each hut young RAF wireless mechanics – part of a special new RAF department called '80 Wing' – were fighting a furious cat-and-dog electronic war with the crews of Luftwaffe bombers intent on destroying Britain. They were assisted by technicians from the BBC. Each radio transmitter – codenamed 'Aspirin' – sent out its own radio beams which transmitted a continuous note along the flight path of the German bombers, swamping the Knickebein beams that the German pilots were using, making it impossible for them to navigate effectively.[9] In the invisible battle of technology raging above the skies of Britain, the Allies had delivered the first blow – the 'crooked leg' was successfully hobbled.

But the problem of dealing with the Kampfgruppe 100 equipped with the X–Verfahren system remained. To start with, Jones and his team knew little about the technology and thought it might even be the same thing as Knickebein. This mystery was partly thanks to its great secrecy. One German airman was heard telling a colleague 'you get your head chopped off even if you discuss it',[10] and most airmen outside Kampfgruppe 100 genuinely knew very little about it. In another conversation, recorded on 19 June 1940, a Luftwaffe pilot confided to his colleague:

They are experimenting in dropping bombs blind. Can you imagine that? It works quite independently of the human brain, for when the wireless beams intersect at the correct angle, then the bombs are released and score an exact hit. There's no need for me to say, 'Now I must be over London so we will drop the bombs' . . . I can only tell you the theory of the thing. I have never seen it and don't know if it is being or is going to be used. I mean to say it is still a great problem, one of the problems of the future of the air force. Blind-bombing – dropping them on a pitch-dark night or through the clouds and so on – that indeed would be wonderful.[11]

Fate – or rather carelessness – handed Jones and his team the breakthrough they needed. On 6 November 1940, a Heinkel from Kampfgruppe 100 crash-landed on a beach off the coast of Dorset after the crew got lost. The three airmen were captured and their aircraft searched, where the onboard equipment for the system was discovered and taken away for analysis. It wasn't ideal – an inter-service squabble between the army and the navy about who was responsible for salvaging the wreck had wasted valuable hours and the rising tide had destroyed some of the equipment. But the somewhat waterlogged X-beam receivers they found allowed the British scientists to fill in some gaps in their previous suspicions.

Later, three POW Luftwaffe airmen – including one crew member from the shot-down plane – chatted in the ornate surroundings of Trent Park, not knowing they were being recorded. Both X–Verfahren and Kampfgruppe 100 were mentioned by name, as the other two German airmen tried to learn more about this elite unit and its tech-nology, and all three speculated as to what the Allies knew. After revealing some key details, the Kampfgruppe 100 airman said: 'Those things are strictly secret.' 'But apparently not secret enough,' one of the other POWs remarked.[12]

After gathering up the various intelligence and joining the dots, Jones and his team wrote a report about X–Verfahren, confirming it was different to Knickebein and that it was being used by the Kampf-gruppe 100. They codenamed the new system 'Ruffian'. Fresh intelligence from Bletchley Park revealed beam-transmitting stations on both the Brest Peninsula and Pas de Calais, which created the cross beams so crucial for the success of X–Verfahren. The report was sent to Churchill. It was time to act.

A plan was agreed to jam the X–Verfahren beams through a transmitting device codenamed 'Bromide', which after a slow start began to effectively hamper the impact of Kampfgruppe 100. By May 1941, only a quarter of German aircraft were getting the automatic 'bomb drop' signal from the beams.[13]

Yet, tragically, Bromide failed to help save the people of Coventry who had been targeted by the German pathfinders in November 1940. Although Bromide jamming devices were already in place by the time of the Coventry raid, it was later discovered that some of the Kampfgruppe 100 aircraft flew almost directly over them without being put off course. In a rush to set them up, the transmitters had been pre-set incorrectly by engineers and so proved useless. Jones later said that 'whoever had made such an error ought to have been shot'.[14] Although, given the stunning moonlit night, who knows if Bromide would have made much difference in stopping Kampfgruppe 100 finding their target.

Nevertheless, Churchill knew just what a close-run thing it had been and how brilliant his boffins were in cracking the German pathfinding technology before it was used more widely across Britain. 'If we had not mastered its profound meaning and used its mysteries even while we saw them only in the glimpse, all the efforts, all the prowess of fighting airmen, all the bravery and sacrifices of the people, would have been in vain,' he said later.[15]

Debate has also raged for 80 years as to what Churchill knew about the Coventry raid in advance and whether enough was done to try and prevent it. Three days before the raid, a Luftwaffe prisoner was covertly recorded revealing that an imminent raid was planned on Coventry or Birmingham, to coincide with the full moon between 15–20 November 1940. German signals also referred to a major operation with the codename 'Moonlight Sonata'. But there was no firm evidence to connect the major operation with Coventry. Only the word 'Korn' [or 'Corn'] was used, and the British didn't know this was the codename for the city.[16] According to some schools of thought post-war, Churchill was informed of all this and decided to sacrifice Coventry in order to keep the existence of the top-secret code breakers hidden. But what did Churchill really know before the raid?

After lunch on the day of the Coventry raid, 14 November 1940, Churchill climbed into his government car and set off for Ditchley Park – a grand country house in Oxfordshire which he used once a month when the moon was full and Chequers, the Prime Minister's official country residence, was vulnerable to German bombing. As the car sped through the London streets he opened the yellow box containing the most recent reports marked 'Top Secret' and began to read.

A decrypted German message suggested the likely targets for the big moonlight raid as central London or a number of towns in the south-east of England. More worryingly, it revealed that Göring himself had been involved in the planning, an indication of how important this particular raid was to Berlin. 'If further information indicates Coventry, Birmingham or elsewhere we hope to get out instructions in time,' the note concluded.[17] This was enough for Churchill. He immediately ordered his driver to turn the car around and headed back to London, convinced that the capital – and not Coventry – was the most likely target of German bombers that night. 'I am not going to spend the night peacefully in the country while the metropolis is under heavy attack,' he told his private secretary alongside him.[18]

Arriving back in Downing Street, Churchill sent his female staff home and packed his private secretaries off to 'the burrow' – his sumptuous personal air-raid shelter under a nearby underground station. 'You are too young to die,' Churchill told them.[19] As they enjoyed a supper of caviar, Perrier-Jouët 1928, 1865 brandy and Havana cigars, Churchill made his way to the Air Ministry roof in Whitehall and waited. But the bombers never came to London.

Even if Churchill had known for sure that Coventry was the target for a major raid that night, it's unlikely he would have ordered an evacuation of more than 200,000 people. As it was, the city was protected by over a hundred fighter planes, dozens of barrage balloons and anti-aircraft guns – reinforced just six days previously on Churchill's personal order: 'ACTION THIS DAY.'[20] But no one – including Churchill – had conclusive evidence Coventry was the target for that night's massive attack. And little did he, or anyone else, realise just how effective the work of the Kampfgruppe 100 would be.

As devastating as the raid was for the people of Coventry, the political and military ramifications were to prove far greater. The raid on Coventry had set a number of hares running, which would be crucial to RAF Bomber Command's eventual decision to create its own pathfinder unit.

First, it had given legitimacy to a greater focus on bombing towns and cities. 'There is a growing demand for reprisals on German towns,' said one local police report six days after the Coventry raid.[21]

A month later, the RAF sent a force of 134 aircraft – its biggest of the war yet – to Mannheim. It was a perfect moonlit night. The raid was spearheaded by eight RAF Vickers Wellington bombers carrying nothing but incendiaries. The rest of the RAF aircraft following were to use the fires started as an aiming point to inflict maximum damage to the centre of the town. But the Wellington bombers failed to accurately identify the target. The German authorities estimated 240 buildings were destroyed, with 34 people killed and 1,266 bombed out of their homes. Mannheim hadn't exactly been 'Coventrated'.[22]

Second, the raid on Mannheim brought home once again to the RAF high command the continuing challenge of bombing accurately in the dark. It was clear that, unlike their German counterparts, with no electronic bombing aids to help them, they were in no position to up the ante yet. But the Germans had shown them what could be done with cutting-edge technology.

While the impact of the Kampfgruppe 100 was certainly one of the contributing factors which led to the formation of the Pathfinder Force in 1942, the failure of the Mannheim raid and the inability of Bomber Command to exact effective raids could be traced back to its overall bombing strategy from before the war.

Bomber Command's strategy was based on something called the 'Western Air Plans' – a series of 16 plans outlining what the force could do, which included targeting a German advance by hitting supply and communication lines and airfields and attacking factories in Germany's vast industrial heartland in the Ruhr Valley – an area the size of Greater London which accounted for 60 per cent of Germany's vital industries.

Initially, Bomber Command flew during the day. Crews used maps to navigate. Over Britain, some relied on 'Bradshawing' – following railway lines detailed in *Bradshaw's*, a railway reference book named after George Bradshaw, the nineteenth-century English cartographer.[23] Commanders thought that by using bombers armed with their own guns and by flying in tight formation, they could defend against attacks from enemy planes. But this was a fallacy, and RAF crews – mainly comprising pre-war professionals, RAF reservists and early volunteers – were hacked down from the sky, the odds stacked against them.

In the early months of the war, Bomber Command consisted of 33 operational squadrons and 280 aircraft which were largely unsuitable for the new war they faced.[24] The Fairey Battle, for example, had an all-metal fuselage which one crew nicknamed the 'tin Lizzie'. The three-man crew sat under a long, glazed canopy that resembled a Victorian potting shed. Slow and cumbersome, armed with a brace of .303 machine guns, it was a sitting duck for more advanced German fighters. In one operation over the Ardennes in May 1940, 40 Battles were shot down out of a force of 71.[25]

Other front-line aircraft in Bomber Command's inventory included the Bristol Blenheim, the Armstrong Whitworth Whitley and the Handley Page Hampden. Although they were reasonably modern and all had their brief moments of glory – mainly down to the skills of the crew flying them – they were outclassed in daylight raids by an enemy using high-performance fighters. Perhaps the only exception was the Vickers Wellington, which was given the affectionate moniker of 'Wimpy'. Made of a lattice-like structure which creaked and groaned as it flew, the Wimpy had a crew of five or six and could carry 4,500lb of bombs up to 700 miles, powered by two Bristol Pegasus engines with a top speed of 250mph. Nevertheless, in one raid half a force of 24 Wellingtons were lost – along with their valuable crews – ten times the acceptable casualty rate Bomber Command could afford.

The Luftwaffe, meanwhile, had a fighter force of over a thousand Messerschmitt Bf 109 interceptor fighters and Messerschmitt Bf 110 Zerstörer (destroyer) heavy fighters that ripped into the British bombing fleet, exposing their puny defences. In the first four months of the war the percentage of Bomber Command losses per operation were almost three times greater than at any other point in the conflict.[26] 'We rather expected to be blown out of the sky,' said one British airman.[27]

And while moves had been underway since 1936 to eventually replace most of these aircraft with better types and long-range heavy bombers, in the interim their outdated combat performance was matched by the conditions facing the crews flying them. Returning to Britain after a leaflet-dropping mission over Frankfurt and Düsseldorf in 1940, a crew flying a Whitley almost froze to death because there was no heating. The navigator and his commanding officer resorted to the almost farcical measure of repeatedly headbutting the metal floor and the navigation table in order to experience some form of alternative pain, hoping to take their minds off the frostbite.[28]

With losses mounting, by the middle of 1940 Bomber Command was forced to fly largely by night, knowing that at that stage German aircraft lacked electronic navigation to prevent night attacks. But this shift to darkness brought even greater challenges. Less than one in ten training flights by Bomber Command pre-war had taken place at night.[29] The crews just weren't used to this pioneering form of warfare. And, like Britain, mainland Europe was plunged into darkness with a widespread blackout. Some targets were attacked from heights of 8,000 to 12,000 feet, with crews first dropping flares by parachute to try and light up a specific target, or by using the moonlight. But, on average, only 10 per cent of the moonlight falling on the ground was reflected back, making accurate bearings from rivers or coastlines very difficult.[30] The moonlight also increased the chances of attacks from German fighters, whose pilots could spot the British aircraft more easily. For the rest of the time, when there was little or no moonlight or the ground was covered by cloud or haze, navigating accurately was a pipe dream. It wasn't unusual for aircraft to be buzzing about for up to an hour, groping to find the target.

Little wonder, given the tools to hand. To navigate at night, the RAF used a combination of methods, including dead reckoning – essentially working out how long it should take to arrive over the general area of the target based on distance and the speed and direction of the wind. But this could leave bombers 30 or 40 miles adrift from most targets in Germany.[31] Another favoured device was astro-navigation from a sextant – an instrument originally invented more than 200 years before, which relied on taking in-flight 'fixes' from the stars and planets and using complex mathematical calculations. One airman likened the process to 'sitting in a freezing cold stair cupboard with the door shut, the Hoover running, and trying to do calculus'.[32]

The contrast between a Bomber Command observer fumbling about in the vibrating fuselage hoping to get a sextant fix and a German pathfinder attacking Britain using cutting-edge radio beams couldn't have been greater.

German technology had also been called upon to create early warning radar which alerted fighters and flak batteries to incoming bombing raids. Although they weren't above resorting to less technical measures to try and stop Bomber Command: if they could not see the enemy in the dark, why not simply light up the sky? By June 1940, over 4,000 searchlights were positioned around key industrial areas in Germany. Bombers had to fly through probing fingers of white light which joined together to form cones, instantly turning night into day and exposing aircraft to flak and fighters.[33]

Darkness, enemy fighters and flak combined with the regular bad weather over northern Europe to make effective bombing almost impossible. Many crews were close to cracking. Raids were small and only one third of aircraft despatched reached their targets. Most of the bombs – too puny in size to cause much damage – fell in open countryside. 'The constant struggle at night is to get light onto the target,' said one RAF Commander, who foresaw 'a never-ending struggle to circumvent the law that we cannot see in the dark . . .'[34]

In other words, there was little point in having an air force unless it could hit the targets it wanted to, which could only happen with better-trained men, improved aircraft and sophisticated navigation. That struggle would continue until the formation of the Pathfinder Force in 1942, and before then Bomber Command would face even harder times.

Nevertheless, despite these limitations, in 1940 Bomber Command was still the only force which could attack the heart of Germany and prevent the initiative from passing entirely into the hands of Hitler. The restricted bombing strategy began to be lifted when Winston Churchill became Prime Minister on 10 May 1940. Churchill was less squeamish than Chamberlain about attacking targets in urban areas, so long as they had a military value. This view was solidified during the Battle of France, as the need to strike harder at Germany's war industry in the Ruhr ever clearer. On 15 May 1940, the British War Cabinet authorised Bomber Command to send 99 bombers to attack oil and railway targets in the Ruhr. And so began perhaps the most continuous and gruelling operation of the entire war, lasting for the next five years.[35] Bomber Command was ordered to target urban areas in Germany in greater scale – including chipping away at the morale of civilians – eventually paving the way for full-scale area bombing of cities from 1942. 'The Navy can lose us the war, but only the Air Force can win it,' Churchill told his Cabinet and Chiefs of Staff. '. . . the Fighters are our salvation, but the Bombers alone provide the means of victory.'[36]

A vast expansion programme was underway. While the Germans produced more aircraft than Britain between 1934 and 1938, in 1939 the figures were equal, and the following year Britain was outproducing Germany in airframes and engines by 50 per cent.[37] The creation of a Ministry of Aircraft Production oversaw a drive to build a powerful air force. Soon, the skies would be filled with a new generation of four-engine 'heavies', including the legendary Avro Lancaster – each with a crew of as many as eight men, all with specialist roles – and the lighter but very fast twin-engine de Havilland Mosquito.

New recruits were urgently needed to fly these new aircraft, and between 1940 and 1943 the RAF issued a worldwide call to arms, embarking on a push to attract more young men on 'hostilities only' commissions. Bomber Command would become a vast force of united nations – men and women signing up only for the duration of the war before returning to civilian life afterwards. And although they didn't yet know it, many would become Pathfinders, spearheading the largest aerial bombing force the world had ever seen.

CHAPTER THREE

Flying like Icarus

C OLIN BELL WASN'T THINKING of flying as he walked towards Hampton Court Bridge in the warm autumnal sunshine late one afternoon in October 1940. Instead, he was looking forward to a fun evening out with his new girlfriend in south-west London. But the 19-year-old's romantic endeavours were rudely interrupted by the piercing whistle of a German bomb, which fell on a house a hundred feet away. There was a 'flash of violet light and an almighty crash,' remembers Bell. 'Everything was blotted out in a cloud of smoke and dust. I heard cries from inside the house and almost immediately rescuers arrived and pulled the poor victims out.'[1]

This was Bell's first experience of the Blitz, as waves of German aircraft hammered the capital. Born in London in 1921, Bell was the son of a civil servant, whose family moved home regularly 'because my mother had permanently itchy feet', which made conventional schooling impossible. For Bell, boarding at a private school was out of the question. 'I had a thing against public schools because, as my mother delicately put it, she had no wish to send her son to a school to be beaten and buggered.'

Instead, Bell and his older brother were educated at home by private tutors. Naturally, being cooped up at home together led to sibling tensions. Bell and his brother 'fought like dogs' and he was usually on the losing end. But it toughened him up, so when he was occasionally enrolled in a school he became well accustomed to fighting his own corner. 'It gave me very thick skin,' said Bell.

One of the many suburbs Bell's family lived in was Hendon, in north London, which happened to be next to an RAF aerodrome. Like numerous boys growing up in the 1920s and 30s, he became fascinated with the biplanes buzzing overhead. One year, Bell's father took him to see the annual Hendon air display, an early summer event attracting crowds of over 100,000.

The display ended with a mock bombing attack by biplanes on a fort overrun by enemy tribesmen and then gallantly re-taken by intrepid soldiers. For a young boy, it was gripping stuff. 'How I longed to be a Royal Air Force pilot in that fantasy world!' said Bell. His near miss from the German bomb in October 1940 merely cemented that desire to volunteer. 'I wanted to be a pilot anyway, but that sort of gave me added impetus and made me think, *I want to have a go at them.*' When he was old enough, Bell signed up with the RAF with the ambition of becoming a pilot.

Like Bell, thousands of young men and women answered a call to arms and volunteered for the RAF. While their paths were destined to converge as part of Bomber Command's Pathfinder Force, their initial inspirations for wanting to take to the skies were as varied as the backgrounds they came from and the countries they were born in.

Sometimes that trigger to 'have a go' was prompted by more visceral experiences. The day after German bombers had pounded Coventry in November 1940, 19-year-old John Trotman arrived in the city to be greeted by a hellish scene. Trotman was a cadet RAF pilot stationed at a local airfield, who had been asked to help the Civil Defence teams in the clear up. Armed with picks and shovels, loaded onto lorries and driven into the city centre, Trotman and his fellow cadets bore the brunt of the gruesome operations, occasionally rescuing trapped survivors but more often removing bodies.

He remembered the 'pervading smell' of burnt flesh. 'The whole scene was horrific and stomach turning, but we had a job to do, and by nightfall I was surprised at how hardened I had become to the terrible scenes,' he recalled. Seeing the German bombing raids with his own eyes hardened Trotman's feelings against Nazi Germany and fuelled his desire for revenge.

'I had no compunction about bombing Germany later in the war,' said Trotman. 'As far as I was concerned, I was giving back the same treatment which they had dished out to the people of Coventry and the other towns and cities of Britain which were bombed.'[2] Neither Bell nor Trotman yet knew it, but the seeds sown in those few hours in London and Coventry would bear fruit four years later, when they were flying hair-raising RAF Pathfinder missions deep over Germany, piloting one of the fastest bombers in the world.

Sometimes it was this patriotic desire to defend their homeland that motivated young men to enlist, but more often, given their youth, it was simply a romantic sense of adventure. Flying was still new and glamorous, and even if you ended up flying a bomber instead of a fighter, it gave many boys the chance to do in real life something they had only ever dreamt about. Knowing they were up against the poster child of Fighter Command, Bomber Command's public relations department regularly printed pamphlets which attempted to make it sound more exciting for potential recruits. In one, aircrews were described as 'Gentlemen of the skies, minions of the moon'.[3]

Some future Pathfinders were inspired by dashing aviators who had become household names. Alec Cranswick wanted to fly despite a family tragedy which had brought home its dangers. Cranswick's father Philip was an RAF pilot based in Wiltshire. Growing up at the family home in Oxford, whenever Alec heard a plane he would rush out to the balcony. If the plane circled the nearby church three times and dipped its wings, he would yell: 'Come on up, Mummy, it's Daddy flying over.'[4] But in June 1928 – when Alec was nine years old – his father was killed in a mid-air collision over Salisbury Plain. Alec was devastated. Nevertheless, the aviation bug had already set in. Five years later he was sent as a day boy to St Edwards, a public school in Oxford, whose alumni included both the First World War aviator Louis Strange, who had pioneered the use of machine guns in aerial combat, and Douglas Bader, the future Battle of Britain ace. One of Cranswick's fellow pupils was Guy Gibson, the future Dam Buster. The spirit of such figures galvanised young Cranswick's adventurous hutzpah and would prove essential when he eventually became a Pathfinder pilot.

Tall and good-looking with dark brown eyes and an easy smile, Cranswick was sporting and – like many future pilots – a dexterous horse rider. His mother Maia ran an English-speaking school for foreign students in Oxford. Using her contacts, young Cranswick was sent abroad in his holidays to stay with the parents of her pupils. In Bremen and Hamburg he saw Nazi Stormtroopers marching through the streets, and Hitler Youth boys in massed countryside rallies. After leaving St Edwards he briefly joined the police. But after seeing the rise of Nazism first-hand, Cranswick volunteered for the RAF. His mother was worried – she'd lost her husband to the air and now her only son would be risking his life too – but hid her fears, telling him '. . . whatever you do, decide for yourself, and I will not worry.'[5]

Most future Pathfinders, of course, had not seen Nazi Germany with their own eyes, nor were they necessarily driven by the same ideologies to join the RAF. Dick Raymond was a fresh-faced 15-year-old when war broke out. He had to leave his grammar school to join the family bakery in Barnstable, a small rural town in Devon, where he drove a horse and cart delivering bread. Before long, the mechanically minded Raymond had got a job as an apprentice at the local garage. The war seemed remote down in the west of England and life didn't move particularly quickly. The furthest Raymond had ever been was Taunton, 50 miles east in the neighbouring county of Somerset. But even down there, news of the Battle of Britain sparked a need for something different.

'I don't think that the majority of people joined through patriotism, they joined through boredom,' reckons Raymond, who went down to his local RAF recruiting centre in Exeter in 1942, only to be told he wasn't fit for service.[6] Raymond was baffled – as far as he was concerned he was fit and healthy, but he was destined for ground duties as a flight mechanic. Sent to an RAF centre in Blackpool, Raymond was horrified to find himself lumped with veterans from the '14/18 War'. Spurred on, he passed the course and was sent to technical training college in Halton, Buckinghamshire, to train as a fitter engineer, where he spotted an advert for Bomber Command aircrew flight engineers. 'I thought *Christ! Who knows? I'll volunteer.*' This time, he passed the medical, and could realise his dream of flying – albeit not sitting in the pilot's seat.

Raymond's change in fortunes was thanks largely to a massive shift in what Bomber Command required. When war broke out initially the demand had primarily been for pilots, but as aircraft advanced and with the increasing use of heavy bombers, so aircrew were needed for specific roles. In addition to the pilot, aircraft increasingly included a navigator to help the aircraft find the target and a bomb aimer to drop the bombs, as well as a flight engineer – a highly skilled technician who kept the aircraft flying – a wireless operator communicating with base, and two air gunners to man guns at the rear of the aircraft and midway along the fuselage.

The narrow educational requirements for aircrew also pivoted as the decision-makers began to realise that potentially decent flyboys were not being selected because they didn't meet the standards set. The initial requirement for candidates to hold a School Certificate, which was taken by 16-year-olds, was dropped. Instead, to get through the door and onto the first rung of the training ladder, volunteers had to sit a simple RAF aptitude examination and aircrew medical. And while the largely public-school, upper-class make-up of the pre-war Bomber Command would soon be washed away by a huge intake of men from lower classes, misconceptions of what was required still remained.

In 1938, Ernie Holmes cycled from his home on Tyneside in northeast England to an airfield outside Sunderland and asked the adjutant if he could join the RAF Volunteer Reserves. When he was asked his age and told the adjutant he was 16, Holmes was given a firm rebuke: 'Go home laddie and get the whippings [slang for nappies] off ya backside!' said the adjutant. 'I'd cycled 12 miles and I cried all the way home,' recalls Holmes, whose reasons for joining Bomber Command were pragmatic as much as patriotic.[7]

Holmes had grown up in relative poverty as his family battled the impact of the Great Depression. His father had worked in the shipyards but was out of work for much of the time. Holmes left school aged 14 and got a job as a message boy. He was bright and ambitious, and used his meagre pay cheque to fund night classes which he hoped would enable him to eventually enrol on a City and Guilds Masters Certificate in painting and decorating. In 1940 Holmes volunteered again. 'There was a war on. I could either go down the pits. Go to the army. Go to the navy. And I thought, *I want to fly*. It was a new thing. I could see there was a future in that,' said Holmes. Reassured he wouldn't be turned away again, because he was now 19, he was still nevertheless worried by his lack of qualifications.

'I didn't have a university or private-school education. I didn't have any school leaving certificates apart from the Northern Counties Schools technical examination.' But Holmes needn't have worried. A corporal spotted his potential and moved him into the operations room of an RAF station in Cheshire, where he mixed with the pilots and got to know the basics. He was soon asked to see the aircrew examining board in London, who pushed him through for pilot training. Before long, the young Geordie lad who had gone home crying with his tail between his legs would be commanding heavy bombers for the Pathfinders over Germany.

The diverse backgrounds of the crew rooms of Bomber Command were echoed by the huge role played by Britain's Dominions and colonies. While many countries had started the journey towards independence from the UK there was a still powerful lure to volunteering in the fight against Nazism. Almost 40 per cent of the airmen who served in the RAF – more than 130,000 – volunteered from Dominion countries and the wider Empire. One in four of Bomber Command's aircrews was from overseas and an estimated 15,661 lost their lives,[8] including 10,000 from Canada – which even had its own Pathfinder squadron. Smaller nations played their part too, including the Caribbean island of Trinidad.

In 1941, 24-year-old Philip Cross – known as Ulric – was one of 250 Trinidadians who sailed across the Atlantic to fly in the RAF.[9] Born in Port of Spain on 1 May 1917, Cross was the second eldest of nine children and the son of a civil servant working in the post office. Raised in a settled, middle-class household, Cross was particularly close to his mother Maud, who encouraged him to sit the annual scholarship that promised a free education at one of the island's finest schools. Soon after, 'I remember my mother coming into my bedroom with a newspaper, crying. I had come first on the island,' recalled Cross, who was sent to St Mary's College, a Roman Catholic school in Port of Spain.[10]

Bright and eager to learn, Cross read voraciously, translating Latin and Greek texts, and devouring everything from Shakespeare to Biggles, the fictional adventures about the heroic First World War flying ace. Cross dreamt of one day emulating his hero, and scrawled 'Flight Lieutenant P.L.U. Cross DFC' in his copies of *As You Like It* and *Kennedy's Latin Primer*. 'To me that was the height of anybody's ambition, to be a flight lieutenant in the Royal Air Force and to get the DFC [Distinguished Flying Cross],' said Cross. 'Most of my friends thought I was mad.'[11]

But his life was turned upside down when, in 1930, Maud Cross died in childbirth, and soon afterwards his father left the family to work in Venezuela, leaving Cross and his siblings to be raised by an aunt. Cross was heartbroken by the death of his mother and it affected his studies. He left school aged 17, working briefly as a proof editor at the *Trinidad Guardian* before becoming a clerk at a firm of solicitors, where his knowledge of Spanish helped with various clients. But his life seemed to be drifting, until greater events played their part.

Despite the remote location of Trinidad, Cross was highly aware of the political turmoil in Europe in the late 1930s. At school he had formed a left-wing book club with some friends which had even published its own magazine, the *Dawn*. 'We had read *Mein Kampf* and had Hitler down cold. We knew what he was about. We knew of Kristallnacht in 1938, when the Jewish businesses in Germany were attacked and looted. We knew of the Japanese invasion of Manchuria in 1931 and the setting up of the puppet state of Manchukuo by Japan. We were appalled by the Italian invasion of Ethiopia in 1935 and the Spanish Civil War which started in 1936,' said Cross.[12] 'The world was drowning in fascism . . . I suppose we were premature anti-fascists . . . we were not as ignorant as people in Europe think. We knew what was going on and in my reading group particularly we realised it . . . the whole idea that the world was going to be dominated by Adolf Hitler and the Germans for the next one thousand years was obviously unacceptable.'[13]

Wanting to play their part, being 'young, adventurous and idealistic', Cross and six members of his book club joined the RAF because 'after the Battle of Britain nobody wanted to join the army or the navy'. Cross admitted his dream of leaving the earth and 'flying, almost Icarus-like . . . was a very romantic notion'.[14]

As Cross made his way towards Britain, destined to become a navigator flying Pathfinder Mosquitos, on the other side of the world in Australia, Robert Maxwell Bryant's adventure had also just begun.

'Well here I am an airman without (as yet) a uniform or anything,' the 20-year-old wrote in a letter home to his family in May 1941, after he had volunteered to join the Royal Australian Air Force (RAAF). Known to everyone as 'Max', Bryant was one of 10,000 Australians to serve with Bomber Command in the war, knowing they would be travelling across the world and risking their lives for freedom. 'By the way, in case of casualty, I have nominated father as the bloke wot gets the telegram,' he added at the top of his letter.[15]

Bryant was brought up in Cowra, a small farming town 200 miles west of Sydney. A third-generation Australian whose maternal great-grandparents emigrated from Scotland on the *Victory* in 1849, Bryant was close to his parents Jack and Estelle, his brother John and his sister Mona. Jack Bryant had left his job as a farmer to enlist with the army in the First World War, serving in the Australian Light Horse and the artillery before returning to Australia in 1917 on medical grounds. Estelle had grown up on a 12,000-acre sheep and arable farm near Cowra, and Max hoped to own his own farm someday.[16] He excelled at both his studies and sports at the local school – working in a firm of solicitors as an articled clerk before joining up. Good-looking and thoughtful, he was a popular with both his male friends and the opposite sex. Like many of the young airmen across the world, he was a voracious letter-writer to his family, which not only helped break up the quieter periods of training, but acted as a cathartic release to let off steam or share good news.

On 25 May 1941, he arrived at RAAF Bradfield Park – a station in New South Wales, and home to the No. 2 Initial Training School. Life as an air cadet had begun. Like all his fellow airmen, Bryant trained under the Empire Air Training Scheme, which had been set up in 1939 to help train aircrew from across the Dominions and wider Empire for eventual transfer into the Royal Air Force. Over the course of the war, over 37,000 Australians were trained under the scheme.[17] If Bryant passed the initial course, he would be progressed to the next stage at an Elementary Flying Training School, before being sent to Canada to complete his advanced training. Then, he could finally join a squadron in Britain and see action over Germany.

After a lunch of stew and mash followed by pineapple and custard, the cadets were given their bedding and shown to the wooden huts which would be their home for the next ten weeks. To the frustration of the young men champing at the bit to get into the air, there was no flying yet. Instead, they would learn the basics of air force life – including drill, small-arms training and lectures on aviation – with exams and an interview with a 'category selection board' that would decide whether they'd continue the course as pilots, navigators or gunners.

At the end of July, Bryant's dream of being a pilot was well on track. He had passed the first part of the course and arrived at the Elementary Flying Training School in Benalla, Victoria, where he would experience flying for the first time just three hours after setting foot on the airfield. Bryant and his fellow recruits changed into their flying overalls and walked onto the tarmac, which was littered with Tiger Moths – a two-seat biplane with an open cockpit and dual controls, where the student sat in the front seat with the instructor behind. Bryant was shown how to correctly put on a parachute, before climbing into the front seat of the aircraft, making sure he didn't put his feet through the delicate canvas fabric of the wing. The instructor communicated to Bryant through a 'Gosport tube' – a mouthpiece and headphones attached either end of a rubber tube.

The Tiger Moth was a go-to wartime basic trainer in both Britain and Australia. Designed in the 1930s and made from wood and canvas, it had basic instruments, including a throttle to control the power, an altimeter, an airspeed indicator, and a fixed undercarriage. Although a forgiving little aircraft in the air, it didn't have wheel brakes, and it was not unknown to see one careering across the airfield with a hapless student flapping away madly in the cockpit. It was powered by a 145hp Gipsy Major engine. As Bryant settled himself, the mechanic on the ground called out 'contact', telling the pilot to switch on the magneto – a sort of ignition – before 'swinging' the two-blade wooden propeller until the four cylinders burst into life in a puff of white smoke.

The instructor taxied to the end of the airfield, turned into the wind, and opened the throttle to pick up speed. As the tail rose, the fuselage levelled out onto the two wheels, immediately improving the view ahead. Bryant felt the roar of the engine and the airframe vibrations increase, as the tarmac below whizzed by in a blur of grey. Then, the vibrations immediately ceased as the airflow increased just enough over the wing surfaces for the plane to climb unsteadily into the air. Every second that passed, the view improved, revealing more of the countryside as it slipped by underneath like an enlarged map. For many new pilots, it was the first time they had ever flown, and a hugely exciting experience.

'Like to take over?' the instructor asked Bryant over the Gosport tube after they'd been flying for ten minutes. 'Sure, if you tell me what to do,' spluttered Bryant. 'She's all yours,' replied the instructor. Bryant 'made a dive for the stick and she bucked and rolled like a mad horse!' But after a few minutes he began to get the feel and the 'attitude' of the aircraft. He found that pushing either foot on the pedals – called the rudder bar – would swing the nose of the aircraft to the left or right, while gently pulling the stick back or pushing it forward controlled the elevators and forced its nose up or down. Moving the stick to the left or right dropped each corresponding wing by moving the ailerons – the hinged sections on the trailing edges of the wings. By combining all these controls, Bryant could, with time, learn the basic building blocks of flight.

After 30 minutes in the air, Bryant and his instructor landed safely. 'The seat on a Moth is pretty cramped and windy but for all that the first flip was grand,' Bryant wrote home later. Over the following days he flew intensively with the instructor, doing various mid-air manoeuvres which gave the young cadet 'plenty of sky and nothing else. I didn't feel sick but I felt plenty of other things . . . he seemed to tell me about 1000 things yesterday and I can't remember half of 'em!'

But by the middle of August, Bryant had to share the news that his dream of becoming a pilot had been shattered:

Dear Mum and Dad,

I'm sorry to have to write this letter, because I have to tell you that I've been scrubbed, washed up, as a pilot, and am consequently feeling pretty terrible. I went up with my instructor first thing on Monday morning, and got on to the landings straight away: he sent me up with the flight commander, but I made a mess of the test – flew badly.

Bryant just wasn't cut out to become a pilot. And as gutted as he was, his flight commander was clear, reporting: 'If this trainee were allowed to continue training, it would result in his early demise.' He was recommended instead he train as an observer – a role which, ironically, would almost be more important by the time Bryant became a Pathfinder.

Like so many young men who had set their heart on flying but whose pride had been dented, Bryant pleaded with his parents not to share the news with friends, but put on a brave face and promised his father he would 'get the old nose down . . . after all it's a team show, and so long as you're in the team just what you are isn't so important . . . I suppose it would be quite easy to get down and moan all day, but by a little application of the chin up theory, I'm pretty cheerful.'

He was relieved to receive a sympathetic letter from his younger brother John, and wrote back: 'My Dear John, Thanks very much for your letter, to be frank I was a bit scared that young brother of mine might be inclined to feel a bit disgusted with his big brother. I'm very glad you're not . . .'

Finally, on 18 September 1941, Bryant was sent to Melbourne, where he boarded the *Monterey* – an 18,000-ton American passenger steamer requisitioned by the military as a troop carrier. 'Our great adventure began this morning,' he scribbled in the opening page of his secret diary, which he would write in throughout his war:

> To say we were astonished by the splendour of our cabins would be a great understatement – we were doing more gaping than anything! I am in a 2-berth cabin on the port side of the ship . . . we've two portholes, a double dressing table, two wardrobes, hot + cold water, two clean towels, private latrine, 3 cane chairs, reading and dressing lamps, shaving cabinet & lord only knows what else. How we were lucky enough to catch a trip on the Monterey is beyond me – she's a real luxury liner.

At 11.30am the ship quietly slipped away from an empty quayside and set sail for Canada. On board, 378 cadets thought about the adventures that lay ahead. Max Bryant watched from the deck and wondered when he would see his homeland again. He was one of twenty young Australians who would complete their training together and qualify as navigators in Canada before joining an operational squadron, and for the best – including Bryant – that would mean the Pathfinders.

By the end of the war, fifteen of those men would be dead.

CHAPTER FOUR

The Most Expensive
Education in the World

LONDON, OCTOBER 1941. JOHN Kelly was feeling nervous as he walked through the famous old gates of Lord's cricket ground in the north of the city, after arriving by train at Waterloo station from Portsmouth, where he lived with his parents. The blond-haired, blue-eyed 22-year-old had spent three years working in Portsmouth dockyard after attending the local grammar school. His brother Jim, four years younger, had already joined the RAF, destined to become one of its youngest Spitfire pilots. Kelly was keen to follow in his little brother's footsteps, and signed up to the RAF as a 'PNB' – pilot, navigator, bomb aimer – to await his fate over the coming months. Kelly didn't know if he would end up flying in Fighter Command or in Bomber Command, and although throwing a fast fighter around the skies might be sexier, his aptitude shown on the course and pilot demand on the front line would decide if he was instead destined for bombers.

For Kelly and many future Pathfinders, civilian life ended and RAF life started when they strolled past the old red-brick pavilion at Lord's. For much of the war, the home of cricket and the neighbouring luxury flats overlooking Regent's Park were used as sleeping quarters for RAF Abbey Wood – one of a number of aircrew reception centres across the UK – where cadets received their uniform and were given medicals and a basic examination. Meals were prepared in the kitchens down the road at London Zoo. After a month of drill, physical education and lectures, cadets were posted to an Initial Training Wing (ITW) elsewhere in the country for the next stage of their journey to becoming Pathfinders.

Learning to fly wasn't cheap. Bomber Command aircrew received 'the most expensive education in the world' at a cost of £10,000 per man – over £500,000 today – enough to send ten people to Oxford or Cambridge for a full three-year degree course, according to one estimate.[1]

New recruits who had met just minutes before were abruptly thrust into a military life which left very little to the imagination. This included the 'free from infection' venereal diseases check-up in the Lord's club room, where the medical officer ordered men to drop their underpants before, as one cadet later recalled, 'using his swagger stick to manipulate any highly suspect genitals for a better view'.[2] Not surprisingly, many found adjustment to RAF life pretty difficult. Gone were the familiarities and luxuries of peacetime life. Young men from different backgrounds and regions were thrown together in a new, unfamiliar world. Some had never spent a night away from home and homesickness was common. They were now being asked to perform tasks which were new and alien, learning the art of biting their tongues and accepting orders without question.

Non-commissioned officers, or NCOs, ran the everyday lives of the cadets and got them used to military life. They were feared by some, scoffed at by others, but regarded with curiosity by the majority. Bullying happened, but, in reality, their bark was usually louder than their bite. They were salt-of-the-earth RAF men, career servicemen – mostly from working-class backgrounds – who had risen through the ranks in the pre-war service. Most were too old to serve in the front line so were given the task instead of knocking discipline into the heads of the young volunteers through drill, menial tasks and rigorous daily inspections to ensure spotless lockers and neatly folded beds.

Despite the petty discipline, some of the future aviators learnt to beat the system and have some gentle fun at the NCOs' expense. In late 1941, Ulric Cross and his fellow Trinidadian, and former schoolmate, Kenrick Rawlins arrived at RAF Abbey Wood, after reaching Britain from the Caribbean following a ten-day crossing of the Atlantic. Cross was garrulous, with a wicked sense of humour, warm eyes and a killer smile. Rawlins was a gentle giant at six foot two. The two were billeted in a room together. This gave them an idea. 'Depending on the ignorance of the English, we decided Kenrick was an African prince and I was his spokesman,' remembers Cross.[3]

When a Cockney corporal swaggered into their room on the first morning and ordered Cross and Rawlins to make their beds to the exact standards of the RAF, they both feigned ignorance. 'But Corporal, how does one make a bed?' enquired a wide-eyed Cross.[4] The corporal was completely wrong-footed. Worried he would 'get in the shit' if an officer saw their beds were unmade, he replied: 'OK, I'm going to make your bed today, but from now on see what I do.' But to Cross's amusement, the corporal made their beds every morning for the entirety of their stay. 'They really didn't know what to do with us,' he said.[5] One fellow West Indian aviator advised Cross that the best approach if people questioned their background was to tell them 'you came on a boat, it took ten days, you're a very quick studier and that's where you learnt English.'[6]

Cross reckoned his acclimatisation to UK life was helped because he had an uncle who was a doctor living in Bolton, Lancashire, who'd sent newspaper cuttings back to Trinidad for years. 'I knew I wasn't coming to an unknown land, in fact I rather took advantage of this,' said Cross. 'We knew ten times more about the British than they knew about us.'[7] Even so, compared to the wide, tree-lined avenues and colourful gardens of Trinidad, the little rows of terraced houses and mansion blocks in Britain bemused Cross. 'We couldn't understand how people knew where their house was because every house in the street looked exactly the same.'[8]

Despite an influx of volunteers from Caribbean countries in pre-Windrush wartime Britain, seeing anyone who wasn't white was rare. As they travelled through Britain, Cross and Rawlins were stopped by schoolboys and asked for the time. 'Some of them had never spoken to a black person in their lives. They wanted to hear what language you were speaking,' recalled Cross later.[9] It worked both ways. Having lived a 'gentle life', the first thing he noticed in the RAF was the language. 'I had never heard four-letter words used so frequently.'[10] Cross was one of nearly 6,000 West Indians who served with the RAF – around 5,500 as ground crew and 300 as aircrew.[11] Prejudice and racism existed, of course, but Cross never appeared to notice them – or really care. He was treated well, perhaps aided by the fact he was in uniform and accepted as a serviceman when huge numbers were arriving from across the Empire.

Despite Cross's wish to become a pilot, he was told he was being trained instead as a navigator. After one month in London he was sent to RAF Hemswell, in Lincolnshire, home to a number of Polish Wellington squadrons, whose airmen loved it when Cross took his turn manning the radio in the control tower – 'because you're the only one whose English we can understand'. Cross was next posted to an elementary air observers' course in Eastbourne before a spell at RAF Cranwell in Lincolnshire studying wireless. He spent the final six months of the year-long course up in West Freugh – a windswept RAF base on the west coast of Scotland, surrounded by green hills and moors frothing with masses of purple heather. Here, he flew around the Western Isles in Anson aircraft, honing his navigating techniques.

By November 1942, Cross had successfully completed his training and was ready to join an operational training unit and then a front-line squadron, where he'd hopefully see action. All ranks were automatically promoted at the end of their training. The majority – about two thirds, became sergeants. The rest were commissioned as officers, with a salary of £30 a month. Pilots, navigators and bomb aimers were more likely to be commissioned as officers than the so-called 'trades' – the air gunners, wireless operators and flight engineers. A commission depended on a successful interview with the station commander, who would assess the individual's 'officer-like qualities' – a policy which some thought was an archaic, class-based hangover from the pre-war old-school-tie era that still pulsed strong through the RAF. Advocates of the system, however, argued that the characteristics they were looking for in an officer included intelligence, a capacity to lead and the ability to set a worthy example, regardless of background.

In that respect, Cross's timing was perfect. The day before he was due to see the commander the whole station shut down and everybody went on a six-mile cross country run, which Cross won. The next morning, he nervously marched into an office and saluted the Group Captain behind the desk. The Group Captain leant forward and shook his hand. 'Congratulations on a splendid race yesterday, Cross,' he said. Cross was not expecting his next question. 'Cross, do you know Learie Constantine?' referring to the West Indian fast bowler.

'I said yes. So we talked cricket. I got a commission,' remembers Cross.[12] There's no doubt Cross had succeeded because of his ability and fierce intelligence, but – as is so often the case in life – charm had played its part too. In any case, he was edging ever closer to becoming a Pathfinder, where his newly acquired navigational skills would be critical.

John Kelly also made it past the first stage of life in the RAF and in November 1941 was sent up to the ITW in Scarborough – the seaside resort on the east coast of Yorkshire. Coastal towns were preferred for training centres because they often had a ready supply of hotels, holiday camps and guest houses that could be easily requisitioned by the RAF. By the middle of the war, the RAF had twenty-three ITWs in Britain, providing a three-month ground school course before cadets – who were grouped into one of two or more squadrons, with each squadron containing three or four 'flights' of fifty men – even climbed into an aircraft. The syllabus involved more than 500 hours of intense instruction to prepare the trainee aircrew for life in the RAF, including Morse code, meteorology, aircraft recognition and yet more physical exercise.[13]

The training school in Scarborough centred around the Grand Hotel – a vast 12-floor Victorian Baroque building towering over the town's South Bay. Cadets were billeted in the 365 rooms, some of which boasted magnificent views over the North Sea, making it one of Britain's finest seaside hotels in peacetime. But as Kelly and his fellow cadets found out, experiencing Scarborough in one of the coldest winters in living memory was no holiday.

His biggest initial concern, he wrote home, was trying to find a private dentist 'before the RAF "dentist" gets a chance . . . he has nearly murdered several of our fellows . . . everyone has had dental treatment prior to joining, but this fellow has collared about 60% of us for further treatment. I believe he must get paid commission on the number of teeth he pulls.'[14]

The day began with breakfast 'or breakfasts, according to whether the corporal notices us first time', parade marching and lectures on subjects such as signals and anti-gas and armament. In the evening Kelly played table tennis or copied up notes from the day's lectures. At 8pm, 'it seems that no sooner does my head touch the pillow than someone is calling "wakey-wakey"' the following day.'

It's little wonder they were so tired, given the RAF's obsession with physical exercise, including regular cross country runs against students from Leeds University and 20-a-side football match on Scarborough beach, as the grey, rolling waves crashed nearby. Arms and legs were shredded on snowy football pitches frozen hard 'just like a nutmeg grater'. Bemused locals, 'wrapped up in big overcoats, stare at us when we gallop through the town every day in vests and running shorts.' All that exercise was hungry work. Kelly and his fellow students were fed well on cake, Welsh rarebit and bread and butter, and many received welcome parcels of goodies from home, such as chocolate and tea, and sweets.

Life was basic and boisterous, and as Christmas approached in December 1941, the young men amused themselves singing carols and bashing dustbin lids in the corridor outside the other dormitories, which ended in mass water fights using stirrup pumps. Once they escaped the walls of the Grand Hotel, wartime suburbia wasn't exactly bursting at the seams with entertainment. For a shilling, they could buy a seat at a local music hall, which, together with fish and chips and a couple of pints, pretty much used up their pay of two shillings and sixpence a day. And without the bounds of family or school, many discovered alcohol in quantity for the first time. Binge-ups in the local pubs of Scarborough were popular ways to break the monotony of camp life. For Kelly, the subject would often turn to 'our girls and the relative merits of the local brews of ale'. For all that, sexual experiences with the opposite sex – or for that matter the same sex – were the exception rather than the rule, beyond a drunken fumble or the odd kiss. Although one or two of the older men were married, and some might claim to have 'casual skirt' or sweethearts back home, most were, for the main, pretty innocent.

Kelly's *amour* was focused on Edna, a 21-year-old woman from Plymouth. He was happy to discuss with his parents – perhaps wisely, one assumes, without her knowledge – how the relationship might develop, including the 'pros and cons' of asking her to marry him.

'I know you and Dad will like Edna,' he wrote home, '. . . she is certainly not the glamorous type, but a nice average-looking girl. There is something very sincere and genuine about her that counts for far more than looks. I know she is fond of me, though goodness knows what she can see, and I think we are of sufficiently different temperament to get on well together. I think she has a wonderful smile, in fact that is the first thing I noticed about her.'[15]

With love in the air, cadets could be forgiven for forgetting there was even a war on. But that illusion was shattered one morning when an aircraft swooped low overhead as the cadets marched through the town. At first the young cadets took little notice, assuming it was friendly. But when it continued to circle, they decided to try out their newly learnt aircraft recognition skills, only to realise with horror it was a feared German Junkers Ju 88 dive bomber. Their commanding officer ordered everyone to scatter and dive into the doorways of nearby houses.

'After about ten minutes the locals began to laugh at us, and a crowd of Leeds University undergrads had a good time making derogatory remarks about the RAF,' recorded Kelly.

But Kelly had the last laugh when the aircraft dropped its payload: 'you should have seen the undergrads go down when the bombs reached earth and went off. I believe they thought the end had come.'[16]

Ten minutes later, three Spitfires zoomed over the town in hot pursuit, but the German aircraft had long gone. The incident shook up the people of Scarborough, who were not used to being attacked from the air. A campaign was started to black-out half an hour before nightfall. 'If it had been at Pompey [Portsmouth] they would have shot the machine down in about half a minute and recognised it afterwards,' Kelly wrote home.

*

By the beginning of 1942, Kelly's course at Scarborough was over. He'd passed his exams, been promoted to the rank of Leading Aircraftman and was about to start his flying training. Like all recruits he was issued with a flying kit – an exciting moment in an aviator's fledgling career, given it was the first tangible sign of what he was actually there to do. It comprised a thick padded inner suit and a heavy outer grey-green suit, a helmet, headphones and a microphone, oxygen mask and tube, leather gauntlets, woollen gloves, silk gloves and lambs'-wool-lined flying boots. 'There is a pair of smashing goggles too,' Kelly wrote home. 'It is lovely stuff. The lot costs £80, the silk inner gloves costing a guinea.'

At this stage, all the men finishing the ITW course were filtered into various categories. Would-be pilots went to flying school to continue flying training. Alec Cranswick and Ernie Holmes, for example, were both sent to RAF Desford near Leicester.

Other trainees who would one day make up the crews in Bomber Command and Pathfinder squadrons diverged to specialist schools. Trainee flight engineer Dick Raymond joined the No. 4 School of Technical Training at RAF St Athan, in Glamorgan, which provided specialist training for the flight engineers needed for four-engine heavy bombers.

Air gunners ended up in bleak outposts like Morpeth in Northumberland and the Isle of Man, learning theory about 'nose attacks', the 'characteristics of machine gun fire' and 'deflection shooting' – the term given to the 'aim off' needed by a gunner to hit another moving aircraft from his own. The theory was put into practice when the trainee gunner squeezed into the dustbin-sized gun turret of a training aircraft. They'd pass instructions to the pilot for evasive action to avoid the mock attacks of a Spitfire pilot, all the while trying to ignore, as one gunner later put it, 'the nauseating smell of fuel-oil, dope and the sickly reminder of the turret's previous occupant'.[17] Despite the gripes, however, all the men were getting that bit nearer to tasting action, and most were eager to crack on and 'have a go' at the enemy.

John Kelly was sent up to Perth, in Scotland, to start his flying training at one of the Elementary Flying Training Schools dotted around the country. He was issued with his flying logbook – a service bible in which was recorded every single hour's flight made until he stopped flying, either when he left the RAF or when he was killed. The air station in Perth was dominated by a huge hangar next to a large grass airfield, which had been camouflaged with fake hedgerow lines in an attempt to fox any wandering German bombers. Airmen lived in wooden huts built in rows. John Kelly was one of eight cadets in his dormitory, with the relative wartime luxury of baths and showers with hot water. They even had their own study, dominated by a large fire to keep the biting Scottish winter at bay, and they could belt out tunes on the piano, listen to the radio or play table tennis.

Two weeks after his first flight in a Tiger Moth, Kelly had become enthused, telling his parents:

> It is a wonderful feeling to be up, you really feel on top of the world. There is no sensation of speed until close to the ground and then oh boy! I had to make a practised forced landing without using the motor this afternoon with the satellite airfield. The instructor switched off the engine 2000 feet and told me to glide around until I have no sufficient height to make a normal gliding approach. It was hard to resist a very strong temptation to close my eyes and wait for the bang as we hit the ground. The earth moves very slowly when you are well up but it rushes up at an alarming rate when you come into land, however I think I'm getting the hang of this flying business very well. I'm finding a hell of a lot more in the actual flying than I ever thought there was. I'm enjoying every minute of it.

He also spent many hours practising instrument flying in the 'Link Trainer', a sort of early version of the modern flight simulator which helped pilots get used to flying at night. The participant sat in a wooden box mocked up as a cockpit, which had instruments and controls and mimicked the basic principles of flight. Although it wasn't actually like flying the real thing, it gave pilots the practice they needed and saved lives. For Kelly it was 'an absolute marvel and electrical engineer's idea of heaven. I could play with it for hours. It does everything except leave the ground and is far more sensitive than an ordinary plane is to its controls.'

In March 1942, Kelly had passed elementary flying training. He was one step closer to flying for Bomber Command and, ultimately, becoming a Pathfinder. All that lay in the way of his winning his precious flying Wings was a final intense period of training to master a more powerful single-engine aircraft. Like many fellow airmen, this would then allow for a smoother transition to bigger two- or four-engine bombers in a conversion unit or finishing school. And while some – such as Alec Cranswick, Dick Raymond and Ulric Cross – were trained entirely in Britain, as the war progressed the RAF increasingly sent cadets overseas, where they could train in peace in uncrowded skies without risk of enemy attack. More than 137,000 RAF airmen – including Ernie Holmes and Max Bryant – were sent to Canada, which made sense, given that the regular shuttling of shipping across the Atlantic could carry trainees west and trained flyers back.

Much less well known is how many future Bomber Command and Pathfinder pilots were trained in the USA, as part of America's Lend-Lease agreement with the Allies. Using American facilities was deemed so vital that Churchill wrote to President Roosevelt personally, praising the 'welcome addition' to RAF training which would 'greatly accelerate our effort in the air'.[18] Some men, including Colin Bell, were trained in the warm skies of Florida under the Arnold Scheme, named after a general in the US Army, in which RAF cadets trained alongside US Army Air Corps pilots. Meanwhile, six British Flying Training Schools were also established on US soil in 1941, under an initiative called the 'All Through Training Scheme', which saw 6,600 trainee pilots qualify throughout the war.[19] Perhaps the most dramatic of the air stations was located on the edge of the Mojave Desert, just a few miles from Death Valley in California – the hottest place in the world. Only a stone's throw from Hollywood, for men like John Kelly, who was used to living in a war-torn country with years of blackouts and rationing, life was about to take on the excitement and glamour of – quite literally – a Hollywood film set.

CHAPTER FIVE

Hooray for Hollywood!

'OH BOY! LOOK OUT California, here we come,' John Kelly wrote home in early April 1942, after making his way across the Atlantic to start his advanced flying training.[1] Around fifty ships were used throughout the war to transport thousands of trainee airmen between Britain and North America. Some requisitioned passenger ships formed a shuttle service, zigzagging back and forth across the Atlantic. With their powerful engines and speed, the unescorted journey was made in four or five days, putting them out of reach from the hunting packs of German U-boats. But their numbers were limited. The slower troop ships needed military convoy protection, and took up to two weeks.

Life on the high seas was basic. In common with many young RAF airmen, Kelly found both the food and conditions were 'lousy', and the crossing was plagued with bad weather. 'Most of us were too ill to care if the ship floated or sunk. "Death where is thy sting" was our uppermost thought for a long time . . . Oh boy were we glad to set foot on terra firma!' he wrote home.[2] Colin Bell, meanwhile, had made the journey over the previous summer after completing his initial training in Scarborough, first embarking on a 'shocking old vessel' called the *Duchess of Ethel*, which promptly broke down, before re-embarking on the *Empress of Scotland*, a fast liner which 'went like an arrow' across the Atlantic.[3]

Most RAF cadets arriving in Halifax, Nova Scotia, or New York were immediately transported by train to the 'Personnel Despatch Centre' in Moncton, New Brunswick, a holding centre sleeping 800 which allowed the RAF to regulate the flow of men to and from the various flying schools in both Canada and the USA. Moncton was a typical little Canadian town. Small wooden houses perched on neat lawns framed by manicured trees. Shiny American cars sat in every driveway. Some cadets stayed in Moncton for a day or two, others for up to two months, depending on the weather and the demand from the flying schools.

It is hard to overestimate the impact of arriving in North America on young men used to a life of bombs and blackouts. Although America had entered the war following the Japanese attack on Pearl Harbor on 7 December 1941, on the face of it, in everyday life, the nation didn't appear to be mobilised for war in the same way Britain was. Both materially and culturally, this was a land of milk and honey for the new arrivals. Colin Bell replaced meals consisting of a doorstep of rough bread, a lump of margarine 'like chalk' and a dollop of jam with 'incredible food, the like of which we hadn't seen for years and years . . . all of a sudden it changed and I was living the life of luxury.'

John Kelly wrote home to his mother in April 1942: 'Whenever you feel at all down in the dumps about the war, Mother, just try to visualise the North American continent. Old Winny never spoke a truer word than when he said "Westward look the land is bright". Any doubts or fears that I ever had have been swept away . . . Boy! When North America gets going and they only seem to have just started they will certainly help us hold the torch.'

While Bell was sent down to train in Florida, Kelly left Moncton for a six-day, 4,000-mile train journey across the North American continent, gazing in awe from the window as the train snaked its way westward through a smorgasbord of scenery – from prairies to wheat fields, to national parks and deserts. On the final leg into California, the 'San Joaquin Special', a silver streamlined locomotive pulling luxury air-conditioned Pullman coaches, climbed over the Rocky Mountains, 10,000 feet above sea level. 'Three times as high as I have flown,' noted Kelly, who leant out of the coach door with a friend holding his trouser belt to take some keep-sake snaps as the Colorado River roared through a gorge 300 feet below. Finally, Kelly and five fellow cadets from the course at Scarborough arrived at No. 2 British Flying Training School, a few miles west of Lancaster town, on the edge of the Mojave Desert.

War Eagle Field, as it was otherwise known, sat in a sea of scorched earth. An airfield surrounded by mile after mile of flat, lunar-like rocky landscape, bleached white through the intense, rasping heat of the Californian sun, with the only sign of life being a few green cacti and Joshua trees. Death Valley was a four-hour drive away. Summer temperatures regularly reach 49°C in the shade. Dry winds whipped up dust and tumbleweed.

The air station had been built by the Polaris Flight Academy – a civilian flight school – before being earmarked for use by the RAF in 1941. It was dominated by two large metal hangars. A whitewashed brick control tower with 'War Eagle Field' painted on the front looked out over two 2,400-feet-long bitumen runways. Cadets wore US Army tropical kit, comprising khaki shirt and slacks. Climbing into an aircraft cockpit the pilot would often find the controls of the plane too hot to touch, as it had been sitting in the hot sun. Cadets learnt to switch on the engine and hold the headphones and microphone in the propeller's slipstream to cool off before they could be used. For the blinking, mostly pasty-white new arrivals, the hot, arid, relentless heat of their new home took some getting used to.

By contrast, cadets found the facilities inside were second to none and superior to many of the RAF's British establishments. They lived in air-conditioned bungalows and relaxed in a communal recreation room with a table tennis table. A jukebox blasted out the latest records by Frank Sinatra, Benny Goodman and Billie Holiday at five cents a tune. The well-stocked shop sold a wide range of items, from bottles of ice-cold Coca-Cola to radio sets and silk stockings, which the men sent to their mothers, wives and sweethearts back home. Listening to local radio was a popular pastime, although for the British recruits more used to the somewhat dry BBC it was frustrating that a show was interrupted with advertisements every ten minutes. From 5am to 10pm all instructions and announcements played over the base's loudspeakers were accompanied by bugle calls.

Perhaps the biggest change for all the men who had emerged from the monotonous diet of war-weary Britain was the food on offer. 'Pardon the interruption,' Kelly wrote in a letter home, 'but a beautiful voice, apart from the twang, has just announced that lunch would be served at twelve. They use a public address system here. Lunch comprised, ham, lettuce, young carrots and greens of some sort, milk, coffee and cream, biscuits, ice cream, bread-and-butter. We just help ourselves. Oh boy if I had a bigger appetite.'

While the enticing facilities were far superior to training schools back in Britain, this wasn't an altruistic gesture of goodwill towards the cadets, but rather was designed to soften the blow of an intense flying syllabus which took around six months. On completion, pilots gained a total flying experience of around 200 hours before being awarded their Wings and sent back to Britain for active service.

Flying training was split into primary and basic-advanced stages, each taking around 14 weeks. For the primary training, new arrivals flew five days a week in the Boeing Stearman, a two-seat 450hp biplane with an open cockpit and dual controls, nicknamed the 'yellow peril', since its bright colour warned that a rookie flyer was at the controls. If they passed, the flying moved on to the basic-advanced stage in the Vultee Valiant – a 450hp monoplane with more advanced controls than they had hitherto experienced – before finishing on the Harvard, a 200mph monoplane powered by a 600hp Pratt & Whitney Wasp radial engine, which was renowned for the tearing noise caused by its propeller tips reaching the speed of sound.

When they weren't in the air, cadets attended ground school, learning the likes of armament and navigation. Lectures were given by visiting aviators, including a heavily decorated wing commander and former Battle of Britain Spitfire ace who surprised the recruits by telling them 'the official policy' of the RAF was to 'machine-gun any Hun' who bails out unless he is in home territory. Fifty new cadets started every 20 weeks, a new batch coming in as the senior batch qualified. Aside from a skeleton staff of RAF officers, the support staff and instructors were all American civilians. For the most part they got on well with the cadets, although Kelly's instructor was forever teasing him about the British and would often say 'ripping old boy' or 'how about a spot of tea old man?' in a supposedly British accent. A small number of American Army Air Corps cadets also received their training on the base, sharing the communal areas with the RAF train-ees, who tried to wind them up by belting out renditions of 'Rule, Britannia', 'Land of Hope and Glory' and Vera Lynn's 'White Cliffs of Dover' around the piano.

Despite the plush facilities, the flying standard was extraordinarily high and successfully passing the course was tough. Kelly admitted he wasn't looking forward to seven months of 'frazzling' in the desert and hoped he could stick it out. 'Somehow the USA training seems very unpopular amongst the pilots here,' he wrote home soon after arriving on the airbase:

> Typical of the feelings is this joke I heard at a recent camp concert. Three pilots have been killed on ops. They rung the bell at the gates of heaven and Saint Peter came out to see them. When they told him they wanted to come in, he asked the first pilot where he had been trained. 'England' was the reply. 'Sorry old man,' said St Peter. 'But you'll have to go to hell.' He then asked the second pilot where he had trained. 'Canada,' was the reply. 'Hm!' said St Peter. 'Very sorry, but I think you'll have to go to hell too.' Finally, he asked the third pilot, who said he'd been trained in the USA. 'Come right in,' said St Peter, 'for you've been through hell already.'[4]

Students were designated a flying instructor who subjected them to regular 'checks'. Two failures meant elimination from the course – throughout the war 23 per cent were 'washed out' – although some instructors occasionally allowed a cadet more time if they believed a fail was due to a minor fault which could be ironed out with practice. Having come so far, failing at this stage was gutting for wannabe pilots. Kelly was keen not to become 'elimination minded', as many of his colleagues had, and by mid-June 1942 he had 50 hours flying time under his belt, flying solo and attempting various aerobatics, such as loop the loops, snap rolls and chasing tails, where pilots met up in their own planes, as he described for his parents in a letter home:

> I had some fun the other afternoon, we arranged a rendezvous when we would both be solo, and met at 5,000 feet in the practice area. We

had a grand time trying to get on each other's tails, and showing each other how to do aerobatics. Mike thought I was pretty good because I did two snap rolls in quick succession. But little did he know that I only meant to do one – gosh did my heart miss a beat when the ship whipped over on its back a second time. Aerobatics are extremely thrilling especially when experimenting up so early but actually they are fairly safe owing to the height they are carried out at. The RAF set great store by them as they are invaluable should you run into any trouble on ops.

While flying a Lancaster for the Pathfinders two years later, Kelly would find out just how vital aerobatics could be in getting out of a scrape.

While most aerobatics were encouraged, unauthorised low-level stunt flying – nicknamed flat-hatting or warping – was forbidden. But for 20-something aviators let loose like boys with their toys, that made it all the more irresistible. One set of British students dive-bombed the small Californian town of Lancaster with loo rolls. Another favourite trick was to swoop down low over fields and chuck empty Coca-Cola bottles at grazing cows, although few bottles hit the right field, let alone the cows.

One Wednesday afternoon, during a cross-country flying exercise with nine other aircraft, Kelly and his friends had some fun diving on cars and lorries driving along a desert road, before landing back at War Eagle Field and thinking nothing more of it. Little did they know, however, that one of those on the receiving end of the dive-bombing was a US Civil Aeronautics Authority inspector who had been forced off the road by the first wave of flat-hatters. Before he could get back on the carriageway, five more aircraft had dived on him, missing him by inches.[5] The miffed inspector managed to scribble down the aircraft identification numbers and promptly reported Kelly and his colleagues to the air station commander. 'Personally, we think he should be very grateful that he still had his life,' Kelly wrote home later, and after all the cadets admitted their guilt, they were lucky to escape with no more than a ticking off. But the novelty of all the training was wearing off. 'You can see, Mother, why most of us have lost the edge of our keenness for Wings and don't much care what happens for after all we joined up to fight Germans,' Kelly wrote home.[6]

While Kelly laboured through his frustration, down in Florida, Colin Bell was finding the discipline and rules 'rigid in the extreme'. After all, he too had signed up to fight the Germans, but he and his fellow recruits now found themselves thousands of miles from the front line adhering to petty whims. Unlike John Kelly, who received his training at one of the six British Flying Training Schools, Bell was trained under the Arnold Scheme run by the US Army Air Corps, where cadets had to adhere to the draconian system called the West Point rules, which encouraged them to 'grass' on contemporaries for tiny infringements such as dirty shoes or failing to salute properly, under the eyes of often sadistic teachers. For Bell, the treatment was harsh: 'They ridiculed you, almost spat on you and the only consolation I had was that they treated the American cadets even worse than they treated us,' he said. He passed the various stages on the flying course but kicked against the discipline and was marked down as a bit of a rebel, until an older Scottish cadet on the course took Bell under his wing and completely transformed his attitude to the training.[7]

Bell wasn't unique in experiencing friction with the American hosts. When he had arrived in the States in mid-1941, public opinion in isolationist America remained opposed to entering the war and RAF cadets wore civilian clothing. But on 7 December 1941, Japan launched an audacious raid on the American naval base at Pearl Harbor in Hawaii, sinking four battleships, damaging four more and killing or wounding more than two and a half thousand Americans. The dramatic change in attitude – certainly outside the training school – was almost immediate. Bell was out having supper with some local girls in Tampa when they heard President Franklin D. Roosevelt on the radio, proclaiming the attack as 'a date which will live in infamy'. 'I turned to one of my chaps who was with me and said "We've won the war,"' remembered Bell. 'But our girlfriends of course were distraught, as they all had brothers and fathers, and their attitude was totally different.' A few days later, Bell was walking across the airfield when an American flight mechanic walked up to him and shook his hand, declaring, 'Well, we are allies now.'

By February 1942, Bell had passed the course, been given an officer's commission and awarded his precious flying Wings. He was looking forward to returning to Britain to see some action. But his skills as a pilot had been spotted and instead he was ordered to stay in America as a flying instructor, training US Army pilots. Bell was hugely disappointed, but if he was going to stay on, he was going to do it his way. At the flying school in Alabama, he immediately set himself apart from the US instructors, telling his pupils, 'I know what your American system is like because I've just finished training . . . my system is different. You can take it from now that unless you disobey what I've asked you to do, I shall help you along as much as I can and you will all graduate.'

'This rather amazed them,' recalled Bell, 'because it was quite the reverse of the American system. I was very much my own man even at that age. It made them better cadets because instead of being frightened all the time they knew that they were going to succeed.' It would be more than two years before Bell climbed into a Mosquito as a Pathfinder, and by then he would be itching for a chance to put his training into action.

America's entry into the war in 1941 ensured almost overnight that RAF airmen training all over the continent were – for the most part – made to feel welcome. Everywhere they went people would offer to buy them drinks or meals and entertain them. Nowhere was this felt more than in Hollywood. When John Kelly and his fellow cadets weren't training their socks off, they hitch-hiked 70 miles to enjoy all that West Coast hospitality could offer, rubbing shoulders with some of the biggest film stars in the world.

On one of his first visits, Kelly ended up at the swanky Beverly Hills Hotel, where he met Marjorie Reynolds, who was doing a swimsuit photoshoot to promote her latest film, *Holiday Inn* – made famous by her duet of 'White Christmas' with Bing Crosby – before partying with some US Army air cadets until 5am. 'I don't know whether I could even begin to describe Hollywood, Mother,' Kelly penned in May 1942. 'It is a very lovely spacious city, Hollywood Boulevard and The Vine and Sunset Boulevard being the most important streets. The people live by the bottle and really are what Americans call "screwball". The women must be the most beautiful in the world and do they adore the RAF.'[8]

Most RAF cadets were invited to eat with local families, keen to show their hospitality. At one evening supper in Beverly Hills, Kelly and his friends were treated to numerous whiskey and sodas and enjoyed juicy T-bone steaks. 'After the war Dad will have to build a barbecue-grate in the garden,' Kelly wrote home. 'The place for it will be just down behind the dugout and when steaks once more become plentiful he can don a white apron and then will the neighbours' mouths water.'

A few weeks later, Kelly and a friend, walking through Hollywood, decided to thumb a lift, and moments later a big Cadillac pulled in, driven by Johnny Weissmuller, the Tarzan star. As they drove along streets lined with palm trees, Kelly plucked up the courage to ask Weissmuller to name his favourite leading lady. 'I just take them as they come,' replied Weissmuller. 'All I have to do is climb a few trees and bellow.'

'He seemed a swell guy,' observed Kelly (clearly warming to the idea of using American slang), '. . . and [looked] just as powerful as he does in the films, though he could've done with a haircut.'

Weissmuller dropped the boys off outside the British American Club, dubbed 'a little piece of old England' and frequented by the likes of Sherlock Holmes actor Basil Rathbone and David Niven, where servicemen could get rooms for the night, sandwiches and cups of tea, poured from a real teapot by an elderly waitress affectionately known as 'Gran'. Using the club as a base, RAF cadets explored Hollywood and took tours of the various film studios. Kelly and a friend had a tour of Warner Brothers and watched Bette Davis filming her latest 'picture'. To their delight, when the scene had wrapped Davis wandered over and chatted for two hours, sharing drinks and allowing them to light her cigarettes. 'It was wonderful to sit next to her and watch all the little mannerisms that you see on the screen. She is really beautiful and after a few moments you feel you have known her for years. She is exceedingly pro-British and was really thrilled at the way the British are carrying on,' Kelly told his parents.

This was just another of the seemingly endless number of drinks Kelly enjoyed with Hollywood actors and actresses. The glitterati, it seems, were falling over themselves to meet the young RAF cadets. In reality, for some, it was probably the last thing they wanted to do, but they quietly knew it did their careers no harm to be seen to be 'doing their bit' now America had joined the war.

After watching Marsha Hunt and Franchot Tone filming the propaganda film *Pilot No. 5*, Hunt invited Kelly and a friend into her dressing room for drinks and sandwiches. 'You can imagine how thrilling it was to be waited on by a real live film star,' he said afterwards.[9] On another occasion, Kelly and a friend were invited for drinks with Greer Garson, the British-born star of *Mrs Miniver*, the romantic war drama she had just finished filming, and a performance for which she would scoop an Academy Award for Best Actress later that year. At 6pm, Kelly and his friend arrived at Garson's home – a mock-Tudor mansion on Stone Canyon Road in Bel Air, a smart leafy neighbourhood in the hills overlooking Los Angeles – and nervously rang the bell. Garson's mother Nina answered the door, and showed them through to the vast wood-panel sitting room, before Garson herself sashayed in.

'Boy! What a woman,' Kelly wrote later. 'She is about twenty-three or four and has marvellous reddish gold hair. She is very pretty but the most marvellous thing about her is her voice. She ordered some drinks and then she wanted to know all about England. At some things on which she feels pretty strongly she spoke quite forcefully, and it was almost like watching a private play, to sit beside her and watch her talk.'[10] Kelly was smitten: 'Greer Garson is the nicest person in movieland, she is an extremely pretty, charming, and unaffected English girl.' After two large whiskey and sodas, he and his friend said their goodbyes and headed to meet Lupe Vélez, the Mexican-born actress, who, Kelly observed, 'was very nice', and Luise Rainer, who, he concluded, somewhat bitchily, was 'definitely not very pretty'.

But, for all the hospitality, for all the hanging out with film stars, for all the glamour, as the weeks ticked by Hollywood and America began to lose their thrill for Kelly and the other airmen. The Allies were ramping up their bombing campaign over Germany and many of Kelly's contemporaries from school were in the thick of the action with the army, navy or RAF – yet here he and the other airmen were seemingly living the high-life, five and a half thousand miles away on the west coast of America. They knew from letters home that Britain was still being bombed by Germany and at least one of Kelly's fellow cadets was keen to get back to England to 'even scores up with Jerry' after his mother was killed in a raid on London. Kelly spoke for many when he told his parents he was getting tired of America, where everything was a daze of bright lights, plenty of food, lots of money and no one seemed very conscious of the war. 'It all seems so "phoney" and we are getting very impatient to get back to England and get on with the "job".'[11]

Finally, with 210 hours of flying time under his belt, Kelly received his Wings in November 1942. 'All the boys feel thoroughly exhausted ... It's been a hell of a course and I don't think I would have the heart to go through it again,' he wrote home. Kelly was recommended by his commander to fly four-engine bombers with Bomber Command, a role which he reckoned was an 'immense responsibility' in looking after the lives of eight or nine men and £40,000 worth of aircraft. 'A lot of people crack the navigator up as being the most important man, but when it all boils down, it is only the pilot who can kill everyone off by making an error in judgement,' he told his parents. Like hundreds of other young men making their way to Britain after months of training, Kelly couldn't wait to get into action. 'I think that if the German people can see the air crews on the training here, they would chuck up the sponge now,' he wrote home at the end of 1942. 'Boy oh boy are they going to get it in the neck.'

Up in Canada, Aussie Max Bryant might have challenged Kelly's assertion about the navigator not being the most important man in the crew, certainly if the intensity of his navigational training was anything to go by. After a three-week sail across the Pacific from Melbourne, Bryant arrived in San Francisco in October 1941 and made his way north by train.

Like all future navigators who were destined to serve in Bomber Command, Bryant would spend the next six months training at a variety of air stations, gaining his qualifications, before being shipped back to Britain for action. At this stage, he was still technically an 'observer', training in navigation, bomb aiming and gunnery. Only later in the war – and by the time he joined an operational squadron – would he be in a specialist navigator role. The first stage was a twelve-week course at the No. 2 Air Observers' School, based at the airport in Edmonton, which sat on the North Saskatchewan River, 140 miles north-east of the Canadian Rockies. Here, they learnt the basics of navigation, combining ground-school subjects such as map reading, calculating wind speeds and meteorology, with flight training in Avro Anson aircraft. Over the following weeks Bryant and his fellow cadets spent hour after hour in the skies, honing their skills in freezing aircraft cabins.

The Australian cadets were more used to the vast flat wilderness than the British trainees, who had only experienced the patchwork fields of home, but the tables were turned with the onset of the Canadian winter. When the first snow started falling one mid-October evening, Bryant and the other Australians 'flew out of bed to inspect the miracle, sure enough tiny white stars were drifting from the heavens.' The following morning the whole airfield was covered in a blanket of snow, in which the giddy Australian cadets had a huge snowball fight, much to the bemusement of locals looking on. As the Canadian winter set in, with heavy blizzards and temperatures sometimes down to -30°C, flying was often cancelled and cadets had time on their hands.

Before the ship had left Australia for North America, Bryant had met Don Charlwood, a young writer from Melbourne six years his senior. The two men got on instantly, forming a close, brotherly friendship. When volunteers had been sought for training in Canada, they glanced at each other and both stepped forward. Charlwood admired Bryant's good nature and intellect. 'At that stage he was a forlorn youngster for he had not long been failed as a pilot. I think he found me a sympathetic elder; to me he became like one of my young brothers,' recalled Charlwood later.[12]

On their first night in Edmonton, the cadets discovered they would train in pairs – each pair were to share upper and lower bunk beds in the barracks. In mock deference to Charlwood's age, Bryant jumped on the upper bunk. The next morning, as Bryant walked past the orderly room, a message came in from a local woman inviting two cadets for supper that night. Bryant leapt at the opportunity, and that evening they sat down with the family, including their pretty daughter Nellie and her girlfriend, Billie. It wasn't long before they became a foursome, with a romance blossoming between Charlwood and Nellie, who would later marry.

With Billie and Bryant remaining just good friends, he struck up a romance with a local woman called Marge, whom he spent Christmas Eve of 1941 with. 'I'd almost forgotten what it felt like to hold a girl in my arms,' he wrote in his diary. But like many romances at this time, despite a natural desire to take things further, 'thinking of the girl's reputation' meant Bryant made his way back to the aerodrome.

In January 1942, Bryant turned 21. Nellie and Billie organised a surprise party, including a birthday cake topped with 21 candles. 'Don and Nellie gave me a copy of a selection of Rupert Brooke's poems and Billie a photograph album,' Bryant told his sister Mona. 'No doubt about these Canadians – they really make you one of the family.' A few days later, Bryant, Charlwood and the rest of the Australian observer trainees left Edmonton for the next stage of their course in the town of Lethbridge – 350 miles further south in Alberta – which would focus on bombing and gunnery. At the railway station, Nellie and Billie turned up to see the boys off. 'I think Don was wishing that a dark wall would close about him and Nellie,' observed Bryant. 'We were standing yapping when the train started to move . . . Don kissed Nellie, and she also hopped on. I don't think they could part. I was just about going to push her off as the train was gathering speed when she jumped off of her own accord – I guess she was very upset.'

Rushed goodbyes and stuttering romances were familiar to hundreds of young airmen, who tried to keep in touch through letters or phone calls, but more often than not romances withered away, were forgotten about or replaced. However, while Bryant had helped Charlwood slip out of the camp for illicit meetings with Nellie, ruffling his sheets to make it look like he had slept in his bed – his own personal life was more complicated. For Bryant, his mind was torn about relationships he had left 6,000 miles away, back home in Australia. He berated himself for becoming close to a girl called Jan, 'whose passionate caresses still haunt me', and another called Heather, 'of the shining hair and sparkling eyes . . . if I could only fall in love with her all things will solve themselves . . . How we clamour for the things we cannot have – or worse, having once had, have lost!' he wrote.

The teaching at the bombing and gunnery school in Lethbridge was intensive and included flights in ancient Fairey Battle aircraft, which were 'cramped' and came with a 'stink', where cadets used machine guns to target drogues pulled by other aircraft. 'You all know what difficulty I had even in potting a sitting rabbit,' Bryant wrote home. 'Even for a good shot, machine gun fire directed at a 20 foot drogue 200 yards away, which wavers a bit, is a tough job.' Winds regularly reached 100mph or more, making flying conditions hairy. The cadets had just two days off in six weeks, and there was little time for socialising with the locals, although if they wished they could attend the church service to hear sermons on such subjects as 'Can we be Christians and Kill?' But the base's remote location made the war seem particularly distant, which in turn made it all the harder hearing about news of the war back home when they could do very little about it.

In February 1942, the Japanese captured the British naval base at Singapore and were threatening to sweep south towards Australia: 'though we had been expecting it, it was still a sickening blow. Nothing stands between the invader and Australia now, and I suppose we must face up to the fact that our beloved country is for it,' Bryant wrote in his diary. 'Life doesn't seem so good now with all the danger to our homeland, our armed forces overseas, and my own petty bothers. I cannot see the light ahead – where all this is going to finish is beyond me.'

As Japanese forces inched ever closer to Australia, launching bombing raids on the northern port of Darwin, Bryant and his fellow Australians felt helpless sitting in Canada. 'Heard last night Darwin had copped it,' he wrote in his diary. 'So it has come at last – first time since our country was founded. The Japanese are so numerous and apparently so thoroughly prepared, it doesn't look as though anything can stop them, and our worries for our country – and our people – grow deeply. And our women folk – that's the big worry.' His mother Estelle tried to reassure her son in a letter. 'We are all very well and do not worry about us as we hope to get along quite well in these troublesome times,' she wrote. 'We all feel as though we would like to be able to take an active part but think the job on hand is to prepare ourselves now for the time when we might be needed.'

It wasn't wise to dwell on one's fate, but as a four-day blizzard blew outside and the men were confined to barracks, Bryant confided in his diary that his mind was 'a mixture of feelings':

> . . . am beginning to realise that my training period is nearly over, and soon I'll be in the thick of it. Which means – it must be faced – a fair chance of crossing the Styx soon. Life is very sweet, more so when I realise how it may soon be gone. I want to go home to do my little bit towards my country's freedom before the race is run and as yet do not know where I am to be sent. Life holds so much as yet untasted and it is hard to keep to the straight way.

At the end of February 1942, Bryant and his fellow cadets stood in the snow as a commanding officer pinned Observer's Wings onto their chests, before going into Lethbridge for a graduation piss-up. After a final four-week navigation course at the No. 1 Air Navigation School in Rivers, Manitoba, he learnt he had finished in fourth place out of all the training schools in Canada, and would soon be flying back to Britain as part of the RAF Ferry Command – a scheme set up in 1941 to fly urgently needed aircraft from Canada to Europe. He warned his parents in a letter that once he reached Britain he'd not be 'hopping into a bomber and scooting for Berlin almost immediately' but would first be sent to an operational training unit 'to put on the final polish before we wade in'.

And, much to his frustration, it would be four months before Bryant made the journey, so he made the best of the time by playing golf and exploring the area. He also took a tour of John Inglis and Company – a huge arms factory in Toronto which manufactured Browning pistols and Bren machine guns destined for Britain. Walking around, Bryant saw guns 'transformed from shapeless lumps of metal to glittering machines of destruction' and was stunned by the technology. 'We saw blocks guaranteed to hold their size within 6/100,000 of an inch and a machine to measure to one millionth. We were even allowed to fire Bren guns on the range and were told production figures for shipments to Australia . . . we began to see what "heavy" industry means. Huge crankshafts towering to the roof quite overwhelmed me.'

In common with most airmen with this leave period, Bryant succumbed to the magnetic pull of New York, where he visited the Empire State Building, watched shows on Broadway and enjoyed beers with friends. One evening, Bryant was invited to a dance, where he met Evelyn, an 18-year-old Columbia University arts student, who he thought 'an attractive brunette with a fund of intelligent conversation and ready wit'. She had a gorgeous southern accent which would occasionally reveal itself with a 'you'all'. The two immediately hit it off and spent the next few days visiting sites around the city. 'The old heart was beginning to rock a bit,' Bryant penned in his diary. '. . . sunlight was filtering through golden windows on to her face and hair, delicately tinting them with gold dust. I must have stared for a long time.'

In an experience shared by numerous British and Australian flyboys spending time with American women, Bryant found them more open and not afraid to discuss a variety of topics which might well be taboo back home. 'Our talk soon ran into deep channels such as the pros and cons of sexual intercourse, what we wanted in our married partners and so on. Evelyn speaks quite frankly on these subjects, which makes her all the more astonishing. She is one of God's finer creations,' he confided to his diary. Another evening they found a park. 'Soon we were luxuriously stretched full length, talking quietly of all sorts of things. I was playing with Evelyn's lovely soft hair, kissing her now and then, and feeling very much at peace. Quite by accident my hand once brushed across her breast . . .' But the relationship went no further. Following a passionate kiss at Grand Central Station, when, for Bryant, 'the world almost stood still', he made his way back to the airbase in Canada.

Finally, on Tuesday, 23 June 1942, after a haircut and one final shopping spree, including purchasing some silk stockings 'in case I meet a really nice English lass', 'the great morning dawned'. With the final flight plan checked – and co-ordinates of secret bases in Ireland plotted in the event the aircraft drifted off course – he climbed on board the American Ventura on Dorval airfield, just outside Montreal, and watched the pilot push the throttles slowly and evenly forward. 'Soon we were screaming down the runway – now up and away!' Their destination – via Newfoundland and Iceland – was Britain.

For Bryant, his destiny now lay with Bomber Command and, ultimately, the Pathfinders – a new force which would be formed just eight weeks later, following one of the biggest and most acrimonious internal rows of the Second World War. A dispute that went right to the very heart of government, and would have a major impact on the Allies' bombing strategy for Germany.

PART TWO

The Making of
the Pathfinders

MAY 1942 – FEBRUARY 1943

CHAPTER SIX

We Guide to Strike

L ATE EVENING, 30 MAY 1942. In his office at Bomber Command's headquarters, Arthur 'Bert' Harris was feeling tense. At that very moment, around 5,000 young men under his command were flying to Germany in the biggest show of air power the world had ever known.

It was the first in a series of huge raids on Germany known as the 'thousand-bomber raids', where practically every squadron in Bomber Command was squeezed dry. With only 400 front-line aircraft available, planes and pilots from training and conversion units with little operational experience were called upon to make up the numbers.

A few days before, Harris, the new commander-in-chief of Bomber Command, had visited Winston Churchill at Chequers, where the two men had chatted until 3am about a bold new bombing plan. Churchill had finally agreed to Harris's idea. But the stakes were huge. Harris was committing the whole of his front-line strength and all his reserves in a single battle. If anything went seriously wrong, Bomber Command would be wrecked. It was crucial the operation succeeded.

Between 10.30pm and midnight, 1,046 bombers rumbled into the sky from bases dotted around eastern England and headed towards Cologne, Germany's third largest city. Rather than flying to the target and bombing independently, the aircraft tried a new tactic, closing-up in a concentrated 'bomber stream' with the aim of overwhelming the German defences. Over the course of an hour and half, 1,455 tons of incendiary and high-explosive bombs poured from the bellies of almost 900 aircraft, destroying or damaging more than 12,000 buildings. Around 470 Germans were killed – a deadly new record for an RAF raid – more than 5,000 more injured and 45,000 civilians were bombed out of their homes. The raid hadn't been cheap for Bomber Command either – 40 aircraft were lost, the highest in the war so far, at the hands of German fighters and anti-aircraft guns, hacking down a British bomber every seven or eight minutes.[1]

Harris called Churchill, who had travelled to America, and broke the news. The Prime Minister was delighted. Many admired the sensational audacity of the raid – codenamed Operation Millennium – including the British media, which printed dramatic headlines. '1,500 PLANES IN BIGGEST RAID: 3,000 TONS BOMB STORM' announced the *Daily Mirror* in its front-page splash the next day. The *Daily Express* reported: 'SKY OVER COLOGNE AS BUSY AS PICCADILLY CIRCUS'.[2] News of the raid even made the headlines over in sunny California. 'We were all tremendously thrilled on Sunday to see the newspaper headlines announcing the elimination of Cologne,' John Kelly had written home. 'I was on Hollywood Boulevard at the time when the papers came out. I give myself full marks for self-control that I did not get drunk for everyone was offering to buy us drinks,' he added, although he must have been kicking himself he couldn't be a part of it.[3]

The feat was repeated two days later, when 956 aircraft bombed Essen in the Ruhr, followed by a final massive attack on Bremen at the end of the month. The sheer size of the attacks dwarfed anything Bomber Command had attempted before. Cologne was three times larger than Coventry, but the weight of the attack – one ton of bombs per thousand people – was the same. Cologne had been 'Coventrated'. Churchill too – despite his initial uncertainty about how far bombing raids would force the Germans' hands – had his imagination fired up at the prospect of the thousand-bomber raids.

The idea of using a vast air armada was the brainchild of Harris, a former First World War Royal Flying Corps fighter pilot, who had taken up the reins of Bomber Command in February 1942, just before his fiftieth birthday. His plan was all the more extraordinary given there were so few serviceable aircraft, following two years of failure in Bomber Command which had left the force threadbare and airmen's morale low. 'I realised something had to be done to let them see they were getting dividends,' Harris said of the raids. '. . . to let the crews realise that they could do something really effective if only they had the numbers and equipment to do it with.'[4]

Harris was a short, robust figure, with a comb-over of strawberry-blond hair and a neat little matching strawberry-blond moustache perched on a plump, pink face. Gruff and prone to flying off the handle at any perceived criticism, he had served in Iraq between the wars – exercising iron discipline over the local tribes with bombing raids – before taking a job in Whitehall, gaining experience at the Air Ministry. When war broke out he became commander of 5 Group in Bomber Command, followed by a stint in Washington. Supporters saw his appointment to head up Bomber Command as a testament to his shrewd intelligence, aggressive single-mindedness, and the ability to get on with the job. But he could easily rub people up the wrong way. One senior Air Ministry colleague told Harris that after working with him for 18 months he had become accustomed to his 'truculent style, loose expression and flamboyant hyperbole'.[5]

Known as Bert to his peers, Harris was soon given the moniker 'Butch' by the crews – short for butcher – a wry reference to his willingness to shed their blood in his desire to bleed Germany dry too. Harris was based at Bomber Command's headquarters, nestled in beech trees near High Wycombe in Buckinghamshire, so few airmen ever actually saw their commander-in-chief, except perhaps when he paid flying visits to airfields, yet many regarded their boss with affection and awe. Harris had to arrange a major battle every day and watch it develop every night. He simply didn't have the time to tour the air stations.

Although Harris later became a hate figure for those who despised the policy of area bombing German towns and cities, the decision to shift the bombing offensive had been initiated at the end of 1941 by Sir Charles Portal – who was Chief of the Air Staff – well before Harris's appointment. It was Portal who chose Harris for the grim task of laying waste the industrial and administrative heartlands of Germany. 'The directive when I took over was that I wasn't to specifically aim at anything unless ordered to do so, except to blast the German cities as a whole,' Harris said after the war.[6]

This strategy was summed up in a frank Air Ministry memo issued in September 1941, which insisted that Bomber Command needed to bomb a town in such a way as to 'break the morale of the population which occupies it' by making it 'physically uninhabitable' and for German people to feel in 'constant personal danger'. The immediate aim of bombing, the paper concluded, was to produce 'destruction' and 'the fear of death'.[7]

Separate British analysis, meanwhile, suggested the demolition of people's houses by bombing actually had a greater adverse effect on their morale than even the death of a relative.[8] Nevertheless, while Harris's tactical remit came from above, he still appeared to have an iron-cast stomach and an apparent indifference to ordinary Germans who might be killed in the process. 'We have got to kill a lot of Boche before we win this war,' he wrote soon after taking up the post,[9] a mantra he would controversially pursue with his trademark vim and vigour until the end of the war. The Ministry of Economic Warfare drew up a list of important industrial targets, based on a points system depending on importance, with Berlin at the top. This table eventually listed over a hundred cities. It was kept in blue books at Bomber Command's headquarters, where Harris crossed through each city as it was attacked.

A few days after the Cologne raids, Harris recorded a short speech which was broadcast on the newsreels. 'The Nazis entered this war under the rather childish delusion that they were going to bomb everybody else and nobody was going to bomb them,' he said to the camera. 'At Rotterdam, London, Warsaw, and half a hundred other places, they put that rather naive theory into operation. They sowed the wind and now they are going to reap the whirlwind.'[10]

'Bomber Harris', as he became known to the public, had laid down the gauntlet. As well as the raids being a necessary evil to rid the world of Nazism, many also agreed with Harris in seeing them as revenge for the Luftwaffe raids on London, Coventry and scores of other towns and cities across Britain. One major counter-argument, of course, was why, if months of German bombing over Britain had failed to break the moral of the British people, and if anything, strengthened their resolve, would things be any different in Germany? But there was a genuine, if rather naive, feeling amongst many senior airmen and staff that the Brits were made of sterner stuff than the Germans, whose supposed lack of moral fibre would see them eventually capitulate under sustained and heavy bombing.

The aggressive shift in Bomber Command's tactics in the early summer of 1942 was cheered by the British public at a time when the Allied war effort had reached a low ebb. Britain's naval presence in the Far East lay in tatters and Japan had redrawn the map. While the Japanese navy had tasted its first defeat to the Americans at the Battle of Midway in early June 1942, its new pop-up empire still covered almost 3 million square miles and contained 88 per cent of the world's rubber, more than half of its tin, a third of its rice, and the rich oil fields of the East Indies. In North Africa, meanwhile, General Rommel had run rampant across the desert, pushing British forces out of Libya and earning his promotion to field marshal. German U-boats continued their deadly assault on merchant and naval shipping, squeezing the vital supply lines across the Atlantic, and in Berlin, Hitler had turned his focus from Britain after opening a new front in the east against the Soviet Union, the latest phase of which had German troops racing across the vast plains towards Stalingrad.

This uncertainty had a direct impact on Bomber Command, with some calls for the force to be broken up and redistributed to other theatres, such as North Africa, the Far East and RAF Coastal Command. Churchill had not been completely convinced as to how effective a continuing strategic bombing campaign against German cities might be in bringing the war to an end, but remained committed to the campaign. The previous July, after German forces had poured across the Soviet border in the biggest invasion in history, he had promised Joseph Stalin, the Soviet leader, that the RAF would bomb Germany night and day. And given Bomber Command's high profile, plus the vast resources in terms of aircraft and manpower that were now being poured into its expansion, it was too late to reverse the bombing campaign anyway. The huge publicity around the thousand-bomber raids helped silence the doubters, ensuring it remained a critical part of Allied war planning.

Yet, while the first thousand-bomber raid on Cologne inflicted vastly more damage than the 1,364 sorties sent against the city over the previous nine months, for all the positive publicity, the two subsequent attacks of similar size were a bit of a let-down. Over Essen – the intended objective of the second raid on 1–2 June 1942 – crews struggled to find a target covered by haze or low cloud, and more Germans were killed by bombs scattered on eleven neighbouring towns than in the city itself.[11] In the raid on Bremen on 26 June 1942, operational training aircraft flown by inexperienced pupils bore the brunt of the casualties. Some struggled with their navigation and drifted away from the main group of bombers to be eagerly picked off by German fighters, or ran out of petrol in the air after getting lost. One returning British heavy-bomber crew crash-landed after getting lost in bad weather. Assuming they were in enemy territory, some of the crew hid in ditches while others surrendered to three rather surprised-looking women speaking a foreign language, only to discover the language was in fact Welsh and they had ditched in rural Wales.[12]

Despite the headlines they created, the thousand-bomber raids were a fig leaf, vainly struggling to hide the undeniable fact that Bomber Command wasn't very good at regularly finding or hitting its targets.

A little under a year earlier, in July 1941, Churchill's scientific adviser Professor Lindemann had decided to investigate bombing accuracy, to establish once and for all what on earth was going wrong. He instructed 24-year-old David Bensusan-Butt, an economist in 'S-Branch' – the Statistical Section of the War Cabinet Offices, comprising a crack team of statisticians – to lead the investigation.

Like R.V. Jones, whose work on radar was proving so effective, Butt was another young intellectual high-flyer from Oxbridge who influenced the wartime thinking of those at the very heart of power. Born in Colchester in Essex, he was educated at Gresham's School in Norfolk – where he was a contemporary of the composer Benjamin Britten – before reading economics at King's College, Cambridge, as a pupil of John Maynard Keynes. Indeed, Butt compiled the index to Keynes' 1936 magnum opus, *The General Theory of Employment, Interest and Money*. In 1938, after a spell at *The Economist* magazine, he joined the civil service, where he became Lindemann's private secretary.

Butt was not a typical economist. His childhood heroes were Montaigne, Voltaire and Hume. He was an accomplished pianist who adored Haydn and Bach, and a keen amateur artist, inspired by his close friendship with Lucien Pissarro, the impressionist painter. According to one friend, he was 'urbane, cultivated, erudite but also witty, charming and generous'.[13] In short, Butt's analytical and open mind made him the perfect man for the job and his persuasive and charismatic personality ensured Lindemann would listen closely to the findings of his research.

In early August 1941, deep in the bowels of the Air Ministry in London, Butt carefully examined over 650 photographs taken by Bomber Command night bombers in the previous June and July, from over 500 operational sorties in 100 raids against 28 targets. Most RAF bombers carried an onboard camera to capture bombs exploding over their targets, the area around the blast illuminated for a few seconds by a very powerful flare dropped from the plane called a photoflash. The resulting images were somewhat grainy but allowed an analysis to be made as to the bombs' accuracy. Butt also studied operational summaries and other documents from hundreds of sorties. On 18 August he handed his report to Lindemann.

It was nothing short of dynamite.

According to the paper, only one in five RAF bombers sent on operations to Germany and France got within five miles of their target. Of those planes recorded as actually bombing, over crucial targets in the Ruhr Valley, this fell to one in ten, and a target in the Ruhr was four times as difficult to locate as one elsewhere in Germany – not surprising given the industrial haze that constantly hung over the region. Even in the bright silvery light of a full moon, only two fifths of the aircraft reported to have attacked their targets had got within five miles. On moonless nights, this proportion fell to one fifteenth.[14]

The bitter truth from Butt's findings – and one which probably wouldn't have come as much of a surprise to some airmen carrying out the dirty work over the skies of Germany – was that hundreds of supposedly successful attacks had in fact resulted in nothing more than bombs being dropped in open countryside. The average crew was unable to locate targets other than in perfect conditions – and even then not very often.

Butt had given Bomber Command a firm shake and some RAF top brass bristled with defensiveness, questioning his report's validity. However, while even Butt himself admitted his research wasn't infallible, he insisted the broad picture his report presented was correct. Crucially, when Lindemann showed it to Churchill, he agreed, and sent a note to Sir Charles Portal, his Chief of Air Staff. 'This is a very serious paper, and seems to require your most urgent attention,' Churchill wrote, before adding in a separate note to Portal a few days later: 'It is an awful thought that perhaps three quarters of our bombs go astray. If we could make it half we should virtually have doubled our bombing power.'[15] Butt's findings were confirmed by a second, smaller report in October 1941, which found that only 15 per cent of aircraft bombed within five miles of the aiming point.[16] Churchill, privately, was appalled. 'Unless we could improve on this there did not seem much use in continuing night bombing,' he said later.[17]

By the winter of 1941, as German anti-aircraft guns and fighter, plane defences grew stronger, Bomber Command aircraft losses were almost 5 per cent – any higher and it would struggle to find replacement men and aircraft. Bomber Command's headache was neatly captured by one group commander in a scathing report simply entitled 'Facing Facts', which highlighted a tissue of failures attributed to a lack of training, inaccurate weather forecasts, the effectiveness of enemy defence measures and a lack of decent navigation technology.[18] It was all pretty depressing stuff. Richard Peirse, Bomber Command's commander-in-chief, was promptly booted out and replaced by Harris, whose subsequent thousand-bomber raids in May and June 1942 had saved his organisation from the hangman's noose – for now.

But the elephant in the room hadn't gone away. If Bomber Command was to succeed in helping the Allies defeat Hitler, in effectively sowing 'destruction' and 'the fear of death' in German towns and cities, it needed to actually find those towns and cities in the first place. And it needed to do so using large numbers of aircraft over a short period of time in order to swamp enemy defences and cause carnage in the streets below. The question was – how?

By 1942 it was widely accepted that to find an enemy target in darkness in the face of heavy flak, searchlights, fighters, smoke screens and bad weather was too much for all but a tiny number of the more exceptional crews. The idea of using a specialised flying force made up of specialist crews to locate and mark the target had been floating about in various aviation circles since the beginning of 1941. Everyone had seen how effectively the German Kampfgruppe 100 used technology to find and firebomb Coventry to guide the main force.

Individual Bomber Command squadrons began experimenting by dropping flares and incendiaries over targets. But pushed ever higher by cones of powerful searchlights, aircraft were forced to search and bomb from heights of 14,000–16,000 feet, while flares dropped to illuminate and locate a target burst at 10,000 feet, making them far less effective.[19] Also, while some squadrons devised their own tactics using flares, it was impossible to achieve a concentration of bombers over the target – a critical ingredient for a successful bombing raid.

A new piece of kit called Gee, which used radio signals and was nicknamed the 'goon box' – 'because any goon can use it' – was introduced in 1941. It provided the navigator with a 'fix' which he could plot in a few minutes and initially seemed promising. But it only had a range of 350 miles, and while it was great for helping crews find their way home, it would only be a matter of time before the Germans learnt how to jam it, rendering it useless as a target-finding device over mainland Europe. This made the need for accurate navigation even more pressing.

A few days after Lindemann had first briefed Churchill about the explosive findings in the Butt report, he wrote to his boss and friend again recommending that Bomber Command explore the idea of using well-trained men armed with the latest navigation technology to locate and firebomb targets, citing the German Kampfgruppe 100 as a benchmark. Sir Charles Portal agreed and had raised the idea earlier in the year. A paper written by Bomber Command's Navigation Section in November 1941 also recommended something similar. When it was circulated to group commanders the response was split – some liked the idea, others were worried that removing their best crews would weaken morale.[20]

One of the loudest advocates for a crack target-finding force was a young group captain called Sydney Bufton. 'Buf', as he was also known, was a 33-year-old wing commander who had joined the Air

Ministry as Deputy Director of Bomber Operations in November 1941. Crucially, he was unusual amongst more senior desk-bound officers because he had recent combat experience commanding two bomber squadrons and an RAF air station, and had flown many missions as a pilot. Bufton knew more than anyone just how difficult targets were to find, illuminate and accurately bomb, but had also seen some success on a small scale when experienced crews guided the rest to the target. After his appointment to the Air Ministry he sat down in his central London office in King Charles Street and drafted out his plans for a single target-finding force brought under one roof, with the aim of delivering more effective target-finding.

Bufton envisaged the force comprising six squadrons, which he labelled the 'cavalry of Bomber Command', with one or two first-class crews requisitioned from each existing squadron. The six squadrons would work closely together and operate as one force.[21] He proposed the creation of a 'Bomber Development Unit' attached to the target-finding force with its scientists 'drinking the same beer' – in other words, using workshops close to hand so the boffins could test the very latest high-tech navigational and target-marking equipment with the target-finding squadrons.[22]

Bufton was perfectly aware some squadron commanders hated the idea their squadrons might be diluted and filleted of their best crews, but he also reckoned that even the best crews were currently disheartened at their lack of success. For Bufton, the strengths outweighed the pitfalls. A target-finding force would result in more Coventry-style attacks on Germany, creating a positive effect on crew morale throughout Bomber Command. The increase in overall efficiency and determination would eclipse any small dilution of other bombing squadrons. 'Unless this step is taken we will never succeed in our aim,' he argued.[23]

But if his idea was to succeed, Bufton had to marshal support from the Air Ministry big guns. On 27 February 1942, five days after Harris was appointed commander-in-chief of Bomber Command, Bufton wrote to his boss John Baker putting forward the idea that the current widespread criticism of Bomber Command in Parliament and by some members of the public was down to a failure in bomber-force tactics. Bufton reckoned that only through the urgent formation of a target-finding force could they 'cut out the dead wood' and tighten control so that the bomber force could be wielded and directed as a sharp, flexible, hard-hitting unit.

Baker agreed, but despite support from Lindemann and Portal, when Harris found out about the idea in early March, he booted it out of the park. Harris wasn't against a target-finding force per se, but favoured instead target-marking crews or 'raid leaders' in each existing Bomber Group, which he thought would lead to healthy competition where new ideas could be more easily tried out. Bomber Command was still a small force and Harris cited concerns – with some justification – that by creaming off the best crews a target-finding force would simply become a *corps d'élite*, creating jealousy and uncertainty in the other squadrons and denting morale. That's assuming squadron leaders were even prepared to release their best squadrons in the first place. And besides, many airmen were in the middle of tours – why would they want to leave and start all over again?

But Bufton wouldn't give up that easily. He had a second chance to push his case in person when, on a bright spring morning in March 1942, Harris convened a meeting of his group commanders, senior air-staff officers, and Bufton and Baker at Bomber Command's headquarters near High Wycombe.

Harris started by outlining various arguments against a target-finding force. In addition to his concerns about morale, he suggested that if the best crews were collected from various existing squadrons to create a special squadron, they would lose their possible chance for promotion. Sitting across the table, a red mist suddenly descended on Bufton. Not only had he recently seen action personally, but both his brothers had been shot down. He knew promotion was the last thing on the minds of most serving airmen. 'Sir, you will never win a war like that!' he declared, dramatically slamming his fist on the table as he made the point. 'These people don't know if they will be alive tomorrow and they couldn't care less about promotion!'[24] In the face of such an outburst from a junior officer, to his credit, Harris simply looked at his watch. 'Perhaps it's time for lunch,' he said, before strolling out of the room. Bufton hadn't exactly sold his case for the formation of a new target-finding force, but Harris's point about promotion must have cemented in his mind the fact that the commander-in-chief was out of touch with the men on the front line.

An hour or so later, the whole group reassembled. 'I called this confer-ence to discuss the very emotive subject of a target-finding force,' resumed Harris, who then couldn't resist a put-down of the junior upstart: 'I was almost assaulted in my office over this matter this morn-ing, but nevertheless, I would like your opinions. I need hardly tell you that I am totally and fundamentally opposed to the idea.' Over the next hour, the men discussed the plan in detail. Harris was supported by all his group commanders in his opposition, and Bufton and Baker promptly returned to the Air Ministry with their tails between their legs.

The following morning, a somewhat downcast Bufton was strolling into the King Charles Street building when a Bentley pulled up at the kerb. Harris climbed out. Bufton saluted. 'Good morning, Bufton. What are you going to do to me today?' asked Harris, smiling. 'Well, I didn't plan to do anything, sir,' replied Bufton. 'Well, if you've got any ideas, write to me,' said Harris.

If Harris had meant his comment as a throwaway line, Bufton was having none of it, and jumped on this third chance. He rushed back to his office and immediately began drafting a three-page note directly to Harris outlining his plan in more depth. He emphasised that forty good crews would need to be withdrawn from Bomber Command, the equivalent of just one crew per squadron, after which the supply of crews could be maintained by selecting the best newcomers from operational training units. Based together they would hone their tech-niques and have access to the best navigation technology, which could be quickly fitted to a few aircraft in the force without waiting until there were enough supplies for the whole Command. 'The ability to find and actually see their target would be an inspiration to the rest of the Bomber Force,' wrote Bufton.[25]

However, with so much at stake, Bufton needed to garner even more support from the men who mattered – those who were actually flying night after night in the skies over Germany. His team sent out a paper and a questionnaire to over half a dozen operational squadron leaders and air-station commanders whom they knew well, to canvass their views about the target-finding force. Over the next few days, the replies came flooding in, and they didn't hold back.

'Objections to the formation of a T.F.F. cannot possibly seriously be entertained by anyone other than the academic degenerate,' wrote one commander, who believed Bomber Command had been taught a painful lesson by the German pathfinder force. 'The sooner we acknowledge this lesson, pocket our pride, and copy their tactics, the sooner we will inflict the necessary degree of damage upon their industry.' He finished – aiming a pointed jibe at Harris's generation of desk jockeys – by arguing that such a new force's composition and success depended upon 'youth and a vigorous mind' rather than the older men who should be swept from the board and whose experience of the last war was 'valueless' because the new conflict was so different.[26]

Meanwhile, the station commander at RAF Scampton in Lincolnshire – who the following year would be closely involved in the famous Dam Busters raid – was particularly outspoken in his response, reckoning that in an average Bomber Command squadron only one out of five crews were 'sufficiently courageous' to mix with the flak and searchlights over the Ruhr and bomb the target, while the remainder were 'fringe merchants' who 'fling their bombs away'.

'There is no doubt about it, flak and searchlights frighten our people beyond measure and many crews go completely to pieces,' he added, arguing that thanks to the law of averages, the one crew that did find the target regularly would quickly be shot down by flak or fighters, but that if they were put into a crack target-finding force where they and thirty or forty other ace crews would all find the target at the same time, the same defences would be saturated. A few of the good crews might be lost, but not half as many as if things were left as they were. 'I am certain that it is the formation of a K.G. 100 [Kampfgruppe 100] which is required at the present time as much for this reason as for any other,' he said. As for Harris's objection to the formation of a target-finding force that it would dent morale, 'I don't think I have ever seen anything quite so wet,' wrote the commander.[27]

Not all the replies were positive. One air-station boss warned that his crews viewed the idea of an elite force 'with some sarcasm' and would prefer to have their own illuminating force kept in the squadron. Another reflected the views of the majority, by telling Bufton something needed to be done urgently 'when the Russians are clamouring, the British public are clamouring and the Gods of the weather seem to have set their faces against any large scale operation by Bomber Command'.

One of the reasons the feedback had been so brutally honest is because the squadron commanders had thought it was anonymous. Determined to make his point, Bufton sent it all in a long note to Harris. Surely now Harris would see the merits of such a force with all this compelling evidence? But, once again, Bufton was firmly rebuffed. Harris argued that while he still had an open mind about a target-finding force and appreciated hearing the ideas from 'the lads who really do the work', he had simply spoken to a set of other station and group commanders who supported *his* view. Besides, Harris argued – firing back his own jibe – those on the front line operated in 'comparatively narrow spheres' with little idea about the bigger picture.

On 8 May 1942 – three weeks before the first thousand-bomber raid – Bufton threw everything into a final, forceful plea in a report marked 'Secret and Personal', which contained yet more evidence of inaccurate bombing from recent raids. He played a straight bat at one of Harris's key objections. 'There seems to be magic inherent in the phrase "corps d'elite" which immediately conjures up battalions of vague and nebulous antagonisms,' Bufton wrote.

> No one, however, would dream of trying to defeat the rival school by turning out the best House team. That is what we are doing now. It is essential we put the best men in the first team, and even that is not enough. They must train and co-ordinate their tactics as a <u>team</u>. Until we do this we cannot start to beat the enemy defences.[28]

In the final pillar of his argument – one which must have irritated Harris the most coming from a junior rank – Bufton suggested that the reason Harris objected to the formation of a target-finding force was the manifestation of a much wider issue – age and experience. 'It has often been said that this is a young man's war . . . that only the young men have the quick reactions needed to fight [using] our modern weapons,' wrote Bufton. The older officers, he added, were reluctant to accept and use advice from younger men whom they 'often benevolently' regarded as inexperienced. 'It is this attitude, I feel, which now prevents the formation of the Target Finding Force.'

Bufton's cause was aided by a new independent report by the High Court judge Sir John Singleton, who had been asked by the Cabinet to review the effectiveness of the bombing campaign, and concluded it had been pretty dismal, with little hope for improvement in accuracy unless things changed.

Bufton sent his report to Harris, and waited. And waited. A month later, on a warm June Saturday morning, he was sitting at his desk at work pondering why he still hadn't received a reply, when Air Marshal Sir Wilfrid Freeman, who was standing in for Charles Portal on leave, poked his head around the door.

'Good Morning, Bufton, any problems?' he asked. Bufton explained the impasse with Harris and lent Freeman all the correspondence he'd had on the subject. An hour later, Bufton's telephone rang.

'This last letter, have you had a reply?' asked Freeman.

'No, sir,' replied Bufton.

'Do you know why?'

'No, sir.'

'Because there isn't a reply,' said Freeman. 'You've beaten Bert at his own game.'

Ironically, Freeman did not initially like the idea of a target-finding force, but realised something had to be done when Portal had failed to move the debate on.[29] He promised to talk to Portal when he arrived back from leave. 'We've got to have a Pathfinder force and I'll talk it over with him,' he said.[30]

The following day, Freeman met with Bufton and Sir Henry Tizard, who added his support, and Freeman drafted a letter in Portal's name which was sent to Harris, arguing that a target-finding force would immediately open up a 'new field for improvement', raising the standard and morale of the whole force. As for Harris's concern that creaming off the best crews would affect the morale of the rest, Tizard told Harris: 'I don't think that the formation of a First XV at a school makes the small boys play rugger any less enthusiastically.'[31]

Harris met with Portal and Freeman and reluctantly agreed to form the new force. For Bufton, it was victory after months of bruising lobbying and dogged persistence. He wrote to his girlfriend Sue: 'WE HAVE WON!!!! Bert came to see the Head Man today, and he hadn't a leg to stand on. It's a shattering result . . . So you see, it was worthwhile after all.'[32] Bufton had every right to be delighted with playing a central role in creating the Pathfinders. But, in truth, others had also played an important hand and Freeman's intervention played a major part.

Harris was bitter about being overruled and the decision created a resentment that would have huge ramifications for the Pathfinders. For now, however, he set about getting the wheels in motion, telling his commanders that 'we must accept the decision loyally and do our best to make it a success.'[33] He refused to call it the Target Finding Force, the name which had been used by the Air Ministry, and instead christened it the Pathfinder Force. Its motto would be: 'We guide to strike'.

It was acknowledged that an elite squadron required special elements to lure the best men, and so Pathfinder crews would be required to complete a tour of 60 operations – later reduced to 45 – in one go, rather than the usual two tours of 30 sorties with a break in between. Operations completed in their previous squadron before being posted to the Pathfinders counted towards the total. All Pathfinder airmen would be automatically promoted one rank and receive a pay rise – in other words, danger money. After around four to ten successful operations, Pathfinders would be awarded a special Pathfinder Force badge – a gilded golden eagle, especially made by J.R. Gaunt & Sons of Regent Street, worn on the left-hand breast, which would, according to one senior airman, be 'highly prized' and give the individual a 'hall mark' in his future career – assuming he lived to see it.[34]

Although he was generally against automatic awards, Harris made it clear that no Pathfinder airman should be denied his badge 'unless for some very special reason you consider he has not earned one'.[35] No one was under any illusion about the increased dangers the Pathfinders would face. Potential recruits were reassured that 'physical or nervous failure after he has completed a total of 30 sorties will not be regarded as a lack of moral fibre', illustrating just how uniquely challenging and difficult the Pathfinders' work was considered to be.[36]

Most importantly of all, for such a *corps d'élite* to work, it would require an exceptional leader. One who could stand up to his seniors but also garner respect and inspire the men who served under him. For that role, Harris had just one person in mind: a young Australian called Don Bennett, whom Harris would later describe as 'the most efficient airman I have ever met'.[37]

Yet little did Bennett realise that even as he took charge of the fledgling Pathfinders, Harris was already plotting to go his 'own sweet way' by moulding the force into his own vision, even if that meant going behind Bennett's back.[38] Harris knew it couldn't be done immediately, but as Bennett would discover, as if transforming Bomber Command's air war against Germany wasn't a tough enough proposition, he would also soon be fighting an ongoing battle for the heart and soul of the Pathfinder Force against the very man who had invited him to lead it in the first place.

CHAPTER SEVEN

The Don

JULY 1942, BOMBER COMMAND Headquarters, High Wycombe. 'I have opposed the idea of a Pathfinder Force tooth and nail,' Bert Harris told Don Bennett, as the midsummer sunshine streamed in through the windows of his office. 'I do not believe it is right to weaken the best Command by taking its best crews in order to form a corps d'élite as a leading body . . . I did everything I could to stop the idea . . . but I have been given a direct order from the Prime Minister through the Chief of Air Staff, and since it was forced upon me I insisted that you should command it.'[1]

If Bennett was excited at being asked to lead such a prestigious unit as the Pathfinders, then his meeting with Harris had swiftly brought him down to earth with a resounding thump. Harris's attitude to the Pathfinders set the tone of his relationship with Bennett for the duration of the war. On the surface, the two men got on pretty well – after all, they shared similar traits. For Bennett, Harris was 'very often right' and his disapproval of those who were wrong 'was generally well justified'. Except, of course, when it came to the Pathfinders. Bennett claimed he liked Harris personally, although sitting across from his boss on that July day, Bennett couldn't help observing he was 'getting a little fat' and 'like most "copper knobs" he had a very short temper, and was very outspoken and indeed rude when he so chose.'[2]

But over the following months, as the pressure of the war over Germany intensified and the two men increasingly clashed over how the

Pathfinders should be best used, Bennett's initial professional respect for Harris would be tested to the limit.

The two men had first met a decade before, when Bennett – then a young pilot aged just 22 – served under Harris in an RAF flying boat squadron. In many ways Bennett was ideal for the job of running the Pathfinders, but he couldn't be more different from the usual breed of RAF officer. Born in Queensland in 1910, Bennett was a single-minded cowboy from the Australian outback who loved surfing waves along the Gold Coast and had learnt to drive a car by the age of eleven.

The son of a successful cattle rancher, young Bennett spent his first holidays on the family's 180 square miles of parched, sandy farmland. His childhood was dominated by farming, where he recalled the 'smell of burning flesh' as red-hot irons branded the writhing young steers and heifers. He learnt to ranch cattle on horseback and slept under the stars with a saddle for a pillow, listening to the howl of the dingo and the raucous screams of the cockatoo. 'It taught me the toughness of an outdoor life,' he later said.[3]

Bennett was fascinated with cars, stripping and assembling engines from a young age and sitting on his father's knee steering a Ford Model T. 'My life was a mixture of horseflesh and austerity on the one hand, with steel and comfort on the other.' One childhood friend recalled how Bennett was 'crazy about speed' and would tear up and down in a sports car lassoing a hat on the ground as he drove by.[4]

Bennett, brown-haired and slight of build, was the youngest of four brothers, who between them forged successful careers in law and medicine. His parents' desire for him to go into medicine too was thwarted by his being, by his own admission, 'somewhat of a loafer' at school. 'Nobody will make me swot,' Bennett told his mother, and when the family moved to Brisbane, Bennett left school and split his time between working for his father's property-estate office in the city and spending months at a time on the family's ranch, 180 miles west.[5]

But while he was sublimely happy working as a 'jackaroo' in the countryside, for Bennett it was utterly devoid of prospects. His failure to follow his older brothers' career paths gave Bennett a self-confessed inferiority complex, which in turn fuelled a steely determination to forge a successful career on his terms and a need to be the best. He joined the Royal Australian Air Force in 1930, inspired by his love of adventure and aviation. At first his parents were reluctant to back his career choice, declaring him little more than an 'aerial bus driver', but Bennett persisted, influenced by flight pioneers such as Amy Johnson. Aviation was still new, and if those only a few years his senior could be pioneers, why couldn't he? For Bennett, flying was as much a science as it was a thrill. He came top of his training class and set sail for Britain to join the RAF, aged 20.

Bennett was not a typical boisterous flyboy like many of his contemporaries. His English-born mother had been brought up a strict Methodist and Bennett inherited her teetotalism and didn't smoke. His grandfather had told him 'the only crime an Englishman cannot forgive is to be right' – an attitude that would set Bennett on a spectacular collision course with both his superiors and peers throughout his career.

Over the following four years, Bennett served with various RAF squadrons – including flying under the command of Harris – honing his aviation skills in 21 different types of land and sea planes. But land or sea, it made little difference. As far as Bennett was concerned, aircraft were aircraft. He gained first-class qualifications in flying, navigation, mechanics, wireless operation and instructing. By the mid-1930s he was one of the most qualified airmen in the world. But he was getting itchy feet serving in the peacetime forces, and in 1935 Bennett left the RAF to pursue a career as a commercial pilot.

He also made a homemade aeroplane out of various aviation odds and ends, in which he would visit friends at weekends. On one occasion, after a spot of lunch, Bennett climbed back into his little aircraft which he'd landed in a Wiltshire meadow. The wind had dropped completely and the field was very short for a take-off run, even with a headwind. As Bennett opened the throttle, the aircraft climbed into the air and cleared a stone wall by six inches. A clump of elms loomed. One observer later wrote: 'My heart stood still as Bennett somehow banked round them. I do not think a dozen other men living could have made that take-off that day.'[6]

Given Bennett's obsession with flying, it is little wonder he hadn't much time for anything else. But one April evening in 1935 – before he left the RAF and while stationed as an instructor at the seaplane base in Calshot on the south coast of England – he and some fellow officers decided to watch a play staged by the airbase's amateur dramatics society. It didn't exactly sound like the most scintillating night out, but it was one that would change his life.

A female character in the play required a French speaker. It just so happened that a pretty young Swiss woman called Ly Gubler was living with the family of the commander at RAF Calshot as an au pair. *Et Voilà!* Ly trod the boards that night, and later, as performers and the audience mingled over drinks in the crowded officers' mess, her eyes locked with Bennett's. The charming officer gave her a beaming smile which made her heart melt.

Bennett promptly asked his commander about the 21-year-old, blue-eyed blonde girl, and the two were introduced and fell in love almost immediately. Their first date a few days later was a drive around the Hampshire countryside in Bennett's Talbot. Ly had been sent to England by her parents to perfect her English, which Bennett, naturally, was eager to help with. It was a blossoming romance and Calshot's commander wrote to Ly's jeweller father back in Zurich reassuring him Bennett was the real deal.

In June 1935, Bennett proposed and two months later they married at the registry office in Winchester, Hampshire. After a whistle-stop tour of Switzerland to visit Ly's family, they set sail for Australia on board the SS *Hobson's Bay* for a honeymoon and to introduce Ly to her new in-laws. Ever the romantic, during the six-week cruise from Southampton to Brisbane, Bennett asked Ly to help him write a book about aerial navigation. *The Complete Air Navigator* would become an international bestseller and was adopted by the Air Ministry as an official textbook.

The fact that Bennett decided to use his honeymoon to pen a book on the scintillating subject of navigation chimed with widespread opinion that he was an arrogant aviation obsessive. Others thought him difficult to work with, one who had little time for people intellectually slower or whose opinions differed from his own. Harris opined: 'He could not suffer fools gladly, and by his own high standards, there were many fools.'[7] One post-war account described Bennett as a man 'aloof and humourless in his demeanour, he made few friends'.[8]

While there's no smoke without fire, the reality was more nuanced. He *did* only expect the best from people – an element which would be essential in making the Pathfinders a success – and possessed a short manner that easily ruffled feathers. But Bennett was a brilliant tech-nical navigator and airman who could also be warm and charming, possessing a more human side most people never saw. As the ship approached Brisbane, he was so nervous about introducing his new wife to the Bennett clan waiting on the quayside, he mistakenly squirted out a large blob of toothpaste onto his hand rather than shav-ing soap – much to Ly's delight.

Ly's reaction told a story in itself. Bennett had married a woman who could set the room alight with her beauty and intellect, who spoke seven languages and excelled at outdoor sports, but who was not afraid to occasionally set her husband straight. This included Ben-nett's fashion sense, which Ly wasted no time in tackling on the cruise to Australia by surreptitiously chucking various items from his ward-robe overboard. But she provided support and counsel, traits which would be invaluable when he was leading the Pathfinders in the dark-est days of war.

And despite his nerves at introducing her to his family, Bennett need not have worried. Ly went down a storm. Her picture was printed in the society pages of the leading Brisbane newspaper, announcing their marriage, with one diary reporter writing that Bennett's arrival in Australia was 'considerably stimulated by the acquisition of his Swiss bride':

> . . . first impressions are frightfully important and Ly couldn't have created a better one than she did from the deck of the *Hobson's Bay*, where the family turned out en masse to be on hand . . . Mrs Bennett made a charming picture as she stood on the deck clutching a huge sheaf of red lilies. She is most attractive, slim, fair-haired and sun tanned, and wore a frock of coarsely woven white linen, navy facings, a navy-blue beret and navy shoes.[9]

Any lingering doubts his parents had about their son's desire to fol-low his dreams evaporated. Six weeks later, the newlyweds sailed back to Britain so that Bennett could start his new adventure as a pilot for Imperial Airways, in January 1936.

After captaining regular services from London to destinations across Europe, Bennett was posted to Egypt. He flew four-engine sea-planes from Alexandria across Africa and Asia, landing his aircraft on crocodile-infested waters and wowing passengers by flying low over herds of elephants in Sudan and around Mount Kilimanjaro in Tanzania. He also set a series of aviation records, such as flying from Egypt to England in one day. Another record set under Bennett's command was for carrying an infant the longest distance in a seaplane – who happened to be Bennett and Ly's daughter Noreen, born in Alexandria in November 1936. 'BABY FLIES 2000 MILES' reported one newspaper after the plane had landed in a wet, rainy Southampton. The article was accompanied by a picture of a distinctly unimpressed brown-eyed baby being lifted from the aircraft in a wicker basket.[10] Noreen was joined by a younger brother, Torix, 18 months later.

Ever on the lookout for more milestones to set, in 1938 Bennett applied to fly the *Mercury*, the smaller of two combined four-engine seaplanes called the Short Mayo Composite. The aircraft took off from water with the smaller *Mercury* attached to the top of the larger *Maia*, looking like two flies mating, before separating in mid-air. As the larger plane circled back and landed, the *Mercury* – which had been too heavy to take off on its own – flew non-stop across the Atlantic. It was the first commercial flight to carry half a ton of mail to North America and was greeted on its arrival with a media frenzy. In October that year, Bennett also broke the world long-distance seaplane record, flying the *Mercury* nonstop for 42 hours in a 6,000 mile flight from Scotland to South Africa, and the following year inaugurated a regular two-way transatlantic commercial service using mid-air refuelling, in a 24-ton flying boat called the *Cabot*.

Among the more unusual cargo Bennett carried across the Pond were a brace of grouse which had been shot on the Scottish moors early one morning and were intended for the White House, two black beaver pelts presented to King George VI by the Hudson Bay Company following his recent visit to Canada, and a small box containing 3,000 live insects destined for Palestine to be used as crop pests.[11] Noreen and Torix became the first children to be flown across the North Atlantic. Thanks to Bennett and his team, the transatlantic flights became routine, although they were not without their dramatic incidents, such as when Bennett and his navigator took it in turns to crawl into the fuel tank in the wing in mid-air to repair a leak.

*

Despite the gathering clouds of war, the transatlantic flights continued. On the day Britain declared war on Germany, 3 September 1939, Bennett captained a flight from Ireland to Canada. As darkness fell, he received an abrupt and urgent message from the radio operator who had picked up an SOS from the SS *Athenia*, a British steam liner carrying over a thousand civilians to North America. The ship was sinking having been torpedoed by a German U-boat – the first submarine strike of the war – 200 miles off the north-west of Ireland. But in the darkness Bennett was helpless to rescue any survivors, and could only pass on the message and continue his flight. Over a hundred people died.

For Bennett, the brutal reality of the new war had struck home 'like cold steel through the heart', and with its outbreak the young Australian was inevitably sucked into the action with a series of hair-raising missions. In June 1940, under orders from Churchill, he flew Polish Prime Minister in exile General Władysław Sikorski from Britain to Bordeaux to rescue members of the Polish government, who had escaped from their homeland and were evading capture from approaching German forces. After Bennett had landed the seaplane in a lake a few miles south of the city, Sikorski and an aid set off armed with pistols while their pilot spent a sleepless night by his plane listening to German tanks rumbling along the roads nearby. At first light, four cars screeched around the corner loaded with Poles led by Sikorski. Bennett rushed them aboard, started the engines and soon the seaplane was soaring over the Bay of Biscay and safely back to Britain.

Shortly after his jaunt to France, Bennett was called to the Air Ministry in Whitehall and told he would be leading the first in a regular formation of American bombers across the Atlantic. For the next seven months he ferried various aircraft from North America to Britain as part of the Atlantic Ferry Organisation – a civilian outfit set up to equip the ailing RAF with much needed planes bought from America. No one had succeeded in crossing the North Atlantic by air in winter and breaking the so-called 'winter barrier'. It was tough and demanding flying which required expert navigation.

In 1941, Bennett was released to the RAF, given a commission as a pilot officer with the acting rank of wing commander and posted to a bomber squadron on operations over Germany. He had amassed over 5,000 hours of flying time and Bomber Command finally had their hands on one of the most experienced airmen in the world. After a number of operations over Germany with 77 Squadron, in April 1942 – three months before he would be asked to lead the Pathfinders – Bennett was given command of 10 Squadron and briefed for a secret mission to destroy Hitler's pride and joy – the German battleship *Tirpitz*.

At 7pm on 27 April 1942, Bennett pushed the throttles of his four-engine Halifax bomber through the gate and felt it hurtle down the runway of RAF Lossiemouth and into the darkening, moonlit skies above north Scotland. He set a course for Norway and thought about the mission ahead. On paper it seemed almost impossible. Bennett was flying one of twenty Halifax bombers from two squadrons, each carrying four 1,000lb spherical mines. *Tirpitz* lay in Fættenfjord, a steep-sided lake ten miles north-west of Trondheim, in the north of Norway. Bennett's objective was to approach the fjord from the west at just 200 feet and release the mines at exactly the right moment so they rolled down the side of the fjord, crashed into the 10ft-wide gap of water between the shore and the ship and exploded under its hull. If the *Tirpitz*'s propellers were successfully damaged, the ship would have to be towed into the open seas and back to port for repair, where it could be attacked by British air and naval forces. The fjord was a natural fortress and even for someone of Bennett's ability it seemed like a tall order, needing a fine degree of accuracy without any of the electronic technology or flares that would become such a hallmark of the Pathfinders later in the war. And as if that wasn't hard enough, the whole area around the ship bristled with anti-aircraft guns.

The two Halifax squadrons – with seven crew to each aircraft – were preceded by a brace of Lancaster squadrons, which approached the fjord from the south just before midnight. The Lancasters began their own attacks to divert attention, dropping 4,000lb bombs around the *Tirpitz*. The Germans, having been given ample warning, switched on smoke generators which sent up vast plumes across the fjord, covering the ship like soap suds in a bath.

Four hours after he had taken off, leading his aircraft in the second wave at low level, Bennett was still forty miles from the target when anti-aircraft fire opened up. A shell from an AA battery on the Norwegian coast smashed through the fuselage of his Halifax, injuring the tail gunner. Bennett pressed on through the crumps of intense flak which repeatedly peppered the aircraft and set the starboard wing alight, attracting yet more shellfire. As they dived down into the fjord to a height of 200 feet, the bomb aimer, lying on his belly in the front of the aircraft, reported he couldn't see anything because of the smoke. A split second later the ship's superstructure whizzed beneath them in a smoky blur. Bennett tried to turn the aircraft round for a second attack, but the fire in the starboard wing was now so bad it was only a matter of time before it crumbled, sending the Halifax into a deadly spin.

Bennett had to concede defeat and save his men. He released the mines into the fjord and banked the aircraft towards neutral Sweden.

'Prepare to abandon aircraft,' he shouted to his crew over the radio.

'Cheerio chaps, this is it, we've had it,' replied one terrified crew member.

'Shut up and don't be a fool,' ordered Bennett. 'We're perfectly alright but we'll have to parachute.'[12] But he realised almost immediately that the ailing plane wouldn't clear the 3,000-foot mountains looming ahead. Bennett yanked the steering controls hard to port with all his strength and shouted, 'Abandon aircraft! Jump! Jump!' He struggled to keep control long enough for his crew – including the wounded tail gunner – to leap out. He was about to do the same when he realised there was just one hitch – he didn't have his parachute with him. But his flight engineer appeared from behind and clipped it on his chest. Bennett jumped through a hatch as the wing collapsed and immediately pulled the ripcord, plunging into deep snow as his parachute canopy bloomed open and the stricken Halifax crashed and exploded a few hundred feet away.

Miraculously, Bennett had escaped with barely a scratch. His first thought on landing was Ly. 'I said out loud a few words addressed to her, and suddenly realised that I should rather be getting on with the job of trying to get back to her,' he reflected later.[13] The area would soon be crawling with SS frontier guards, police and German soldiers, so Bennett quickly covered his parachute harness with the white silk of the canopy and began the trek east through the deep snow towards neutral Sweden, around 40 miles away. After an hour on the run, with dawn beginning to break, Bennett was walking along a stream when he heard the crunch of footsteps on snow. A dark figure appeared in front of him. He assumed it must be a German and reached for his service revolver. But he realised it was his wireless operator, who'd landed nearby. 'It's all right. It's your Wing-co, it's your Wing-co,' Bennett reassured him in a hushed voice. Together the men hiked for three days and nights, walking over steep mountainsides and through snow waist deep, crossing streams of fast-flowing icy water to shake police dogs off their scent. Although they'd escaped injury, they began to suffer from frostbite in temperatures of −15°C and were hallucinating, surviving on a meagre ration of Horlicks tablets and barley sugars from their escape kit and drinking from streams or melted snow.

As they became so weak with hunger and exhaustion that they would soon no longer be able to continue, the airmen stumbled across a little farmhouse where a friendly Norwegian – who by luck had lived in Australia and spoke English – invited them in. The two fugitives fell asleep by a warm woodstove and were fed stew before being guided to the Swedish border. After an anxious half-hour walk over the frontier, Bennett came across an alpine house with light streaming out of the window and music playing inside. He was greeted by two men. 'Welcome to Sweden, and come inside,' they said in English, sitting the two scruffy and exhausted airmen down in the warm kitchen. A village dance was in progress, and before Bennett knew it, he was greeted by the somewhat bizarre sight of ladies in glamorous evening dresses pouring into the room to hug and shake their hands.[14] Following a generous dinner, Bennett and his crewmate were formally arrested by a Swedish army captain and sent to an internment camp.

Bennett had lost weight and was riddled with frostbite. But he wanted to get back to the war – and his family. It was knowing that one day he would get home to his wife and children that kept him going. Aided by a diet of silver-fox meat and 'coffee' made from ground fir kernels, he soon regained his strength and demanded to be released, threatening to sue the Swedish government if they resisted. He was promptly let go and flew back to Britain to be reunited with his family in May 1942, one month after being shot down. Back home, Ly had laid a place for her husband at supper every evening, praying he'd return.

The mission to damage the *Tirpitz* was a failure. Five aircraft were shot down, killing 15 airmen. But Bennett's flying skills had saved the lives of his crew – three made it to the Swedish border and four were captured and became POWs – and his extraordinary escape with his wireless operator caught the imagination of the media. The *Daily Telegraph* described their 'superhuman feats of endurance' in scaling alpine fells 'as good as impassable', while the *Daily Mirror* headline read 'RAF MEN FOIL NAZIS' and the *Newcastle Chronicle* reported how Bennett 'BALED OUT IN NORWAY BUT ESCAPED HUNS'. Bennett was awarded a Distinguished Service Order.

As the spring turned into summer, Bennett was posted back to 10 Squadron and then told he was to fly to the Middle East to assist in the bombing of the Italian fleet. He said goodbye to Ly and the children, but just half an hour before he was due to take off, he received an urgent message telling him to report to Bomber Command HQ immediately, where he was informed he would be leading the new Pathfinder Force.

As soon as he left Harris's office on that July day in 1942, Bennett set to work. The formation of the Pathfinders wasn't a complete surprise to him, of course. He had attended a series of meetings with Air Ministry figures over the previous 18 months about how bombers could better navigate to the target, and had suggested creating a force of experienced navigators using the latest technology and 'fireworks' to lead the main force. He later claimed – with his trademark modesty – that this was the first seed which was sowed on the subject of the Pathfinder Force. In reality, while Bennett played a key role in running the new force, the formation of the Pathfinders germinated from a number of people. Nevertheless, by appointing Bennett to lead the new squadrons – whatever his own misgivings about their shape – Harris knew the bar would be set high from the off.

Over the next month, as the finer details were thrashed out, Bennett fought hard to create his new force in the face of a total lack of enthusiasm and sense of urgency from some RAF group commanders, who were unwilling to relinquish their best crews. For others, the promotion of this brash but talented young officer to arguably the most interesting command job in Bomber Command left a bitter taste in the mouth. Yet while Bennett was a Marmite character to his contemporaries – there's no doubt he could be bloody hard work – his pre-war aviation exploits and his *Tirpitz* adventure had cemented him as something of a *Boys' Own* hero in the ranks. One fellow airman observed, 'He is a bundle of energy. Never still. The fellows under him think the world of him',[15] while another reckoned, 'If you were not religious you thought Bennett was Jesus Christ. If you were religious, he was the next best thing.'[16] Indeed, Bennett acquired a new nickname: 'The Don'.

All the new Pathfinder airmen were volunteers (albeit not always willingly), and ideally Bennett wanted those who had completed at least 12 ops over Germany and excelled at navigating and bombing accurately. Crews from operational squadrons were expected to have 'proved determination in pressing home the attack', a high standard of proficiency and an adaptability to new methods. Every crew member was expected to know his job inside out but also be expert in map-reading at high altitude. Bennett, or one of his small team of five, would personally interview every man to check his suitability and knowledge. Any not making the grade would be sent back to their unit. It was also planned that a third of the new crews would comprise the best of the pupils graduating from Bomber Command's operational training units, who were expected to be 'strong of character', intelligent and quick learners.[17]

For now, the Pathfinder Force would not have its own group status but would instead work under the direct control of Bomber Command HQ, with orders being sent through 3 Group. By 15 August 1942, the new force had been scraped together, comprising five existing bomber squadrons – 7 Squadron, 35 Squadron, 83 Squadron, 109 Squadron and 156 Squadron – one from each of Bomber Command's groups, which were moved to four new bases in Cambridgeshire and

Huntingdonshire. Like most Bomber Command squadrons, they typically comprised around eighteen aircraft – split into three flights of
six – although sometimes their numbers were swelled.

In an ideal world, Bennett could have done with a few more days to
prepare his men, but Harris turned the screw. Just three days later –
with new crews still arriving – he ordered the fledgling Pathfinder
Force to face a baptism of fire.

CHAPTER EIGHT

Blooded

EIGHT-THIRTY PM, TUESDAY, 18 August 1942. In his new headquarters at RAF Wyton in Cambridgeshire, Don Bennett waited nervously as 31 aircraft from his fledgling Pathfinder Force rumbled off the runways at Wyton and three other aerodromes in eastern England and headed towards Germany for their maiden mission. Earlier in the day, Bert Harris had sent Bennett a signal:

> Tonight the force under your command makes its debut in the vitally important role for which it has been raised. I am confident that the selected crews under your command will achieve all that skill and determination makes possible of achievement. All the crews of Bomber Command now look to The Pathfinders for a lead to their future objectives which will ensure the maximum infliction of damage on the enemy with the greatest economy of force. They will I know not be disappointed. Good luck and good hunting.[1]

While it was always nice to get an encouraging message, Bennett knew full well that many people – including his boss and some group commanders – were totally unconvinced about the Pathfinders and wouldn't lose much sleep if they failed. It was crucial this first mission was a success to prove the doubters wrong.

On paper, compared to some missions over Germany, reaching the target should have been relatively simple. The Pathfinders were leading a force of 118 aircraft to bomb Flensburg, a small town in the north of Germany on the Baltic coast. Coastal cities and towns were generally easier to navigate because of the coastline and inlets. However, the winds were stronger than forecast, pushing the Pathfinders north into Denmark. It was a dark night with a lot of ground haze, making accurate navigation almost impossible. Arriving in the area around midnight, some crews flew around for 40 minutes desperately trying to find the town while avoiding flak and German night fighters. Other planes dropped to 2,000 feet in an attempt to see through the haze but still couldn't see the target. A few simply turned back with their flares and bombs unused.

Sixteen Pathfinder crews claimed to have dropped their flares on Flensburg, on which 78 planes from the main force then dumped their bombs. In fact, the little town had completely escaped damage and instead the force bombed two Danish towns and a large area of Denmark, 25 miles north. As if it wasn't bad enough hitting the wrong town, it appeared this new band of supposed elites couldn't even find the right country. It couldn't have been a worse start for Bennett.

'Great joy was generated in the command and outside the command because of these phoney Pathfinders,' recalled Hamish Mahaddie, an extrovert Scotsman and one of the most experienced pilots in the new force, having already completed one tour with Bomber Command. 'We were these people that were going to find the target. Now we were only Pathfinders by name'.[2]

The 31-year-old had jumped at the chance to join the Pathfinders, but the veil fell from his eyes after the Flensburg raid, which was 'an absolute disaster'. Mahaddie had only arrived at his new squadron in Wyton from Scotland the night before, where he'd been training crews to fly Whitley bombers. With less than 24 hours' notice he'd been asked to captain a Short Stirling heavy bomber. 'I had come into a completely new crew, in a strange aeroplane that I had never flown . . . that didn't bother me, I was a very experienced pilot, but I was not experienced as a Pathfinder. None of us were. We were "makey-learny", and that Flensburg trip was really desperate,' he said later.[3] 'We felt rather like a star footballer, purchased at some enormous transfer fee, who fails to score a goal during his first season.'[4]

Soon after joining a Pathfinder squadron, one navigator walked into a local pub only for the other airmen to beat a march out on the bar, singing 'Here come the Pasture Finding Boys! Ta-ra-ra-ra!' – a suggestion that all they could hit was open countryside. He felt the force had no common tradition. It was all so new. But the mickey-taking acted as a spur. 'When we heard the others singing "Here come the Pasture Finding Boys" we became all the more determined to make the Pathfinders into something to be proud of. "Hell," we thought. "We'll show them." '[5]

Over the coming nights various ops against targets over Germany came and went as the Pathfinders tried to get to grips with their new role. Rumours about the new force were beginning to swirl around Bomber Command. One morning, in the mess of RAF Coningsby in Lincolnshire, Guy Gibson – the future Dam Buster – and a group of his squadron colleagues got chatting to an airman who had landed at the airfield with engine trouble the night before and who was about to be posted to the Pathfinders. The young airman told Gibson he was looking forward to operating out of one of the Pathfinder airfields in Cambridge, where 'the beer's good and the girls aren't bad', and explained about the merits of gaining the Pathfinder badge, 'to a chorus of sarcastic cheers' from the rest of the assembled group, noted Gibson afterwards.[6]

Gibson got to see the work of the Pathfinders for himself on a raid to bomb Saarbrücken just two weeks after the force had formed. Piloting one of the main-force Lancaster bombers, he arrived in the target area early to observe their technique. 'Sure enough,' said Gibson, 'the Finders laid their long string of flares, the Illuminators hovered around and then dumped bunch after bunch of flares right over the town; the bombs, incendiaries at first, began to fall thick and fast, about a thousand tons of them. Soon the whole area was one mass of flames.'[7]

Gibson's crew dropped their 8,000lb bomb on the target and returned safely home, with Gibson impressed by what he'd seen from the Pathfinders. The next day, however, they received bad news from the photo-reconnaissance unit. 'The Pathfinder Force had boobed,' wrote Gibson. Instead of hitting Saarbrücken, the raid had bombed Saarlouis, a tiny town thirteen miles to the north-west situated in a similar bend on the River Saar. 'The Recco boys said that judging from the photographs there wasn't even a signpost left standing there. Those thousand tons had removed the place from the map.'[8]

The raid, which killed 52 Germans, would have inflicted a much greater death toll if the local inhabitants hadn't been able to take shelter in unoccupied concrete positions of the Siegfried Line – the huge concrete defensive structure built during the 1930s that happened to run around the town. According to local reports, the community was said to be 'enraged' at being targeted, but the residents had witnessed something which would become all too familiar to thousands of Germans as the war progressed: watching flares appear overheard before the bombs started exploding a few seconds later.[9]

And in that respect, it wasn't all bad. As Harris told Bennett, they may have hit the wrong town again but at least the Pathfinders had done a damned good job in finding a target for the main force to pummel. But the unintentional bombing of Saarlouis illustrated the challenges faced by Bennett. By the end of August he had lost 15 aircraft on missions – the equivalent of 9 per cent of the force's total strength – with vitally experienced crews being shot down and killed.

And Mahaddie was right. What the early missions had shown is that they were only Pathfinders by name. Because, in reality, nothing much *had* changed. There was no magic bullet. A few selected squadrons had been pulled together with no extra training, no special equipment or technology. Although many were experienced crews, all they really had was enthusiasm and a desire not to let the rest of Bomber Command down. Bennett would need to fight tooth and nail over the next few months to get the technology, planes and men he knew were required for the dice to roll in his favour. He was confident he could prove the doubters wrong, but the clock was ticking.

First, Bennett had to consider the aircraft. In August 1942, the five founding squadrons sent to the Pathfinders – like the rest of Bomber Command – were primarily of a mishmash of medium and heavy bombers.

At RAF Warboys, 20 miles north of Cambridge, the crews of 156 Squadron flew the two-engine Vickers Wellington bomber, widely used by all groups in Bomber Command and in operational training units (OTUs).

But the Wimpy's vulnerability was ruthlessly exposed in a typical incident witnessed by Australian Max Bryant soon after he arrived back in Britain following his successful training as a navigator in Canada. Bryant was still five months away from being posted to a Pathfinder unit, and after a brief stint in Scotland he was posted to an OTU in Staffordshire, where crews learnt 'on the job' by taking part in operations over Germany. Bryant's best friend Don Charlwood had also been posted to the station following his training, and in fading light one September evening in 1942, Bryant walked Charlwood out to a Wellington and gave him a hand with his preflight checks, before shaking his hand, wishing him luck and heading to the watch office to see the aircraft take off for the mission to Bremen.

A few minutes later, just before midnight, with the last two Wellingtons just about to take off, there was a yell over the radio from the control tower. 'Stand by ambulance and fire wagon – aircraft coming in with port engine on fire.' One of the Wellingtons had lost power from an engine soon after take-off and was returning to base. Bryant's thoughts immediately turned to Don. 'Get ready to move, here he comes,' said the controller, as the incoming Wellington approached the runway, its green starboard light blinking. Bryant watched as the aircraft suddenly turned steeply on one engine – the light vanished, there was a loud crash and a great cloud of flame burst thirty feet into the air. Bryant heard the controller yell: 'Get cracking – too late' and then an exasperated: 'These fucking Wellingtons! Get those other aircraft in the air immediately. There are bombs on that aircraft. Tell them to hurry up.' The ambulance and fire engine rushed towards the burning plane. 'The case was hopeless but my heart contracted at the thought of these gallant blokes going in their line of duty to a blazing crate, loaded with bombs,' wrote Bryant in his diary later. 'The flames were leaping skyward, and there were bright flashes and explosions as flares and ammunition blew up. I was feeling ill; my heart seemed encased in ice for I thought it might be Don. It was a sickening sight.'

A few minutes later, Bryant was relieved to learn it wasn't Charlwood's aircraft. However, a fellow Australian cadet who had trained in Canada had been killed. 'I discovered that the navigator was poor old Joe Turnbull . . . For a few moments I felt sick and shaken. Only after a while did I realise the crew would never realise what hit them – the crash would kill them all immediately'. Later that night there was another explosion as the rest of the bombs went up – four of the fire crew on the ground lost their lives. Nine men gone. 'I crawled to bed and prayed in cowardly manner that I might not die as Joe did,' wrote Bryant. Turnbull was the first of the 20 Australians who'd trained together in Canada to be killed, but there would be 14 more.

Bryant's account illustrates the relative weakness of the Wellington. While it was pretty durable, with only two engines, a limited capacity to carry bombs and lacking powerful armament to defend itself against fighter attacks, the medium bomber was an unrealistic long-term option for a sustained bombing campaign over Germany, especially for the Pathfinder Force spearheading the raids. Ideally, Don Bennett's men needed a decent heavy bomber which could carry a good number of bombs and flares with an operational range to fly long missions deep into Germany. It needed to be manoeuvrable to fly its way out of enemy attacks from fighters, with some defences of its own to fight back. Finally, the aircraft had to be robust enough to absorb enemy fire and to be flung about the sky, with four reliable engines to bring it home again.

Three of the five founding Pathfinder squadrons used three different types of heavy bomber. The crews of 7 squadron, based at the Cambridgeshire airfield of Oakington, flew the Short Stirling. The only aircraft to be originally commissioned as a four-engine bomber in 1936, the Stirling was a monster – as long as three double-decker buses and the height of a two-storey house. In the factory, the fuselage had to be built in sections and shunted together like a train. It had a wingspan of 100 feet and could carry more than 14,000lb of bombs carried in three parallel bomb bays 42 feet long – the equivalent in length of one and a half Spitfires. Its huge wheels were six feet in diameter, designed to support an aircraft weighing over 30 tons when fully loaded. Powered by four 1,595hp Bristol Hercules engines, which gave it a top speed of around 270mph, it was armed with eight .303 Browning machine guns, mounted in pairs in turrets in the nose (with two pairs), tail and on the top of the fuselage. Manned by a crew of seven, some thought it a lumbering giant while others looked upon it with affection.

Yet the Stirling was plagued by technical problems. One of the most common was when the electric undercarriage packed up after the fuse blew, meaning some poor sod would have to wind a handle 600 times to lower the wheels manually – not an ideal situation to be in after a long mission with a damaged aircraft and fuel running low. 'The flight engineer carried a half a copper penny in his pocket and shoved it in the fuse slot so it wouldn't blow,' remembers one Pathfinder airman.[10]

All that weight meant the Stirling had a limited flying ceiling of around 16,000 feet and was vulnerable to flak, enemy fighters and bombs dropped by other Bomber Command aircraft flying at higher altitudes. Of all the heavy bombers, the Stirling had the highest loss rate in the war – both for the Pathfinders and in Bomber Command overall – and would be phased out of front-line operations in the autumn of 1944.[11]

Ten miles to the west of Oakington at RAF Graveley, 35 Squadron flew the Handley Page Halifax – another four-engine bomber originally conceived in 1936 as a twin-engine type. It was beefed up with four Rolls-Royce Merlin or Bristol Hercules engines, depending on the mark, which gave it a top speed of 280mph. The Halifax was 70 feet long – 17 feet shorter than the Stirling – yet it could carry 13,000lb of bombs flying at altitudes of around 19,000 feet, making it marginally less vulnerable to flak. It had three gun turrets, front, mid-upper and rear (the guns in the nose were removed in later marks), and a crew of seven, comprising the pilot, navigator, flight engineer, bomb aimer – who also manned the front guns – a wireless operator, mid-upper gunner and tail gunner. Crews affectionately nicknamed it the 'Hallybag' and it was a workhorse of Bomber Command.

But, like the Stirling, the Halifax was beset with flaws, especially in the early versions. Its handling wasn't always brilliant and if pilots needed to try any evasive manoeuvres to avoid enemy flak or fighters, they were warned the fuselage might break apart. Flames from the exhausts on the side of the engines could be spotted from up to 500 feet away, acting as a beacon to attract enemy fighters. Early marks also had a tendency to spin at low speeds. 'We had little confidence in the capabilities of the aircraft,' recalled one Pathfinder bomb aimer. 'Nearly every trip was faced with one big (though unspoken) question by us: "What would go wrong this time?"'[12]

Nevertheless, whether they liked it or not, both Harris and Bennett knew the Stirling, Halifax and Wellington all provided a stopgap until they could be replaced by the best heavy bomber of all – the Avro Lancaster.

The 'Lanc' was already being used by 83 Squadron when it arrived at Wyton in August 1942 to start life with the Pathfinders. In almost every area it was simply leagues above all other heavy bombers – a masterpiece of British aviation.

Like the Halifax, it was originally designed as a two-engine bomber, named the Manchester, but was thankfully redesigned in late 1940 with two more engines and rechristened the Lancaster. The smallest of the three heavy bombers, coming in at just shy of 70 feet long, the Lancaster had a much better performance thanks to four 1,460hp Rolls-Royce Merlin engines and a top speed of around 287mph. It could reach an altitude of 24,000 feet and still fly over 1,600 miles when carrying up to 22,000lb of bombs. Like the other heavy bombers, it carried a crew of seven or eight, and was armed with a brace of .303 Browning machine guns in both the nose and dorsal turrets, and four guns in the tail turret. Even counting motors and turrets as a single part and excluding nuts, bolts and rivets, the Lancaster comprised 55,000 separate parts and over three miles of electrical wiring. Yet it still took fewer man hours to make than the Halifax and the Stirling and dropped more tons of bombs for every plane shot down.[13]

'Its efficiency was almost incredible, both in performance and in the way in which it could be saddled with ever increasing loads without breaking the camel's back,' recalled Harris, who pressed hard to increase the production of the Lancaster at the expense of the other types.[14]

The Lancaster also made a lasting impression on new pilots setting eyes on it for the first time. John Kelly returned from his training in Hollywood in early 1943 and was destined to join 83 Squadron after converting from Wellingtons. At an operational training unit in Rutland, he walked up to a Lancaster for the first time, swung his legs up into the belly of the great machine, turned right and inched himself into the pilot's seat on the left-hand side of the cockpit. Compared to the Wellington, which Kelly reckoned was a 'regular chamber of horrors with levers and dials all over the place', the Lancaster seemed beautifully simple.[15]

'The Lancaster is really a colossal size and when sitting in the "office", even with the machine on the ground one gets an impression of being airborne,' he wrote home to his mother. The cockpit was almost 20 feet above the tarmac, with a single seat in front of the steering column and a vast bank of engines. 'I am fast becoming reconciled to the idea of flying four motor stuff, in fact I think I could really enjoy it. These Lancs really are tremendous machines, it almost makes one dizzy to look down from the cockpit. There are dozens and dozens of instruments and "gadgets" but strange to say I find myself familiar with most of them. What makes things look so complicated to the stranger is that there are four of most things – Four throttles, four starters, and of course there are four times as many engine gauges, plus a lot of extras,' said Kelly.

There was no co-pilot – second pilots had been scrapped in the spring of 1942 to economise on aircrew – so the flight engineer sat below him to the right on a fold-down seat. 'I was surprised, though I had heard rumours, that there is only one pilot seat, for no second pilot is carried nowadays. Fortunately, a flight engineer is carried. He relieves the pilot of a whole instrument panel and just leaves a mere 60 other things to look after,' Kelly wrote. He was also impressed by two Lancasters in his squadron that between them claimed to have destroyed 37 enemy night fighters. 'You can imagine there is great rivalry between the crews, and the boys who have shot down the 19 are always very rudely telling their rivals to go and get some shooting practice in.'

For most bomber pilots, flying the Lancaster was a revelation compared to preceding heavy bombers. Ernie Holmes – who had picked up the nickname 'Sherly', short for Sherlock – had started his bombing career flying Halifaxes, and found the Lancaster a joy to fly by comparison: 'What a difference it was. It was a beauty to fly. You could throw it around the sky like a Tiger Moth.'[16]

Yet as special as the Lancaster was, there was one remaining type of aircraft flown by one of the five founding Pathfinder squadrons that rivalled it, and it couldn't have been more different. A few select crews of 109 Squadron flew one of the most remarkable machines to take to the skies anywhere in the world during the Second World War. If the Lancaster was the workhorse of Bomber Command, then the de Havilland Mosquito bomber was its greyhound. And its arrival with the Pathfinders in the autumn of 1942 would be as important as the Lancaster in transforming the fortunes of Bomber Command.

The Mosquito came from the drawing board of the British aircraft designer Geoffrey de Havilland in 1938. Its smooth, rounded lines were lauded by aviators, but it was initially pooh-poohed by the Air Ministry as a serious military aircraft, until Air Marshal Sir Wilfrid Freeman championed its performance, ensuring it gradually began to be used by the RAF in greater numbers, as both a fighter-bomber and a bomber. Most remarkably, the two-man plane – comprising a pilot and navigator – was made almost entirely of wood and given the moniker 'the Wooden Wonder' – a well-deserved sobriquet, for it could fly faster than every bomber and fighter of the time, thanks to two 1,460hp Rolls-Royce Merlin engines. Little wonder it went like the clappers, reaching speeds of almost 400mph, given it was basically a plywood frame with two Spitfire engines attached. As a result, the Mosquito's designers decided it didn't need any guns or defensive armament, but could instead rely on its speed and agility to escape enemy skies virtually unscathed. In fact, although it was made mainly of wood, by the time this had been compressed via a mould into the iconic Mosquito shape and laminated, the fuselage churned out of the factories was pretty strong – certainly not that far off the thin aluminium which covered most other aircraft. Many 'Mossies' would return from missions shredded with flak holes. But its tiny losses said it all – from the beginning of 1943 to the end of the war, the Pathfinders would lose just 1.1 per cent of the Mosquito aircraft despatched.[17]

Initially only available in small numbers, the Mosquito would soon be taking a 4,000lb bomb to Berlin in around two hours with only the slimmest chance of being shot down. Bennett knew how important the plane could be for his new force, but still had to convince the powers that be at the Air Ministry of its potential impact. Some couldn't believe a wooden aircraft would stand a chance in the maelstrom of gunfire over Germany and argued that it couldn't be landed at night because of the blinding glare from the flames licking out of the exhausts which flanked its nose.

So Bennett decided to do what he did best – in the autumn of 1942 he quietly borrowed a Mosquito from the de Havilland headquarters in Hatfield and took it for a spin himself, flying tests day and night from Wyton. A few weeks later at a crunch meeting in Whitehall, Bennett sat down opposite senior Air Ministry figures and listened as they listed various reasons why the Mosquito shouldn't be used. He batted them all back, before they finally said, 'Well in any case it is all academic, you can't fly a Mosquito at night because the exhaust flames blind the pilot.'

'I'm very sorry,' replied Bennett, 'but if I had only known I would never have flown it as I have for the last 6 or 8 days every night.' There was a hushed silence and Bennett got his Mosquitos.[18]

His crews were overjoyed. 'It was fun to be in because you skitted around so fast,' recalled one 109 Squadron navigator.[19] For Colin Bell, who returned from training pupils in America in mid-1943 via a conversion unit flying two-engine Blenheim bombers, it was a revelation. 'Let's put it this way, if you took off in a Blenheim you might position yourself in relation to the airfield before you set course. When you took off in a Mosquito, when you looked back, the airfield had disappeared. It's like getting into a racing car. It could outfly anything in the air force.'[20]

Which was just as well. Because Bennett was about to use it for a top-secret project which would revolutionise bombing.

CHAPTER NINE

Boffins

WYTON AIRFIELD, SUNDAY, 20 December 1942. In the gloom of the chilly winter afternoon, the little tractor chugged into the hangar towing a Mosquito Mark IV bomber belonging to 109 Pathfinder squadron. It was being prepared for an operation that night. But then – disaster struck.

'You're too close. You're too close!' shouted a desperate armourer to the tractor driver. It was too late, and before he knew it, the Mosquito's wooden wing had hit another aircraft with a loud crunch. The ground crew swarmed over the plane, worried the aircraft would have to be scrubbed from the mission.[1] Thankfully, the damage was superficial – a smashed navigation light, which was easily and quickly repaired. However, the prang illustrated just how nervous and excited everyone was. This was no ordinary night.

A few hours before, the whole squadron had been paraded in a hangar and addressed by a commanding officer. 'You are engaged in a very special operation and if I hear the word Oboe mentioned in any pub around this district,' he said, 'your feet won't touch the ground.'[2]

At around 5.30pm, after the preflight briefing, pilot Hal Bufton – brother of Sydney – the commanding officer of 109 Squadron, and his Australian navigator Edward Ifould climbed into their now thankfully repaired Mosquito. The little cockpit was cramped but comfortable. Bufton sat on the pilot's seat to the left, in front of the steering column and display full of dials. Ifould was in the navigator's spot, positioned to Bufton's right, checking through his maps and route plan. Red-blue flames licked from the exhausts as the 12 cylinders in the two Merlin engines burst into life before settling into a comforting purr.

The ground staff removed the chocks from under the wheels and after a thumbs up, Bufton gently pushed the throttle forward and carefully taxied down to the start of the runway. When he saw the light of the green Aldis lamp flash from a little caravan next to the runway, Bufton released the brakes and pushed the throttle forward.

The Mosquito gathered speed, reaching 125mph before Bufton pulled back on the steering column and the plane gently rose into the black sky above Cambridgeshire. Climbing at 2,500 feet a minute, in a short while it had reached 26,000 feet. It was one of six Mosquitos from 109 Squadron cruising at 300mph towards mainland Europe.

Their target was innocuous: a coking plant in the town of Lutterade, 270 miles from Wyton in the south-east Netherlands. Yet the method of bombing was anything but. Packed into the nose of each Mosquito was a little piece of clever new technology called Oboe. At about 7.27pm, flying over the Netherlands, Bufton and Ifould picked up a signal in their headphones. They were on track. At 7.37pm they heard another signal through their headphones and Ifould immediately pressed the bomb-release 'tit'. Four 500lb bombs plummeted from the belly of the aircraft towards the target, 26,500 feet below. The Mosquitos banked for home and landed back at Wyton an hour later to eagerly await the photo-reconnaissance pictures which would be snapped by another high-flying Mosquito the following day.

The results of the raid were mixed – some bombs landed just 200 yards from the coking plant while others were up to a mile and a half away. And Oboe had failed to work properly in three of the aircraft.[3] Yet, despite the teething troubles, the partially successful deployment was a sign of things to come. On another December evening the device was tested on a target in Belgium, where Pathfinder Mosquitos struck the headquarters of a German night-fighter unit. The attack was observed by Belgian resistance fighters, who sent back a report to London confirming bomb craters had been smoking just a few feet from the target.[4] In both cases, the most remarkable aspect was that the crews hadn't even seen their target.

It was clear that Oboe could be extraordinarily accurate. No longer would a cloudy sky or a pitch-black night provide a blanket of protection for targets in the crosshairs of Bomber Command. Don Bennett reckoned Oboe was 'probably the most effective single instrument of warfare in our entire armoury', and knew just how important the device might be in transforming Bomber Command's fortunes.[5]

Just as remarkable was the little-known background of Oboe's inventor. Alec Reeves was a 40-year-old engineer who before the war had helped invent the first commercial transatlantic telephone and developed something called 'Pulse Code Modulation' – technology that allowed Churchill and Roosevelt to talk securely between London and Washington during the war. Educated at Reigate Grammar School in Surrey, City and Guilds Engineering College and Imperial College London, Reeves moved to Paris in 1925, working for the International Telephone and Telegraph company.

As boffins sometimes tend to be, Reeves was an unusual man to say the least. His father was a mapmaker who had been deeply involved with spiritualism and attended sittings with great mediums of the day, including Estelle Roberts, whose 'spirit guide' was an American Indian named Red Cloud. Reeves inherited his father's love for the paranormal, believing he was in regular contact with the nineteenth-century inventor of electrical generation, Michael Faraday.

A keen climber and skier who loved chatting modern art with the French cubist painter Georges Braque, Reeves claimed to have played in the French tennis open championship before the war, but fled Paris in 1940 as the Nazis were rampaging through the country, reaching England via Spain on a coal freighter and losing most of his possessions along the way.[6] Despite being a committed pacifist, he accepted the need to defeat Hitler and entered the world of scientific intelligence, working first for R.V. Jones, where he played a significant role in the 'battle of the beams' – helping detect and destroy the radio beams that had been used so effectively by the Luftwaffe on Coventry and London – before moving to the Telecommunications Research Establishment (TRE) in the Midlands town of Malvern, where he started developing Oboe.

The TRE was the main British centre for radar innovation and development in the war, staffed by 1,500 of the country's brainiest scientists busily working on a wide range of radar and other radio-based technology. On the second floor of the Preston Laboratories in Malvern College, Reeves and his team worked around the clock to find a solution to Bomber Command's night-navigation conundrum. Like many ingenious inventions, Oboe was fantastically simple, and although it operated slightly differently, part of its origins lay in the X-Verfahren system used by the German pathfinders which Reeves had worked to counteract.

Two transmitting stations were built in England. One station, codenamed 'Cat', was based in Trimingham in Norfolk, the other, 'Mouse' 116 miles away in Walmer on the Kentish coast. A device on board the plane received pulses transmitted from the two stations, amplified them, and sent them back again, allowing a fix of the air-craft's location to within 50 feet – even if it was flying at 300mph, five miles in the air and up to 270 miles away. When the plane was about ten minutes flying time from the target and had reached the previously agreed position then, with luck, the pilot started to hear a constant tone through his headphones that sounded like an oboe – hence the name – indicating he'd picked up the invisible arced tramline from the Cat station. He then flew carefully along the arc – rather like if the plane was an air valve on a slowly spinning bicycle wheel and the Cat station was the nut at its centre – which would eventually bring him over the target. The invisible arced track was only 175 yards wide and required skilful and steady flying. If the aircraft drifted off course either side, the constant tone in the pilot's ear was superimposed by dots or dashes, depending on whether the plane was too near or too far away from the station, so he could adjust his course accordingly.

As the plane approached the target, the pilot was given a series of Morse code warnings through his earphones. Finally, when the plane intersected a straight line from the Mouse station – which measured the distance between it and the aircraft to determine how far along the arced track it had gone – the pilot heard a final signal of five 'dots' followed by a 'dash', indicating they'd reached the correct aiming point and it was time to drop the bombs.[7]

A special air-pressure chamber was built to simulate how the Oboe equipment would perform at high altitudes. 'Time and time again the chamber ascended, with anxious Boffins surrounding the sacred set, prodding with long screwdrivers in an encouraging manner,' wrote one observer. Again and again 'a flash and a puff of smoke came from the set as 35,000ft was reached' and the set broke down. However, their patience was eventually rewarded when they ironed out these initial faults.[8]

But, as clever as it was, Oboe wasn't a panacea for all Bomber Command navigation problems. Because of the curvature of the earth, it only had a range of about 270 miles, meaning the RAF could hit most targets in the Ruhr Valley but no cities beyond, such as Berlin. It also required an aircraft to fly at around 26,000–30,000 feet, ideal for the Mosquito but ruling out heavy bombers. Once a crew had picked up the radio pulse to take them to the target, they needed to maintain a level trajectory and constant speed, making them more vulnerable to enemy attack. Finally, the Oboe system could initially only control one aircraft every 10 minutes, negating any chance of using it alone for saturation bombing.

Nevertheless, Oboe would prove to be the most accurate blind-bombing system of the whole war, with an error margin the equivalent to the length of a football pitch from bombs dropped two miles above, and about three football pitches from a plane flying five miles up – astonishing statistics bearing in mind that just a few months before it was operational two thirds of crews were struggling to get within five miles of a target.[9] For lower-level precision attacks nearer Britain – targeting V1 and V2 rocket sites and gun placements in the run-up to D-Day in 1944, it would be even more accurate and 'the cat's whiskers as a navigational tool', according to Harris.[10]

Yet, despite its potential, Oboe wasn't churned off the production line. Each set was handmade by Reeves and his assistant Frank Jones and assembled on circuit boards before being fitted to Pathfinder aircraft. It would increasingly be used by Bennett's Mosquitos as the war progressed, but by the beginning of 1943 there were still only 16 Mosquitos available as target markers. In reality, Oboe's production was an eccentric affair and really rather apt, because – by and large – the boffins at TRE in Malvern and its nearby testing airfield in Defford were an unconventional bunch.

At the Rose and Crown pub in the village of Severn Stoke, twelve miles west of Defford, they'd gather for beers to let off steam and chat tech. On one occasion an observer recalled how one scientist wore his work shoes without socks – the height of 1940s sartorial daring. Then there was the young Scot who could not ride a bike. After a few pints his colleagues would take seemingly endless pleasure in plonking him on the saddle and pushing him down a hill, where he'd wobble and eventually tumble off, prompting widespread guffaws. Other japes were less vanilla. A pilot testing some of the boffins' equipment got so merry at a lunchtime drinking session that he climbed on board his Lancaster bomber and flew it under the Severn Bridge in Shropshire. Thankfully he landed safely with the mid-upper gunner looking 'somewhat shocked'.[11]

In addition to Oboe, the experts at Malvern were working on a second important blind-bombing device to help the Pathfinders try and see in the dark. H2S was a sort of airborne radar housed in a rotating scanner in a dome attached under the fuselage of an aircraft, which sent out a fan-shaped beam that scanned the ground. The returning echoes – or 'backscatter' – were strongest from built-up areas, less strong from open countryside and weakest from open water. They created a shadowy map of the terrain below that appeared on a cathode-ray tube housed in a set in the fuselage. By comparing the image with a detailed map, a navigator could – in theory – identify his aircraft's location both en route and when they were over the target. It was especially effective at distinguishing between land and water, and tended to be used more effectively against targets by the coast – such as Hamburg – or next to large rivers or lakes.

Unlike Oboe, H2S didn't rely on 'talking' to ground stations but worked independently, with the bulky kit fitted in individual aircraft. Its use, therefore, was limited only by the range of the aircraft which carried it – meaning it could target Berlin when deployed on a heavy bomber. However, like Oboe, H2S was far from perfect. It suffered countless technical teething problems, often during ops and sometimes as the aircraft was approaching the target. In the early months of 1943, only around half of the planes fitted with H2S arrived over the target with serviceable sets.[12] It was tricky to operate because the radar returns on the cathode screen often gave poor resolution – little more than a fuzzy blur which made the identification of landmarks difficult. In time, bomb aimers were retrained as H2S specialists – referred to as 'Nav 2' or the 'Y-operator' – working with the navigator as a two-man team, and flight engineers doubled up as visual bomb aimers.

The H2S was fitted with a highly secret magnetron valve. Air Ministry fears that it would fall into enemy hands were realised just a month after it was first deployed over Europe in early 1943, when the Germans captured an intact unit from a downed British bomber in the Netherlands, unravelling its secrets to develop their own radar so that Luftwaffe night fighters could track and home in on Pathfinder bombers.

But H2S was a damn sight better than what the RAF had before when the weather conditions outside were appalling, and from being used in just a couple of dozen Pathfinder heavy bombers in January 1943, by September that year it had been fitted in all Pathfinder heavies.[13] One newspaper described it as the 'Magic "Black Box" of the Skies'.[14] Crucially, because it could be fitted to many more aircraft than Oboe, H2S also had the potential to increase the 'estimated weight of attack' – in other words, more bombers over the target at once to swamp the defences – a pillar in the success of Harris's area bombing. One Pathfinder commanding officer even reckoned that by using H2S, Bomber Command could more accurately bomb targets at night than the US Eighth Air Force could by day.[15]

With his hands-on approach, Bennett kept a close eye on the development of H2S and Oboe and made regular visits to Malvern. On one occasion in the summer of 1942, during H2S trials in the dawn skies above Defford, Bennett threw a Halifax around with an H2S set in the back to recreate the rough and tumble of operational flying to see if he could lose the signal. 'I managed to hang on,' Dr Bernard O'Kane, one of the H2S inventors, sitting in the rear of the aircraft monitoring the set, later scribbled in his diary, before Bennett continued to put it through its paces so much that 'unfortunately the gear blew up'.[16] Passions ran high – later, O'Kane and Bennett had a full-blown argument about H2S in front of the band during a dance at Wyton.

Nevertheless, thanks to the boffins, by the beginning of 1943 Bennett and the Pathfinders had both Oboe and H2S to help them take the fight to the Germans. 'The Pathfinders without boffins would have been an improvement,' said Bennett, due to better crews, more training and superior aircraft, 'but they would have not have been half as good as they were with the boffins,' he admitted.[17] Bennett now needed to think how best to use the new technology. He devised a policy of using Oboe on targets close to Britain and in the Ruhr Valley and H2S on targets further afield, such as Berlin. But it wasn't much use if only the Pathfinders could accurately locate the target, and many aircraft in the main force behind were without their own cutting-edge navigational devices. They still needed to be shown where to aim their bombs. And for that, Bennett turned to another little known boffin – whose speciality was fireworks.

CHAPTER TEN

Fireworks

T HE REPORTER FROM THE *Daily Express* looked up as the aircraft rumbled over Wyton airfield. It was late. The sky was pitch black. But then, quite suddenly, everything changed.

'A cow blinked in the garish night light,' the journalist later wrote.

> Fields and farms blazed with brilliant colours. The highest hedged country lane reflected more light than pre-war Times Square in New York. Expanding marker flares drifted slowly in the sky as though dragging at anchor; multi-hued target indicators reflected crazy shadows on the earth below. The night was dark . . . but the Pathfinders brought daytime to this secret spot. At that moment I knew the feeling of helpless nakedness that must come to people when first they see the Pathfinders in the vanguard of 800 bombers.

The journalist had been invited to Wyton to watch the trials of the latest Pathfinder flares and target markers. The story made a page lead in the paper and ran with the headline, 'R.A.F. LIGHT UP A BIT OF ENGLAND'.[1] The use of flares and markers by the Pathfinders to light up many bits of Germany was just as important as the latest navigation technology and bombs in turning the fortunes of Bomber Harris's strategic bombing campaign. Yet despite their playing such a crucial role, the details of who invented the markers, how they were made, or how they even worked is often overlooked. It was all top secret.

Bomber Command had been experimenting with dropping flares to illuminate and identify targets since before the war. The theory was simple, even if it very often hadn't worked in practice. If a town or city was brightly illuminated and the sky was clear, then a bomb aimer looking through the bombsight from the nose of his plane had a good chance of knowing where to aim. But bad weather, cloud, smoke and haze often made this impossible. And besides, even if the leading aircraft accurately bombed the target, once it was on fire, the crews following up tended to simply dump their bombs on the blazing, smoky mass below. And human nature being what it is, if they were flying through heavy flak or under attack from enemy fighters, they bombed on the back edge of the conflagration and got the hell out of there. Some referred to those crews as 'fringe merchants', and they caused a phenomenon known as 'creep-back', where the fire caused by the bombs moved steadily away from the initial target towards the direction of the incoming bombers as the raid progressed.

The Germans also created dummy towns and suburbs made from canvas and plywood which, to the British crews thousands of feet up, looked remarkably like the real thing. They were designed to draw the bombs and incendiaries of the RAF planes away from the real targets. They worked too – in one RAF raid on Berlin in 1941, RAF crews dropped 43 times more high-explosive bombs and 47 times more incendiaries on a dummy installation than on the city itself. Construction crews built a replica of the famous Brandenburg Gate and government buildings east of the Spree River. The German capital was surrounded by sixteen such sites. The Germans also constructed fake airfields, complete with hangars and runway lights, on moors and lakes around Berlin. Other sites were even filled with combustible materials and set alight before or during a raid, so that from 10,000 feet they looked like burning buildings.[2]

Hitler's Minister for Propaganda, Joseph Goebbels, mocked the RAF's 'grotesque' claims about successfully hitting various targets in Germany. 'Perhaps they even believe them themselves,' he wrote in his diary in July 1941. 'They give us a certain pause to catch our breaths.' Wisely, Goebbels' department didn't publicly refute the RAF numbers. Why alert them to the error of their ways?[3] Although Goebbels didn't know it, the RAF was fully aware of the dummy sites. After a raid on Mannheim in May 1942, Harris berated crews for bombing flaming decoy sites thinking they were the real target. The fires had a magnetic attraction for his bomber crews. 'Somehow or other we must cure this disease, of wasting bombs wholesale upon decoy fires,' he told his commanders.[4]

To try and counter this, in the first few months after being formed, the Pathfinders began using two types of rudimentary marker bombs to try and help the main-force crews bomb in the right place. Once they'd located the target, they dropped a 'Red Blob Fire' – a 250lb incendiary bomb stuffed with benzol, rubber and phosphorus, which landed on the ground and burnt with a red glow. Its big brother – the Pink Pansy – was a 4,000lb bomb casing filled with the same ingredients and coloured pinkish red, so the initial flash produced a brilliant, vivid pink which could be spotted from high in the sky.[5] These were only stopgaps, however. The Germans soon began to produce their own imitation markers to fool British bombers. It was a game of pyrotechnic cat and mouse, and the British boffins needed something better to outsmart their German counterparts.

The man tasked with helping the Pathfinders find the firework solution was an unassuming former chemistry teacher from County Durham. Wilfred Coxon was born in Newcastle upon Tyne in northeast England and brought up in the little village of Ryhope, on the edge of Sunderland. After gaining a PhD in chemistry from Nottingham University, Coxon joined the chemical company ICI as a research chemist, before becoming a teacher at a grammar school in Birmingham, where he taught the subject to sixth-form pupils. Following a stint as a lecturer in chemistry at the Regent Street Polytechnic in London, in February 1940, aged 29, he joined the Directorate of Armament Development as a technical officer.[6] With his chunky woollen jumpers and tweed sports jackets, Coxon was an unlikely saviour of Bomber Command. He had no experience with explosives or armaments, and sometimes felt he was more like a nuisance to be tolerated by his new colleagues than a valued contributor. But his knowledge of flares and pyrotechnics was second to none.

Coxon began working on a marker bomb in 1940 – knowing Winston Churchill took a personal interest in developments. At his workbench, he worked long into the night – cardigan sleeves rolled up, glasses perched on the end of his nose – experimenting with various fuses and mechanisms. But he struggled to find a workable version, partly because he lacked a fuse which was able to eject the flares at altitude. He was certain it would only be a matter of time before he made a breakthrough, but the Air Ministry and his bosses disagreed, ordering all attempts to be abandoned. Unconvinced, Coxon continued conducting his own, totally unauthorised experiments in secret, alongside his normal work for the Directorate of Armament Development. Sitting in his workshop one day, it dawned on the Tynesider that the armament department was long in empty shell cases. That is when a brainwave hit him – why not simply turn the bomb into the marker using the shell cases?

At a ground-based trial at Boscombe Down in Wiltshire in June 1941, he watched as incendiaries successfully exploded from the bomb casing, producing a fiery oval pattern which could be easily seen from a spotter plane circling in the sky above. Now he needed a way to repeat that in the sky. Coxon scored a second breakthrough shortly afterwards when an engineering friend he'd approached fitted a fuse to the marker bomb that worked at different altitudes. This was followed by more clandestine tests at Boscombe, aided by a photo-reconnaissance commander who was officially testing flares. Coxon was getting somewhere. But it was all too much for the officialdom of the Air Ministry. Despite his breakthrough, when they found out what Coxon had been doing, he was formally charged with carrying out illicit trials which they claimed had endangered the aircraft and its crew. The charges were soon dropped, but Coxon's card had been marked.

Nevertheless, Coxon's determination burnt as bright as his pyrotechnic markers. He had spotted an action report on a failed raid over Essen in March 1942, in which an RAF observer was impressed by sticks of flares dropped from a Stirling. 'If similar sticks of incendiary bombs could be given a distinctive colour or colours they would form an ideal marker bomb,' stated the report.[7] Following the raid, the RAF airman approached Coxon with his observations and, armed with this nugget, Coxon wasted no time.

In a series of trials, Coxon set about filling the shell cases of 250lb bombs with 60 magnesium pyrotechnic candles, each 12 inches long.

The bomb was to be dropped from the aircraft and, when it reached 3,000 feet, 5oz of gunpowder and a clever little barometric fuse reacting to the change in air pressure blew off the tail, ejecting the candles inside. The candles cascaded at 150 feet per second like drops of water from the rose of a watering can, hitting the ground after 20 seconds and fizzling for around two and half to three minutes in a diameter of about 100 feet. If the bomb was fused to eject the candles at 1,500 feet, their fall was even more accurate – around 60 feet in diameter. The candles burst in different colours – red, green or yellow – depending on the job required, although in the later stages of a raid when a target was burning ferociously, green markers would need to be used as they were more conspicuous in the smoke and flames. The three-minute burn time could be extended to around 12 minutes depending on how the casings were filled and through delayed ignition. Some even had explosive charges to hinder attempts by people on the ground to put them out. These sorts of markers – called ground markers – would be dropped in clear weather in salvos of four or six.[8]

But ground markers were useless if the sky was thick with cloud – a regular occurrence in northern Europe. So Coxon and his team also developed sky markers, which burst at a predetermined height and floated down on parachutes at between 500 and 700 feet a minute, lighting up the cloudy sky above the target, meaning, in theory, the target could be bombed from thousands of feet above irrespective of weather conditions. In reality, these markers drifted in the wind, so the aircraft using them would have to allow for this by dropping them upwind, so that they would float across the target as they burnt. Target indicators could also be also used as route markers to guide a bombing force to the target and keep the bomber stream together, and as orbiting markers, which aircraft could use to fly around until they began their attack.

Coxon had the fireworks. He now needed to garner the support. He visited Sydney Bufton at his offices in Whitehall to explain his progress. Bufton knew just how important this could be for the Pathfinders and, using his clout as Deputy Director of Bomber Operations, days later he put in a formal request for the marker bombs to be officially trialled by Bomber Command. In early July 1942, Coxon demonstrated his bombs to both Bufton and Frederick Lindemann, Churchill's scientific adviser, in a series of midnight trials at Boscombe Down and the British Army's Larkhill artillery range in Wiltshire. Both men liked what they saw.[9]

But Coxon still needed to win over Don Bennett, newly installed as the Pathfinders' chief. Such were their importance to the success of Bomber Command, Bennett had been given special powers to approach the Ministry of Aircraft Production directly for development and design of new target markers. A liaison officer was installed permanently at the Ministry to co-ordinate the Pathfinders' requirements and to liaise with private companies to circumvent official production and design channels, which could be lengthy and bureaucratic.[10]

What the Pathfinders required, Bennett explained to Coxon, was a target indicator which was difficult to imitate and had good ballistic properties to ensure accuracy, but which was bright and colourful enough to illuminate the target area and provide a mark to catch the eye of crews who didn't want to grope about searching in vain. Once the Pathfinders had correctly identified the target, they needed to ensure the rest of the bombers knew where to accurately drop their bombs too, otherwise the whole raid would be a waste of planes and people. The pressure and responsibility on young Coxon's shoulders were huge. But with some more tinkering, he reckoned he had the answer.

Soon, the various types of target markers were ready for their final test. In the fading light of a bitter early January afternoon in 1943, Coxon's car gingerly turned through the gates of Rushford bombing range near Thetford in Norfolk. He joined a small group wrapped up in greatcoats at the side of the vast, snow-covered range, and waited nervously in the chilly evening. Looking on were representatives from both the Air Ministry and the Pathfinders. All Coxon's work would live or die in the next few minutes. Just before 6pm, the distant throbbing of eight Merlin engines drifted on the wind. A couple of minutes later, two Lancaster bombers roared over the range at 7,000 feet. Quite suddenly the black sky was transformed into day as bright flares fizzed down, bringing the wintry landscape to life. Over the next hour, the Lancasters made eight more runs, each time dropping different types of flares and target indicators.

The following morning, Bennett held a conference at Wyton to assess the results. To Coxon's delight, the trial had been a resounding success. For Bufton, who'd done so much to help Coxon, getting the target markers into action as soon as possible was a matter of urgency. 'These weapons,' he told colleagues in a memo, 'might well constitute the "missing link" in our night bombing operations and, if successful, might have a profound effect on the ability of the bomber force to achieve the concentration essential to success.'[11]

The process hadn't been entirely smooth, of course, and like many boffins, Coxon wasn't without his occasional mishap. On one occasion, he was experimenting with a dazzling combination of target-indicator candles at Wyton when things got out of hand. 'Talk about technicolour,' recalled one of his assistants later.[12] Thick black smoke billowed through a neighbouring hangar containing Lancasters and Mosquitos, causing someone to call the fire brigade, thinking that the hangar was on fire. Coxon could have been brought up on charges but instead received a serious dressing-down for his antics.

Better news was to come, however, and on 16 January 1943 – eight days after the final trial at Rushford – the new target markers were first used by the Pathfinders on a raid by 200 bombers over Berlin. They proved an instant success. It was now crucial that a steady supply was maintained. The markers were initially made through the Ministry of Aircraft Production and various ordnance-filling factories across Britain. Their research, development and production soon triggered a whole separate industry involving some of Britain's leading fireworks companies, who just a few years before had been manufacturing Jumping Jacks and Catherine Wheels to delight children. Now they would be used to help reap death and destruction. Firms including Aladdin Industries, the Crystal Palace Fireworks Co. and Standard Fireworks won lucrative contracts. A contract with Aladdin Industries alone was worth over £600,000 – the equivalent to an eye-watering £28 million today. Brocks – another fireworks firm – also supplied pyrotechnics, although it probably did no harm that the Pathfinder Force armament officer happened to also be a director of the company.

At the laboratories of the General Electric Company in Wembley, north London, scale models of towns were built in huge tanks filled with water with a window at one end to mimic the view from an air-craft flying at 10,000 feet. Fog, mist and haze were simulated by adding Dettol, a disinfectant which went milky when it entered water. 'Clouds' consisted of puffs of cotton wool wedged flat between two panes of glass. Small electric lamps dropped down from rails on the side of the tank represented flares, allowing observers to calculate their effective-ness before testing the real thing, with the aim of making them perfect for operations.

When they were in action over a target, bomb aimers in the main force were instructed to ignore the target itself – even if they could clearly see it – and instead bomb at the centre of the markers laid by the Pathfinders – or the 'mean point of impact', as it was known. As the target became covered in thick smoke and raging fires, fresh markers were dropped by more Pathfinder planes 'backing up' so the main force could continue to accurately drop their bombs through the duration of the attack. The smoke tended to clear after about 15 min-utes as the fires really took hold, but as they spread, smoke drifted up from new areas. So some markers were designed to ignite at a height of up to 10,000 feet, with the candles taking over a minute to drop to the ground and spreading over a wider area – especially effective if smoke was pluming from a target.

The light from fires, searchlights and anti-aircraft tracer could be as great as 100 million candlepower per square mile – eight times as vivid as the light given off from streetlights on a modern motorway.[13] The brightness of the sky on a dark night over a flaming, fire-raged target at 20,000 feet was greater than the moonlit brightness at the same altitude. Little wonder RAF bomber crews felt so vulnerable to attacks from German night fighters. The target markers dropped by the Pathfinders needed to be extraordinarily intense to be spotted by the main-force crews flying above.

Even with their intensity, target indicators on the ground were often obscured – they could glance off buildings and burn harmlessly in high-sided, narrow streets, smash through fragile roofs, land amongst trees or quickly be extinguished by alert fire wardens on the ground. The RAF estimated that as a plane approached, four miles from the target flying at 20,000 feet, the bomb aimer laying on his belly in the front of the plane looking through his bombsight at an angle of about 45 degrees could expect to see between 10–50 per cent of the candles dropped. If the markers fell in woodland as little as 5 per cent of the light given off was visible to bombers, depending on the time of year and whether the trees were deciduous or coniferous. For targets surrounded by woodland, green markers were chosen over red as the chlorophyll in the leaves absorbed more red light.

As the war progressed, various simulators were built for bomb aimers to practise bombing on different target indicators dropped by the Pathfinders. One, called the Air Ministry Bombing Teacher, used various ten-inch coloured lantern slides showing different patterns of target indicators depending on the type of raid, and the correct aiming points. Based on intelligence from real missions, the slides were judged by operational crews to give a pretty realistic effect.

The Camouflage Branch was asked to make a 10 feet by 9 feet 1/2,500 scale model of a raid in progress, simulating a town about three miles across undergoing an attack involving bombs and target indicators. On another version, bomb aimers in training stood in a viewing room simulating their cockpit and looked down on a 12 foot turntable with interchangeable 6 foot centrepieces showing different types of target with lighting effects for various attacks. The model buildings were made from wood and hessian cloth. Ground-up coffee granules served as tarmac, corrugated cardboard painted matt brown simulated newly ploughed fields, while cotton wool painted green resembled the tops of woodland. Electric lights shone through perforated holes in the base of the model, simulating clusters of target indicators, with the effect of smoke and glow produced by covering the holes with silk floss, dyed in red, green or yellow. The glow on the atmosphere was recreated using mosquito netting about a foot above the model, and crumpled sheets of gauze painted with a grey dye mimicked a smoke screen when seen under flare light. Although somewhat rudimentary, the models were built by staff who had done a good deal of flying over Germany, and worked pretty well in practice.

Scientists from the University of Cambridge even investigated the psychology behind why bomb aimers dropped their bombs on certain patterns of target indicators – although if they'd asked the average bomb aimer what he was thinking over a target he'd have most likely turned the air blue with his reply. But for much of the

Don and Ly Bennett relaxing on a beach in southern Queensland, Australia, during their honeymoon in 1935–36.
(Credit: *The Bennett family archive*)

Don and Ly Bennett visiting her family in Switzerland in 1935.
(Credit: *The Bennett family archive*)

Don Bennett with son Torix and daughter Noreen, 1939.
(Credit: *The Bennett family archive*)

King George VI, Queen Elizabeth and Princess Elizabeth inspect crews from 83 Squadron on a Royal visit to the Pathfinder air station at RAF Wyton, May 1943. (Credit: *The Bennett family archive*)

John Searby, left, and Don Bennett leaving headquarters of RAF Air Defence at Bentley Priory, Middlesex, after a conference before the Peenemünde raid in August 1943. (Credit: *The Howard Lees Collection via Chris Coverdale [8 Group Path Finder Force author and historian]*)

Allan Ball and Brenda Bridger in the summer of 1943. A few weeks later Ball was shot down over Berlin. (Credit: *Juliet Stockford*)

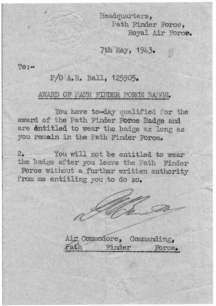

Headquarters,
Path Finder Force,
Royal Air Force.

7th May, 1943.

To:-

P/O A.R. Ball, 125905.

AWARD OF PATH FINDER FORCE BADGE.

You have to-day qualified for the award of the Path Finder Force Badge and are entitled to wear the badge as long as you remain in the Path Finder Force.

2. You will not be entitled to wear the badge after you leave the Path Finder Force without a further written authority from me entitling you to do so.

Air Commodore, Commanding,
Path   Finder   Force.

After around six to ten successful operations, Pathfinder crew could qualify for a special Pathfinder Force badge. Allan Ball was awarded his in May 1943, as signed by Don Bennett. (Credit: *Juliet Stockford*)

Ernie Holmes, fifth from left, pictured with other airmen and WAAFs ahead of a raid on Hamburg in July 1943. (Credit: *David Holmes*)

I. Will Remember

When the sun sets, and darkness falls, I will remember.
When the sun rises, and another day is born, I will remember.
For remembrance, is all that I possess, of those I knew so well.
Those who flew, with me, into the silent night, to fight the foe.

They asked not for bloodshed, nor did they start this fight.
But when they heard the bugle call They jumped to fight for right.
Often they prepared for missions, flying into the sleepy night,
To bring death and destruction to those who called right-might.

They did their job right, they did it well, but this couldn't last
For on the 23rd of May we fell, and became as the past.
Four of the eight are missing. These we know are dead.
Three more are accounted for, but the eighth man is still ahead
Making his way for his own homeland. Keep going my friend.

Tommy, Johnny, Mac and Jock, have left this earth
But we who live, will remember. I with Derick and Ron.
From the setting of the sun, till the rising of the same
We will think of those, who kept up Englands fame
Will you in England remember?

The poem penned by Ernie Holmes as a prisoner of war in Stalag Luft III in the autumn of 1944, after his Lancaster was shot down over Holland in May 1944, killing five of the eight crew. (Credit: *David Holmes*)

Fons Van der Heijden, a Dutch farmer who helped numerous Allied airmen including Ernie Holmes evade capture after they had been shot down, by providing food and shelter on his farm. (Credit: *David Holmes*)

Alec Cranswick, taken soon after Cranswick had successfully flown on the raid to Peenemünde on 17 August, 1943. (Credit: *The Howard Lees Collection via Chris Coverdale [8 Group Path Finder Force author and historian]*)

Dick Raymond in 1942. When he first met his new station commander, Raymond recalled: 'He looked at me and said: "How old are you my man?"; "I'm nineteen, Sir"; "Good God" he said.' (Credit: *Dick Raymond*)

(*Right*) John Kelly was one of only a handful of RAF cadets to be trained in Death Valley, California. The gruelling training was tempered by adventures in Hollywood where Kelly rubbed shoulders with movie stars. (Credit: *RAF Museum X004-2500/013*)

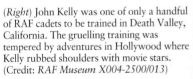

Gwen Thomas at her teleprinter machine in the signals section at RAF Upwood, 1944. Thomas experienced both love and heartache working with the Pathfinders.
(Credit: *Wendy Carter*)

(*Left*) Ian Bazalgette in 1944, proudly wearing his Pathfinder badge.
(Credit: *Pathfinder Collection within the RAF Wyton Heritage Centre*)

John Ottewell (*far left*), Charlie
Sergeant, (*second from left*) and
Charlie Shepherd, (*second from
right*) with some of their crew in
1944. 'As far as we were concerned
it was just another raid,' recalled
Ottewell of the raid on Dresden in
February 1945.
(Credit: *Chris Ottewell*)

(*Right*) John 'Doc' Macgown,
the group medical officer of the
Pathfinders. A former First World
War fighter pilot, Macgown
garnered the respect of young
Pathfinder airmen by accompanying
them on dozens of operations over
Germany.
(Credit: *The Macgown family*)

After gaining his flying Wings in Florida in early 1942, Colin Bell so impressed his instructors they asked him to stay in America to train US Army Air Corps pilots. In 1943 he returned to Britain and converted to twin engine Mosquito bombers. (Credit: *Colin Bell*)

VE Day, 8 May 1945. Don Bennett and a group of somewhat bemused Russians visiting RAF Wyton gather outside the station mess. Noreen and Torix Bennett stand with Pathfinder airmen and WAAFs in front of effigies of Hitler, Mussolini and Hirohito.
(Credit: *The Bennett family archive*)

war the only real way bomb aimers could practice was on operations, and seeing a mass of target indicators over the target could be a confusing and mesmerising experience for inexperienced crews in the main force.

As a Bomber Command Halifax approached Hanover one night in October 1943 on just its sixth mission with 109 Squadron, the bomb aimer watched in awe through the thin Perspex of the canopy at the unfolding sight 15,000 feet below. First he saw yellow target indicators dropped by the Pathfinder planes ahead floating down through a circle of searchlights. 'Now the red TI's were going down and a moment later a number of greens cascaded around the target,' he recalled in his diary afterwards. 'The fires were beginning to take hold now and what had been sticks of bright incendiaries were taking in the compact red tone of the true fires. I could see no ground detail.' As they neared the aiming point, the bomb aimer put his eyes to the bombsight and his fingers automatically felt for the panel of switches he would press to release the bombs.

'The smoke was pouring out of the centre of the target but I spotted a red marker on the southern edge of the clear centre of smoke,' he recalled. He ordered the bomb doors to be opened as the red marker inched ever nearer to the cross hairs of his bombsight, before relaying instructions to the pilot. 'Left! Left! Bags of left, left! OK. Steady her up. Here she comes! Steady! Steady! Steady! Bombs going – One, two, three, four, five, six, seven – Steady Skipper! – nine, ten – OK. Bombs gone.' The aircraft lurched up as the 2,000lb of bombs and incendiaries dropped away. 'Then as I looked again at the target I saw the most remarkable eruption I had seen so far,' he wrote.

> From the south-west quarter of fires it came, lighting up the whole place and the inside of the machine a deep blood red . . . it looked for all the world like the volcano in Walt Disney's *Fantasia*. It came up out of the smoke like a great thrusting forearm and clenched fist – a terrible, solid column of fire and smoke that must have been at least 200ft in diameter and risen to close on 2,000ft. It was the most amazing sight to see it rolling, writhing, thrusting out of the lesser fires, dull brown in the body of smoke, flecked and feathered with sprays of intense red light for all the world like lava issuing violently upwards

from a crater. It rolled majestically upwards while the light from it got steadily brighter for some 5 or 6 seconds and then the light died down again.[14]

Realising the effectiveness of the Pathfinder Force's target markers in helping the RAF main force bomb more accurately, the Luftwaffe was quick to try and create fake flares and target indicators to draw the unsuspecting bombers away. By March 1943, they had built rocket-launching sites around many decoy dummy towns. Each site was operated by 20 Luftwaffe personnel in 12-hour shifts. When a raid was imminent, they fired off rockets simulating the target indicators in a variety of colours from wooden crates built on concrete launchpads.[15] It was all pretty rudimentary, but even if they diverted just a few bombers away from the real targets it was worth the effort. In turn, Wilfred Coxon and his team regularly changed the ingredients in the target markers or made them ever more elaborate to keep the German scientists on their toes. One flare ejected seven stars in differing shades of red, green and orange every 20 seconds, each burning for eight seconds. Another ejected 28 candles which changed colour between green and yellow every 15 seconds for six minutes.

As pretty as they were, for the German civilians on the ground, these fantastic starbursts of colour were a prologue to terror. A German schoolboy from a small town in the Ruhr recounted seeing a single Pathfinder aircraft flying ahead of the main raid. He and his friends nicknamed it 'The Iron Gustav'. It dropped 'Christmas trees' – so named because the dropped target indicators fanned out to resemble lights on a festive tree – which 'looked like giants with light-bulbs that marked the whole area'.[16]

Handouts were circulated to firefighters and members of the public in cities across Germany urging them not to be afraid of the fizzing target markers dropped by the Pathfinder planes but to instead 'get them first' and put them out before the main-force bombers had the chance to see them and release their bombs.[17]

The Pathfinder crews thousands of feet above were fully aware of just what an impact the markers must be having. John Kelly wrote to his mother admitting German civilians would be shaken 'when they hear a commotion and rush out into the garden to find a whacking great crimson target indicator there, shooting off stars in all directions. Only be a couple of minutes before main force arrive and deliver their payloads on the spot.'[18]

Marker bombs were the keystone in the construction of all Pathfinder tactics, but it wasn't just a case of dropping the markers and considering the job done. Don Bennett created a complex system for his crews in which they followed a strict hierarchy and were only trusted to carry the precious markers as they gained operational experience.

In its very simplest form, this hierarchy dictated that anything up to 15 minutes before 'zero hour', when the main force was due to arrive over the target, Pathfinder 'illuminators' – made up of the most experienced crews – lit up the target area like daylight using strings of very powerful white flares. These aircraft were accompanied by 'supporters' – normally relatively inexperienced newbies to the Pathfinder Force who didn't carry markers but instead dropped bombs to help saturate the defences and take some of the pressure off the marker crews. Following closely behind were the 'primary markers', comprising Pathfinder crews with most accurate bomb aimers, who identified the target in the light of the first flares dropped by the illuminator crews, before dropping the first coloured target indicators. Once the aiming point was marked, more Pathfinder crews called 'backers up' had to estimate the mean point of impact of the primary markers before dumping more target markers – usually of a different colour – on the aiming point. If the ground couldn't be seen because of cloud or haze, then the target was located using Oboe or H2S – this was known as 'blind marking'. Now it was time for the main-force bombers to fly in. The target markers were refreshed every three minutes throughout the raid by Pathfinder 'recenterers' dropping fresh target indicators, partly in an attempt to prevent creep-back.

By their very nature – the fact they arrived first over a target and had to mark accurately – Pathfinder crews gained a reputation for being 'press-on types', given their task of accurately marking in grim weather or under terrifying conditions, including cones of search lights, flak exploding all around and enemy fighters waiting to pounce. What passed as a 'straightforward' mission was recorded in the notepad of one Pathfinder pilot soon after a raid to Ludwigsfaven on 17 November 1943:

> Took off at 1705 in 'D' & climbed to 20,000 ft on track. Severe internal icing all the way, started at freezing level (2000 ft) and didn't clear until we descended on way back. I kept my cockpit windows free by continually wiping them with a handkerchief soaked in glycol. The mid-upper gunner was hardly able to see out of his turret the whole trip. The rear gunner's oxygen froze up and his guns wouldn't depress. But we carried on! Low cloud during the whole trip but it cleared over the target and we were able to get a photo. Opposition was negligible, we saw no fighters & very little flak. Searchlights caught us once but couldn't hold us.[19]

As experienced as many of the Pathfinders were, a calm voice was still needed. So in mid 1943, Bennett introduced a 'master bomber' to proceedings. To be a master bomber crew member was one of the most dangerous jobs in aerial combat in the Second World War. The master bomber was normally a Lancaster or Mosquito with a highly experienced crew monitoring the whole operation from above and instructing the main force – and if need be other Pathfinder crews – over radio on where to aim their bombs. Most crews knew the way to survive was to get in and out as quickly as possible. But the master bomber arrived first and was often the last to leave, circling the combat area like a conductor or master of ceremonies.

The captain of a master bomber crew – the man actually issuing the instructions – needed to be a natural leader and issue clear, calm decisions under quickly changing circumstances. Success or failure depended on the human element, and encouragement and advice from the master bomber could tip the scales. When it worked, it improved the concentration and accuracy of bombing, reduced wasted bombs and boosted morale. Main-force crews especially said they felt reassured by hearing a calm, authoritative voice providing guidance to new crews, and it also relieved main-force crews of major decision-making responsibilities.

It could also be inspiring in the heat of a raid. During one operation, a flight engineer looked down from his Lancaster at 21,000 feet as the master bomber flew down to personally re-mark the target, 19,000 feet below. 'From what we could see all hell was being let loose at that lower level,' he recalled later. 'Looking down into the heart of the target, which by then was well lit up with other flares, we could see the silhouette of a Mosquito of the master bomber . . . he was coming over on the R/T [radio transmitter] as calm as could be, telling people to come in and bomb his northern markers and that it was a piece of cake.'[20]

Organising the raids was far from a piece of cake. Differing aircraft with varying performance, speeds and operational heights added to the complexity of the operations. With over a hundred Pathfinder aircraft required for larger raids, meticulous planning was required by Bennett and his team night after night. If the Pathfinders arrived at the target after the main force, hundreds of aircraft in an orderly bomber stream could be exposed to flak and fighters while circling around or bombing randomly. Minutes, seconds even, mattered and getting there too early could also affect a mission. When a Pathfinder navigator arrived back at base after what he thought was a successful bombing operation on the northern Italian city of Genoa, he was given a roasting by his squadron commander. 'He seemed to think that we had bombed half a minute before our time. "Hell," I thought, "we fly about 700 miles and you make a fuss about 30 seconds!" But I could see the point all right.'[21]

The final piece of the complex jigsaw of when and how targets would be marked by the Pathfinders was the age-old foe – the weather. Bennett knew some missions would require target marking by sight, and in others the target would be marked by Pathfinders using H2S and Oboe. So he devised three rather obscure but memorable code-names to be given to crews on their preflight briefings.

One morning Bennett called a squadron leader into his office in Wyton. 'Pedro, where do you come from?' asked Bennett. 'Wanganui,' replied the young Kiwi officer. Bennett made 'Wanganui' the code-name for operations where the target was completely obscured by heavy cloud, and sky markers would need to be dropped by Pathfinders using H2S to identify the aiming point. Bennett decided that the codename of the second technique should be taken from a town in Australia. When the target was covered in low cloud, fog or haze, but ground markers could still be dropped using H2S as their glow would be spotted through the murk, the codename 'Parramatta' – after a suburb of Sydney – was designated. Finally, Bennett needed a third codename for missions where ground markers could be dropped on targets in clear weather after being lit up by conventional flares and visually identified by crews through their bombsights. Bennett pressed the bell on his desk and called in his personal secretary. Corporal Ralph, otherwise affectionately known as Sunshine because of her blonde hair and breezy manner, strolled into the office and saluted. 'Sunshine, where do you live?' asked Bennett. 'Newhaven, sir,' she replied, looking slightly puzzled. And that was the final codename decided.[22] If any of these operational names were preceded by the word 'musical' it meant Oboe-equipped Mosquitos would first mark the target.

By the end of 1942, the Pathfinders had flown just over a thousand sorties for the loss of fifty crews. It had been a tricky opening six months with mixed results, but as the new year came in, they finally had the crews, the navigational technology and the target markers. On 8 January 1943 the Pathfinder Force became its own separate bomber group – 8 Group. Bennett's men were here to stay. And despite attempts by some from the Air Ministry to insert their own choice for commander, with Harris's backing the 32-year-old Australian was promoted to Air Commodore. With his new Group in place, Bennett ordered the first of regular reports to be circulated to all Pathfinder crews summarising the previous month's operations. It had a sketch of the Pathfinder eagle above a target with an arrow in its bullseye and the words 'Total Tenacity'.

'Our responsibility grows every day,' wrote Bennett in a note on the cover. 'With the advent of ground marking methods and new equipment, the reliance placed on us by the main-force crews is greater than ever. Perfect precision and unshakable reliability are the essentials of our existence. We must press on with them.'[23]

The wider war was turning. On 2 February 1943, the German army was forced to surrender to the Soviets at Stalingrad, and before long Axis troops in North Africa would be defeated by British and American forces. Now it was time to turn the screw in Hitler's backyard.

Winston Churchill met US president Franklin D. Roosevelt and his chiefs of staff in Casablanca to discuss how the bombing campaign should proceed. The role of Bomber Command was decided, with Harris later being told: 'Your primary objective will be the progressive destruction and dislocation of the German military, industrial and economic system, and the undermining of the morale of the German people to a point where their armed resistance is fatally weakened.' The American Eighth Air Force, meanwhile, would take off from airfields in Britain to bomb German targets by day. 'At long last we were ready and equipped,' said Harris.[24]

Following a brief but unsuccessful diversion of Bomber Command to bomb the German U-boat pens in north-west France, that spring Harris began his strategic all-out destruction offensive against Germany by attacking the Ruhr – a vast network of towns and cities along the Rivers Rhine and Lippe which provided Germany with most of its coal and half of its electricity. Bomber Command had targeted the Ruhr before but its success rate had been poor, as it was covered with a perpetual industrial haze from factories and protected by heavy flak defences and the most experienced Luftwaffe fighter units. Now, thanks in part to the new navigational merit of the Pathfinders and helped by the fact that nearly all the targets in the Ruhr were in range of its Oboe technology, Harris could start again. Defending German industry and civilians, meanwhile, were hundreds of crack night fighter aircraft and thousands of anti-aircraft guns. The level of death and destruction – on all sides – was about to increase dramatically. But who would blink first?

PART THREE

The Bloody Ruhr

MARCH 1943 - JULY 1943

CHAPTER ELEVEN

Essenised

EARLY AFTERNOON, FRIDAY, 5 March 1943, RAF Graveley, Huntingdonshire. Allan Ball was nervous and excited. Earlier in the day he'd strolled over to the operations room to see if his crew was listed for operations that evening. It was. One of six crews from 35 Squadron which would be flying into the dark enemy skies in just a few hours. Now, it was a case of waiting until the briefing later in the day to see exactly what fate awaited them.

Tall and brown-haired with Hollywood good looks, Ball had been in 35 Squadron since the previous January. Before volunteering for the Pathfinders he'd completed a tour of operations as a wireless operator with 77 Squadron – including an attack on the Renault Works in Paris in a Whitley bomber flown by Don Bennett – before converting to Halifax bombers and being reunited with his old colleague.

Ball was just the sort of man Bennett wanted in his force. Born in 1922, he was the oldest of three children brought up in a comfortable middle-class suburb in the Kirkstall area of Leeds. His father, a clerical officer in the accounts department at the Ministry of Labour, was a strict Edwardian type who did not like the noise of children around. This instilled in young Ball a determined drive and desire to better himself. He would lock himself away in the loo to practise his 'BBC English', worried his northern accent might hinder his chances in life. Perhaps he wanted to prove a point to his father too. In 1940, aged

18, Ball ran away from home with a few shillings in his pocket and joined the RAF.

But his motives to become a Pathfinder weren't entirely altruistic. One of Ball's best friends in 77 Squadron was a 22-year-old rear gunner called Larry Bridger. In October 1942, the squadron was posted from Devon to a new airfield in Yorkshire. Bridger gave Ball a lift in his Ford 8 car and suggested they break the journey up by calling in at his family home, a gamekeeper's cottage and six-acre smallholding perched on a hill on the Knebworth estate in Hertfordshire. Bridger was the oldest of four siblings – his two younger brothers were still boys, and his grandparents also lived on the farm. The family kept cows, a bull, pigs and chickens. They were always playing practical jokes. On one home leave, Bridger and his friends put beehives down the middle of the Great North Road, which ran past the farm. Their life was a total antithesis to Ball's strict upbringing back home. He loved the welcoming family, the relaxed, happy atmosphere and the whole way of life, full of noise and laughter. Everyone was welcome at Sunnyside.

It was there that Ball also met Bridger's young sister, Brenda. The same age as Ball, she dreamt of being a model and was proud of her 24-inch 'wasp waist'. Friends said she resembled the Hollywood actress Jane Russell. When she and Ball were introduced the air practically crackled. For Ball especially it was love – and lust – at first sight. The following day they went shopping in London. Ball bought Brenda the latest Glenn Miller records from Selfridges, before dropping a bombshell – would she marry him? She didn't say yes, but she agreed to go out with him. Ball instantly knew that this was what he wanted for his future. It was everything he had dreamt of and a complete contrast to his life so far. When he arrived at Graveley to join 35 Squadron two months later it meant not only was he part of Bomber Command's *corps d'élite* but more importantly just a short motorbike ride away from his new *amour*. He and his squadron mates would occasionally 'beat up' the farm by flying their giant bombers at rooftop height, causing Brenda to dive to the ground.[1]

35 Squadron had been founded in 1916. Its crest was a winged horse's head, commemorating co-operation with the cavalry during the First World War. Its official motto was *Uno Animo Agimus* – *We*

Act with One Accord. However, after three years of war, its airmen had
come up with their own, unofficial version: 'If it is possible we will do
it. If it is impossible, it will take a little longer.'[2] Ball's squadron mates
included Alec Cranswick, who had completed two main-force tours
and won a Distinguished Flying Cross for bravery – despite a nervous
breakdown due to exhaustion – before volunteering his crew to join
the Pathfinders in January 1943. Cranswick was considered one of the
finest pilots in 8 Group. Quiet and reserved, his closest friend was his
Alsatian dog Kluva, who would accompany him on training flights,
curling up in the wireless operator's compartment with the headphones from a spare flying helmet pressed against his head so he
might listen to music picked up on the bomber's radio. 'Sergeant
Kluva' even had his own logbook – filled in by Cranswick after each
flight – and once joined him on an operation in France when the plane
was targeted with heavy flak. When the aircraft's undercarriage collapsed at the end of the runway after landing, and Cranswick slithered
out of the escape hatch clutching Kluva, he vowed not to take the dog
on a bombing raid again.[3]

On that Friday, 5 March, as cigarette smoke danced on the rays of
the sunshine streaming through the windows of the briefing room,
Ball sat with dozens of other young airmen and waited. Briefings were
always tense affairs. Like so much of this job it was the not knowing,
the anticipation, that was almost more unbearable than the actual op
itself. At one end of the hut was a large map of Europe with a black
cloth over it. A group of senior officers filed in. The crews stood up. 'Sit
down, gentlemen,' said one officer, as the black cloth was whisked
away to reveal their target that night. Red threads of wool pinned on
the map led back and forth to the German city of Essen. Groans and
catcalls went up, as they often did for a 'hot' target. Then it was down
to work.

For the next hour crews were briefed on various details of the
mission. The target was the giant Krupp plant – a crucial jewel in
Hitler's industrial crown, manufacturing armaments for the Nazi
war effort, and one of the most heavily defended targets in Europe.
The plant lay in the centre of the city, surrounded by built-up areas.
Little wonder the RAF had tried but failed so many times to deliver
a knockout blow.

Beginning at 9pm, eight Oboe-controlled Mosquitos from 109 Squadron flying at 28,000 feet would take it in turns to drop red markers directly over the plant every two to three minutes, interspersed with up to 22 Pathfinder heavies operating at around 19,000 feet which would also be dropping markers. Ball's crew – one of six from 35 Squadron on duty – were given the crucial job of backing up the Mosquitos by raining green target markers on the reds to ensure the visibility of the aiming point for the 400 main-force aircraft. The weather was expected to be fair over Essen – perhaps a little stratocumulus cloud at 1,500 feet – with little serious haze, although crews were warned they might run into patches of mist and fog on their return to England.

In air stations all over eastern England the scene was being repeated. Main-force crews were told that the method of placing the red markers was 'a new and very accurate one' and ordered to aim at them with the greatest precision.[4] If no red markers could be seen, they were told to aim at the greens with equal care. At RAF Elsham Wolds in Lincolnshire, Max Bryant – who had completed his operational training in four-engine bombers and joined 103 Squadron flying main-force Lancasters – summed up his feelings in his diary: 'There was a good deal of knee knocking when we learned that the target for the evening was Essen. Reputedly the hottest spot in Germany, we did quite a bit of nail chewing while waiting for take-off time.'

Bryant's fears were well founded. Essen was one of the most heavily defended targets in Europe, with hundreds of anti-aircraft flak batteries and searchlights operating around key industrial areas within the Reich itself and along the western approaches in France, Belgium and the Netherlands. In the first six months of 1943 the Wehrmacht spent a whopping 29 per cent of its entire weapons and ammunition budget on flak weapons and 14 per cent on flak ammo, all with one purpose in mind – to blast the hell out of the Pathfinder and main-force planes flying overhead. By June 1943, there were 1,089 heavy flak batteries and 738 light flak batteries protecting Germany – mainly around towns and cities – with 350 searchlight batteries in place by the end of that year.[5] They were operated by thousands of young Germans recruited for military service to free up soldiers for front-line fighting. Women were also recruited, although Göring was forced to issue a warning to Luftwaffe commanders when he was told certain flak and searchlight supervisors had attempted to 'enter into love affairs' with female teenagers under their care, adding that they would be punished with the 'fullest severity under the law'.[6]

Each flak battery could comprise up to twelve guns, with some operated by radar and predictors, which tracked the incoming planes flying overhead and fed data to the gun crews, who in turn would set their fuses and sights accordingly before firing. Radar crews painted the silhouettes of successfully downed bombers on the radar dish next to the date of the victory. The light flak was typically heavy machine guns or 20mm cannon which pumped up thick gunfire – ideal for engaging fast, low-flying aircraft. The heavy flak, meanwhile, was single shot guns ranging from 88mm to 128mm, which didn't have the same intensity as the light flak but could reach altitudes of 30,000 feet.

Flak was designed to scare as much as kill. An estimated 322 Bomber Command aircraft were lost to flak between March and July 1943, but many more were badly damaged or prevented from bombing.[7] And as if flak alone wasn't bad enough, the British bombers also faced the increasing threat from the *Nachtjäger* – the German night fighters. The Germans had almost 400 night fighters available, crewed by highly trained and brave young men. Like their British counterparts, the most pressing concerns for the majority were defending their homeland and simply surviving in the forbidding, violent skies above mainland Europe. While a vast number of British bombers were shot down by a small number of highly skilled flying aces, many German fighter crews never downed an enemy aircraft – known as an *Abschüsse* – at all, and it could take as many as fifty operational flights before that first success came.

The *Nachtjäger* initially flew three types of aircraft, all converted from their original purpose of operating during the day. The Messerschmitt Bf 110 was a twin-engine heavy fighter which was quite popular with its crews thanks to its speed and manoeuvrability, and was armed with two 20mm cannons, four 7.92 mm machine guns and a single rear-firing 7.92 mm machine gun. The Dornier Do 217, meanwhile – an ugly twin-engined converted bomber – was slow and cumbersome. Perhaps the best of the three was the Junkers Ju 88, a smaller and more manoeuvrable aircraft than the Dornier, armed with one or two 20mm cannons and three 7.92mm machine guns. Some models were also fitted with two *Schräge Musik* upward-firing 20mm cannons. This allowed the aircraft to quietly position itself in the blind spot underneath an unsuspecting bomber, before opening fire into a bellyful of high explosives and incendiaries, the resulting explosion vaporising metal, bone and flesh alike. In contrast to the carnage it could reap, one German pilot remarked that his Junkers Ju 88 was so comfortable to fly, it was as if he were 'at home by the fireplace'.[8]

By 1943 a well-established German night-fighter defence had been set up, based around the Kammhuber Line, an invisible belt stretching from the German–Danish coastline in the north, through Belgium and down to the Swiss border, through which the British bombers would have to fly to and from targets in Germany. Positioned along the belt were a series of more than 70 three-dimensional radar-operated fighter boxes which the Germans called *Räume* (rooms) – each one covered an area of 20 miles by 15 miles and was controlled by a fighter-control room on the ground staffed with Luftwaffe personnel. They had innocuous-sounding codenames such as Oyster, Quail and Polar Bear.

When the British bombers were detected on the Freya radar – which had a range of about 100 miles – German night fighters scrambled from their airfields and took to the skies to await further instructions. As the British bombers flew through a *Raum*, they appeared to fighter-control officers – known as the *Jagdwaffe* – down on the ground as blips on a cathode-ray screen. Like a lion stalking its prey, the fighter-control officer selected the blip of the best-placed bomber. They then turned to a second radar system, with a range of 30 miles – called a Würzburg – one of which tracked the progress of the bomber, while another directed the orbiting night fighter to it. In the fighter control room the movements of the two aircraft were plotted on a glass table with a red marker for the bomber and a blue one for the fighter. The controller's aim was to radio instructions to vector the night fighter to within about two miles of the bomber, at which point its crew switched to their onboard Lichtenstein radar to close in and get visual contact with their quarry, before commencing their attack using machine guns and cannon fire.

The system was limited because a fighter box could only direct one interception at a time, and Bert Harris hoped that by squeezing his aircraft into a tighter bomber 'stream' – something which the Pathfinders were key in helping to achieve – he could swamp the German defences and sustain fewer casualties. Thanks to improved training and navigation, Bomber Command bombing rates steadily increased from 40 planes per hour passing over a target in 1941, to 30 per minute in 1943. The aim was to try and get the concentration of aircraft as high as one aircraft per cubic mile. Nevertheless, Bomber Command lost almost 500 aircraft to night fighters between March and July 1943.[9] Many of these were on the return journey after the bomber stream had been thrown apart over the target and was far more spread out, meaning night fighters could pick off stragglers. One estimate suggested a bomber was twice as likely to be shot down on the way home.[10]

Around major targets like the Ruhr, British bombers also faced a combined night-fighting zone using flak, searchlights and night-fighter aircraft. Some night fighters also used the vast columns of light from radar-controlled or manual searchlights to home in on bombers. When bombers become 'coned' and trapped like a moth in a light beam, the night fighters would strike.

One airman recalled: 'In Ruhr Valley there were about six or seven towns clustered together and they all used to give you a walloping as you went in.'[11] Another Pathfinder airman said of the Ruhr: 'They were like cities and towns of steel, searchlights all round, anti-aircraft guns everywhere, fighters floating about. We were glad to get in there and get out.'[12]

Many wouldn't be so lucky.

As darkness fell on the evening of the 5 March, Allan Ball and his fellow airmen were in their final preparations for the mission on Essen. Earlier in the day they'd flown their night-flying test to check all was well with the aircraft and gulped down their supper of eggs and bacon. Ball, as wireless operator, had safely received his 'flimsy' on which the radio frequencies of the night were printed, so he could communicate with the base once in the air. Then it was time to change into their flying gear. Long woollen underwear, fleece-lined vest and trousers, flying boots, a white rollneck jumper, a leather jacket, a helmet with attached oxygen mask and intercom lead and silk scarf and gloves. Collecting their parachutes and Mae West life jackets – so named by Allied airmen across the world because some wag had once joked they resembled the generous bosom of the American actress – they grabbed sandwiches, a flask of coffee, slabs of chocolate and barley sugar for the return journey, and waddled out into the crisp night air.

There wasn't much to see, of course. It was getting gloomy. But other senses kicked in. The cold wind on the face whipping across the airfield. The crunch of the hard concrete under the feet. The sharp tang of coal smoking from the stoves in the Nissen huts, mingling with the comforting aroma of fried food from the canteen drifting on the wind – supper for those lucky enough to not be flying on ops that night. The smell of petrol from the bowsers refuelling the aircraft, the tractors towing the bomb trolleys, and the buses waiting to carry the men to their aircraft. And climbing onto the buses, the sound of nervous chatter and laughter – perhaps an exchange of words or a clumsy flirt with the WAAF driving the bus, before the crunch of gears and a jerk, and they were off.

Graveley was a typical Bomber Command airfield, with three interlocking concrete runways – one more than 2,000 yards long, the other two around 1,400 yards, positioned in a triangle shape. The accommodation blocks – made of wood and asbestos – were situated to the north of the airfield next to the technical area where two vast hangars allowed for major repairs. A concrete track ran around the perimeter, with 36 dispersals – pan-shaped areas of concrete which looked like little white mushrooms from the air – on which aircraft were maintained, fuelled and armed.

When the bus reached the dark outline of the Halifax 'R for Robert', Ball and his crewmates piled out, to be met by a little army of mechanics, fitters, riggers and armourers, their grease-stained and dirty overalls betraying the work they'd been doing for most of the day preparing their aircraft. Tonight it was armed with 6,000lb of bombs and all-important green target indicators, carefully ferried across the airfield by tractor-drawn trolleys from the bomb dump on the south of the airbase, before being winched very carefully into the bomb bay of the waiting plane.

The pilot did a quick circuit of the aircraft to check all was in order, signed the form 700 for the ground crew corporal (with all the red tape and formalities in the wartime RAF it's a wonder they had time for any flying), and after a final good luck pee on the rear wheel, the crew squeezed themselves through the side hatch – not easy with all their gear and parachute on – making sure they didn't bang their heads on the frame. While the tail gunner turned right down to his tiny dustbin-sized rear turret, Ball and his five other crewmates clambered the other way through the skeletal fuselage towards the nose of the plane, which smelt of cold metal and oil. Passing the pigeon cage to the left – all bombers carried two messenger pigeons in case they ditched at sea – and the flight engineer and navigator's position, Ball reached his crew station: a little cubby hole to the port side near the front of the plane, directly underneath the pilot, always an occupational hazard if the pilot decided to relieve himself mid-flight by aiming – or not – into the little bottle provided.

Ball settled himself at his little desk in front of the radio – a big black box with three blue, red and yellow dials on either side, which he used to keep in contact with the formation and ground crews. It was one of the more comfortable positions on the Halifax, and he now set about tuning in to receive messages on the weather, wind speeds, and any other information.

Ball heard the fitter beneath the wing shout 'Contact!' and the spit and crackle of the first of the four engines starting up, shuddering the whole airframe. The hatch to the aircraft was shut and the wheel chocks pulled away by the ground crew. The big plane eased forward and slowly taxied its way around the airfield to join the other heavies lining up at the top of the runway, taking off at the rate of one a minute. With a full load of fuel and bombs, they needed the full length of the runway just to get airborne. Taking off was always a dicey affair. The fuel tanks in each wing held 1,800 gallons of petrol, which crews nicknamed 'liquid dynamite'. The pilot glanced at the instruments one final time, put the aircraft into fine pitch, lowered the flaps and set the compass for take-off, and switched the oxygen flow to 20,000 feet so they wouldn't all pass out. 'Everyone all set?' he asked the crew. 'OK, here we go.' When the Aldis lamp from the chequered signalling caravan at the end of the runway flashed green, the wheel brakes were released and the great roar of the engines barrelled them down the runway. Ball heard the strain on the engines as the plane finally lifted off with a few feet of runway to spare and lumbered slowly into the sky. The time was 19.03.

Across England more than 430 aircraft made their way east, over the North Sea, soon crossing the coast of mainland Europe at 20,000 feet in a giant stream. The temperature in the cabins soon plummeted to −30°C. Ball opened the curtain of the little observation window and stared out at the blackness, occasionally punctuated by the vast outline of another bomber. Their Halifax would also occasionally be buffeted about by the slipstream of another flying just a few hundred feet away. Funny to think of all those other planes out there, full of ordinary blokes like him, with their own thoughts and fears.

And then, as they crossed the Dutch coast, still around 40 minutes from the target, ahead of them the ghastly white fingers of the search-lights began to probe the sky. Before long, these were joined by the flashes and deep crumps of flak exploding all around them. The bombers weaved from side to side to try and reduce the chances of being hit as the 88mm guns hurled up 18lb shells exploding into 1,500 red-hot jagged splinters which could prove lethal to anything within 15 yards. Crews joked that if you saw them it was fine – it was the explosions you couldn't see you had to worry about. Occasionally a close one would send tiny pieces of shrapnel rattling against the fuse-lage, which sounded like hail on a car roof, followed by the acrid smell of cordite. The whole plane bumped up and down. Some men were seemingly ambivalent to flak. It felt somehow impersonal. It was firing at the aircraft. But the night fighters were different. They were aiming not at your aircraft, but at you. And now they began to attack, scyth-ing into the bomber stream and shooting down three Halifaxes and a Wellington in a few short minutes.

Ball's plane made it through and there, ahead, were the twinkling red markers dropped by the leading Pathfinder Mosquitos from 109 Squadron. They couldn't see the target, which was covered by thin cloud at 16,000 feet. But that didn't matter, they were on their final run in. As the ruby target indicators drifted into the centre of the bombsight the bomb aimer released the plane's load. Ball felt the

Halifax surge up as their bombs and green target indicators tumbled out. They had to fly straight and level for another 30 seconds – the longest thirty seconds of their life – to wait for the photoflash bomb they had also dropped to ignite, allowing their onboard camera to record the accuracy of their marking. Then it was time to head for home, with the pilot banking the aircraft and everyone praying they'd not collide with another plane in the stream.

A few minutes later, with the target now well alight, the main-force bombers started their run in. One rear gunner in a Wellington bomber on his first mission in the Ruhr admitted to being 'terror-stricken' at the 'sheer weight of metal' being thrown into the sky from the German guns. 'It was as we approached the Ruhr Valley for the first time that I realised I had made a mistake in volunteering for aircrew,' he admitted. 'It was a scene from Dante's *Inferno* brought into reality'.[13] Another later said 'Smoke was pouring up to 7,000 feet . . . one huge blazing area of over a square mile. It was a wonderful concentration; only two dropped their incendiaries outside. In the midst of this veritable hell could be seen the red TI markers.'[14]

Max Bryant's Lancaster, in the third and final wave of bombing, began its run on the target, which was now well lit up with fires. There were the green and red markers drizzling down, as they'd been told. 'There was certainly plenty of flak about, but we made our run in and out without being hit,' he wrote in his diary. 'And so home, after leaving Essen in a mess. The Lancs were on the last phase and when we left the target area was a mass of concentrated flame. In our own words, it was a wizard prang.' It had been a successful night for Bryant and his crew. Another mission chalked off. As the bomber approached the squadron airfield it was ordered to orbit the Pundit Beacon (all airfields flashed Morse code via a beacon so crews could identify their home airfield) to help the control tower 'stack' the planes before landing them every minute or so. But Bryant's crew didn't mind. They were in high spirits, and made up a song, 'Circling the Beacon' to the tune of 'Waltzing Matilda', as the giant Lancaster circled the black sky.

Just over four hours after they'd taken off, Ball's Halifax also touched down safely back at Graveley. He was weary, and after a debriefing with a cup of coffee laced with a tot of rum, followed by bacon and eggs, he sank into the soft, welcoming sheets of his bed, dreaming of seeing Brenda again. By the early hours of Saturday, 6 March, the bases of Bomber Command were quiet. Although fourteen bombers had been lost – ten to night fighters – many crews reckoned the raid had been a success, with large fires across a wide area and spectacular explosions. The Pathfinders had dropped their markers on the button and three waves of main-force bombers had pounded the target over the next 40 minutes, with 75 per cent bombing within three miles of the city centre. Most remarkably, at no stage did any of the bombers see – or need to see – the actual target, which had been covered in cloud and haze.

Photo-reconnaissance pictures taken over the next few days confirmed devastating damage to the centre of Essen and the Krupp works. An area of 160 acres had been 'laid waste' and three quarters of the buildings had been demolished or damaged by high explosives across a further 450 acres. Thirteen buildings in the Krupp works were in ruins and 53 workshops affected, mainly by fire.[15] Inevitably, there was a human price to pay. More than 5,000 houses were destroyed or damaged, and over 500 people had been killed on the ground. Seventy-four Bomber Command airmen were dead, including fourteen Pathfinders.

But Harris was delighted. The raid inspired him to create the verb 'to Essenise' as the benchmark when talking about razing targets to the ground – and as a satisfying riposte to the German 'coventrieren'. He despatched a punchy signal, commending the airmen for their 'great skill and high courage', adding that the attack on Essen would 'take historical precedence as the greatest victory achieved on any front'. 'You have set a fire in the belly of Germany which will burn the black heart out of Nazidom and wither its grasping limbs at the very roots.'[16]

It was stirring stuff. And the raid had certainly shaken the Germans. Senior officials in Hitler's inner circle, including Joseph Goebbels and Albert Speer – the ministers responsible for national morale and war production respectively – were quick to visit the scene, promising relief and rehabilitation. The sudden accuracy of the bombing – after so many botched attempts on Essen – horrified Hitler. He wanted answers. He ordered Hermann Göring, the Luftwaffe chief, to immediately fly from Berlin to the Berghof, Hitler's sumptuous chalet overlooking the Bavarian Alps near Berchtesgaden, which he used as his country headquarters. Göring was accompanied by Wolfgang Martini, the man in charge of Germany's radar defence.

On the flight down that night the two men discussed their forthcoming meeting with the Führer. 'Is it possible the British are using some radio method to find the target?' Göring is said to have asked Martini. 'I believe they are,' replied Martini. 'We've got some evidence to suggest they are developing new techniques for bombing.' 'Well when we see the Führer you don't tell him that, you keep your mouth shut. I'll do the talking,'[17] Göring told his junior, conscious perhaps that it was only four years since he had arrogantly bragged, 'If one enemy bomber reaches the Ruhr you can call me Meyer.'[18]

The following day the two men met Hitler. 'How did it happen?' Hitler asked. Göring explained it was an 'unfortunate incident'. The RAF bombers were flying over thick cloud, a gap appeared, there were the Krupp works. It was a target of opportunity. Hitler turned to Martini. 'Don't you think they have some other method?' he asked. Martini said there was no evidence to prove it. Göring then rapidly changed the subject by talking about Hitler's rocket programme.

The story, which was recounted by Martini after the war, was a significant claim if true. Had he and Göring had been able to chat more freely to Hitler, it might have altered their response and had a significant impact on how the Pathfinders used Oboe. As it was, however, Bennett's men were allowed to continue using it to spearhead a series of crushing raids on Ruhr targets over the coming months, and it wasn't until November 1943 that the Germans knew enough to jam the technology, and even then not very effectively.[19]

On 6 March 1943, as the Krupp works lay smouldering, the crews were ordered to Essen once again. More than 400 aircraft were detailed to fly. Harris wanted to make sure once and for all. Preparation went on as usual. The weather over the target looked like thick cloud all the way up to 20,000 feet, but the crews got dressed and made their way to their dispersal points and waited by their aircraft, ready for the final thumbs up. As the sun went down, Max Bryant spotted a couple of vans approaching. 'We pricked our ears, and found it was a scrub!' he wrote later. The bosses had decided after all that the weather over the target was likely to be grim, and a raid wasn't worth the effort. It had been 'scrubbed' – RAF slang for cancelled. 'It was like the lifting of a great weight – we all yelled with the relief,' said Bryant. 'We presented some of our chocolate to the people on the farm next to our dispersal, salvaged what coffee the ground crew had left, and departed in high glee to get undressed. I did not realize just how strong had been the strain until sudden and unexpected relief showed it up.'

Two weeks later Bryant would be in the Pathfinders. And the strain was about to get a whole lot worse.

CHAPTER TWELVE

The Horse Thief

L ATE AFTERNOON, MONDAY, 22 March 1943. Max Bryant looked at the flat, monotonous countryside through the window of the Bedford bus as it rumbled along the A414 out of Huntington. His destination was RAF Warboys – home of 156 Squadron. This was Pathfinder country. Mile upon mile of fenland between Peterborough and Cambridge. Boring to look at, but perfect for the Pathfinder boys flying operations over mainland Europe.

Could it really only be nine months since he finished his training in Canada? It had all been such a blur. His route through Bomber Command to the Pathfinders since he arrived back in Britain was a typical one, followed by thousands of young men. It had started with a three-month course at an OTU in Staffordshire, where individuals who had completed their various training courses were forged into crews. The process, known as 'crewing up', was simple in theory: chuck a load of men from different roles into a room and let them get on with it. Of course it wasn't always that easy. Personalities clashed. Sometimes it took a few days because there was a shortage of certain aircrew positions. But soon Bryant had his crew, which he recorded in his diary.

Captain-Pilot: Sgt Lay. Owns a pub in Melbourne and is quite a typical Aussie.

Navigator: Sounds like me.

W/Op.: Sgt Bill Drake – a English bloke with blue eyes and fair hair – like his type.

Bomb-aimer: Sgt Don Bauman, an English bloke also; bit of a bludger,
extra keen on the women, but may possibly make a good man.
Rear Gunner: Sgt Bill Forster. Quiet English lad, keen, should be OK.

Bryant's crew was a typical mixture of nationalities and backgrounds. They would now be spending most days and nights with one
another. Life or death might depend on split-second decisions made by
each man. In time, when they progressed from flying Wellingtons to
Lancasters via a heavy conversion unit, where they practised flying
four-engine bombers for around 30–35 hours, the crew would be joined
by three more – a flight engineer, a mid-upper gunner and a second
navigator. The aim of the OTU was to weld the new crew into an efficient fighting machine. This process involved intense training both in
the aircraft and in the classroom. It was often tedious and dangerous –
during the war over 8,000 crewmen were killed in training accidents,
more than one sixth of Bomber Command's wartime fatalities. The
skies over Britain were often covered in thick low cloud. Death was
only one miscalculation away, as one of Bryant's fellow crews had discovered when they had broken cloud and crashed into the side of a hill.
Bryant and most of his crew vomited on their first flight as the Wellington was thrown around the sky. On another occasion, taking off
laden with training bombs, the Wellington struggled into the air. A big
chimney and some trees loomed ahead, but 'by great providence' Lay
managed to fly the aircraft between them. 'I was sitting in front, watching the sloping ground rushing towards us, wondering with a strange
detachment whether we'd hit and what it would be like,' wrote Bryant.
'I cannot remember feeling scared – just a strange curious and semi-
resigned feeling. Ken was too busy at the time to feel anything, but on
the ground he confessed he thought we'd had it.'

They'd escaped death thanks to some deft flying, and from early on
Bryant's crew displayed the skills which would propel them into the
Pathfinders. In the OTU, Bryant scored 96 per cent in his navigation
exam – top of the class. Although he didn't immediately take to his
bomb aimer personally, Bryant observed 'he can do his bombing and
photography'. The wireless operator he reckoned was 'a bit of a wizard', while the rear gunner was a 'good lad who knows his gen
backwards'.

'The other day he flattened the Armament Section by stripping and re-assembling a Browning in 1m 55 secs. Not bad eh?' Bryant wrote in a letter to his friend Don Charlwood.

Charlwood had flown over from Canada a few weeks ahead of Bryant but the two close friends were reunited at the OTU. As Bomber Command losses mounted so OTU crews were increasingly thrown into the cauldron to take part in operations over Germany. One evening Charlwood's crew was detailed to fly to Düsseldorf.

'Much activity on the station,' Bryant wrote in his diary.

Apparently it is a big 'do'. There was bustle everywhere. Wimpys were being tuned up, swung, bombed up and air tested. Squadron Leader blokes were tearing about on motor bikes. Everywhere activity. I could not see Don – except for a brief moment when he whispered 'Dusseldorf' to me – until after tea . . . Down to the flights – the take-off was 20.00 and the boys were hastily pushed out to their kites. Too hastily really as they did not have time to properly prepare flight plans, etc . . . A couple of crews went past in a lorry to their dispersal – they were Aussies and were singing lustily – 'She'll be wearing silk pyjamas when she comes'. There was no undue panic . . . Eventually the starting signal came – a hasty handshake and Don was swallowed up inside his Wimpy.

Bryant watched as the planes took off:

The air was tense as take-off hour came. The light was green and the first Wimpy came thundering up the runway, lumbering heavily, lifting off at the end. I watched them go off – one up – two up – three up . . . my thoughts a bit mixed. Going to war in a Wimpy – not much fun. Lots of good pals in those dark moving shapes – Don, Harry, Blue, Keith – many others. At last they were all gone and the night was silent again. The watchers began to disperse – six hours before the boys were due home.

Later Bryant returned to see them land:

The mist was closing in a bit. Pyros and rockets were shooting up. After a while, the boys started to drift in – Col beaming, Blue with a kite full of little holes and tales of flak and 'bloody great fires' – Harry telling me about the fireworks display – all down and still no Don. Finally I learned he had had to turn back with engine trouble, as had Keith and others. Just got to bed when Don came in to tell me of the 'do'. Apparently they had got well into Belgium – been shot up by a flak ship but missed. Jeff was worried about one engine – its temperature was 240 and the maximum permissible is 235 for 5 minutes. So after a while he yelled into the intercom: 'You blokes may think I'm yellow, but this engine's too hot – all in favour of going home say Aye!' There was a unanimous 'Aye!' So they turned back and just as well, for the old Wimpy was starting to limp a bit. Don says it was a good introduction to the war.

Bryant's first operation, by contrast, had been quiet – a 'local' do over northern France, in which they'd barely seen any flak, but after they arrived back safely with their spirits high, they'd sunk a glass of beer. It was a good feeling to enter their first operation in red ink in their logbook. In early January 1943, Bryant's crew had joined 103 Squadron, based at RAF Elsham Wolds in north Lincolnshire. The squadron, part of 1 Group, flew Lancasters, news which was 'received with beaming smiles by the boys'. Once again his journey echoed that of his friend Charlwood, who had already completed 12 ops with 103 Squadron.

Bryant was seemingly more concerned that Charlwood would get through his tour unscathed than he was about his own future. This was partly because he'd seen just how important Charlwood was to his girlfriend Nellie back in Canada – his death would drive a stake through her heart. As his friend ticked off the ops so Bryant marked them in his diary. It's not like Bryant could even be with Charlwood in the action. One January evening he had sat in the mess in front of a warm fire with the gramophone playing the *Warsaw Concerto* and *The Nutcracker* suite as the waiter brought over cocoa and biscuits. 'While we sit here and loaf in luxury,' Bryant wrote,

> Don is somewhere over the other side twisting and diving twenty thousand feet up, sucking oxygen into his lungs, dodging flak and fighters. It is a strange existence. Somehow I feel he is all right tonight,

and often I've felt he'll get through easily. The thought of Don going is quite unreal to me. Perhaps the wishful thinking I do on his behalf and Nell's has something to do with it . . . he is more than halfway through now and I know he has enough inspiration from Nell to carry on.

Bryant's fears for his own future were less optimistic. 'I don't know whether Mum and Dad realise just what chances I will have once I get on ops,' he told his brother John in a letter.

> I never write to them about it, for it would only distress them unnecessarily. To you I can speak freely, though rather in confidence. My chances of getting through my operations are by no means good; on the other hand, it is no suicide squad. With a good knowledge of our job, and a fair share of luck, we may make the grade, and just as easily not make it. I want one of the family to fully realise the possibilities, so that in the event of us packing in you'll be prepared. For the same reason, I want you to be as careful as you can, consistent with your job, so that Mum and Dad will have one of us left afterwards. Don't think I've developed into a morbid type with a drooping moustache – far from it. There's just a little motto we once had in different settings – 'Be prepared.' Before I burst into tears, I'll say cheerio . . .

Such feelings were made all the harder because Bryant's parents lived on the other side of the world. Bryant confided in his brother that he was struggling with not being able to see his parents for over a year and had pangs of homesickness. Like many men, his voracious letter-writing home was a way of helping to keep that at bay. Bryant had also been interviewed by a local radio station for a Christmas broadcast which was aired in Australia a few weeks later. 'At last the boys began to speak,' his mother Estelle wrote in a letter to Bryant. 'You were one of the last but I can tell you it was wonderful to hear your voice. I am glad you sent me the photo of your "flight" as I picked the boys out as they spoke and I felt as though I knew all of them. I sent word up to Grandma Bryant so I hope she listened in too.'

Like many whose sons were in Bomber Command, Bryant's parents must have been aware of the dangers he faced, but probably not just how alarming the stats were in terms of survival. It was probably for the best. One of Bryant's first missions on an operational squadron had been to Cologne on 26 February 1943, part of a raid of 430 planes. The Pathfinders were late getting to the target, and Bryant was 'sweating blood' waiting. Finally, the green markers went down, and they weaved in to attack. He recorded later what he saw: 'The place was a blaze of light. There were three large cones of searchlights, and umpteen stray ones. Jerry was belting a crossfire of light flak into the cones. Heavy flak was mostly below us, but we were rocked a couple of times by near ones. There were many patches of brilliant light just like a handful of tinsel scattered on the ground and blinking like electric light. We felt as naked as a newborn babe.'

A few days later they attacked Berlin – 'the Big City' – for the first time. The run in and bombing had been smooth, but as Bryant's crew flew home, with the fires of the German capital still glowing 150 miles away, the inside of the aircraft was suddenly flooded in the bright white light of a searchlight. 'Hell seemed to burst loose,' Bryant said later. 'Flak flew all around us and we could not get out of it. Ken put the throttles through the gate and weaved like mad.' Bryant held on to the airframe for dear life and watched as the altimeter dropped to 4,000 feet. 'With flak everywhere I thought it was curtains at last.'

Don Bauman, Bryant's bomb aimer, clambered up from the front of the aircraft. Blood was streaming down his face from a two-inch piece of shell which had smashed through the Perspex and hit him below the eye just as he'd ducked behind the front guns. Bryant bandaged Bauman up as best he could, his blood 'spattered on the maps, logs, and my arms', and sent him to the rear of the aircraft to the canvas bed. They landed safely just after 3am, 'everyone feeling done in' but 'damned lucky to get away with it . . . thanks to a combination of Ken's cool handling of the situation and our splendid aircraft, we were home again'.

Perhaps it was that operation – their 'press-on spirit', the ability to drop the bombs on the target and fly back in one piece through 'muck', as Bryant called it, and still get home safely – which caught the eye of their commanding officer. For, two weeks later, Bryant and Charlwood had returned from a Sunday morning church service when Ken Lay walked up and dropped a bombshell. 'About 11am Ken gave me a great shock; we were posted to Pathfinders without any choice at all. To me especially it was a bitter pill for it meant leaving Don after seven short weeks and moving right down south out of 1 Group. The Winco [wing commander] had conveniently absented himself and there was nothing we could do about it.'

That evening, Bryant and Charlwood went to the cinema and chatted over supper about Australia and Canada, the present and the future. They had a final drink in the mess, watching dreary Sunday-evening entertainment, ranging from a WAAF singing 'Ave Maria', to a lumbering male sergeant pretending to be a 'young lady' taking a bath, before going to bed. 'Neither of us was very cheerful,' wrote Bryant. 'I suppose we should soon have been separated in any case, for Don is nearly finished ops. All the same I felt very peeved just to be hurled away.'

Charlwood viewed Bryant's sudden parting to the Pathfinders with foreboding. 'All through his Air Force life, Max Bryant had been a young enthusiast – articulate, dedicated, personable. This and the fact that he was commissioned, meant he was bound to be noticed by senior officers. These things, probably more than any other crew factor, led to the sudden change in their fortunes,' he later wrote.[1]

The following Monday afternoon, as the late March sun was setting, the Bedford van carrying Bryant and his crew swung left off the main road, under the raised barrier and past the sign which said: 'RAF Warboys'. After stopping at the little shed to check all personal papers were in order, the van drove to a collection of long narrow Nissen huts which would be their new billets and living quarters in 156 Squadron, nestled amongst trees tinged with the first green shoots of spring.

Max Bryant's reaction at being told he had been selected to become a Pathfinder was not surprising. While many saw the Pathfinders as the elite force of Bomber Command, if a crew was happily established in a main-force squadron and had made close friends and established roots – as Bryant had – there wasn't always much attraction in moving on, even if it was to become a Pathfinder.

In the autumn of 1943, Dick Raymond – who had completed his training as a flight engineer and joined a main-force squadron – was told by his pilot the crew had been volunteered as Pathfinders and would be joining 83 Squadron. 'I said "What's Pathfinders?",' recalled Raymond. 'I had no bloody clue what the Pathfinders were. I'd never even heard of them and they were supposed to be the elite of Bomber Command.' Once he'd found out, rather than being elated he was wracked with nerves at what being a Pathfinder crew would entail. After taking off on his first mission he was violently airsick. 'That's not easy when you're wearing an oxygen mask. That was the only time I was ever airsick.' Raymond soon fitted in to Pathfinder life, although with his cherubic features it was sometimes hard to believe he was even old enough to fly. When he first met his new station commander, Raymond recalled: 'He looked at me and said: "How old are you my man?"; "I'm nineteen, sir"; "Good God," he said, and walked off.'[2]

While individuals were occasionally chosen, by and large whole crews transferred either after being volunteered by their commanders or after the pilot – who was the commander of the crew – put in a request on their behalf, and not always with their knowledge. Technically those men who weren't happy could stay in the main force with another crew, but more often than not, saving face, not 'letting the side down' and staying with their friends, meant the other crew members reluctantly agreed. In many cases they were not even volunteers.

By contrast, many others were all too aware of the significance of 8 Group – the official Pathfinder group. 'I jumped for joy,' said one airman when he knew he'd been selected to become a Pathfinder,[3] while a navigator agreed to join after being urged by his pilot: 'How would you like to give the dames a treat and go about with a lot of scrambled eggs on your hat?' (Scrambled eggs was the slang for the gold embroidery on the peak of a high-ranking officer's military cap.)

A wireless operator who went on to fly 14 operations with the Pathfinders was lured by 'the glamour of the little gold wing on your pocket . . . We were hearing stories about all their equipment and what they were doing . . . I thought, *Well it would be rather fun and it would be interesting and quite exciting.* We all thought Pathfinders were the elite. I thought, *Why not have a go at being among the elite if you can get it?* And luckily I got it.'[4]

For others, it was often a case of honour and prestige, and with one eye on their career after the war. 'Dear Mum and Dad,' Halifax pilot

Albert Arter wrote in a letter home in June 1943, 'I am shortly going to be posted to a Pathfinder Sqdn. More honours for the family. The Wing Com. [Wing Commander] selected 5 captains this morning at conference from whom he wanted one volunteer. No one seemed keen; so he said "What about you Arty boy?" Well I couldn't say no when he said it like that and one of us five had to go so I said, "Yes, I'll have a crack." … There's bags of unit flying opportunities after the War from this job and I feel it is another step up the ladder of the family's successes. Cheerio for now hope you share my elation at such an honour.' The 20-year-old was killed flying for the Pathfinders over Berlin two months later.[5]

During a military parade in the Essex market town of Chelmsford in the summer of 1943 – which was a chance for the town to proudly show off their local lads – amongst the Battle of Britain fighter boys and autograph hunters, an airman 'wearing the golden symbol of a Pathfinder' was interviewed by the local paper. The journalist drew comparisons with the work of James Fenimore Cooper, the nineteenth-century author, in particular his novels of *The Last of the Mohicans* and, indeed, *The Pathfinder*, both about the fictional frontier hero Natty Bumppo: 'But the Pathfinder of today tracks his way not through the dim and sinister forest where the Indian lurks, but through the illimitable space of the sky, where the night fighter waits for his prey. This young man – and he is again a fine-looking fellow – has now been over Germany no fewer than twenty-five times. That is a record in which the town as well as his father can take pride.'[6]

A newspaper sketch about the Pathfinders published by a paper in Lancashire sought to encapsulate the hard-earned attachment between a Pathfinder airman and his badge: 'There is a story of an RAF policeman who charged a Pathfinder with being improperly dressed and tried to take the eagle off the man's tunic. I was told that the policeman is still doing as well as can be expected'.[7]

However, as the Pathfinders' reputation soared it was sometimes used for more nefarious purposes. Such was the social allure of the Pathfinders that one 22-year-old man from Cheltenham pleaded guilty to impersonating a Pathfinder navigator after being challenged by military police while wearing a Pathfinder badge and an RAF uniform. The man's solicitor pleaded for leniency, citing his tragic life, including the 'disability of a withered hand', but the magistrates branded his impersonation a 'disgraceful offence, due to the stupid conceit in trying to be something he was not'.[8] In Newcastle, meanwhile, a 26-year-old man was sentenced to six months hard labour after impersonating a Pathfinder bomb aimer – complete with Pathfinder badge and military medals – using it to as a foil to enjoy the finest hotels and clubs, stealing from women he seduced, and blagging his way into various RAF bases where he pilfered items from officers' quarters before selling them. He had been treated as a hero and claimed to have been on 67 operations and wounded in action – only for the rather more mundane truth to later emerge that he had been hurt by the wire of an anti-aircraft balloon cable.[9]

The desire to wear the golden Wings of the Pathfinders was not always shared by the main-force group commanders or squadron leaders, who were asked to send their best crews as reinforcements. Not surprisingly, the average squadron commander did not want to bleed his squadron of its best blood to supply the Pathfinders. Volunteers wishing to join met local opposition. When replacements were demanded by Bomber Command, often the worst and not the best crews were sent. While some were all too happy to put forward strong crews, others used the Pathfinders as a skip in which to dump weaker performers. 'The idea was to send off the best crews but in practice the awkward squad was often posted to Pathfinders,' said a navigation instructor who served with 8 Group.[10] According to one internal RAF report, one 'selected' Pathfinder crew contained 'a night-blind rear gunner, a constitutionally airsick wireless operator, and pilot and navigator who were waverers. The mid upper gunner was just mentally slow.'[11] Some of this obstruction was due to squadron pride, some jealousy because of the increased rank and pay, some due to friction between higher-up officers.

By the spring of 1943, Don Bennett was sending back more new crews than he was keeping. But with losses mounting as the operations over the Ruhr intensified – at an average of five crews lost per squadron per month – something needed to be done.[12] Bennett appointed Hamish Mahaddie – the ebullient Scottish pilot who had been with the Pathfinder Force since it was created the previous August – as his Group Training Director. Small, chippy and confident, with the ability to turn on the charm like a tap but equally pile on firmer persuasion, Mahaddie was the ideal figure for the job of touring the main-force squadrons to identify and recruit the best crews for the Pathfinders. He'd also had a 'hot war' – winning four military medals in the space of just four months – garnering respect amongst his peers.

Mahaddie's method was to examine bomb-aiming photographs from the previous evening's raids to identify the top crews, before using his charisma to approach group and squadron commanders and crews themselves. Speaking to crews directly, he found some had volunteered for the Pathfinders but had their applications rejected by their senior commanders. After a few strong words from Mahaddie, this decision was usually reversed. This didn't always go down well. One training commander wrote to Harris raising the subject of Mahaddie's 'powers of mischief' and complained that Mahaddie's approach 'smacked of Gestapo methods'.[13]

But, once the call had been made, it was only a matter of time. John Kelly, no doubt still dreaming of sunnier climes in glamorous Hollywood, had ended up on 207 Squadron after returning from his pilot training in California. 'Apparently my nomination for PFF [Pathfinder Force] did not come from our wing-co but from group headquarters and now the wing-co is trying to keep me here,' he told his parents in a letter home. 'Whether he will be successful or not I do not know, I expect he will only succeed in delaying things.' Kelly's instinct was right, and a few weeks later he was off to join Bennett's men.[14]

But, while Mahaddie had permission to overrule objections from senior commanders, he claimed he never forced a crew to join if they didn't want to. He also toured air stations and navigation training schools giving lectures to aircrew in the hope of luring some away. One crew coming to the end of their main-force tour were keen not to be split up, and saw the Pathfinders as a way of remaining together for longer. Worried about the force being nothing more than a 'suicide club', they listened to Mahaddie with bated breath. 'When we found out the Pathfinders were not a suicide club, a sort of noble six hundred charging across an aerial valley of death, but designed as a highly scientific instrument, we decided to volunteer,' said one airman.[15]

As well as crews, Mahaddie swooped on individuals. One experienced navigator who had already completed a tour of operations was subsequently stuck in a dead-end but important role as a navigation instructor at an airbase in Oxfordshire. When he got a tap on the shoulder, his senior officers forbade his transferring and even put him under close arrest so he couldn't leave the air station. They were simply delaying the inevitable. 'Bennett and Mahaddie could get anybody from anywhere. They couldn't stop me . . . it was wonderful to get out of this training and back on operations where I was doing something far more useful,' he said.[16]

This view was shared by Ian Bazalgette – a tall, good-looking Canadian-born pilot who had also been posted to a windswept, bleak OTU in Scotland after a tour of operations in the main force, but was desperate for more action and saw the Pathfinders as a way in. Bazalgette was the great-grandson of the famous civil engineer Sir Joseph Bazalgette, and was destined to become a Pathfinder legend. He wrote to Mahaddie with a self-confessed 'pathetic appeal from the frozen north – my six months OTU tour expires at the end of this month and I must get to 8 Group at once. I feel that if I cannot break away now, I have "had" my second tour. It is my dearest wish to have another personal affair with Germany.' He added that 'a few keen types scattered around the group are anxious to get back with me', so he could form a crew. Mahaddie warmly replied a few days later, promising Bazalgette he would soon be a Pathfinder, but to 'please take no action officially until my own horse dealing methods have been completed'. As for the other men, Mahaddie reassured Bazalgette that it wouldn't be much difficulty. 'Once I get the Skipper, the others follow quite easily.' He signed off: 'Well, cheerio Bazal, and may I wish you in the near future good Path Finding.'[17]

But, even with his persuasive powers, Mahaddie sometimes met stiff opposition that even he couldn't shift. In the spring of 1943, Guy Gibson, the commander of the newly formed 617 Squadron, gave Mahaddie a list of 20 pilots and warned him to 'leave my bloody crews alone'. When a young Australian ace pilot was posted to the Pathfinders, he was almost immediately whistled away 'in the dead of night' by Gibson from under Mahaddie's nose. 'That was the sort of the jiggery-pokery that was going on all the time,' said Mahaddie, although little did he realise then that Gibson was assembling his crews for the famous Dam Buster raids, which would take place in May 1943.[18]

Nevertheless, over the following three years, Bennett's self-styled 'horse thief' Mahaddie recruited around 16,000 men to the Pathfinders, with around half from Commonwealth countries, a few Dutch nationals and even a sprinkling of Americans – including a Texan who wore cowboy boots on operations until Mahaddie had his crew forcibly hold him down one morning, enabling them to saw two inches off the high heels so he wouldn't injure himself if he bailed out on operations. Mahaddie brought a strong positive vibe to the Pathfinder Group. And with things hotting up in the bombing war over Germany, that would be needed more than ever.

CHAPTER THIRTEEN

Happy Valley

RECRUITING MORE CREWS TO 8 Group became increasingly necessary as spring moved into summer in 1943, and Harris's desire to batter towns and cities across the Ruhr intensified. The 'Battle of the Ruhr', as Harris dubbed it, had begun with the attack on Essen on 5 March and would last until the middle of July. Over that time, Bomber Command would launch 43 major raids – two thirds on targets in the Ruhr and the rest scattered across Europe, including Berlin. But, as cities such as Cologne, Düsseldorf and Dortmund were pounded, the Pathfinder and Bomber Command losses began to mount. In April, Bomber Command lost an average of five aircraft per squadron on operations.[1] Between March and May alone, 459 Pathfinder airmen were killed in action.[2]

One Halifax pilot on just his third Pathfinder mission later recounted a raid on Cologne from the period: 'As we approached it, it looked rather terrifying, with very many searchlights and a heavy flak barrage. I thought it looked suicide to go through . . . saw about 15 aircraft go down in flames – five at the same time.' A Halifax bomb aimer later recalled a raid over Essen: 'It was a hot one and they were ready for us. The damn flak was like lightning flashing in daylight all about us as the searchlights grabbed us over the target. The shell bursts made a squeaky, gritty noise. The smell of cordite was strong and you had the feeling that someone was kicking your undercarriage, keeping in time with the bursts.'[3] Another pilot, on his sixth operation, wrote in his diary: 'Somebody got shot down by a fighter, crashed and burst into flames on the ground. Another crew mistook this for a Pathfinder flare and went in and bombed the burning aircraft.'[4]

Little wonder, with the usual dark humour of the armed forces, the crews named the Ruhr 'Happy Valley'. One popular song in the Pathfinder's mess took the tune of 'The Quartermaster's Store' – originally a Scout song – and adapted the lyrics:

> There was flak, flak, bags of fucking flak, in the Ruhr, in the Ruhr,
> There was flak, flak, bags of fucking flak, in the Valley of the Ruhr,
> There was fighters, fighters, full of Nazi blighters, in the Ruhr, in the Ruhr,
> There were fighters, fighters, full of Nazi blighters, in the Valley of the Ruhr.[5]

Max Bryant's move to 156 Squadron in Warboys coincided with this increase in the tempo of raids – and deaths. Crews came and crews went. Some hardly had time to unpack their kit. Others were old stagers with tough trips behind them. 'I wonder what plan it is that picks one chap and leaves another? Every time one of the boys goes, it makes you wonder whether you'll see another dawn yourself,' Bryant confided in his diary. However, the young Australian settled in quickly, drawing his flying gear and making himself at home in the room he shared with one other officer in the officer quarters, while the rest of the crew, as non-commissioned sergeants, messed and slept in separate quarters. Bryant was cheered up too by the arrival of three more Australian officers, which prompted a few glasses of beer and a singalong to 'Waltzing Matilda' in the mess-room bar.

The following morning, Bryant and his crew were addressed by the squadron wing commander, who reassured them they had been picked as Pathfinders for being a 'better than average' crew. 'Being all blessed with suspicious minds, we mentally classed this as soft soap and wondered where the catch was,' Bryant wrote home. Their early action, they were told, would take the course of a typical Pathfinder crew: a few 'ordinary trips' carrying just bombs to get the feel for operations, before acting as supporters dropping target indicators for the main force to bomb on. 'Our job is more responsible than it was before, and the road ahead is much longer than it was,' acknowledged Bryant. They would do anything from five to a dozen trips then sit for the Pathfinders exam – comprising various questions in front of a board of senior commanders, depending on what trade they were in. If they passed this, they were entitled to wear the Pathfinder badge and go on until they'd completed 45 trips. After 30 operations, however, they had a three-week break or could refuse to go on and have six months' rest, but they would be stripped of the Pathfinder badge. If they completed 45 trips they kept the badge come what may, and were entitled to stop operating. But if they got that far most crews were encouraged to stay for a second Pathfinder tour – their experience was vital. 'It seems we have been pooled into a job which (a) ruins all chance of getting home for ages; (b) will keep us busy for the duration!' reckoned Bryant.

In many ways, life at Warboys was much the same as being on a main-force squadron – an airfield surrounded by low buildings; the focus on the mess; the increasingly frantic activity most days as the station geared up for that evening's operations. In the first few hours of the day, many airmen were still asleep from the previous night's operation. Life was almost peaceful. The long day for the ground crew had already begun, however, working on the bombers perched on their concrete dispersal pans dotted around the perimeter of the airfield. Fitters and mechanics could be seen standing on scaffolding-style platforms swarming over the engines and airframes of *their* aircraft.

By lunchtime, the target for the evening was usually decided by headquarters, and into the afternoon the whole mood of the station shifted, ramping up a gear to ensure everything was ready in time for take-off. WAAFs drove tractors ferrying bombs around the airfield, before the payloads were painstakingly winched into the bomb bays of the aircraft. Planes were filled with fuel, engines tested and aircrew briefed. There would be flying during the day, mostly to test aircraft, but sometimes to give new crews a chance for a quick outing.

And then, for the crews, the empty hours before take-off, filled by writing letters, playing cards or flicking through a magazine without really taking the words in. For the ground crews, final aircraft inspections to ensure the machines were ready for that night's adventures.

Although Warboys was only a few miles down the road from Wyton – the Pathfinders' headquarters – Bryant found life more informal, without many of the petty disciplines. They were too busy concentrating on the responsibility involved in operations. 'We are stationed on a satellite aerodrome, a sort of sidekick to the parent station,' he said in a letter to his grandmother.

> This has the great advantage that life is more free and easy. There is practically no red tape, we are just here to do a certain job and that is all anyone worries about. The Commanding Officer is a very decent type of man, and is well-liked by everyone on the Squadron. This is of course a deciding factor in the life of any station – what kind of bird the CO is. The atmosphere is very happy here, and though we suffer lack of some things through being a satellite, it is an efficient squadron.

The first two weeks after they arrived revolved around an intense flurry of lectures and air training. As Pathfinders, the entire crew were encouraged to learn the basics of navigation – a clear sign of Don Bennett's influence – but also have a better understanding of each other's jobs too. 'Much of the talk was on PFF methods and equipment and was far above my head. Rather left me with a frantic desire to get back to Elsham,' admitted Bryant.

Bryant's first operation as a Pathfinder, on 2 April 1943, was a damp squib – a small raid on St Nazaire on the west coast of France in which all their thousand-pound bombs had 'hung up' – meaning they didn't release – and the crew 'fiddled about' over the target area and the Channel trying to get rid of them. The only consolation is that they'd got their thirteenth operation safely out of the way. How many ops had been completed was always on crews' minds. It was better not to dwell on the odds – many didn't for fear of 'cracking up' – and it wasn't much talked about by many crews. The reality was stark. The average loss rate for the Pathfinders at this time was about 5 per cent. That meant that, in five trips, 25 out of every 100 aircraft went missing, and after 20 trips the original 100 – statistically – would all be lost. In terms of the losses, the first five trips were the worst. If you got beyond those, you felt like your chances of making it increased.

And those losses were just due to enemy action. Wartime flying was a dangerous business full stop. According to a secret RAF memo, in Bomber Command alone in 1942, 1,920 aircrew were killed in accidents, and almost the same number again were injured or missing – representing a potential loss of 6,000 operational sorties. Across twelve months, 3,700 aircraft were damaged or destroyed, at an estimated cost of £33,700,000 – enough to pay for a staggering 727 new heavy bomber aircraft.[6]

Luckily for the airmen at Warboys, when they were not flying on ops there were some opportunities to let their hair down in the local village. A typical evening might start at the Pelican before a pub crawl sampling beers at the Cross Keys, the Red Lion and finally the Horse in Harness. If they'd been joined by some WAAFs along the way it was not unusual to wobble home on bicycles before finishing the evening drinking beer and eating pies on the road outside the mess. But that was nothing compared to the comparative excitement of a night out in Cambridge. 'We were goggle-eyed at the array of youth and beauty in the town after the semi-isolation of Elsham and Warboys – it was almost too much for our fainting hearts,' observed Bryant.

Most men tried to make the best of longer leave, if they had a few days or even a week, by visiting London or seeing girlfriends. Max Bryant had been dating a land girl called Brenda Champion since the previous summer. Brenda's parents had a large country house near Wolverhampton, which they had opened up to entertain servicemen on leave, including Bryant. Brenda worked on a dairy farm in Warwickshire, and Bryant would stay in a house nearby and help out on the farm. Bryant loved it there. 'One thing about ops is that it makes one more internally glad to be alive, more conscious of blue sky and green grass and the peace behind a few old hens busily scratching in the fowl yard,' he noted in his diary. The relationship soon blossomed into something more serious, with the couple spending their evenings in an 'orgy of wrestling holds and passionate kisses' in the farm's hayloft.

Bryant had a strong moral compass, and felt angst at the growing physical attraction he felt for Brenda. He wrote in his diary:

> We had a very long and candid talk on moral aspects and our own particular relationship, but it did not do us much good. It clarified the fact

that fundamentally, we think the same and want the same things but just how we are to achieve them was not to be discussed.

Bryant's obvious frustrations were matched by a more material challenge. One evening he read a book about sex which had been lent to him by a friend. For Bryant, it 'illustrated to me my abysmal ignorance of the subject and passages of it gave me cause furiously to think'. But he was aware too of the ephemeral nature of war. And while for many the urgency and immediacy of wartime living often loosened sexual morals, for Bryant it appeared to strengthen his resolve. After a Valentine's supper with Brenda 'looking more lovely than I have ever seen her', the couple chatted and 'made a resolution to keep our friendship on the rails so I could always know that should the morrow take me, I would leave her virgin'.

After another romantic supper, Brenda told Bryant she loved him, but he could only respond with, 'Tonight I love you; in the morning I won't be sure.' He was torn – as many were – by the brutal reality that he would either be killed on operations or return to Australia. Before he knew it, his leave had ended and the train was drawing in to take him back to ops. 'A whistle, a long kiss – and Brenda was gone again. I could not help thinking as I watched her grow smaller, "Shall I see you in six weeks, or never . . .?"'

As the Battle of the Ruhr intensified and the strain of operations increased, when Bryant went to stay with Brenda in mid-March 1943 he tried to explain the reason for his unhappiness – a combination of sadness that so many friends had been killed, worry that one day he might lose his close friends Don Charlwood and Bill Charlton, fear of the future and the strain of ops.

'I can't find any sympathy for you,' Brenda had replied, starkly. She had three brothers in the RAF, one of whom had just completed a tour. 'I just don't let myself worry about them,' she said.

'She is lucky to have such control of her feelings – I have not. If she had no real sympathy a little manufactured for the occasion would probably have done the trick,' Bryant wrote later. 'I had two bad pictures in my mind – of Brenda hard, unsympathetic, self-reliant, untouched by war and its horror; of myself as a weak, drivelling coward, pouring out a lot of introspective rubbish into cold ears. Not a very pleasant brace of thoughts.'

More arguments followed the following day – not helped when Bryant rather untactfully accused Brenda of having 'a carburettor for a heart'. On his final day of leave, as they hoed cabbages together in the garden, Bryant cautiously tried to apologise for his rudeness and pleaded with Brenda 'not to despise Australia and Australians merely because of me'. Then, with his train due once again, Bryant collected his belongings and said goodbye at the gate of the farm. 'We both made a few remarks on the stupidity of human beings, but could say nothing else. I kissed her goodbye, the response tender; my thoughts were still a hopeless confusion. The only clear feeling was one of emptiness and regret.' Bryant was self-deprecating enough to be privately sympathetic towards Brenda. Talking to a squadron mate 'on life, women and sex' one evening, he admitted that his friend 'found me not at all comprehensible. He is scarcely to be blamed as I cannot understand myself. No wonder Brenda had such a hard time of it.'

Back at Warboys a few days later, Bryant heard 'the worst news the war has brought me', that Bill Charlton – one of the original twenty recruits who had made the initial boat journey from Australia to Canada – was posted as missing after an op over Stettin.

'No, Brenda, there's nothing to worry about in Ops!' he scrawled sarcastically in his diary. The news had brought to him 'a sense of weariness, of futility, of littleness. In one breath I felt I must give it all up, must run away and hide before some new blow found me. In the next I felt a surge of anger, something that drives me to want to operate, to seek revenge for my cobbers. There is always the chance Bill is a prisoner, but on that raid I don't think there was much hope. Too much sea crossing.'

Bryant sent Don Charlwood the news via a wire:

> That is nine of the twenty. It is with a strange sense of detachment that one sees the list narrow, and wonder if you will be the next. Now and then I feel it is all a bad dream and that suddenly I shall wake up and find myself back in the canteen at Edmonton, with the juke box playing 'Concerto for Two' and all the boys lining up for a toasted tomato sandwich and hot chocolate. Bill, the gentlest, hardest working, most conscientious and most lovable of all – now a name in the casualty list. To those of us who knew him, a flame that will burn steadily in our

memory until ever we hold on to life. Life goes on – if we did not have
something to fill our minds we should go crackers.

A few weeks later Charlton's death was confirmed. Bryant called
Don to break the news. 'He took it with a kind of dull resignation – I
don't think anything can hurt any of us now,' wrote Bryant. 'He told
me Ron Hendy and Ron Wheatley were both gone, so that just half of
the twenty are left.'

A few days later, on Anzac Day – the annual day of commemoration
for the Australians and New Zealanders lost in the Gallipoli campaign almost thirty years before – Bryant let his hair down with
dozens of Aussie and Kiwi Pathfinders from the neighbouring airbases. A busload of thirsty airmen arrived at a pub in Huntingdon and
the beer began to flow, with spirited renderings of 'Waltzing Matilda'
and 'Along the Road to Gundagai', before the haka was performed.
On the way home Bryant realised he was, 'for the first time in my life',
stinking drunk. 'It was the usual thing,' Bryant told Don Charlwood
in a letter, '. . . bags of beer, spirited if tuneless singing and hakas. By
the end of the evening I was quite incapable and remember scarcely
anything of the trip home. I have dim recollections of George holding
me up while I became ill, uttering words of consolation,' before Bryant, 'steered a most erratic course for my room, undressed and
collapsed into bed'.

By May 1943, Warboys was bathed in warm summer sunshine. In
the surrounding countryside, hedges blossomed with white and pink,
newly cut haystacks sat in fields waiting to be collected, and other fields
burst green with new crops. On airfields across Pathfinder country, aircrews assembled for operations surrounded by idyllic pastoral scenes.
One ground-crew mechanic on a Pathfinder station rejoiced to be
working on aircraft in pleasant temperatures after months of wind,
rain and snow. But he also became conscious of a 'sinister background'
in the change of season. 'I began to realise that these warm balmy evenings constituted a sort of mocking backcloth for a number of our
aircrews. These idyllic conditions could forecast for them a night of
fear, suffering and possible death. One particular summer evening
could be the last that some of them would experience on this planet . . .'[7]

Max Bryant and his crew had steadily stacked up the operations, with targets ranging from Pilsen in Czechoslovakia – which had been something of a Pathfinder boob – to Stettin, Düsseldorf and Stuttgart. The crew had successfully completed its Pathfinder probation and was now backing up the primary target markers. Better still, they had earned their golden Pathfinder badges. Don Charlwood had completed his tour – much to Bryant's relief – and they'd enjoyed a few days' leave together walking on Exmoor, in the West Country, before taking the train back to Wolverhampton, where he and Charlwood had parted with a 'be good' and 'look after yourself'.

'A real friendship does not need many words,' he wrote later. After saying goodbye to his friend before heading back to ops, Bryant also managed to steal an hour with Brenda – 'We talked for a while. Brenda admitted to a still-confused mind. I gave a lot of advice which I can't even keep myself. Fortunately, Bren is young and has plenty of life ahead of her. We kissed goodbye – her kisses are still the same' – before getting back to Warboys just in time to watch Vera Lynn putting on a concert in the mess.

A week later, on the morning of Sunday, 23 May, the airbase was alive with activity as it prepared for the biggest operation since the thousand-bomber raids a year before. The target was Dortmund, in the Ruhr. This would be the largest raid in the Battle of the Ruhr, with more than 800 Allied aircraft, including 662 four-engine bombers. 'We were all a bit staggered by those figures – the previous top list of heavies had been nothing like it. Bomb tonnage was over 3,000, more than twice the thousand [tons] raid on Cologne,' observed Bryant.

The mission was a success. The Pathfinders marked the target accurately in clear weather conditions, and before long large areas of the city were being blasted by the main force. The Hoesch steelworks – the key target – was badly hit. Bryant's crew touched down safely in the early hours of the morning and after the usual round of interrogation and breakfast, finally plonked into their beds at 0630 as the sun was rising. 'That is twenty-two trips now, almost half way,' Bryant wrote in his diary. 'After the next one [I] will have turned the corner.'

After a decent number of operations, a Pathfinder crew could expect to be working as a well-tuned unit. They trusted each other, and in turn that gave some reassurance against the dangers. 'I have the greatest confidence in our kites. They can absorb lots of flak and still fly. The real danger these days – or nights – is to run foul of a night fighter, but with Jock in the rear turret I don't feel unduly worried,' wrote Bryant after one operation.

> One of our trips was in brilliant moonlight. On the way home I went back to the end of the kite to relieve nature, and stood there for a moment watching. The rear turret was moving steadily from side to side, guns rising and falling. I knew that behind the guns there was a cool head and steady eyes and went back to the 'office' feeling very secure. It was a grand feeling to know there is someone way back in the tail keeping ceaseless vigil.

Over the next fortnight, bad weather over Germany meant operations were scrubbed night after night. Airmen hated this the most – so much of the job was about getting into the right state of mind. Once the operation started they could concentrate on the job at hand. Effort was put into practising target marking and bombing. On the morning of Friday, 11 June 1943, the signals burst into life as the orders came in from Bomber Command HQ in High Wycombe. 'The old battle cry "Ops tonight" has been raised again,' wrote Bryant.

> If the weather were not so good I should snicker nastily and mutter 'Oh yeah!' Just to think that when we last came back from leave we had 21 ops in. It looked a piece of cake to do nine in the next six weeks, and so have our long leave. Here we are with just two weeks to leave, and seven ops to go! Not a chance of getting them done. Oh well, why should we worry? I can't control the weather or the mighty brains at Bomber Command.

A large raid on Düsseldorf was planned, with almost 800 bombers. For Bryant and his crew, a special assignment to attack the railway works in the German city of Münster beckoned. When the crews gathered to be briefed, they learnt the Münster raid would be the first all-Pathfinder raid, using 72 heavies from 8 Group in a mass trial of H2S technology. Thirty-three Pathfinder bombers would mark the target with the rest carrying conventional bombs. Accuracy and speed were key. They would be in and out of the target as quickly as possible. The weather held good. That evening all around eastern England aircraft took off and headed for mainland Europe. Bryant's plane took off at 11.38pm carrying four red target indicators and was in the leading force of markers. Two hours later red flares drizzled down over the marshalling yards, allowing the rest of the Pathfinders following up to drop their bombs right on the mark. As the aircraft made their way back to England, five were shot down, including a Lancaster which was seen to go down in flames near the small Dutch town of Lemmer after being shot at by two German flak positions.

The force attacking Düsseldorf, meanwhile, was met with strong opposition from the Luftwaffe night fighters, which made 70 sorties in clear and almost cloudless night sky, helped by the milky light from a half moon. One Halifax bomber of 35 Pathfinder Squadron, flying towards Düsseldorf at 18,500 feet, was pounced on by a night fighter from the portside quarter, firing long bursts of tracer fire from 800 yards away. The bullets ripped through the rear and the middle of the lumbering bomber, hitting the mid-upper gunner and starting a small fire in between the starboard engines. At the rear of the aircraft in the tiny turret, bullets from the attacking plane also smashed through the Perspex and thudded into the right leg and stomach of the rear gunner, splattering the turret with his blood and causing him to wonder if his leg had been blown off. His guns were still working but the mechanism that rotated them to the port side had been damaged. The pilot immediately put the Halifax into a violent corkscrew manoeuvre to try and shake off the fighter, only for a second enemy aircraft to start its attack. The Halifax was a sitting duck and the crew prepared to bail out.

But the German fighters had messed with the wrong plane. The rear gunner was Norman Williams, a 28-year-old Australian and something of an ace shot who had already earned two military medals for his sharp shooting. Despite his wounds, Williams shouted to the pilot through the intercom to turn starboard so he could bring his guns to bear on the rapidly closing twin-engine night fighter. He opened fire with a four-second burst and watched with satisfaction as the enemy attacker immediately stopped firing and, seconds later, exploded and fell towards the earth in flames. Almost immediately, the first plane made a second attack from dead astern. Williams was only just regaining his night vision after the bright flash of his first victim and fired off 500 rounds in a six-second burst. The enemy fighter kept coming. Was it trying to ram them? Williams fired again and finally the nose of the fighter dipped and shot underneath the Halifax, missing it by just 20 feet before disappearing into the clouds, seemingly out of control, with pieces falling off. Bleeding heavily and in great pain, and unable to move his legs, Williams insisted on staying at his guns until the aircraft crossed the English coast, before being cut out of his turret after the plane crash-landed. Williams survived, and spent several months recuperating from his injuries. He was awarded the Conspicuous Gallantry Medal by King George VI, before the two shared a bottle of beer. 'I was told I would have got the Victoria Cross if I had died,' he later said.[8]. His crew gave him the bomber's turret door as a memento, which contained 37 bullet holes.

The rest of the bombers began to land as the sky was brightening in the east and had their usual interrogation before a bite to eat and flopping into bed. And then, a few hours later, the well-oiled wheels of RAF administration began to whirl. A secret RAF report on the Münster raid concluded that 'Navigation to and from the target has been consistently good. Navigators did well to fulfil the requirement regarding the duration of the attack, viz that 72 aircraft taking part should all bomb within five minutes.'

It was indeed a remarkable effort. Meanwhile, a WAAF clerk typed out each crews' interrogation reports in the operations record book. Next to Lancaster 111, serial number ED935, she wrote, 'Task: Munster' and then: 'THIS AIRCRAFT FAILED TO RETURN.' Five simple words that were about to rip apart the lives of dozens of people. The captain of the Lancaster was listed as 'F/Sgt Lay'. The navigator: 'P/O R.M. Bryant'.

At Warboys, as the warm summer sunshine blazed onto the low Nissen huts, members of the RAF's 'Committee of Adjustment' filed into Max Bryant's room. His diaries, camera and clothes were collected up and the bed sheets replaced with fresh linen. Within minutes, it was as if no one had ever been there at all. The bed wouldn't be empty for long. They never were.

Two days later, 10,000 miles away in the little Australian town of Cowra, a three-line telegram addressed to Mr J.J. Bryant was hand-delivered to number 15 Bartlett Avenue.

REGRET TO INFORM YOU THAT YOUR SON SERGEANT ROBERT MAXWELL BRYANT IS MISSING AS RESULT OF AIR OPERATIONS ON 11TH JUNE 1943 STOP LETTER WILL FOLLOW[9]

Bryant's personal belongings were handed over to Don Charlwood, as the men had agreed if Bryant was shot down. Charlwood too had been sent a telegram. 'One word hit me at a glance: "Max", then "missing". The brightness drained from the day,' he wrote afterwards.[10] Charlwood wrote to Bryant's parents:

Dear Mr and Mrs Bryant,
I had hoped that it would never be my lot to write you this letter; indeed, even now it seems impossible to me that Max is not still safe in England. I assure you, I can write of him as one of my own brothers and a brother I would be tremendously proud of. It is not yet a month since he failed to return; so I am still very hopeful that he has managed to bail out and even hope that he will turn up unexpectedly some day in the way that I found typical of him.
. . . Max just didn't make mistakes in the air . . . I can confidently say that their loss would certainly have nothing to do with his navigation . . . I feel very sure that he would wish us to remember, if we do not see him again, that he was very happy and that he did his job well. He did it more than well, he did it splendidly, – but he would not have had us think that.

Bryant's parents, Jack and Estelle, clung on to the hope that their son had bailed out and was now a prisoner of war, but the suspense of not knowing was horrific. A few days later, a letter arrived from his commanding officer at 156 Squadron, informing them no messages had been received from Bryant's aircraft on the night of the attack. Yet the letter still talked about him in the past tense: 'Pilot Officer Bryant was a Navigator of outstanding ability . . . your son set a fine example to his many friends in the squadron . . . it is hoped that there will be news of his safety at an early date.' They were assured that any news of Bryant's well-being would likely come via the International Red Cross in Geneva. That was something to hope for.

Over the coming weeks, the condolence letters flooded to the Bryants' house from friends and relatives, all laced with reassurances. '. . . Max has had a lot of flights so will have experience behind him . . .' '. . . I would not worry too much as there is a big possibility that he had the chance to bail out and would be quite alright . . .' '. . . one must not give up hope until definite news comes . . .' And one, from a child: 'Dear Auntie Estelle, I am learning to type and I writing you a little letter. I pray every night for Max and I know that he will come home to you safely. Love Michael.'

Then, in late September 1943, a letter arrived for the Bryants from the Red Cross Bureau for Wounded, Missing and Prisoners of War. Perhaps it was the good news they had been hoping for at last.

> Dear Mr Bryant,
> Our Central Bureau, Melbourne, have advised us that the following cabled message has been received by them from International Red Cross, Geneva:
>
> 'Berlin cables Sgt. Robert Maxwell Bryant, dead, washed ashore 17 June, 1943.'
>
> It is to these brave and gallant lads who have paid the supreme sacrifice for their country that we owe so much, and in passing this sad news on to you we would like to extend the deepest sympathy, not only of this Bureau, but also of the Australian Red Cross, in your great loss.

Bryant's Lancaster had been shot down over IJsselmeer in the Netherlands – most likely as it was returning from the mission after bombing Münster – killing the entire crew, whose average age was 23. Two German flak batteries claimed the kill in the early hours of the following morning.[11] Six days later, a man out walking with his son found Bryant's body floating in a dyke near the village of Urk. Locals gathered and carried his body into the village and buried him in the little cemetery with a simple service.

The great cogs of war ground on. Back in England, according to the Pathfinders' own group diary, 'from the point of view of encounters and combats June was the most exciting month since the Pathfinder force came into being.'[12] That was one way of putting it. But it had also been a bloody one for the Pathfinders. June 1943 was the costliest month of the war so far for Bennett's men – 194 killed, with 156 Squadron losing 52 men, including Bryant and his crew. In one June week, 7 Squadron lost three commanders. On a single raid against Krefeld, a town north-west of Düsseldorf, 14 Pathfinder aircraft were shot down. It wasn't just the emotional loss – years of combined operational experience wiped out in the blink of an eye. Just more names on the casualty list. 'The heavy flak defences through which the aircraft had to fly from which only little evasive action during target marking is possible is the most likely cause of the increasing hazards when engaged on PFF duty,' concluded one secret RAF report.[13]

As the days grew longer, the sustained bombing campaign against towns and cities across the Ruhr slowed down. It was time to take stock. Between March and July, 774 Pathfinder airmen had been killed, scores more injured and taken prisoner.[14] Over the same period, Bomber Command as a whole had lost just over a thousand aircraft and nearly 4,000 crew were killed or became POWs. The Command had dropped almost 60,000 tons of bombs – more than the Luftwaffe had despatched on Britain in the whole of 1940 and 1941. 'They had ruined the Ruhr,' Hitler remarked in June after one particularly heavy raid.[15] Thanks to the increasing accuracy of the Pathfinders' target marking, raids had been delivered in ever increasing concentration and numbers – 35 raids used 300 bombers or more, with quite terrifying firepower, and more bombs had been dropped in the five months of the Battle of the Ruhr than Bomber Command dropped on Germany in the whole of 1942. Some cities, such as Wuppertal, had seen astonishing devastation. Morale amongst the Pathfinders and Bomber Command was high.

Though Bomber Command had various estimates as to the material and industrial output damage its bombing of the Ruhr had achieved, nothing could be confirmed. Estimates were based on reconnaissance photographs of damage from the air, intelligence from the ground, and the number of industrial 'man hours' lost. Yet it all served to legitimise Bert Harris's city-bombing strategy. The turning of the screw on the German people and industry from the air also, crucially, came at a time when the wider war was pivoting in the Allies' favour.

In May, joint British and American forces had secured North Africa and the Mediterranean, and on 10 July 1943 a combined Allied invasion of Sicily began, signalling the beginning of the end for Mussolini and his Fascists. In the Atlantic, meanwhile, the deadly influence of the once feared German U-boats was waning. Soon the wolfpacks would haunt transatlantic conveys no more. With the Battle of the Atlantic won, the Allies could begin their planning for the second front. Two years of war still lay ahead, however, and July and August 1943 would see Harris turn his attention to fresh targets. Soon, the Pathfinders would spearhead the most destructive and lethal attacks the world had ever seen.

CHAPTER FOURTEEN

In Sickness and in Health

'IT'S DANGEROUS HERE,' SAID the little girl. 'I'm taking my brother to Switzerland where it's safe. Will you open the gate please?' Her round eyes looked up with steely determination at the young RAF sentry manning the main guardhouse. A few minutes earlier, as the air-raid sirens started blaring across RAF Wyton, six-year-old Noreen Bennett had calmly gathered some squash and biscuits, grabbed the Mickey Mouse and Donald Duck gas masks, tucked her five-year-old little brother Torix up in a rug in a wheelbarrow, and set off towards the exit of the base. While raids against the airbase by German planes were rare, the sirens often sounded, and the visitation now making its way unsteadily along the road towards the guardhouse was something of a regular occurrence. The sentry picked up the phone. 'Good Morning Mam. I've got your daughter here. She's apparently taking your son to Switzerland . . . Very good Mam.' A few minutes later, Ly Bennett scooped up the young marauders and took them back home.[1]

For Noreen and Torix Bennett, it was just another fun adventure as young kids growing up on a working airbase, where their father happened to be spearheading Bomber Command's war against Germany. In June 1943, the Pathfinders' headquarters moved to a three-storey eighteenth-century townhouse in the centre of nearby Huntingdon, and 8 Group had swelled in size to 10 squadrons across seven airbases dotted around Cambridgeshire. But the Bennetts' family home remained on Wyton – which was the base for 83 Squadron, flying Lancasters, and 139 Squadron, in Mosquitos – very much a central hub for the Pathfinder Force. 'They flew over my bedroom every night,' recalled Noreen.[2]

Don Bennett may have been known as a stickler for detail and doing things right by his men, but he was far more relaxed about integrating his family life into proceedings. 'We were part of everything,' said Noreen. 'He wasn't the slightest bit worried about segregating work. We were always in the office or in the mess.' As the Commanding Officer's wife, Ly Bennett helped the airmen's wives organise parties for the children and kicked off the WAAF's football matches. Every day she made her husband his favourite chocolate cake – one of the few vices he allowed himself – and occasionally had to remind him to wash his oil-covered hands again before he left the house, such was his passion for tinkering with car engines. The previous Christmas, Bennett had bought the children an Alsatian puppy, which immediately began playing with the decorations on the tree. 'Aw. That's it! He's going to be called Tinsel,' said Ly. 'No it's not!' replied Bennett. 'Yes he is. He's obviously got to be called Tinsel.' Bennett put his foot down, although much to his frustration couldn't explain why that particular name was forbidden – it was the codename used for a highly secret airborne jamming device being trialled by the Pathfinders to block German radio transmissions – so the dog was christened Bombo, and became a permanent fixture at Wyton.[3]

Wyton had been established as an airbase in the First World War, and rapidly expanded in the inter-war years with new hangars, a two-storey officers' mess, accommodation blocks and tennis courts. In early 1942, concrete runways were added, ready for the arrival of the new heavy bombers, and by the summer of 1943 more than 2,000 men and women lived and worked there. According to one account, Wyton was 'as ugly as wartime military bases can be. Endless puddles, barracks, warehouses full of bombs, [and] rusting wreckage of damaged equipment not worth repairing.'[4]

It was certainly more functional than pretty, but in the height of a war it did the job. And it could scrub up well. At the end of May 1943, King George VI and Queen Elizabeth had paid a flying visit to Wyton for an 'informal lunch' with the Bennetts and other senior staff. Noreen and Torix looked on excitedly as a bouquet of flowers was presented to 17-year-old Princess Elizabeth, accompanying her parents. The royal party had a tour of the airfield, walking past a line of Lancasters shining on the tarmac in the early summer sunshine, and met some of the Pathfinder airmen.

The royal visit sprinkled a rare moment of magic dust on Wyton, before it was back to reality. One morning, as Bennett walked out of the house to his car and set off across the airbase for Huntingdon, Bombo raced out of the house, only to rip open his stomach leaping over a metal fire hydrant. 'Stop the car!' Bennett immediately ordered his driver, before gathering up the blood-soaked dog and instructing the driver: 'Take us straight down to Doc Macgown as quickly as possible.'[5] John Macgown was the Pathfinders' Group Medical Officer. More used to dealing with airmen than canines, when he saw Bennett's anxiety he promised to do all he could to save the family dog. The following day, Bombo was wrapped in plaster of Paris and on the road to recovery, much to Bennett's relief, although his blood-soaked uniform hadn't fared so well.

When Macgown wasn't saving dogs, he was spearheading a remarkable medical department within the Pathfinders, looking at everything from how to improve aircrew night vision to the welfare of unmarried pregnant WAAFs. It was his responsibility to ensure that the crews were fit to fly, mentally and physically. Silver-haired Macgown wasn't your usual medical officer. He regularly flew on missions as a pilot or a navigator over Germany and – aged 43 when the war broke out – he was practically prehistoric for an active airman. He was probably the only doctor in Bomber Command to brief a group for operations, based on his work refining techniques of visual bomb aiming at night.

Macgown had already seen enough adventures to last a lifetime. He was born in the small harbour town of Millport on the island of Great Cumbrae off the west coast of Scotland, and his studies at Edinburgh University were cut short by the First World War, when he joined the Royal Flying Corps as a fighter pilot. He was shot down over the Western Front in July 1917, captured by the Germans and imprisoned in Holtzminden in Germany. From his POW camp he wrote home to his sister, telling her:

Have had some most exciting experiences. A shell hit my machine at 3000ft up and I hit the ground rather forcibly. It was rather funny while I was falling, expecting to be an angel in the next few seconds. Suddenly I found myself on the ground with the machine piled up on the top of me and as I couldn't feel any wings sprouting came to the conclusion that I was still in the land of the living.[6]

Feeling rather 'fed up at being out of everything', Macgown escaped twice, first to Russia – from where he was sent back to Germany after the 1917 Russian Revolution – and then, successfully, to the Netherlands. At the end of the First World War, Macgown resumed his medical studies and became a doctor, practising in Hong Kong, where he learnt to speak Chinese and met his wife Marjorie, a nursing sister. He returned to Britain and established himself as an eye specialist in London's Wimpole Street, until the autumn of 1939 when he enlisted in the RAF Medical Branch.

Before he joined the Pathfinders, Macgown had helped start a farm while stationed with a Bomber Command squadron in the north of England, cultivating 30 acres of land. It was entirely self-supporting, providing its own vegetables and salad, plus meat and fresh milk for the bomber crews, while officers paid five shillings a week to ride horses around the base as a form of exercise. It was this aspect of pastoral care – as well as his expertise as an ophthalmologist – which made Macgown an ideal fit for the Pathfinders.

Ahead of Macgown's arrival at Wyton in early 1943, Don Bennett had already made it clear how important his aircrews' health and well-being was in improving their efficiency in the air. Bennett didn't drink or smoke, and while he knew it was unfair to expect the airmen not to either, he advocated plenty of exercise and sports as a way to keep fit for operations. 'Aircrew as a class have never been very keen on taking exercise to keep fit', opined an 8 Group memo on fitness. 'One reason for this is that flying itself, particularly at high altitude, is very tiring although it entails little physical exertion. Nevertheless, in order to get the best out of oneself in operational flying, physical fitness is absolutely essential'. Airmen were also encouraged to play sports to relax the mind, while ensuring they didn't get injured in the process. They were also warned about avoiding catching colds or other infectious diseases. 'Most infectious diseases are spread by the fine droplets of water expelled from the mouth and nose in the acts of speaking, coughing and sneezing. It follows, therefore, that all crowded places are dangerous during an epidemic.'[7]

Bennett saw that his crews received fresh vegetables, especially those containing vitamin D, which, based on various studies circulating at the time – including one where participants were fed a pound of carrots every morning for breakfast – were thought to improve night vision.[8]

He also set about trying to prove his theories with a number of intriguing experiments. First, he investigated the effects of alcohol and fatigue upon aircrews' night vision. Two guinea pigs, a wing commander and a junior medical officer, were kept awake for 36 hours on the trot, including a 'heavy' air station party. Before and after, they were tested on a machine called the 'Livingston Rotating Hexagon', a piece of kit designed to test night-vision capacity, consisting of a dark room with a rotating hexagonal structure, on the panels of which were painted different letters and objects, such as outlines of aircraft or ships. Scores were based on how well participants identified what they saw, and in the case of the two men who had been forced to stay awake for almost two days, there was little difference in their performance. Two more aircrew were tested before and after a large party, when both had become 'moderately drunk', with a similar result. 'Group Captain Bennett was exceedingly keen on investigating any possible operation to increase efficiency in the crews,' observed one RAF report. 'It was a period of research at Wyton which was interesting, if not constructive.'[9]

But Bennett was onto something with the focus on night vision, and under Macgown's steerage, research and development into the subject gathered pace. A night-vision training school was established and Macgown was soon asked to give a lecture on night-vision training to representatives of Allied armies and air forces at the Royal Society of Medicine in London. The problem of cockpit lighting was studied extensively. It concluded that the best results were obtained from red lighting of low intensity, where almost full night vision could be obtained immediately after looking at instruments. Special eye drops which dilated the pupils and improved night vision were handed out. All new gunners and bomb aimers appointed to the Pathfinders were tested on the Livingston Hexagon, and those who didn't reach a certain grade were immediately sent back to the main force. Participants learnt the best way to try and spot an incoming attacking enemy fighter was not to look directly at the point where it was thought to be, but at an angle of 10 to 40 degrees away from it, where their peripheral vision could detect motion best.

Light was as much a challenge as the dark. If a Pathfinder bomber was 'coned' by German searchlights, it was estimated the eyes would take 20 minutes to recover their optimum night vision after escaping the light. In these vital minutes, gunners could fail to spot attacking aircraft. Gunners were warned against staring at blazing targets below. 'Once they have looked down at the fires and incendiaries or searchlights the night vision is temporarily ruined,' said a secret RAF report. Some were issued with special anti-glare sunglasses to wear on operations. In the summer of 1943, intelligence gathered by the Pathfinders suggested a major change in enemy tactics, with enemy fire shifting from flak to fighters, placing an additional responsibility on the gunners. 'It cannot be stressed often enough that gunners must now avoid looking down at the target and commenting on the inferno below, but must keep searching above, for it is from far above that the [German] fighters select their targets visually over the target area, when bombers show up well against the light on the ground.' Gunners were warned not to allow the enemy to 'creep in and right himself' for the attack. 'If only gunners would view a fighter aircraft through their sight at 400 yards and then view a Lancaster, Stirling or Halifax at the same range, they would never allow the enemy to come in below 600 yards,' said a Pathfinder report.[10]

Even with perfect vision, however, it was not always easy to identify enemy aircraft. Men were tested on a synthetic device called a Shadowgraph in which an aircraft silhouette was thrown onto a screen in a darkened room, with the pupil obliged to give the aircraft's name and judge its relative distance. The action of a gunner who couldn't differentiate one aircraft from another, dubbed a 'Hun Helper', could have disastrous consequences. 'This Headquarters is very keen indeed to meet the mid-upper gunner of a Lancaster aircraft who opened fire on a similar aircraft of this Group, seriously wounding our Flight

Engineer,' said one circulated Pathfinder report. Gunners were warned to be certain of the plane they were shooting at before 'getting their men'. This wasn't always easy. Pathfinder research indicated that enemy aircraft could open fire from a range of 800 yards, yet unless it was bright moonlight the average RAF gunner was unable to see an approaching aircraft until it was 500 yards away.

They needed all the help they could get. It was essential that Perspex shields were kept scrupulously clean and free from scratches or oil spots. Some rear gunners simply removed them completely, despite being exposed to plummeting temperatures. Intense cold experienced by crews – especially rear gunners – at 20,000 feet or more could induce fatigue and impact their vision. After a Pathfinder raid on Mannheim, a rear gunner with 35 Squadron was found unconscious by his crew on landing. He died on the way to hospital. 'Cause probably lack of oxygen and cold,' wrote a colleague in his diary.[11] Emphasis was placed on ensuring that aircrew and gunners especially had electrically heated suits, although these didn't always work. One rear gunner destined for the Pathfinders got so cold on a training mission after removing his turret's Perspex screen that the film of water over his eyes started turning to ice. Little surprise, given the temperature had apparently dropped to an astonishing –76°C.

Frostbite could also be a major problem. It was all right for the navigators and wireless operators – their positions tended to be near warm pipes running through the aircraft – but for the bomb aimer in the nose and gunners in the middle of the aircraft and the rear, objects that were innocuous back at base took on sinister characteristics at high altitudes, as the temperatures plummeted. All exposed metal became so cold it could burn bare flesh on contact. Faces, hands and feet were most commonly affected by frostbite. Airmen were reminded to cover all metal parts of their helmets and oxygen masks with adhesive chamois leather, and instructed not to shave for six hours before a flight, thus retaining a protective layer of epidermis often removed during shaving. Even though two sets of gloves were worn, if these were removed – perhaps to connect oxygen after a leak or to assist a crewmate in an emergency – vulnerable fingers were quickly exposed. Aircrew often wore flying boots about the camp before missions, but sweating feet and socks not properly dried greatly increased liability to frostbite, so crews were advised to put on boots at the last minute and to ensure that their socks were dry.

Most instances of frostbite were self-induced, and some were plain idiotic. One Pathfinder rear gunner enjoyed sneaking a flask of coffee into his turret to sip on the way back from operations, but knew that what went in must come out. As he couldn't leave his position in case the aircraft was attacked, he rigged up a portable urinal – a glass milk bottle tied to the inside of his leg, joined to a funnel via an oxygen pipe. Great in theory, until one night, when returning from a mission, the grateful gunner relieved himself only for the liquid in the milk bottle to overflow all over his leg and freeze. By the time the aircraft landed, the dozy gunner had a nasty case of frostbite. 'You bloody fool, you shouldn't have done that should you?' was all his exasperated commanding officer could say.[12]

Macgown identified lack of oxygen as another major factor affecting night vision. Symptoms of oxygen deficiency varied from man to man. It could cause hallucinations or blackouts. One rear gunner at 15,000 feet above a target area suddenly felt his breathing get deeper and faster, followed by headaches. A mid-upper gunner accidentally pulled his oxygen tube from its socket while adjusting a glove. He remembered nothing from the time of leaving the target over Berlin until they reached the Dutch coast. A flight engineer feeling airsick at about 9,000 feet went to the Elsan loo – an open lavatory rather like an oil drum near the back of the aircraft – but forgot to plug in his oxygen. As the aircraft climbed to 20,000 feet, the unfortunate man was found by the bomb aimer slumped in a state of unconsciousness, still sitting on the loo. The sortie was abandoned. A system was introduced whereby the captain of the aircraft called up every member of the crew every 20 minutes and if no reply was received an investigation was started.[13] All crew positions had their own oxygen stations, but if an airman needed to move about the fuselage, a portable oxygen bottle gave about seven minutes' worth of supply.

Crews were issued with instructions on first aid in the air, with an emphasis on treating shock. 'The treatment given in the aircraft by you may make all the difference between life and death,' they were told. Little could be done to treat broken bones, except perhaps a bandage or a sling. Open wounds were dressed with bandages. Most injured men were given morphine and not moved. After dressing wounds as best they could, crew were advised to place injured men in a comfortable position and keep them warm with fluids, offering reassurance until the aircraft landed back at base. Perhaps the biggest challenge was trying to treat shock, which affected 75 per cent of operational casualties. 'A badly wounded man is like a child in that he has lost his grip of the situation and needs someone to give him back his peace of mind,' said an RAF dictum. 'He should never be allowed to know if there is anything wrong with the aircraft, as this will only increase his shock. Even if danger is imminent and these remarks are overheard by other members of the crew, they will understand the reason for them.'[14]

One of the most common ailments preventing airmen from operating was the humble head cold, and at the first signs they were told to go to bed. Decompression chambers were also used to help unblock sinuses of returning crews. The chamber had actually been designed to assess how well crews performed at high altitude, and allowed the operators to have some fun if they suspected the crews inside were being overdramatic about the effects of altitude. More than one airman 'passed out' while still at ground level with the door shut, only to be 'revived' by being taken up to 30,000 feet. Oral medication could also have a strong placebo effect. Another experiment tested three types of 'wakey-wakey' tablets as a means of preventing fatigue during long operations. One tablet was caffeine, the second type Benzedrine and the third simply chalk. On the night of a cancelled operation, there was considerable complaint of the inability to sleep from crews who had in fact taken the chalk. It was concluded that caffeine pills would be best for future use – presumably striking a happy medium between chalk and the probably-too-happy Benzedrine tablets.

Even when Pathfinders were not on operations, the pressure never ceased and they practised intensively. 'I am only just beginning to find out what a lot of hard work there is attached to the PFF, it is constant training even on squadron,' wrote John Kelly to his parents after joining 83 Squadron. 'We do nothing but fly here, in fact occasionally we pay a flying visit to the Earth ... Whenever an aeroplane is spare and the weather fit we are rushed off into the air to fly all over the British Isles, making practice blind-bombing runs on about six different towns each day. It is a binding job for me, and indeed for everyone.'[15]

The Pathfinders set up their own Navigational Training Unit – a sort of navigational finishing school – based at RAF Gransden Lodge, in Cambridgeshire, where new crews embarked on a week of intensive 'postgraduate' instruction, and operating crews visited for refresher courses if required.[16] 'We take up bags of PFF narks with us, who check up on everything we do, from the way we refer to each other on the intercom to the way we can drop bombs,' Kelly wrote home. 'If we do not come up to scratch we get sent back to main force, either for good, or else until we have another six ops, when we can have another try out.'

The focus on navigation was not surprising given Bennett's background, and navigators were suddenly put on a plinth. 'In my old squadron a navigator was an essential member of the crew, but here in the Pathfinders he was almost the King Pin,' recalled one Pathfinder. 'It was no good if your pilot flew like an angel, your engineer knew more about engines than Austin and Morris put together, and the gunners could see in the dark for miles – if your navigation was out by a few degrees and you arrived over the target a little late, then the main force would be kept waiting, and the whole careful plan of attack would be thrown out.'[17]

Bennett himself interviewed many new crews. He told one: 'Well, welcome to Pathfinders, if you make it through the school. But we don't accept one mistake. You guys make one mistake here at the school, you're out. So let's look for the mistake.' For the new crew, the pressure from Bennett helped. 'Pride enters into it, so we didn't make a mistake,' remembered one. 'I used to think, well, you know, we haven't flown all this way over here to bomb Frau Schultz's potato patch. If we're going to come over here we'll do what we're supposed to do.'[18]

When time and machines permitted, Bennett insisted his Pathfinder crews practised relentlessly to hone their navigation techniques. 'Nobody can be a good captain of an aircraft unless he knows where he is going,' he said. He reckoned a captain needed to be 'very strong on navigation, reasonably strong on technical matters such as engineering and on the radar and electronics, and just a little bit on moving the levers . . . 5 per cent.'[19]

Crews were given exercises known as 'Bullseyes', which tried to mimic the conditions of a real operation over enemy territory, where bomber crews had to navigate and 'attack' targets in real towns and cities across Britain, while British fighter planes tried to intercept them. Although they didn't actually drop any bombs, the drills also allowed the bombers to practise evading the probing fingers of search-lights, which doubled up as an opportunity for the British searchlight and anti-aircraft crews down on the ground to hone their own techniques.

Crews were also told to practise marking. In one practice run, a newspaper reporter watching on described the process:

> Somewhere in England a few nights ago the darkness was broken as Pathfinders dropped yellow target indicator bombs on the bombing range. Hanging like huge chandeliers in the sky, they slowly fell to the ground, throwing up a glare which lit up the countryside for miles around. Then from other planes came loads of ordinary illuminating flares which find the target area with a brilliant intense glare. By the light of these flares other aircraft positively identified the target and dropped red target indicator bombs which strongly resembled a rope ladder of illuminated electric candle bulbs . . . the target accurately marked, along came the 'backers-up' with green target indicator bombs . . . so it goes on right through a raid. As one lot of marker bombs die away, another lot of pathfinders come to restore the brilliance with more loads.[20]

The intensive training sanctioned by Bennett was understandable. He wanted his crews to be the best and, in his view, practice made perfect, even if it meant that some crews felt like they were returning to an operational training unit. 'If they want to play at OTUs, well we can do the same,' scribbled John Kelly in a letter. 'I have briefed all my lads on what to say on the intercom, no more "Jack" but "Captain" now. And before we get airborne I am going to insist on inspecting the narks' parachutes etc, see if they know their ditching stations, and then carry out a practice dinghy drill. Duggie [G.J. Duggin, Kelly's Australian rear gunner] is going to report an imaginary fighter attack, I shall corkscrew until somebody is sick, and then Duggie will claim the fighter shot down. I bet they won't want to fly with us the second trip.'[21]

When they weren't operating over Europe, crews were encouraged to carry out training runs over bombing ranges near the Pathfinder bases, with the best squadrons winning a monthly squadron trophy while the worst were presented with a wooden spoon. Despite their extra training, they didn't always hit the spot. Pathfinder crews were warned to take care after their practice bombs missed a range and 'nearly caused an outbreak of red revolution among the local farmers'. However, for many airmen, it was this extra training and the desire of Bennett for his crews to be the best that attracted them to the Pathfinders in the first place. 'I was extraordinarily happy from the start,' said one. 'Throughout the day we were training hard. There was an exhilarating atmosphere of efficiency. One felt that nothing was going to be left to chance.'[22]

The physical dangers of being an airman were obvious. But Doc Macgown was also critically aware that the mental welfare of those he affectionately called 'my boys' was crucial to successful operations. The responsibility Pathfinder crews had to ensure the raids they led were successful created added pressure and stress. If a crew had a bad flight, Macgown joined them on the next operation to provide support and reassurance and to calm any jitters. One of the reasons they trusted him so much was because he'd been through it with them – in two world wars. But he was given no special treatment, and like all other Pathfinder airmen, Macgown had to earn his Pathfinder badge, as he recounted in a letter to his wife in June 1943:

Darling, I got my Pathfinder Wings today. I passed the exam in navigation, flying a Lancaster, use of sextant for finding your position from the stars, use of some secret radio devices for target location, meteorology and beam-approach blind flying. You have to do ten trips with the Pathfinders. I've done 12. They are all very keen here on learning to see in the dark and I've got a better school going here than the one I started at Heyford. [Macgown had briefly been stationed at RAF Upper Heyford in Oxfordshire, where he set up a night vision training school.] Having been over with the boys they listen to what you say because they know that you understand what they have to do and what the difficulties are.[23]

Macgown ultimately decided when Pathfinder airmen were no longer in a fit mental state to fly. 'Twitch', or 'crack up' as it was also known, was an aviator's condition in which a healthy concern for one's safety turned morbid. The word had numerous shades of meaning. A man could be a bit twitchy after a few rough missions and then be fine. At the other end of the scale, severe twitch, which often built up over extended time exposed to the pressure of combat, could render an airman literally a dribbling mess and unable to fly. Sadly, many sufferers were demoted to a menial ground job in some far-flung windswept airfield, or released by Bomber Command completely, under a cloud of humiliation.

More often than not, twitch was kept in check by not dwelling on missions and keeping busy, or through the panacea of alcohol, and there were remarkably few cases reported within the RAF – around 2 per cent, compared to the army campaigns in Italy and northern France where a 10 per cent casualty rate from 'exhaustion' was acceptable.[24] Most of the airmen were in their late teens or early twenties, buoyed along by the idea that it will 'never happen to me'. They knew the dangers, but while they saw many bombers go down, unlike ground troops they were generally spared the sight of the burnt and smashed bodies of their comrades or indeed enemies – unless of course the moment came when their own plane was hit.

But for those who were susceptible, twitch could grow like a cancer, an anxious mental state eating away at the nerves until it overwhelmed everything else. How this manifested itself depended on the man. When crews were debriefed after landing from a mission, officers were trained to pick up on the understandable but 'normal' characteristics associated with the stress of operations, which produced high levels of adrenaline. 'Mentally they are hyperexcitable, emotionally facile, talkative to the point of garrulousness, passing rapidly from one topic to another. Bodily they may have difficulty in keeping still, express their words with actions, and frequently show coarse tremors of fingers and eyelids . . . it would appear that this is a perfectly natural way of releasing emotions which previously have been suppressed,' said one RAF internal briefing.

If a man was cracking up, on the other hand, it tended to manifest itself in behaviour that appeared out of character. People developed tics and idiosyncrasies due to being 'flak happy'. Quiet men became boisterous. Gregarious types morose. A man who usually shunned alcohol began drinking. Some were given sedatives or sleeping tablets, but many medical officers avoided these, preferring instead to talk to an individual to establish whether it was a genuine psychological condition or simply an unwillingness to fly. Twitch rarely showed itself on operations, when men were occupied, but tended to emerge in between missions when they had time to reflect. But there were occasionally dramatic examples of crack-ups in the air.

During a Pathfinder mission over Essen, with the plane bouncing around because of heavy flak on the final run in to the target, the pilot informed the crew he was going around again to ensure they dropped the target indicators accurately. Suddenly one of the crew piped up on the intercom, 'Don't go in there, Tony. Don't go in there. They'll kill us!' The flight engineer and another crew member ended up forcibly tying the distressed man to the bed in the back of the aircraft. When they landed back at base, 'The ambulance met him and I never saw him again or heard anything of him,' said a crewmate. On another occasion, with the same crew, a mid-upper gunner 'went bananas' during an operation. 'He saw aircraft all over the sky and he gave evasive action [instructions] and we're pitching around trying to find these aircraft until it finally occurred to us that there weren't any.'[25]

According to Bomber Command's official policy, when a man refused to fly on operations it was often because he possessed a 'lack of moral fibre'. In other words, he lacked the courage needed to do the job. However, Macgown recognised that in reality the matter was far more nuanced and complex, and differed from man to man. He adopted a more sympathetic and understanding approach to the nerves and mental health of the young airmen. In the summer of 1943, a young mathematician called Freeman Dyson visited Wyton. Dyson worked for Bomber Command's Operational Research Section, and wanted to see how the Pathfinders' radar countermeasures against German fighters were working. But he was also there to study loss rates, and estimated the young Pathfinder airmen had a one in eleven chance of surviving their tours. When he first met Macgown, Freeman was struck by the 'tall, white-haired officer, he seemed to me very old, although he cannot have been much over forty'.[26]

Dyson continued: 'I was astonished, at our first meeting, when Macgown told me he was flying to Berlin that night. He said the crews loved to have him go along with them. It was well known in the squadron that the plane with the Doc on board always came home safely.' Dyson noted Macgown had already been to Berlin and back six times in the previous two months:

> At first I thought he must be crazy. Why should an elderly doctor with a full-time staff job risk his life repeatedly on these desperately dangerous missions? Afterward, I understood. It was the only way he could show these boys for whose bodies and souls he was responsible that he really cared for them. It was the only way he could face the boys who cracked and declare them 'lacking in moral fibre' without losing his own self-respect.

One evening, as Macgown was flying with one of twenty Pathfinder crews on a mission to Berlin, Dyson joined the remaining crews left at base for a beer party. 'The boys drank a great deal of beer and sang their squadron songs. "*We take our bombs to Germany, We don't bring them back … Eighty-three squadron – eighty-three men.*" It was the saddest beer party I ever attended.'[27] Macgown returned, and survived the war. Many years later his widow said of her husband: 'He flew partly to test the accuracy over targets but also made a point of flying with crews who had previously had a bad trip. They all reckoned that as he had survived two wars he must have good luck.'[28] There is no doubt Macgown developed a bond with his men. He wrote home to his wife: 'Our boys have had fairly heavy casualties recently but they keep going just the same. They have a great spirit.'[29]

Another sign of potential twitch was if the same crew began to show a pattern of returning from missions early – ostensibly because of engine trouble or some other mechanical problem, but in reality to avoid the worst of an op over the target. It was pretty rare amongst Pathfinders, but it meant genuine cases of engine trouble came under suspicion. When Colin Bell had to return from three missions in close succession, he fell under scrutiny – despite clear-cut reasons, including his oxygen failing, with his navigator having to bring him round again at 10,000 feet with the emergency oxygen bottle.

'When the third one came up they were beginning to look at me a bit closely,' said Bell. There was never a question of Bell's commitment or mental health – he flew 50 missions over Germany, including 13 on Berlin – and after clearly explaining in each case why he'd had to bring his Mosquito back early, he reassured his superiors at 608 Squadron that he was fit to fly. But he also reckoned he was lucky because he was 'possessed with not too much imagination', and never allowed the spectre of unpleasant thoughts to linger in his head. 'If you dwelled too much on your mortality you were more subject to twitch,' said Bell – a view shared by many other airmen. 'As far as I was concerned it was just a job to be done.'[30]

Not thinking too much was key. But training was also important – especially for Pathfinders. 'It was of little use to live in constant fear of what *might* happen,' said one rear-gunner Pathfinder. 'The proficiency of the crew allowed a hope for ultimate survival, despite the probability of a violent death. And the immediate emergencies of combat left no room in the mind for philosophy, only an automatic reaction that brought to the fore all the skills learned in training and (more important) the later experience.'[31]

Despite this spectre of death, hundreds of men flew many missions without so much as a scratch. But, strangely, for some Pathfinders, being hit actually helped their morale. When the Mosquito of Herbert Dunford, one of Bell's squadron colleagues, was badly hit by flak over Berlin on his forty-second operation, he managed to fly the aircraft home, and felt afterwards that 'it was a relief to have that incident and survive it, because one had seen one's friends go missing and get badly hit and you think *Well, it's got to be my turn sooner or later*, so to actually have it and get through it is quite a relief.' He found his last five missions – which took him up to a total of fifty-five operations over enemy territory – were the most traumatic. 'You wondered if the pitcher had gone too often to the well, and you could make [it through] the last five.'[32]

Officially, 8 Group's policy was one of 'firmness' in handling what were dubbed 'waverers' – often men who'd had relatively little operational experience who were showing reluctance to fly on operations. It asserted that this policy worked exceedingly well once the 'cold plunge' had been taken and the *esprit de corps* of the Pathfinders had a chance to take effect. It cited examples of men who had initially been reluctant to fly going on to win decorations for bravery. And many Pathfinders who survived a tour of 45 missions went on to serve two and even three tours – passing 100 operations.[32]

For all his characteristics as a hard taskmaster, however, Don Bennett ultimately approved of Macgown's approach. At the end of the war, an internal RAF report looking at the way in which 8 Group handled cases of LMF [lack of moral fibre] noted that 'squadron station commanders were very late to take disciplinary action and frequently brought pressure to bear on the medical officers to send the case concerned to a psychiatrist who would almost always find some loophole whereby the person's lack of courage could be attributed to some hypothetical psychological complaint.'[34] Or perhaps Bennett, Macgown and his team realised that for the airmen who did crack up, it was often a far more complicated matter than simply a supposed 'lack of courage'. It says much about both the vast majority of young airmen and Macgown that, as the report observed: 'after a chat with an operational type old enough to be their father most of the waverers decided to have a go.'

One way of dealing with operational stress was seeking pleasure, and when Macgown and the doctors of the other Bomber Command groups weren't dealing with airmen's psychological issues, they had rather more inevitable matters to contend with. At the force's peak in 1944, more than 190,000 male and female ground personnel worked to support around 36,000 Bomber Command aircrew. Between 1942 and 1944, there were more women than men in the service.[35] By the end of war, over a quarter of a million women had served in the Women's Auxiliary Air Force.

Every group had its share of sexually transmitted diseases and the Pathfinders were no different. Doctors knew they couldn't totally eradicate venereal diseases but did their best to control them, with mixed results. In 1943, the infection rate was 9.5 per 1,000 people for ground personnel, just 2.9 per 1,000 for WAAFs, but almost 10 per 1,000 for aircrew. One report detailed how medical officers had 'earnestly endeavoured' to convince men that 'sexual intercourse is not necessary', and the sure way of avoiding VD was to avoid the risk of contracting it. 'Such efforts and dissuasion would appear to have had no positive effects,' the report concluded, rather predictably.[36]

Air stations did their best to promote 'healthy attractions', such as concerts, sports and plays, with the aim of keeping personnel inside the stations during evenings and away from sources of infection in nearby towns and cities, where casual sex and prostitution provided welcome relief from the grim reality of flying. But RAF bosses realised that putting areas out of bounds would only cause 'turmoil and repercussions' resulting in a 'bigger set back to the war effort than the disease itself'. They set about analysing why the rate was so much higher amongst airmen. Most of their conclusions were obvious – the influence of alcohol, the strain of their service and ephemeral life expectancy, more money to spend, boredom, the exuberance of youth and the inexperience of life – but they also included the somewhat harder to prove ' "hero worship" engendered upon them by the character of their duties'. In other words, damn those dastardly infected women who couldn't help but jump on our brave lads. But the majority of airmen knew the perils involved in visiting prostitutes, and few actually risked it. Soon after he'd arrived in Britain, Max Bryant had told his brother John in a letter: 'I have never been accosted by a prostitute, male or female; probably I should be exceedingly embarrassed if ever the occasion arose. I have been very lucky in that all the girls with whom I have made friends have been such good types.'

The fact that the rate of STDs was much lower amongst WAAFs suggests airmen and women tended to look outside their bases for casual sex, in the bars surrounding Pathfinder country. In fact, sex between airmen and WAAFs was less common than between personnel and civilians, although it certainly happened, despite the rather misogynistic views of some airmen towards their female colleagues. One Pathfinder remembered how, 'A few of the ladies were pretty but most were just acceptably plain. All were out for a good happy time with the chaps, whose days in most cases were numbered. Some did, some didn't, and many just teased.'[37] If the views of some men are taken at face value, it's a wonder there were any liaisons at all. One rear gunner recalled that the chief of the WAAFs at one Pathfinder air station was 'shaped rather like a large trout and had a moustache bigger than me'.[38]

The secret, of course, for those willing to take risks, was not to get caught in flagrante delicto on the base. One sergeant at Downham Market, a Pathfinder airbase in Norfolk, was court-martialled after being found guilty of 'improperly introducing an airwoman into his sleeping quarters' and 'occupying the bed therein with the said airwoman'. He was demoted by a rank. It's not known what happened to the airwoman.[39]

When Ian Bazalgette was given the job of 'showing a rather attractive WAAF officer' over one of his squadron's aircraft, they ended up in the pilot seat of a Lancaster, and embarked on 'a course of six easy lessons in love making. It was so hot and in such a strange place we both kept roaring with laughter and couldn't take it seriously!' he wrote afterwards. Bazalgette must have known that such clinches between a WAAF and an airman on an RAF station, let alone in the cockpit of a bomber, were highly forbidden. But it seems the urge had been too much.[40]

Nevertheless, many WAAFs entered into relationships with aircrew members and were broken-hearted when they failed to return from operations. Some women were unfortunate enough to date successive airmen who were killed on operations. Rumours would spread that any aircrew who associated with her would be 'for the chop' and the woman would be labelled a 'chop girl'. WAAFs were given lectures on morality by visiting staff, and although sex wasn't encouraged, in one official RAF report exploring the high rate of depression amongst some WAAFs, the writer concluded it was due to the 'high stress of the job' and 'frustration', claiming: 'The only solution here seems to be to get the war over and allow these young women to lead a normal sex life again as soon as possible.'[41]

For most of the WAAFs stationed on Pathfinder bases, sex outside marriage was unthinkable. 'I worked with lots of chaps all the time but they treated me like a sister. We would play badminton or go down to the village pub. But sex business – no, not in those days,' remembered Gwen Thomas, who had been posted to the Pathfinders in June 1943 and worked as a teleprinter operator in the signals section in both Upwood and at the Pathfinder HQ in Huntingdon.[42]

Thomas had volunteered for the WAAF in September 1942 when she was 18 years old. She didn't want to go into the army but 'liked the uniform' of the WAAF, a view reflected by many young women who found the RAF blue was more flattering than the army khaki. Thomas, the second of four sisters, was born in North Wales and enjoyed a happy upbringing. Her father, an engineer, travelled a lot, and she spent most of her time with her mother, for whom she had a 'deep, deep love'. But in 1936, Thomas's mother contracted TB, and had to be isolated in hospital. Thomas was desperate to see her, but wasn't able to say goodbye: 'in those days you were not allowed to visit under the age of 12 and Mummy died five days before my proposed visit.'

With her father unable to cope, Thomas moved to St Albans to live with her aunt and uncle, and shared half their home with a doctor and his family. Thomas left school and joined secretarial college, but with war raging was eager to do more, so decided to join the WAAF. 'I wasn't streetwise at all,' she remembers, but her bright and enquiring personality would ensure that less than a year after joining up, she was at the very heart of the Pathfinders.

One night, Thomas was about to fall asleep in her room on the airbase at Upwood when she was aware of a man standing over her bed, clearly hoping for a good time. Thomas immediately jumped up and ran at him, and promptly chased him all the way out of the building, only stopping when he'd escaped by running across the main runway into the darkness. She never found out who it was, but he never tried again. 'I think if you were looking to have a sexy time you could find it, but I was brought up that you don't do that sort of thing.'

Thomas was friends with an ambulance driver who had a fling with an airman and fell pregnant. 'Her parents were heartbroken. I should think that marriage lasted a year. But in those days the honourable thing was to marry,' said Thomas. For WAAFs who did fall pregnant, an immediate discharge from the service usually beckoned, while for the airmen responsible, a posting to another part of the RAF. In 1943, 2,234 WAAF personnel across Bomber Command were discharged from the service on grounds of pregnancy, of whom 1,589 were married and 646 were single.[43] Many, barely out of their teens, found themselves alone in wartime with the prospect of trying to raise a child they had never planned.

However, the following year, the medical staff within 8 Group – led by Doc Macgown – proposed a remarkable scheme to provide accommodation, general medical care and 'mothercraft' for unmarried pregnant airwomen who couldn't be looked after – or had been shunned – by their families. While it was directly contrary to Air Ministry policy, an RAF official acknowledged that 'from the humanitarian point of view the scheme was most admirable.'[44] It also underlined Macgown's fearless approach in protecting both the young men and women of the Pathfinders under his care. He needed them to know he had faith in their well-being, even if, privately, he was as weary of the war as anyone. Macgown eventually flew more than 50 operations over enemy territory as a pilot or a navigator. After one mission to Italy, he wrote to his wife: 'The Alps were perfectly beautiful in the moonlight, with Mont Blanc towering over everything like a great white sentinel. It makes one feel how puny are the petty efforts and quarrels of man compared with the great scheme of affairs which guides his destiny . . .'[45]

Gwen Thomas may not have been the type to jump into bed with any man, but she couldn't help falling in love. In the late summer of 1943, at one of the Pathfinder Group dances, she met Bruce Smeaton, a handsome 23-year-old pilot from Warrington whose crew had recently joined 83 Squadron. 'It really was love at first sight,' remembers Thomas. Smeaton's crew was plunged straight into the Battle of the Ruhr and life for both him and Thomas was hectic. But with Smeaton based at Wyton and Thomas working just three miles away at the Pathfinder HQ in Huntingdon, when they weren't on duty – normally if flying operations had been cancelled because of the weather – the two would meet and enjoy long suppers at the local Bridge Hotel and countryside walks with Susan, his cocker spaniel.

Like many airmen with girlfriends or sweethearts, when he wasn't flying Smeaton would give his Wings to Thomas. 'You used to wear the Wings of your boyfriend on your scarf. One night, after what must have been a pretty tough operation, we met up, and Bruce said to me, "Here are your Wings, darling. I don't want to go on an op like that again." He didn't want to talk about it and he didn't dwell on it because the next night they might be going again. They wanted to switch off if they could.'

If she couldn't see him in person, Thomas rang Smeaton at noon every day to steal a quick chat and tell him she loved him, before that evening's operational briefing started and Wyton was locked down from the outside world. Like all WAAFs working at Castle Hill House in Huntingdon, Thomas was billeted in a Nissen hut in the Georgian building's grounds. One night, knowing she was on duty late and might oversleep, she asked a WAAF colleague to give her a shake the following morning to ensure she could make her telephone call to Wyton in time, in case Smeaton was on operations that night and the base was locked down.

'I was supposed to ring him at 12. I'd been on night duty and I said to a girl in the hut, "Please wake me at 11.30." But she forgot and I didn't ring him. I was praying all day they would not fly,' said Thomas. That night, Smeaton took off for Berlin, and Thomas, who had finished her shift at 11pm, went to bed thinking of her boyfriend somewhere over Germany, praying he'd return safely. The following morning, after dressing, she walked into the signals' office. 'I knew by the faces of people that he hadn't come back. I walked next door and it said "failed to return" on the board.'

Everyone hoped Smeaton had been taken prisoner. 'It is a great tragedy that such a good young life has had to go but we shall never give up hope and look forward to seeing that smiling face again. Any tiniest piece of news of him which you may have or get would be most welcome to us,' wrote his aunt to Thomas. But three months after he had gone missing, they received news that Smeaton and his crew had all perished. Thomas was devastated – she had only known her beloved Bruce for nine weeks, but loved him with all her heart – and yet, like many other WAAFs who lost loved ones, she put on a brave face. 'I wondered if they realised I felt let down by someone who hadn't woken me so I could say goodbye to him . . . but you had to manage your sadness and carry on.'

CHAPTER FIFTEEN

Firestorm

MORALE WAS RUNNING HIGH in the Pathfinders at the end of July 1943. While their losses in the Battle of the Ruhr had at times been heavy, they had helped Bomber Command strike some crushing blows, thanks to new technology and skilled crews. But it was time to move on.

At 9am on Thursday, 22 July, in the secret reinforced concrete operations room deep under the leafy beech trees surrounding Bomber Command's High Wycombe headquarters, Bert Harris sat down at the head of the table to discuss the operation for that night. In reality, there was only one target on his mind – Germany's second biggest city: Hamburg.

Hamburg had a population of 1.8 million and was one of Germany's most important ports. Located at the mouth of the Elbe River on Germany's north coast, it was a major shipbuilding city, responsible for constructing around a third of Germany's U-boats, as well as being home to important aircraft and engineering factories and oil refineries.

The city had already been attacked over 130 times by Bomber Command since the beginning of the war, with little impact. Yet Harris now had fire in his belly following the Ruhr campaign, and given the navigational ability of the Pathfinders now at his disposal, *not* to launch a spectacular raid would have been more difficult to explain to his bosses. Hamburg was simply too important a target to ignore.

After being asked for a plan by his commanders for the obliter-
ation of the city eight weeks before, Harris set out the proposal.
Rather than a single raid, his force would launch a series of four
operations over ten nights. He envisaged at least 10,000 tons of
bombs would be required for what he called 'the Battle of Hamburg'.
His overall aim was stark: 'To destroy Hamburg'. Doing so would
achieve 'immeasurable' results in reducing the capabilities of the
German war machine.[1] The raids were given an appropriately
unpleasant codename – Gomorrah.

But it wouldn't be easy. Hamburg had a fearsome reputation
amongst the British crews. It was protected by six night-fighter bases,
over 50 heavy flak batteries and two dozen searchlight batteries,
placed in a circle 20 miles from the city which it took a bomber 15
minutes to fly through. Now more than ever it was crucial that the
Pathfinders accurately marked the route to the city, dropped their
indicators bang on the target and laid a clear path home again, so the
main force could get in and out as quickly and closely as possible.

After a tense two days, when Harris had to postpone the operation
because of bad weather over the target, at 9.45pm on the warm evening of 24 July, almost 800 planes, containing 5,500 young airmen,
began to take off from their bases in eastern England, headed for Germany. En route, the Pathfinders dropped yellow target indicators to
guide the main force. The plan was for the vast force behind them to
attack from the north-west of Hamburg in six waves over a 50-minute
period. The aiming point would be marked by Pathfinders using their
H2S radar – which was ideal, as Hamburg's coastal location gave a
sharp radar image. The Pathfinders would continue to mark the target
throughout the duration of the raid. Despite Hamburg's vast U-boat
yards, the area chosen by Harris for this initial raid was mainly resi-
dential. The intention was brutal. This was about shaking the morale
of the German civilians like never before.

Despite the formidable defences, little did the Germans realise that
Bomber Command was armed with a childishly simple but devastat-
ingly effective new secret weapon, known as Window. Strips of black
paper, measuring ten inches by two inches with aluminium foil stuck
on one side, and held in bundles of 2,200, were manhandled out of
windows or flare chutes by crew. They were released in large batches

every minute as they approached the target, millions of strips in total. It wasn't always a smooth procedure. One airman threw his helmet down the chute by mistake, while another crew was suddenly swamped with hundreds of silver slivers flying around the fuselage when some loose bundles blew back in. But as the millions of little strips fell through the night sky at 400 feet a minute, they blossomed out into a fluttering cloud, swamping the German radar with false echoes.

This crude but highly effective measure was, on the surface, ingenious – and it had an immediate impact. Of around 750 aircraft to reach Hamburg, only 12 were shot down. Pathfinder crews reported radar-operated searchlights groping around the sky, their clueless fingers of light aimlessly looking for targets. John Christie, a 33-year-old Norwegian Halifax pilot flying his first operation with his crew for 35 Squadron, wrote in his diary how 'as we approached the target the flak barrage was furious but all the searchlights were feeling hopelessly around the sky without apparently any sort of system.' Christie added: 'A funny story was told after this raid about the impression it made on the German defences. A radio message was picked up in this country from some German HQ to another. It asked for advice about what to do as about 7,000 enemy aircraft were approaching . . . it must have caused real panic.'[2]

The night fighters were waiting, but for the German aircrews being directed to the bombers, there was panic and confusion. One was heard to remark: 'It is impossible. Too many hostiles.' Another airman – a gunner who sat behind his pilot, turned on his onboard radar to find 'Targets, nothing but targets. I can't understand it. 1.5km dead ahead, the height is correct, then it was gone again – quite suddenly. Another one! And gone again. It went like that ten times. Whatever the course, the targets are always coming towards us. It's maddening. Has the driver no eyes in his head? Or is the equipment unserviceable. I give up. We land.'[3]

The British bombers made the best of their new-found dominance. The weather was fine and the night sky was clear. At 12.57am, three hours after they'd taken off, the pilot of a Pathfinder Lancaster from 83 Squadron told his men over the intercom, 'It's about time someone started this party', and released two yellow target indicators and the plane's bombs over Hamburg.[4] In the streets below, German civilians watched as the first markers dropped by the Pathfinders began to fall. As she ran out of her house with her husband, one woman recalled that they 'could already see the Christmas Trees nearly overhead; they were whitish yellow. They lit up the street so brightly we could have read a book. We knew what these meant and we were frightened.'[5]

Over the following minutes, the first wave of Pathfinder planes dropped jewel-like red and yellow flares through the sky. They weren't all accurate – and some bombers were led astray by German decoy markers – but that didn't seem to matter. Planes backing-up in the following wave dumped 200 more green markers to guide the main-force bombers following in a stream 200 miles long. The mix of bombs and the order in which they would be dropped had been carefully planned by the Bomber Command brains. Research had indicated the buildings would burn well. The main-force heavies dropped 4,000lb bombs to blast open doors and windows, and thousands of 4lb incendiaries and 30lb phosphorus and benzol gel bombs, which ignited the wooden roof beams, joists and floors inside. Some of these were delayed action, containing explosives designed to hamper firefighters. With an average of 17,000 incendiaries falling per square kilometre, Hamburg was soon flaming, with a plume of black smoke towering 18,000 feet into the sky. At 1.55am, the last RAF bomber dropped its load and turned for home.

The Pathfinder marking had been mixed – and less than half the main force bombed within three miles of the aiming point. But a creep-back of bombing six miles long had smashed the central and north-western districts of Hamburg, killing around 1,200 civilians. The Pathfinders, meanwhile, lost no aircraft and the main force just 12 – over one of the most heavily defended targets in Germany. The impact of Window had been nothing short of astonishing – one estimate suggested it had saved at least 78 British bombers, and hundreds of airmen's lives, from being lost.[6]

Three nights later, on 27 July, after the US Eighth Airforce had bombed Hamburg with their Flying Fortresses during the two hot, intervening days, Bomber Command returned with a force of over 700 bombers. The city was still ablaze and smoking from the previous raids as the first markers cascaded from the leading Pathfinders and the bombs started falling once again. This time Bennett's men had done a good job dropping their markers in a concentrated group, and within a few minutes three large fires developed. In the warm July night, with low humidity and little rainfall for weeks, the fires spread. They quickly became greedy for more oxygen to keep them alive, sucking in air from the surrounding streets, creating a massive firestorm covering an area of 10 square kilometres. Airmen tasted and smelt the smoke through their oxygen masks 18,000 feet above. Crews map-read from the light of the fires. One Canadian pilot later said: 'Hamburg was so bright with fires, it looked like a prairie sunset.'[7]

For the German civilians on the ground, the experience was almost unimaginably horrific. People rushed to basements or air-raid shelters, while thousands more cowered in their homes. The emergency services were overwhelmed. A hurricane of hot air blew open doors and windows, uprooted trees and snatched people running for their lives along the streets, turning them into human torches. Some were vaporised in an instant. Others were left without a mark, but suffocated or were poisoned by carbon monoxide as they hid in shelters. The most able-bodied had the best chance of surviving. The elderly and the young, the least. A survivor recalled later:

> Women and children were so charred as to be unrecognizable; those that had died through lack of oxygen were half charred and recognizable. Their brains tumbled from their burst temples and their insides from the soft parts under the ribs. How terribly must these people have died. The smallest children lay like fried eels on the pavement. Even in death, they showed signs of how they must have suffered – their hands and arms stretched out as if to protect themselves from that pitiless heat.[8]

An estimated 40,000 Germans were killed in the firestorm. Four miles above, the British crews weren't immune from thoughts of the havoc the vast inferno must be causing. As one crew dropped its bombs and swung for home, a flight engineer looked down at the mass of flames: 'I said over the intercom, "Those poor bastards down there." I couldn't help myself. It was a terrible, terrible sight. I've never seen anything like it on any other target,' he recalled.[9] Others were less sympathetic, and while most RAF airmen had no personal issue with the ordinary German, they despised Hitler and what the Nazi regime stood for. One Pathfinder pilot said: 'I was full of satisfaction. The more we hammered Hamburg, the better we were pleased at that time.'[10]

But the Pathfinders and main-force crews were not having the same easy time they'd enjoyed three nights earlier. The German night fighters had adapted their tactics, and rather than just patrolling fighter boxes, were instead vectored onto the bombers by controllers on the ground via a running radio commentary on the course and height of the bomber stream. These less constrained *Wilde Sau* (Wild Boar) squadrons became the basis of the Luftwaffe's immediate counter-attack. Soon, a large number of combats were taking place around the target area and crews reported enemy aircraft 'playing' in the search-lights. They were given the nickname 'Cats' Eyes', because the pilots were using the light of the fires, searchlights and flares to spot and attack the lumbering bombers. Other German fighters were attracted by the yellow target indicators being dropped by the Pathfinders. One heavy bomber was attacked before dropping its markers and blew up in a brilliant yellow flash. Another Pathfinder pilot flying a Lancaster with 156 Squadron told his crew to bail out as he wrestled with the controls. Seconds later, the whole plane exploded, and the pilot found himself tumbling through the air. He managed to open his parachute just before hitting the ground.

By the end of the night, two Pathfinder and 16 main-force planes had been lost, but 98 per cent returned safely to their airfields. And while only half the bombs dropped actually landed on their target, Harris was a happy man.

A third raid followed on 29 July, with 777 bombers despatched. Wild Boar fighters once again attacked the incoming bombers, shooting down at least 20 aircraft. After the previous raids – including two from the USAAF [United States Army Air Force] – Hamburg was still burning, acting as a beacon for the incoming bomber stream. One Pathfinder pilot, an American flying with the RAF, reassured his navigator he'd not need to use the H2S in the final run in. 'You can leave that box o' tricks of yours, Dixie. I can see the son-of-a-bitchin' target; it's still lit up from the last trip.'[11] Previously undamaged areas of the city around the docks were hit with 2,318 tons of bombs, causing even greater damage than the firestorm. Around 800 Germans were killed.

In the early hours of the following morning, the bombers returned to England. In the pitch-black skies, Ernie Holmes was piloting a Halifax bomber with 76 Squadron in the main force, and was contemplating bacon and eggs and his warm bed back at base when the cockpit was suddenly flooded with the intense white light of a searchlight. 'I had to get out of it fast, and the only way I could do that was by diving directly down the shaft of light,' recalled Holmes. 'I presume the searchlight operators thought I was dive-bombing them, and eventually the light went out. But my aircraft was reaching 400 knots, twice the speed at which we normally flew, so I had to pull hard on the stick to level out at 6,000 feet and get safely away.'[12] Holmes's quick thinking ensured his crew lived to fight again, following their third raid on Hamburg in five days. With such a cool head in the pilot's seat, it was little wonder that in two months' time they would find themselves in the Pathfinder Force

Thirty aircraft had been shot down that night. Crews were weary and tired. After Holmes had landed back at his base in England, he scribbled in his logbook: 'Ops Hamburg. Clear Sky. Bags of s/lights. Good Prang.'

But Harris needed to deliver the *coup de grâce*. John Christie and other Pathfinders from 35 squadron gathered in the briefing room at Graveley on the afternoon of Monday, 2 August and watched as the commanders arrived and pulled back the black cloth covering the target board. 'We were surprised to see Hamburg on the map again,' wrote Christie, 'as all reports told that the town had literally been wiped off the map.' Nevertheless, later that evening 700 bombers took off for the city. The meteorology boys had warned of a nasty front of thunderstorms heading towards northern Germany, which Harris hoped his force could beat. Lightning was already flickering in the black skies over eastern England as the crews took off.

Sure enough, the weather deteriorated as the armada of bombers flew east, with huge anvils of thunderclouds towering to 25,000 feet.

Nearing Hamburg, the Pathfinders leading the raid were faced with flying through the storm or dropping to below the base of the cloud at 10,000 feet and risking the flak. Most, including John

Christie, took on the storm, battling vicious updrafts, heavy icing of the wings and 'terrific flashes which totally blinded me for many seconds afterwards'. At first, they assumed the lightning was a new German anti-aircraft weapon. 'The whole aircraft seemed to be completely electrified,' wrote Christie. 'There were huge luminous rings around the propellers, blue flames out of wing-tips, gun muzzles and also everywhere else on the aircraft where the surface was pointed . . . electrical flowers were dancing on the windows, until they got iced up, when the flowers disappeared.' Christie's wireless operator looked on in horror as sparks shot across his radio equipment, so they dropped to 10,000 feet and released the bombs 'on something we thought was the target', before turning for home.[13]

It was chaos above Hamburg, as the fierce storm combined with flak and combats between night fighters and bombers. One bomber plummeted to the earth after being struck by lightning. Another was unintentionally rammed by a German night fighter – everyone fell to their deaths. In all, thirty heavy bombers failed to return to England, and some of the airmen were bitter they had been asked to fly in such bad conditions, when Hamburg was already in such a bad state. Christie reckoned the last operation was 'one of the greatest flops in the history of Bomber Command. Well over 200 hundred lives were wasted, probably without achieving anything at all.' When they landed, the crews saw an order of the day from Harris suggesting the war might be over in a couple of months if they carried on. 'Even experts make mistakes,' Christie scribbled bitterly in his diary. 'Everybody in the squadron had had similar and worse experiences than ours and hardly anybody seemed to have done very much better than us.'

The Battle of Hamburg was over. The combined raids had killed an estimated 45,400 German civilians – 82 for every dead Allied airman – and had shaken their morale to the core. The dead included 7,000 children. Two thirds as many people had been killed by bombing in a single week as the Luftwaffe had killed during its attacks on British towns and cities throughout the war. Meanwhile, a total of 552 Allied airmen lost their lives, including 79 Pathfinders.

After their confusion at the hands of Window, in a portent of things to come, the German air defences had put their experimental 'Wild

Boar' tactics to the test, shooting down 59 British bombers. The RAF claimed twelve German night fighters destroyed, and eight German night fighter airmen had been killed. The Pathfinders had lost 13 aircraft – a loss rate of 3 per cent, the second heaviest of the six bomber groups and testament to the conditions they'd faced leading the force. And although in not one of the four nights was there any really concentrated bombing in the intended target area, the initial marking and backing up by the Pathfinders ensured the entire bombing fleet still dropped more than 8,400 tons of bombs in the Hamburg area. Decent route marking by Bennett's men also ensured the bomber stream had swamped the German fighter boxes and a greater concentration of bombers reached the target. It had been a monumental effort by the young airmen.

For Don Bennett, the operation was his proudest moment. 'We could have taken Hamburg with a boy scout patrol at that time, they were so shaken,' he said later.[14] The Pathfinders' group record book for August 1943 pulled no punches. 'The Huns outcry against these raids has been thoroughly hysterical and panic-stricken and there are signs that this panic has already spread to Berlin,' it said. 'Soon it will be spreading throughout all Germany and will go on spreading until our enemy's lowering morale cracks for good.'[15]

There was, in the immediate aftermath at least, some truth in this. After the firestorm, an estimated 1.2 million Hamburg residents poured from the city for the relative safety of the countryside. In time, they spread all over Germany, taking with them shocking first-hand accounts of the bombing. A secret German intelligence report said the raid on Hamburg was 'generally regarded as a catastrophe, far exceeding previous attacks in western Germany in its harshness and extent', which had 'strengthened the feeling of heading towards an annihilation, which only a section of the population will be able to avoid'.[16]

Following eyewitness accounts from his men over the target, Bennett was so convinced at the devastation wrought, he picked up the phone to Bomber Command HQ, suggesting they offer peace to Hitler or land paratroopers in key points in northern Germany. But his suggestion fell on deaf ears at High Wycombe. In fact, while the Hamburgers had been shaken, their morale had not cracked. U-boat building returned to 80 per cent capacity within five months.

Nevertheless, the British estimated up to 27 German submarines were not built because of the damage exacted during the Battle of Hamburg. Submarines which could have gone on to inflict crippling losses on Allied shipping in the Atlantic. While the human cost was dreadful, the raid had military value, and appeared to be a vindication of Harris's area bombing, the overall strategic bombing campaign and of course a vindication of the whole Pathfinder project.

But while the bombing of Hamburg had been a success, its methods were unsuited for those operations where the target was smaller. For that, a new type of precision bombing would be required, using revolutionary techniques pioneered by Bennett and the Pathfinders.

PART FOUR

The Rapier and the Sledgehammer

JUNE 1943 – FEBRUARY 1944

CHAPTER SIXTEEN

The Boffin Bashers

T EN AM, TUESDAY, 29 June 1943, Whitehall. In their secret subterranean complex under the streets of Westminster, Winston Churchill and his War Cabinet gathered to hear the latest intelligence about the Nazis' secret weapons development projects. The evidence was stark. Duncan Sandys, the chairman of the Scientific Advisory Committee, warned the Prime Minister that information gathered by his team appeared to show that the Germans had developed a new rocket weapon.

Although the exact details were still sketchy, there was intelligence that a German research establishment, hugging the coast near the Baltic town of Peenemünde, was building a state-of-the-art rocket called the V-2 – 'V' standing for 'Vengeance' – which was almost 50 feet tall on its launchpad and weighed 13 tons when packed with fuel and explosives. It took only 30 seconds to reach the speed of sound. Hitler hoped that by launching his rockets he would change the course of the war, killing thousands of civilians in Britain and threatening the Allied prospects of invading Europe.

After receiving this fateful news, Churchill turned to Frederick Lindemann, his trusted scientific adviser. Lindemann wasn't convinced by the intelligence, reasoning it was unlikely the Germans had manufactured propellant powerful enough to create a ballistic missile that deadly, and besides, how did they know it wasn't just a bluff and a cover for the development of an even more advanced weapon?

Considering what he had heard, Churchill then asked for the opinion of Dr R.V. Jones sitting opposite, who – the PM reminded his Cabinet – had helped Britain defeat the beams of the German pathfinder bombers two years before. 'Now I want the truth!' Churchill demanded from Jones, who told him in the frankest terms he dared that while the likelihood of an imminent rocket attack was small, the evidence for its existence was stronger than it had been for the German beams which he had presented to him three years before. 'Stop!' Churchill said. Then, turning to Lindemann, he asked: 'Hear that. That's a weighty point against you! Remember, it was you who introduced him to me!' All the professor could muster was a 'rueful half smile', Jones said later.[1]

The evidence – comprising RAF reconnaissance pictures, anonymous tip-offs, intelligence from secret agents, prisoner-of-war interrogations and labourer informers – provided an overwhelming argument to act now. Peenemünde would need to be destroyed. But it wouldn't be easy. They faced formidable fighter and flak defences. Precision bombing with a huge force of aircraft would be required to deliver a knockout blow. Nothing like this had ever been attempted before. It was time for Bomber Command to step in.

The whole operation would be led and controlled by the Pathfinders.

On Monday, 16 August 1943, John Searby, the dashing young commanding officer of 83 Squadron, was sitting down to breakfast in the officers' mess at RAF Wyton when he was handed a memo requesting he immediately report to the Pathfinders' headquarters in Huntingdon. An hour later, Searby, together with his bomb aimer and navigator, walked up the narrow stairs to the second floor at Castle Hill House and through a doorway guarded by military police. The briefing room was dominated by a table with a large model of a factory compound built on a coastline. The three men saluted Don Bennett, who was already in the room examining the model. Without giving any information on the facility's name or exact purpose, Bennett invited them to pore over the model. The details, he said, were top secret and would need to be committed to memory. Their objective was to work out how best the Pathfinders could mark three separate targets within the complex and ensure they could be successfully destroyed by the main-force bombers. The codename for the operation was Hydra.[2]

That afternoon, Searby hired a boat and rowed down the Great Ouse River in the warm August sunshine, pondering the top secret and vitally important mission he had been invited to lead. The 30-year-old had been handpicked by Bennett because he was the ideal man for the job. A Pathfinder veteran of 50 missions over Germany, Searby was calm and collected under pressure and well liked by his squadron, which was on a golden run of 175 sorties without a loss – a damned good record given the intense missions in the summer of 1943. A few days before, he had led a raid over Turin and been briefed to circle over the city to orchestrate the bombing – little realising that it was something of a warm-up. Now, as he watched his fellow airmen in whites playing a game of cricket on the grass in front of the officers' mess, Searby mused again on the strange world they were in, and how the 'likelihood of a sudden exit' – in other words, death – lay just around the corner. 'You could knock up fifty runs before teatime and be wriggling your way through flak and searchlights after supper! Life was full of surprises and each operation was different,' he later wrote.[3] But what surprises would this new highly secret mission hold?

The following morning, Searby was called to Bomber Command's headquarters. Bennett revealed the target's name was Peenemünde, but only that it was the location of an 'experimental radar station'. None of the men taking part would know the true nature of what they had attacked until later in the war. For the first time on such a large scale, the main force would be controlled by Searby acting as 'master of ceremonies', circling overhead to monitor the whole operation and provide instructions to the other crews over the radio.

The use of a master bomber had been tried two months before by bombers from 5 Group against the former Zeppelin works at Friedrichshafen, and on the famous Dam Buster raid the previous May, when Guy Gibson acted as a master bomber directing his force of 617 Squadron Lancasters to help destroy two vital dams in the Ruhr. However, the attack on Peenemünde would involve 30 times the number of aircraft across six bomber groups. Success or failure depended on the human element, and encouragement and firm orders from Searby could tip the scales. It was an intensely dangerous role.

The planning was intricate and pioneering, involving the use of a new, largely untested technique. The most experienced Pathfinder crews would act as 'shifters', moving the target marking from one part of the vast compound to the next at a pre-specified time as the raid developed, so the aiming points moved over three main areas over the course of 40 minutes. It was crucial that the scientists' and workers' living quarters, the rocket factory and finally the experimental works of the compound were all plastered in turn and at the right time with target indicators, so the main-force bombers could then do their stuff with high-explosive bombs. If the crews were unsure about the accuracy of these markers, they would be guided by the instructions of Searby or – if he was shot down – the deputy master bomber circling in another plane.

In addition to their crack navigating and H2S sets, the Pathfinders would be aided by something else. Unusually, Harris had decided to carry out the operation during a full moon, reckoning – even with their navigating skills and technology – the crews would need all the help they could get. The weather was due to be clear, so the Pathfinders would use the 'Newhaven' technique to mark the target. Harris also ordered widespread use of Window, hoping the little strips of foil might once again confuse the German defences as they had a few weeks before over Hamburg.

The Pathfinders had certainly improved Bomber Command's accuracy since their formation a year before, and Bennett sent an encouraging message to the 10 squadrons now under his control, saying the Pathfinders had done much in showcasing how effective bombing can be, adding that the 'quality of our bombing is in your hands. Keep at it and good luck to you all'.[4] But using a large force of bombers to hit a target 500 miles away with such a precision three-in-one-attack, at night, was an extraordinary proposition. And if they failed to destroy the target the first time they would have to return, regardless of casualties, until the job was done.

German fighter defence was expected to be intense, so an hour before the operation was due to start bombing Peenemünde at around 12.15am, a crack flight of Mosquito bombers crewed by the most experienced airmen from 139 Pathfinder Squadron would carry out a 'spoof raid' on Berlin to lure the German night fighters into thinking that was the main target for the night. This was a crucial part of the mission. If it failed, the force attacking Peenemünde would be decimated by the overwhelming firepower of German night fighters using the pale-blue moonlight to pick off the bombers.

The afternoon of the raid, the Pathfinder and main-force crews sat down for their briefing. At Wyton airfield, Searby briefed his squadrons on the operation. He would be master bomber, with two more crews from different Pathfinder squadrons acting as backups – 'if we were clobbered, then continuity was safeguarded,' said Searby. As he glanced to the back of the smoky room, he spotted Bennett standing next to Sandys – who had come up especially from London with a handful of Air Ministry senior figures to watch on – a clear sign of the importance of the operation. As the VIPs circulated with the crews afterwards, one walked up to Searby's flight engineer and asked, 'Do you think there's a better chance of you returning from Peenemünde than the Ruhr or Berlin?' For Searby, it was a stupid question. 'We'll just have to wait and see, won't we?' his crewmate calmly replied, smiling.[5]

A few miles away on Bourn airfield, Arthur Spencer, a Wiltshire-born 22-year-old navigator with 97 Pathfinder Squadron, was anxious. With the nights getting longer, Spencer and his crewmates knew it was only a matter of time before they were asked to strike at Berlin. Earlier in the day, the Order of Battle had been posted up on the notice board as it was on every day of operations. It listed which crews would be needed that night, plus the fuel and bomb loads. The target itself was only revealed in the briefing later in the day. But as an experienced team with 39 operations under their belts, Spencer's crew were pretty good at 'reading' the figures to guess where they might be heading. 'When we looked at the Order of Battle we were horrified. The petrol and bomb loads appeared to be just right for Berlin, and yet it was the night of a full moon. It would be a massacre of the aircraft of Bomber Command by the increasingly skilful Luftwaffe night-fighter crews,' thought Spencer.[6]

When the black cloth was removed in the briefing room later, however, they saw the red tape pinned across the map of Europe, stretched out across the North Sea and over Denmark, but stopping short of Berlin. 'Eventually the target was revealed as Peenemünde, a place none of us had heard of,' said Spencer. The true nature of the target was not revealed, but enough was shared by the various squadron commanders giving the briefings for men to know it was of huge technological and scientific importance to the Nazis. One wag piped up from the back of the briefing room, promising a prize for the first aircraft back with a pair of scientist's spectacles hanging from its undercarriage.

Spencer's crew learnt they would be in the first of three waves, identifying the aiming point and dropping target indicators over the housing estate belonging to the scientists and technicians. The next two waves would target the production works and finally the experimental works. The route took the bombers across Denmark and the Baltic Sea, making it look like they were hitting Berlin – which was over a hundred miles south of Peenemünde – only to peel off and instead attack the rocket works.

Following the briefing, the airmen endured the usual agonising empty hours of waiting, before wolfing down an operational meal of bacon and eggs, writing a 'last letter' home, and walking to the locker room to draw their parachutes and flying gear. Spencer had his own superstitious ritual, brushing his teeth before every mission 'because I thought that if I were shot down and taken prisoner it might be a long time before I could clean my teeth again'. He also wore his mother's silk scarf. 'I would have been very worried to set off on operations without it,' he said. Many airmen carried good-luck charms. One navigator always wore a part of his girlfriend's blue silk petticoat around his neck, until one night when he was wearing a yellow one. 'Why the change of colour?' he was asked. 'Well, we had a little bit of a tiff, and I've moved on,' he replied with a shrug and a smile.[7]

All afternoon, Bourn airfield was frantic with activity as ground crews prepared 18 Lancasters for take-off. Spencer and his crew took a bus to their Lancaster, codenamed J-Johnnie, enjoyed a few deep draws on a last fag, had a pee on the back wheel for luck and then clambered aboard.

It was a beautiful late-summer evening across much of England. One airman observed: 'There wasn't the usual babble and horseplay. I remember coming out onto the airfield, right into the rural surroundings and sunshine and I thought: "This can't be happening to us on such a lovely day." [8] The farmers busily haymaking in the surrounding fields stopped momentarily and gave an encouraging wave as the great planes taxied past. A little knot of watchers – WAAFs, airmen and ground crew not on duty – gathered at the end of the runway to see the bombers off.

Spencer's Lancaster throttled up its engines, waited for a green light from the controller in the black-and-white chequered caravan, and rumbled down the runway into the sky. It was 20.50. Over the next 45 minutes, 120 young airmen from 97 Squadron took off in 18 Lancasters. They were part of a 90-plane-strong Pathfinder force spearheading a total bombing taskforce of 596 aircraft.

Flying alone a few minutes ahead of the other bombers, Searby concentrated on keeping his Lancaster – W for William – straight and level as it barrelled across the moonlit North Sea at just 200 feet. Before long, Searby's bomb aimer – lying prone in the nose of the Lancaster – spotted the shadowy line of the Danish coast. 'Enemy coast ahead,' he called up over the radio. Searby gently eased back the control column and inched up the revs. The four powerful Merlin engines did their job and the bomber climbed to 4,000 feet. Searby looked out at the glowing red exhaust stubs on the side of the engines and reflected on how naked and vulnerable the lone bomber was. He then pushed the thought out of his mind and concentrated on the operation ahead.

As the vast bomber force made its way across Denmark and the Baltic Sea, German night-fighter controllers broadcast an urgent message warning of 'many hostiles' heading towards Germany. 'The head of the hostile formation reported to be close to Berlin, at heights from 19,500 to 22,000 feet.'[9] Dozens of Wild Boar fighters were ordered into the air and headed for the city. The plan was working.

Two hours before, Ulric Cross and his pilot Roy Crampton had climbed into their Mosquito bomber and taken off from Wyton. They were one of eight Mosquitos to take to the skies from the airfield in an eight-minute window.

Cross had already made a big impact since graduating as a pilot officer from RAF Cranwell and arriving at 139 Squadron earlier in the year. In the summer of 1943, the squadron was transferred to the Path-finders and, being based at Wyton along with 83 Squadron, was naturally under the close scrutiny of Don Bennett.

139 Squadron was also known as the 'Jamaica' squadron, given its name because its Blenheim bombers – used before it upgraded to Mosquitos – were paid for by a fundraising effort started by a Jamaican newspaper. This goodwill continued throughout the war, with the Caribbean island sending airmen cases of rum and other local delights. Ironically, given this association, Cross was the only West Indian member of 139 Squadron. However, like many Bomber Command and Pathfinder squadrons, it was a cosmopolitan mix of nationalities, with Polish, Indian, English, Welsh, Scottish, Scandinavian and Dutch aircrew.

Following his arrival in England and swift progress through to becoming an officer in one of Bomber Command's most revered squadrons, Cross had become something of a poster child for West Indians serving in Britain. In 1943, he was featured in a BBC propaganda film called *West Indies Calling*, showcasing the West Indian contribution to the war effort. Cross's gentle Trinidadian accent extolled the vast number of roles West Indians were playing in the forces. He also featured in the society pages of *Tatler* magazine.

When he arrived at Wyton, he immediately made an impact. 'He was very handsome. He was one of the people that we all knew,' recalled Gwen Thomas, who was working at Wyton as a teleprinter operator.[10] Cross's navigation skills were in hot demand. 'He was an excellent navigator. Very much a desired navigator. He never panicked,' said one pilot.[11] Cross garnered genuine affection and respect from his squadron mates, who nicknamed him the 'Black Hornet', yet his popularity also highlighted the importance of the navigator in the Pathfinders.[12]

And now he was navigating the Mosquito in the most important operation of his war so far. Not that he had much time to dwell on it. 'All your flight is busy busy busy. The pilot has more time to be afraid than you do,' said Cross later. 'We were depending for our safety on accurate navigation and speed. You can't be trained not to be afraid but trained to conquer fear. It comes from a belief that what you are doing is right and worthwhile.' Cross wasn't immune to the danger, however, admitting 'when the flak starts coming up at you and you are coned in a searchlight you feel fear. But your job is to get to the target on time and that is what you are preoccupied with.'[13]

Just before 11pm, the eight Mosquitos of 139 Squadron had barrelled across Denmark and the Baltic and were closing in on Berlin. Their route took them within 80 miles of Peenemünde, which triggered the air-raid sirens on the base. But that was part of the plan. Like the boy who cried wolf, raids to Berlin were common and the camp had become somewhat used to the sirens sounding before the all-clear was given a few minutes later. Tonight would be different – but that was all to come.

Like every Mosquito on the operation, Cross and Crampton's was carrying three 500lb bombs and a set of target indicators, plus bundles of Window. It wasn't a particularly large bomb load. But that wasn't the point. This was all about perception. As they approached Berlin, 89 flak batteries across the city opened up, firing a heavy barrage of steel to 18,000 feet, helped by hundreds of searchlights. And as if that wasn't enough to contend with, as many as 150 German night fighters had been ordered to the capital. The idea was to trap the British bombers between the gunfire below and the fighters above. But most of the Mosquitos were too fast and nimble, releasing their payloads over the city while dodging and weaving at speeds of 330mph, before turning to the west to begin their long flight home.

As they flew over Berlin after dropping their bombs, Cross scanned the skies for fighters. All was clear. Then, in an instant, the cabin was flooded with a blinding white light as though it was midsummer's day. It meant only one thing – they were being coned. Crampton threw the little bomber into a series of twists and turns in an attempt to lose the lights. But this wasn't some provincial town. The searchlights in Berlin were operated by skilled crews, and however much they tried to shake off the lights to reach the blessed luxury of darkness, they failed. Flak was bursting all around, yet still they flew on. Crampton's skill as a pilot was showing through. The plane weaved over Brandenburg, a few miles to the west of Berlin. Just a few more seconds and they would be out of the capital's defensive area. But quite suddenly the wooden airframe of the Mosquito jumped with a huge bang. The starboard Merlin engine was hit with shell fragments, piercing the pipes carrying the vital glycol coolant. 'He shot the propeller, didn't he?' shouted Cross. 'We gotta look out for fighters,' replied Crampton, who had managed to shake off the searchlights and pushed a button on the control panel, closing down the starboard engine to reduce the drag by 'feathering' the propeller.

A Mosquito could fly on one engine but not at 25,000 feet, where they'd be safest. 'We've got to come down to 7,000 feet,' said Crampton. 'I suggest we clip on our parachutes. We may have to leave the aircraft.'[14] The two men clipped on their parachutes as the Mosquito lost altitude. 'Give me a course to the nearest aerodrome in England,' said Crampton. Cross quickly set about calculating where they could potentially land. He gave his crewmate a course for Swanton Morley, an RAF base in Norfolk. Crampton levelled out the Mosquito at 7,000 feet. They had no guns and were flying at half the speed on one engine, all on their own. It was going to take all their skill and experience to get home alive.

As Cross and Crampton limped west, the other Mosquitos from 139 Squadron had also finished their bombing runs over Berlin. One had been shot down by a German fighter over the city, but the remaining six would make it safely back to Wyton. Whether they'd ever see Cross and Crampton again remained to be seen. However, it seemed the little operation by 139 Squadron had been a huge success. Long after the Mosquitos had gone, the searchlights continued to weave over the city and dozens of night fighters circled above, expecting the main force of the RAF bombers to arrive soon. They had given the main force now closing in on Peenemünde the best chance of success.

John Searby's Lancaster arrived first over Peenemünde, bathed in bright moonlight. He could clearly make out the three aiming points the Pathfinders would need to mark for the main-force bombers. The Germans had opened the taps of hundreds of smoke canisters, and the smoke was beginning to drift across the target, but there was little flak and most of the German fighters were still over Berlin. Now all Searby could do was to watch and wait.

The raid didn't start brilliantly. At 12.10am, the initial Pathfinder planes dropping red target indicators, called red spot fires – which ignited at 3,000 feet and burnt for 10 minutes after hitting the ground – struggled to identify their positions using the H2S radar and overshot

THE BOFFIN BASHERS 221

the target, dropping their markers two miles from the housing estate. By complete bad luck, these fell on a Polish forced labour camp. Bombers following up dropped their high explosives and tragically killed around 500 workers. However, more Pathfinders dropped their yellow target markers correctly and Searby quickly broadcast over the radio to tell the immediate crews coming in to 'ignore all but the yellows', which were soon backed up by a mass of drizzling greens.

Arthur Spencer's Lancaster from 97 Squadron was now making its run towards the target at 13,000 feet and dropped its seven target indicators and 4,500lb of bombs on the yellow and green markers fizzing below. They managed to avoid the searchlights and flak hose-piping up into the sky, but watched on as another plane was targeted. 'He was coned and blew up as we watched, horrified,' said Spencer.[15]

The target was soon a mass of bursting bombs, ground fires and billowing smoke. The earlier mistake had been rectified by Searby and Pathfinders backing up so that much of the Peenemünde housing estate was burning furiously. 'Christ almighty boys! Just look at the fires – just look at the fires!' exclaimed one pilot.[16] Another later said: 'It gave me a lot of pleasure to hit those bloody buildings.'[17] Others watched in awe as the sea bounced back off the shore due to the pressure waves from the high-explosive bombs. One rear gunner later joked he was sure he'd seen a German scientist flying past his turret.

At 12.31am – fifteen minutes after 'zero hour' when the main force had started dropping their bombs – the raid moved to its second phase. The Pathfinder shifter crews dropped fresh markers, ensuring the aiming point was moved to a brace of 300-foot-long factories where the V-2 rockets were made. Once again, some missed the target, not helped by a strong crosswind pushing drifting markers towards the sea. Searby issued corrective orders to the main force, and over the next 11 minutes 124 bombers pounded the area with 480 tons of high explosives. Although many missed, others hit the spot. 'From our vantage point, circling the target throughout the raid, we witnessed some of the most accurate marking and bombing we had ever seen,' said the navigator flying in the aircraft of the deputy master bomber.[18]

But where were the German fighters?

*

As dozens of German night fighters circled over Berlin waiting for the bombers that would never arrive, they spotted the Christmas trees, or *Weihnachtsbäume,* dropped by Pathfinder aircraft slowly descending in the bright moonlit sky over Peenemünde, 150 miles to the north. There had yet to be any official order over the radio, but with the penny beginning to drop that Berlin was safe, some crews made the instinctive choice to head towards what appeared to be the main action of the night.

A 20-minute flight away, the night fighters arrived over Peenemünde not a minute too soon, just as the third and final bombing wave of 180 Lancasters and Halifaxes was about to start targeting the experimental works. With much of Peenemünde now blazing, the black silhouettes of the low-level attacking bombers presented clear targets for incoming German fighters.

John Searby was circling in his Lancaster looking down at the 'mish-mash' of fire and smoke when his intercom crackled into life, 'Bomb aimer to Captain – look out for fighters. A Lanc has just blown up over the target.' Searby saw the bright flash almost at the same time. The real opposition had finally arrived and the situation was changing rapidly for the worse.[19]

Bomber after bomber was shot down in a frantic, violent few minutes. Planes from 5 Group – which had had been given permission by Harris to carry out their own experimental form of target marking in the final wave, by carefully timing a straight run in to the target using visual landmarks as guides – were particularly badly mauled, despite achieving some of the most accurate bombing of the entire raid.

One Canadian navigator in a Halifax recalled a Junkers Ju 88 – now being used as a night fighter despite its fast-bomber origins – bearing down on his aircraft before it opened fire. 'We went down into a dive, trying to avoid the fighter. Then the aircraft quivered, like in killing poultry you strike the brain with a knife and the feathers release – that is the way the aircraft felt,' he said. In the front of the fuselage 'a horrible smell of gunpowder enveloped the aircraft and the wireless operator lay beside me dying, with his entrails exposed.'[20]

For the first time, the Luftwaffe also used Messerschmitt Bf 110 night fighters armed with *Schräge Musik* upward-firing cannons, which fired almost vertically, allowing the aircraft to attack from

600–800 feet underneath British bombers, in their blind spots.[21] By aiming at the fuel tanks between the port and starboard engines, one volley of cannon fire quickly created a lethal fire in the bomber above. *Schräge Musik* became the Pathfinders' nemesis. One German ace later said: 'As I squeezed off a burst of fire I gently pushed the nose down so that my cone of fire walked through the wing and engines . . . the enemy aircraft would usually burst into flames right away . . . our opponents stood little chance . . . for us night fighters this type of attack was practically our life insurance.'[22]

By 1am the raid on Peenemünde was coming to an end. The vast stream of bombers making their way home in the moonlight continued to be plagued by German fighters. 'They were hopping in and out of the stream of bombers as if they were crossing a busy road,' said a mid-upper gunner. 'They sometimes looked as if they were going to get run over.'[23]

At the rear of the vast line of bombers was John Searby and his crew, who had made an astonishing seven passes over the target in an intense 50-minute window, dodging flak, enemy fighters and even bombs dropped by British planes attacking from above. While Searby hoped his luck would hold, his rear gunner suddenly came over the radio: 'Rear gunner to Captain – fighter attacking from astern and below!' Searby heaved the controls into a sharp turn and simultaneously heard the rattle of machine-gun fire from the rear turret. Red tracer fire from the German fighter whizzed past the cockpit window. Seconds later another fighter bore down from the starboard side, and Searby made a sharp turn towards the attacker, just as his mid-upper gunner shouted with excitement after seeing some of his machine-gun fire hit home.[24]

Thanks to his deft flying and eagle-eyed gunners, Searby skilfully shook off two enemy fighter attacks. He arrived safely back at Wyton in the early hours of the morning, leaving an 'impressive glow' at Peenemünde.

An hour later, six 139 Squadron bombers had also landed safely back at Wyton. That just left Mosquito DZ 465, crewed by Roy Crampton and Ulric Cross. Thanks to Cross's navigation, Crampton had managed to carefully nurse the one remaining Merlin engine so that their faithful plane made it safely across mainland Europe and the North Sea. It was now closing in on the airfield at Swanton Morley, but their drama was far from over. Radio silence needed to be maintained so as not to alert roaming fighters to the ailing plane, so Cross and Crampton had to land in the dark without a flare path or runway lights to guide them in. As they approached the airfield they spotted the faint outline of the grass airstrip in the moonlight. That would have to do. Crampton gently pushed the stick down and throttled back the single engine. The plane hit the grass runway with a hard jolt and bounced back up again. He pushed his feet hard on the rudder brake and held the control stick firm. But the aircraft had landed halfway down the runway, and they were rapidly running out of strip. 'It looks like this is it,' shouted Crampton. 'Yes, looks like it,' replied Cross, who braced himself for the impact. 'We thought we were going to die. We were both rather cool about it,' recalled Cross, later.[25] The plane burst through a hedge at the far end of the airfield, careered into a disused quarry in shower of branches and dust and came to a grinding halt with a bang. There was silence except for the ticking of the hot engine. Both men had banged their heads but appeared to have miraculously escaped serious injury. The time was 2.12am.

The following morning, the Pathfinder airbases were quiet. Most of the men had flopped into bed and were still fast asleep after landing safely from the 1,250-mile round trip a few hours before. At Bourn, Arthur Spencer woke early as he always did, even if he had been on an operation. He had a shower – 'because you always felt dirty after a night out in a bomber' – dressed and made his way over to the deserted mess for breakfast. On a normal morning, Spencer would then wait for the rest of his crew to wake up, write up the operation in his logbook, pen some letters home and perhaps practise his potting in the billiards room. But this morning was different. He only had one question on his mind. Would they need to return to Peenemünde that night? With 'the thought of that threat still hanging over us', he strolled over to the intelligence library to have a look at the aiming-point photographs snapped by the 83 Squadron bombers. Although not totally conclusive, they provided a decent barometer of the mission and indicated it had been hugely successful. They would only have a clearer idea later in the day when the photo-reconnaissance plane returned.[26]

But what absolutely astounded Spencer was the casualties. They'd seen no real defences over Peenemünde and just one bomber shot down. All eighteen planes of 83 Squadron had arrived home safely with barely a scratch. Yet Operation Hydra claimed 40 British bombers – 6.7 per cent of the force despatched – leaving, it would later emerge, 288 Bomber Command airmen dead. Twenty-seven bombers were shot down by night fighters over or on the way back from Peenemünde, as a huge air battle involving 46 separate combats had erupted over the space of 50 minutes.

The Pathfinders escaped relatively unscathed, losing just two aircraft – or 2.1 per cent of the planes sent. This is because most of their effort was at the start of the raid when the German fighters were still being spoofed by the Mosquitos of 139 Squadron over Berlin. When those German planes had arrived at Peenemünde it became a veritable turkey shoot. The bombers of 5 Group and 6 Group attacking in the closing stages of the operation lost 29 aircraft between them – a loss rate of 17.4 per cent. The night fighters hadn't escaped unscathed either, losing 12 aircraft.

Despite the casualties, Operation Hydra was deemed a victory. One airman who had taken part in the raid wrote to tell a friend: 'There was more shit unloaded there in an hour than flows down Barking Creek in a year.'[27]

Back at the Pathfinders' HQ, there was a feeling of excitement at the 'outstanding success' Bennett and his men had helped achieve. 'A very large force went Boffin Bashing at the experimental establishment at Peenemünde,' scribbled the Pathfinder officer writing up a summary of the mission. 'This vitally important target was well plastered with TIs [Target Indicators] and with the bombs of about five hundred aircraft, and the Hun scientists were for once blinded by the science of hitting a small target accurately at night.'[28]

The Pathfinder planes marking the targets had certainly played a vital role, but Searby himself was perhaps the kingpin in the whole operation by keeping the other bombers on track when the initial marking went astray. It would be the most important operation of his wartime career, for which he was awarded an immediate Distinguished

Service Order. There was kudos too for 5 Group. Their own form of 'time and distance' target marking had shown some promise, despite coming under heavy attack from German fighters. But the fact that 5 Group had been granted permission by Harris to carry out its own form of target marking independently from the Pathfinders, pointed to the beginnings of a hairline crack in the differing tactical opinions between some Bomber Command group commanders, which would become a yawning fissure by the following year.

Just how many German boffins had actually been 'bashed' and what impact the raid had on the development of the V-2 rocket bomb would only be discovered later. In cold facts, much of the Peenemünde compound was pounded with almost 2,000 tons of high explosives and incendiaries. Most of the senior scientists managed to escape with their lives by taking cover in shelters in the early minutes of the raid. And while the material damage was huge, vital workshops and design blueprints survived. But while it had not been completely knocked out as Churchill must have hoped, the damage was enough to delay the launch of Germany's V-2 assault on Britain – which started in early September 1944 – by at least two months. This meant around 740 fewer rockets hitting the country, potentially saving the lives of thousands of civilians.

Just as importantly – but harder to quantify – was the knock-on impact of the raid. In the days following, Hitler ordered some parts of the rocket production to be transferred from Peenemünde to huge underground caverns and tunnels 220 miles away in central Germany. Although forced labour would provide much of the manpower at the new factory itself, there is little doubt that moving production on this scale was a logistical nightmare for the Germans, using up valuable resources, and causing substantial disruption which only benefited the Allies.

Many Bomber Command airmen gave their lives for the successful raid, but casualties could have been so much worse had it not been for the tiny but vital contribution from the Pathfinder Mosquitos of 139 Squadron in drawing off the bulk of the night fighters over Berlin. The Luftwaffe later estimated that they might have shot down 200 bombers over Peenemünde had the diversionary raid to Berlin not been successful. Hitler considered it a military failure. The morning after the operation, in an office in the Prussian town of Goldap, General

Hans Jeschonnek – the 44-year-old chief of the Luftwaffe general staff – took out a pistol from his office desk and blew his brains out.

There was a happier outcome for Ulric Cross and Roy Crampton, who had been rescued from their disagreement with a disused quarry and, following an overnight stay at RAF Swanton, were given a flight back to Wyton the following morning. Circling the crash scene they released just how lucky they'd been. Cross hadn't had time to be scared when they'd landed, but looking down in the cold light of day, he saw bits of wood from the Mosquito hanging from trees and the Mosquito itself at the bottom of the quarry. 'Then I was terrified,' he said later.[29] Back at Wyton that evening, Cross was relaxing in his room as Crampton retired for a bath with a bottle of gin, a pack of cigarettes and a good book. When he failed to come out after an hour Cross knocked on the door and found him unconscious – he had delayed concussion and spent the next six weeks in hospital.

On Thursday, 19 August 1943, people across Britain opened up their newspapers to read of the daring airborne operation which had taken place 36 hours earlier. 'OUR BOMBS FERRET OUT A NAZI SECRET. FIGHTER SCREEN DEFIED, VITAL RESEARCH STATION SMASHED' read one headline in the *Birmingham Daily Gazette*. The story was one of daring do:

> Hundreds of Britain's great bombers – Lancasters, Halifaxes and Stirlings – constituting a giant taskforce, smashed their way 700 miles through a German fighter screen in the 'daylight' night on Tuesday to obliterate a vital 'secret' research station which the enemy had hidden in the woods on the Baltic shores . . . They carried with them well over 1,500 tons of bombs which were crashed down within the four-and-a-half miles by one mile target area – the research development establishment at Peenemünde, 60 miles north-west of Stettin . . . It was one of the most important single target attacks the RAF has ever carried out. The huge bomb load was dropped with the accuracy of a daylight precision raid.

But while the Peenemünde raid was a milestone in showcasing the Pathfinders' ability to deliver precision attacks only previously dreamt about, it exposed differences in not only the tactics of Bomber Command's group commanders, but also the methods which Harris used to deploy them. His decision to allow 5 Group to carry out their own marking during the raid irritated Bennett. In reality, the 5 Group bombers had done pretty well, but Bennett would need to have his wits about him. If Harris was having his head turned about marking by other commanders in key raids such as Peenemünde, what else might he be planning behind Bennett's back in future operations?

In the meantime, Bennett had more pressing matters to think about. Eight weeks after the Peenemünde raid, the Pathfinders led Bomber Command's planes on an altogether different operation to bomb a tiny city barely anyone outside Germany had even heard of. Yet, proportionally, the resulting firestorm would cause even greater damage than the hell of Hamburg, and create more headaches for Hitler.

Its name was Kassel.

CHAPTER SEVENTEEN

Oh Tannenbaum! Oh Tannenbaum!

S EVEN PM, FRIDAY, 22 October 1943. In the central German city of Kassel, nestled in a valley on the banks of the Fulda River about 100 miles east of Essen, many of the 225,000 residents were finishing their work and beginning to wend their way home through the chilly autumnal evening. At its centre, crowded either side of the river in the old town, lay a maze of timbered, steep-roofed houses on narrow, winding streets. The west and north-west of the city were dominated by pretty eighteenth-century squares, parks and public buildings, and two- or three-storey townhouses with fine gardens. Outside Germany, Kassel was probably best known for being home to the Brothers Grimm, who wrote most of their fairy tales there in the early 1800s.[1]

But, by October 1943, the city had also become one of the most important centres for armament production in Germany, helping Hitler realise his own Nazi fairy tale. It was dominated by Henschel & Son, a massive heavy engineering works sprawling over 4.5 million square feet – much of it in vast factories occupying the centre of the city – which built the much-feared Tiger tank and was responsible for the largest locomotive plant in Europe, churning out 50 new engines a month – a third of the country's output of steam engines. To the south-east lay the city's other main industry – aircraft production – where its Fieseler firm was developing single-seater fighter engines and the V-1 flying bomb, which Hitler hoped would soon be unleashed on the streets of Britain. Around 61,000 industrial workers lived in and around Kassel. Henschel & Son employed around 25,000 men and women, while at least 9,000 people worked at Fieseler.

The city contained vast marshalling yards and was an important railway junction between central and western Germany, helping to traffic arms to the Russian front. Germany's network of railways were the veins that kept the heart of the Third Reich beating, and destroying its transport system was one of the key objectives of the British and American Combined Bomber Offensive. The Tiger tanks, V-1 flying bombs and locomotives, meanwhile, symbolised the latest in Germany military hardware and were therefore a legitimate target for Bomber Command to hit hard using its own cutting-edge technology and modern fighting machines.

Two hours earlier, at 5.20pm, the first of 569 RAF bombers had begun to take off from airfields around eastern England. The plan was for 78 Pathfinder crews – flying Lancasters and Halifaxes fitted with H2S radar – to spearhead and maintain a concentrated air attack on Kassel, allowing the main force to drop bombs to destroy the hardware in the factories and the people who worked in them. Little did they know, however, that they would soon be met in the skies above Germany by hundreds of Luftwaffe *Nachtjäger* fighters.

One of the most intense air battles of the entire war was about to begin.

The British bombers hadn't even reached the Dutch coast when they were detected by Luftwaffe radar controllers at 6.44pm. But rather than sending the fighters to patrol the Himmelbett fighter boxes, the controllers decided instead to unleash them as a mass of Wild Boars, directing the unhindered freelance fighters onto the bombers in the hope that the sheer numbers would prove devastating. A mixture of aeroplanes – Messerschmitt Bf 110s, Messerschmitt Bf 109s, Junkers Ju 88s and Focke-Wulf Fw 190s – were scrambled from airfields all over northern Germany, bringing the total *Nachtjäger* effort to a massive 309 sorties.[2] They were under the command of General Joseph Schmid, who had been brought in by his close friend Göring to oversee German fighter defence in western and central Europe, despite his somewhat mixed record three years beforehand as chief intelligence officer for the Luftwaffe during the Battle of Britain.

A diversionary raid by 36 British bombers on Frankfurt lured 87 German fighters to the city thinking that was the main target, but as the majority of the bombing force continued inland, it soon became clear Kassel was the main objective. By now, four fifths of Bomber Command's aircraft were strung out in a vast stream 95 miles long and ten miles wide, ranging in height from 11,500 feet to 23,000 feet. The weather was appalling, with heavy rain and thick cloud. Pilots battled to keep their aircraft under control. John Christie, flying his Halifax with 35 Squadron, watched in fascination as electrical flowers 'danced' on the front windows and electrical rain made luminous spots on the windscreen. Only around half of the main-force aircraft had been able to spot the burning route markers, which fell in hilly, wooded countryside or were masked by cloud, but most were still on track. At 8.40pm, as the first Pathfinders were approaching Kassel, the cloud parted to reveal the city awaiting, its violin-shaped lake, ornate parks and tapestry of little streets hugging the river.

The first signals for the operation didn't bode well. The initial Pathfinder aircraft using their H2S radar sets to blind mark the aiming point overshot the target. But the majority of the visual markers that followed realised the mistake and corrected, and soon red and green target indicators blossomed over the centre of the city. On their final run-up to the target, John Christie later noted in his diary how 'the defences were up when we arrived, but just as we were going in everything concentrated on another poor bugger who was even earlier than us. They held him with every searchlight in the place and shot at him with nearly all they had while we were doing our run. He seemed to get away with it though.' Christie's crew dumped their red target markers on the target and turned for home.[3]

Following behind, one main-force bomb aimer was on his fourth operational sortie with 158 Squadron, flying Halifaxes. It was his crew's second visit to the city in three weeks. On the previous raid he'd had to scramble to the back of the plane for a call of nature over the target just before they'd shot down an attacking German fighter. This time, things were going more smoothly. 'As we got nearer we saw the first red markers go down,' he wrote in his diary later. 'We commenced our run 15 minutes from the target. Most of my forward vision was still blocked by ice but this did not trouble me very much. The lights were definitely coning tonight . . . the rest were wandering around for nothing in particular. Light flak came up in long red streams which finished at about 15,000ft or so. We had got up to 18,000ft and the flak was twinkling away merrily at this height.' And there, in the middle of the city, 'was a great red marker like a volcano crater'.[4] He waited until the crosshairs of his bombsight had passed over the marker, then dropped the bombs. The raid on Kassel had begun.

Down on the streets of Kassel, the air-raid sirens had started to wail a few minutes earlier. There was no widespread panic. A few weeks before, the city had been on the receiving end of a Bomber Command raid killing 118 people. Afterwards, one local Nazi official told residents to return to work: 'The enemy wants to keep us away from the work but he will not succeed. Help to remove danger and ease grief wherever you can but above all continue to work where the fatherland has placed you.'[5]

Many treated the latest warnings with an air of resigned complacency. Some decided to stay put in their homes. Others wearily made their way down to their own cellars. But as the distant sound of engines grew louder, one man ran to the roof of his building. 'You could still hear pedestrians in the street as in normal times. The sound of propellers continued strongly and I had the impression that the airplanes were just flying over us because I could see no lights in the sky. I felt spooked, however, and said to my wife: "Come on, let's go to the cellar, something's in the air, something is not right." '[6] Seconds later, the first 'Christmas trees' dropped by a Pathfinder aircraft appeared in the sky. 'A flare left the single plane . . . after it exploded, the city and the sky were lit as brightly as day by smaller beacons. It was so light, you could have read the newspaper,' recalled a 33-year old anti-aircraft gunner.[7]

Hot on the heels of the markers fell hundreds of incendiaries. It was often sheer luck whether an incendiary took hold or not. One dropped through the roof of a house into a full bath tub. The bomb burnt through the bottom of the tub but was extinguished by the water pouring out. Another landed in a larder, melting a lead water pipe which dampened out the fire. To start with – as with the German bombing raids on Coventry almost three years before – locals did their best to douse fires using stirrup pumps. But the sheer number of firebombs falling soon made this impossible, and the fires took hold amongst the winding streets of Kassel's old town. 'It was about as useful as spitting into a furnace,' said an air-raid warden.[8]

As it became clear the raid was more serious than anything that had ever targeted Kassel before, residents ran through the streets and scrambled down staircases to seek shelter in the myriad of cellars under the old buildings. But for thousands of people, the safety they sought by heading underground would instead entomb them for ever.

A 33-year-old, who later wanted to be identified only as 'Clara', had arrived home from her job at the post office and was sitting down for supper with her mother when they heard the sirens sound. She walked over to the window and looked out. 'We'd better go down, the sky is full of searchlights,' Clara said to her mother, and together with her brother and sister-in-law they quickly gathered some belongings and made their way downstairs. When they reached the cellar, a large bomb exploded a few hundred feet away, causing the building to shake, covering them all in black soot from the fireplace, which prompted laughing and teasing. It was still quite fun and exciting, despite the noise. But when more big explosions rocked the buildings, the mood changed. It was clear the cellar might collapse at any moment and they needed to get out, fast. Outside, the street was blazing with fire. They decided to make a run for it to a house opposite. Clara went first with her mother and made it safely across the road, with her brother following closely behind. But as she turned around to check on the others, Clara watched in horror as burning beams fell onto her sister-in-law. 'We both screamed, my brother ran back but I could not leave my mother alone as she was completely exhausted . . . I never saw my brother and sister-in-law again.'[9]

Clara and her mother made it down to the cellar opposite, where 400 people had crammed into three small rooms. One room had a shaft in the middle. The iron cover was removed so it could be used as a lavatory. It was a bit undignified, but everyone was alive. Then, quite suddenly, there was a huge bang, followed by screaming and silence. When Clara woke up it was pitch black. At first, she thought she was lying in her bed at home. 'I wanted to get up and reached around me but it was all very slippery. I kept falling back and did not know what that was [I'd been touching].' She remembered a torch in her coat pocket, fished it out and shone the light around her. 'Then I saw that I had been touching dead people. They had green faces and a thick foam at their mouths.' A woman and her child sat against a wall, struggling to breath with ruptured lungs. 'As my head cleared, I heard wheezing,' continued Clara. It was her mother, who died a few moments later. Clara reached across, gently closed her mother's eyes and prayed for the rescue which would come the following day.

With the air raid on Kassel now in full force in the skies directly above, 90 per cent of the Pathfinder planes had dropped their target indicators within one minute of their allotted time, while four fifths of the main-force bombers released their bombs within the planned 16-minute window. Up to 29 aircraft passed over the Kassel every minute, dropping as much as 527 tons of bombs per square mile – including 4,000lb cylindrical 'blockbusters', which ripped apart whole buildings as if they were made of matchsticks.

The experience was appalling for those sheltering in the cellars under the old buildings of Kassel. Just as he had reached a cellar, one man described how 'the floodgates of hell' opened up in the sky above. 'Without pause or break you could hear hissing, whistling, gurgling, roaring, crashing, thundering, smashing, battering, and hammering so that you could believe that the end of the world had arrived,' he said. Every close explosion blew dust and air in through the holes in the cellar 'so that you would have been forgiven for believing that the house would collapse at any moment'.

> You could hear from the outside the rattling of the window panes and the roof tiles which dropped on the pavement. The bursting and collapsing of nearby buildings made a dreadful sound which we could hear, the terrible thunder of two factory chimneys which both fell onto neighbouring properties. Through the cellar vent we could see a small piece of the sky which shone red with fire.[10]

Many cellars had heavy iron manholes which acted as emergency exits to the streets. Those inside watched on as the air pressure from the bomb waves outside flipped the manhole covers open and shut like bottle tops. People sheltering in basements which took direct hits were 'thrown about like dice'.[11] Others cowered in the darkness without light or water, wondering if they would be next. Kitty Michel, aged 52, recalled how 'The cellar shook, it was easy to believe that it would be impossible to escape from that hell . . . The children were screaming constantly, the mothers were jumping up with every explosion. The older people were exhausted and were lying on the beds.'[12]

One of the biggest cellars was under the Gasthaus zur Pinne, a large, stone Renaissance-style guest house in the old town, where hundreds of people flocked when the air raid started. But although the deep basement protected them from the flames raging in the buildings above, the precious oxygen being used by 400 pairs of lungs was now being gratefully sucked out of the cellar by the fire in its own bid to stay alive. People began to suffocate in the darkness. One 38-year-old woman, sheltering with her two daughters, passed out. 'I came to again, I heard my daughter scream: "Mum, I'm suffocating!" She was lying in the cellar under a pile of dead bodies,' she said later. The woman fainted again. The following morning two soldiers came in to rescue the survivors, including the woman. 'I shouted: "Dear man, please help pull out my child!" They got the older one out and me; the little one was already stone cold.'[13]

Nearby, a 25-year-old woman called Grete was visiting her friend Ilse and her five-month-old baby son when the sirens sounded. Like so many others, at first none of them realised the seriousness of the situation. 'I was knitting a jumper when the sirens started wailing,' she recalled later. 'I didn't feel like going into the cellar. When ack-ack started shooting, we took the child and went into the cellar. It was a terrible din. Maybe 14 people were in the cellar, mainly residents from the building, and a Hitler Youth leader from the self-protection troop stood at the door.' After 10 minutes, 'a terrible cloud of dust came into the cellar and I got really angry about getting so dirty. I hadn't imagined anything like that.'

As the air got thicker with dust and smoke the women wrapped themselves in wet clothes and soaked the baby's nappies to use as makeshift gas masks. A big explosion in the street outside blew the Hitler Youth back down the stairs into the cellar. Grete used a nappy to bandage his bleeding head. The buildings on street level were now burning furiously, so they stuffed a quilt into the window to try and stop smoke pouring in. Grete realised her knees were knocking together in fear. 'Ilse, do you think we'll die in here?' she asked her friend. 'Nonsense; don't talk like that!' she replied. Another bomb exploded directly above, causing bricks to tumble down onto the Hitler Youth. In agonising pain, he took out a revolver and shot himself. Grete vomited. It was pitch black. She whispered to her friend: 'Ilse, are you still alive?' And she answered very softly: 'Yes!' Then Grete recalled: 'The baby started to cough and to cry and I don't know how long it took until the crying and coughing stopped. And when I touched the baby a little later, the legs were cold.'

Some soldiers arrived. 'We have to get out of here, even if we get roasted,' one of them shouted. They pulled the dead Hitler Youth away from the door and dragged Grete onto her feet. Her friend had died. 'As they shone a light on her, her eyes had rolled up and as he touched her hand, she was already cold. Strangely enough, I was very matter-of-fact about her death, which I could not understand afterwards because we had been very close.'[14]

Like all air raids, the evening was littered with personal tragedies. A woman stood in the middle of a basement shelter with her eight-year-old child. Then, in a matter of seconds, the ceiling collapsed and the child had vanished from her side. 'She must still have been alive because she screamed: "Mother!" . . . I don't want to live anymore without a child,' she later said.[15] A former Luftwaffe airman who had crashed in the North Sea and been treated for twitch had come to Kassel to celebrate his engagement with his fiancée's parents. Before the raid started, her mother had told them: 'If it gets hairy, come into our cellar . . . No one's going to drop a bomb on our little house.' The dead bridal couple and her parents were dug out eight days later. Another man had recently moved to Kassel from Essen to escape the terror bombing. His wife and daughter were killed.

Amongst the death, however, there were rare snatches of hope. In one dark cellar, a young woman went into labour. A man nearby washed his hands using what little water was available and delivered the baby successfully.

Not that many of them realised it, but the drama and violence being experienced by the people in the streets of Kassel was being mirrored four miles above as a huge air battle raged between British bombers and German night fighters.

When it became clear where the main raid was targeting a few minutes before it began, German fighters orbiting over Frankfurt were radioed by ground controllers and ordered to immediately fly to Kassel. However, 350 miles away in an unassuming transmitting station near Deal, Kent, someone was having some fun. British scientists had managed to hack into German radio frequencies with a new piece of kit codenamed Corona, which allowed German-speaking operators in Britain to use the same wavelengths as the *Nachtjäger* fighters and controllers to broadcast false or contradictory information. Exchanges between the controllers in Germany and England often became increasingly heated as each tried to convince the pilots of the authenticity of their orders. 'Do not go to Kassel, but remain over FF Otto' (FF Otto was the codename for Frankfurt), the voice over the radio suddenly announced to puzzled night-fighter crews. Clearly irritated, the real controller back in Germany furiously replied to warn his aircraft: 'Beware of another voice . . . on the authority of General Schmid I order all aircraft not to remain by O but to fly to Kassel.' Two minutes later, he was heard exclaiming: 'Don't be led astray by the enemy!' and was incandescent with rage.[16] The spoof voice – clearly warming to his task – remarked: 'The Englishman is now swearing', to which the German retorted, 'It is not the Englishman who is swearing, it is me!'[17]

In the confusion, the leading planes of the British force – including many Pathfinders – were able to drop their flares and bombs without being attacked by fighters. However, within a few minutes dozens of German fighters were arriving over Kassel. Willi Kleebauer, a 22-year-old novice pilot flying a Junkers Ju 88, arrived over the burning city to see the black shapes of the British bombers clearly visible beneath him, like flies crawling across an orange tablecloth. As he and his two crewmates picked out a Lancaster and began their attack, their aircraft was suddenly caught in a huge thermal and pushed up several feet a second. 'What the hell is that,' he wrote later. 'Suddenly we're surrounded by hundreds of strange flying objects, which are climbing up past us at a prodigious rate. We're scared stiff, as we have no idea what they are.' The objects were in fact empty sacks, hurled three miles into the sky by the tremendous heat from the fires. And while that Lancaster they were homing in on had escaped, there were plenty other bombers to choose from. Moments later, Kleebauer flicked his aircraft over to begin another attack. 'A Halifax this time. I dive down on it and open fire with everything. The tracers chew their way into the starboard wing and the fuselage. "Got him!" yells Hans [Kleebauer's crewmate]. The bomber starts to burn and falls away trailing smoke.'[18]

German fighters dropped flares strung out in long, floating avenues of bright light to illuminate the British bombers, and give other German fighter planes a better chance of seeing the prey. One Lancaster was targeted by two German fighters simultaneously. The mid-upper gunner in the Lancaster opened fire with a clatter and 'saw my tracer and the stuff from our tail gun hitting home'. Almost immediately, 'a Junkers 88 was coming at us from the other side,' recalled the gunner straight after the mission. 'I just had time to swing my guns round and give him four seconds. He, too, dived out of the way. I don't think he was one of the keen fellows.'[19]

Towering beams of white light from over 60 searchlight batteries prowled the sky, targeting individual aircraft to aid night fighters and anti-aircraft fire. Moderate and heavy flak was being thrown up in a barrage to 20,000 feet, while intense light-flak burst at 15,000 feet, making the run in to the target insanely dangerous.

One Pathfinder Halifax bomber with 35 Squadron became trapped in the bluish white of a radio-controlled master searchlight. Dozens more searchlight beams greedily locked on and high-explosive shell fire pumped up the centre of the beams. Wilfred Hart, a Welsh wireless operator whose crew had only recently become Pathfinders, felt the fuselage rock and shake. 'It was like being in a tin shed with somebody throwing stones,' he recalled later. 'We were hit by anti-aircraft fire and two engines caught fire.' Hart looked forward only to see a pool of blood collecting in front of him. It was dripping from the pilot sitting above who had been hit in the chest by shrapnel. They dragged the pilot from his seat and replaced him with the bomb aimer, who had failed his pilot training but claimed he could still fly and was the best they had at that moment. When it became clear the best they had wasn't actually good enough to fly the plane, it was time to get the hell out. 'I gave the pilot an injection of morphine from the first aid kit and we threw him out with his hand on the parachute. We were going down and down and we all had to get out. It was quite low when we all jumped,' said Hart, who survived the jump – along with the pilot – and ended up in a POW camp for the rest of the war.[20]

By 9.12pm, the air raid on Kassel was almost over. But while the bombs had stopped, for the people of Kassel, the worst was still to come. The fires had taken hold in the timber-framed buildings of the old town, where its narrow streets were helping funnel the wind to fan the flames, turning them into a firestorm. According to one Swiss journalist in the city, 'a raging sea of fire was spreading over the town.'[21] It tore and sucked its way through the streets, thumping on windows and kicking at doors, belching great funnels of scorching, poisonous air laced with sparks.

A Luftwaffe pilot known only as Otto had been on leave in Kassel celebrating his twenty-fourth birthday with his 19-year-old wife Margarete and her mother. When the cellar they were sheltering in with dozens of other people filled with smoke and fumes, Otto shouted, 'Those who have the courage to follow me can walk behind me.' He wrapped his mother-in-law in his air-force greatcoat and climbed the cellar steps into the street, where the firestorm was raging. 'My wife fell and I had to lift her up. Fire was already on the ground and lay there in burning ash . . . the sparks were flying everywhere in the burning wind,' he recalled afterwards.

> We were separated a bit. Alternately, I supported my wife and my mother-in-law against the storm and rain of fire. Then I saw that my wife's hat and coat were on fire. I tore them off her. My cap was on fire too. I threw it away. Then I saw 10 metres behind me my mother-in-law on fire. I wanted to run back when burning debris, a gable end or something like it, fell on her and she disappeared behind a curtain of fire. I could no longer see her. I had to look after my wife. She was lying

helplessly on the ground and begged me not to leave her. I laid myself
on top of her to protect her from the flying fire so that she would not
burn. Her knees, hands and face were already burnt. It was a moment
– you can't explain to anyone what we suffered and felt. We wanted to
live or die together . . . I took my burning wife in my burnt hands and
carried her through the firestorm . . .

They finally sought refuge in – ironically – the dugout in the garden
of a former synagogue. Otto had third-degree burns while Margarete
'was a terrible mess' with 'burnt and crooked hands'. But they were
alive.[22]

Remarkably, some houses still remained untouched. When one
resident returned home briefly, 'the clock on the wall ticked as if nothing had happened'. Many people were faced with the Russian roulette
of being poisoned, burnt or buried alive if they stayed in the cellars, or
making a dash for it in the firestorm to try and seek safety. 'I still see
my mother running in front of me, through the fire, and I'm thinking:
It's like in the movies; she's running for her life,' said one man, who
managed to reach safety, to be greeted by others muttering: 'Now we
can understand the people of Hamburg.'[23]

Many were too paralysed with fear to leave the cellars. Others were
worried about their appearance. One man remonstrated with a group
of women, telling them: 'You will have to choose between your hairdo
and your coat, and dying.'[24] A 49-year-old wire-fence manufacturer
called Anton was sheltering in a cellar with his wife. They decided
they had to risk the firestorm. He took out a bottle of French Hennessy
cognac which they had saved 'for an emergency', took a swig and
climbed into the street. 'The first sight of the street was a sight of hell,'
said Anton later. 'All the buildings were on fire, nearly every cobble
was on fire, the spring steel factory was collapsing, and flames were
shooting out as if blown by bellows from the buildings on both sides.'
To him, the firestorm was like 'a snowstorm with fire. The sparks flew
into the houses and ate into wooden objects.'

They managed to make their way to the station. There they saw
mothers with small children sitting on the bare ground and sunk over
with exhaustion. A woman was shouting for her husband. 'Have you
not seen my husband?' she pleaded. 'Dear lady, how would I recognise

your husband?' someone replied. 'Well, a man on his own?' she said. Another woman kept shouting: 'I have lost everything, I have lost everything', only to be told: 'Don't drive us nuts; be quiet, we too have lost everything', while a man cried, 'My beautiful cigars, my best cigars!' as his house collapsed. Anton and his wife were alive but had also lost their home. 'Churchill got everything, the bastard,' he said, bitterly.[25] Others countered: 'You can't complain, all our neighbours are dead, we did not salvage anything, not even a handkerchief, but we are alive!'[26]

As dawn broke the following morning, the city continued to burn. At one stage the fire services had been dealing with 3,600 separate fires. A German radio broadcaster announced: 'Overnight, the colourful autumn in the picturesque town of Kassel has been turned into the grey horror of a heavy terror raid.'[27] Vehicles and rescue parties from the surrounding towns and villages streamed into the city, passing cars, lorries and carriages drawn by horses and oxen going the other way. Children were carried on people's backs in rucksacks or laundry baskets. As with Hamburg, thousands fled the carnage.

In the worst hit areas, a grim clear-up began. Dead bodies lay in the streets. People scoured the ruins looking for their families. Children found wandering alone or without any adult supervision were taken to a military barracks, where anxious parents gathered to hear their names called out. Some were reunited with their grateful families, but others were confronted with the dawning realisation that no one was coming to meet them. As rescuers reached trapped cellars, they were forced back by blue flames shooting out as the fresh oxygen reignited the embers inside. 'We found mainly many children in those cellars,' said one rescuer. 'The horse butcher Herrmann in Schäfergasse was completely incinerated and had shrunk to about half a metre. They were like dolls. Other bodies were terribly bloated and defaced. Others were easy to recognise, as if they were still alive, but all were dirty and blackened.'[28]

Oskar Spiess, a 53-year-old hairdresser, lost seven relatives in the raid, including his wife and daughter. When he found his dead grandson in a cellar, he 'did not have the smallest mark on him'. Spiess took the boy away and 'put him in his mother's arms' one final time.[29]

The Pinne hostelry had been one of the worst hit, with hundreds dead. One 13-year-old boy recalled later how he and his 11-year-old sister had run for their lives with their mother to the Pinne's cellar, where they sheltered as people began to suffocate around them. The following morning, as soldiers arrived and piled the dead to one side to concentrate on the injured, the boy was carried out. 'I could see how a soldier lifted my mum. I felt her heart beating at that time,' said the boy. He and his sister were taken to the local sports stadium. 'We never heard from our mum again.'[30]

Over the following hours, huge trenches were dug in public cemeteries. Lorry after lorry arrived carrying corpses, which were shovelled into the mass graves. 'I can't bear the sound of a truck anymore,' said a clerical officer from the Office for Burials, who was responsible for dealing with victims of bombing raids.[31] It was a thankless task. French prisoners of war and interned Italian soldiers were ordered to lift decomposing bodies without any protective equipment, which had been destroyed in the raid. Reluctant at first, they were soon encouraged by a few savage beatings from SS guards armed with sticks. Bodies were stacked three or four high and some tags had become illegible because of the blood, dirt and the 'corpse water'. Because many of the dead had died through suffocation, their faces were purple and unrecognisable. 'We were also brought tubs with bones,' added the clerical officer. Bodies were buried with jewellery and wallets with large amounts of money. One man had at least 6,000 Reichsmarks with him as he tumbled into the ditch. The spoils were too tempting for some. Six people were executed in the street for looting.

There were rare tales of survival. A man separated from his son, assuming he had died, rejoiced as the five-year-old came running towards him near his house. 'Heavens, was that a moment, the boy with his five years pressed himself against me so, that I thought a much older person was squeezing me.'[32]

Afterwards, as he looked around him at his smoking city, Fritz Köhler, a 43-year-old railway conductor, said: 'I have seen so much death, in enemy territory, that nothing can daunt me. But what happened here is inconceivable. You can't see them. I stood for half an hour at the window and saw the fire and heard the bombs and the invisible planes above us and I thought: Is there justice in the world or isn't there? There is none!'[33]

But perhaps Köhler's question could be partly be answered in an order from Nazi officials less than a week after the raid, telling the workers of Kassel to 'remember your duties as Germans. Just as the soldier is not allowed to leave his post you must not stay away from work. This applies even if your family has been bombed out or evacuated.'[34] And therefore, as grim as the raid had been for those in the firing line, in the eyes of the Allies, Kassel was a wholly justified target because many thousands of people who worked and lived in Kassel contributed directly to the armament production of the Third Reich.

Allied analysis later showed that 86 per cent of the main-force aircraft had dropped their bombs within three miles of the aiming point – a remarkable figure – thanks partly to the excellent target marking by the Pathfinders but also to the high standard of timekeeping by the crews of the main force. Writing up his diary after the raid, John Christie reckoned it was 'the best raid the PFF has ever made, certainly the best Newhaven, against a defended German target . . . this means Kassel is now the worst bombed city in the world. At any rate considerably worse than Hamburg.'

Around 1,656 tons of bombs fell on the target – three times the weight of bombs dropped on Coventry in November 1940 – with 65 per cent of these in an area of 17 square miles around the centre of the city. An estimated 94,700 people lost their homes, with 32,400 houses seriously damaged – about 42 per cent of all the houses. The death toll of 6,000 people meant that, proportionally, the raid was even more devastating than the firestorm in Hamburg. And while only around 26 per cent of industrial buildings were seriously damaged by the raid, the real impact came in the subsequent shortage of a functioning workforce. Many of the workers were dead or injured – 8,000 people had been blinded by the effect of smoke and heat. Industrial losses in Kassel amounted to 311,000 man hours per month. Henschel & Son lost at least six to eight weeks in production of locomotives, and two to three weeks in lost output of Tiger tank production. The production of 8.8cm anti-tank guns was also badly hit.

Slowing production of locomotives and Tiger Tanks was not catastrophic for Germany, but it was still a serious blow. The Reichsbahn – the German railway network – was the glue that kept the Third Reich held together. The country had very little fuel, which meant motorised transport was kept to a bare minimum and as much as possible went on the railways. Equally, Tiger tank and anti-tank gun losses were not devastating, but anything that hindered the German ability to fight effectively – especially at a time when its armies on the Russian front needed all the supplies they could get – was a good thing for the Allies. The raid also had a significant impact on the production of the V-1 flying bomb, delaying the launch of the missiles and reducing the scale of the campaign when it eventually came the following year.

The raid hadn't been cheap for Bomber Command, however, with 243 airmen killed – although unbelievably the Pathfinders lost only one aircraft, with two men killed. A total of 43 British bombers had been lost – 7.6 per cent of the force – the majority shot down by German night fighters or flak. Many German crews later talked about their desire to stay over the 'sea of flames' until the last possible moment, their blood raised by the apparent targeting of a civilian population, 'hitting our people where they were most vulnerable'.[35]

But the reality is that many who were killed in Kassel worked in Nazi war production. As unpalatable as it might seem 80 years later, popular opinion at the time was that they were fair game, even if they were civilians. Back in 1940, the British public had been shaken to the core as the German air force bombed cities across Britain. Bert Harris had warned Hitler he would 'reap the whirlwind'. Britain could, and would, fight back. For many, Germany and its people were now getting their just deserts. 'Kassel was a horror on the scale of Hamburg . . . For once I felt sorry for the folk in that city,' said one Pathfinder pilot who had flown on the raid with 97 Squadron. Even with regrets, however, he summed up the feelings of most Bomber Command airmen at the time, intent on defeating Hitler and the Nazis: 'Would I do it again? Yes. We were at war. All war is evil, but more evil is to submit to evil. For me it's as simple as that.'[36]

In some ways, the grim reality of what the people of Kassel had experienced under the bombs was not unique – their stories would have been familiar to those who had also been targeted by air bombing, from London to Leipzig and Coventry to Cologne. But what was remarkable – and new – was the sheer weight, concentration and accuracy of the firepower in such a small amount of time. And while it was still far from perfect, the raids on Hamburg, Peenemünde and Kassel had shown that – thanks to the Pathfinder Force – Bomber Command had been turned from a weak, leaflet-dropping flying circus into an iron fist, with the ability to accurately find and pummel small military targets or raze whole cities to the ground in minutes. As far as Harris was concerned, his force was finally delivering what he had always hoped, and was grinding down the enemy. For him, thanks to the Pathfinders and the H2S radar, the raid on Kassel was a 'remarkable success'.[37]

Now – on Harris's orders – it was time for Don Bennett's men to open a new front, by striking at the heart of the Third Reich: the 'Big City', Berlin.

CHAPTER EIGHTEEN

Tommy Oil

ON THE AFTERNOON OF 24 August 1943 – a few hours after Bomber Command's first raid on Berlin for almost six months – Brenda Bridger opened her diary and began to write.

'It has happened. Allan hasn't come back from Berlin last night – the bottom has fallen out of my world. There is only one person for me – that is Allan. I realise that now – I love him so – he has got to come back.'[1]

Earlier that day, Brenda had received the news she always prayed would never come – her fiancé Allan Ball, flying with 35 Squadron, was missing after a trip over Berlin in the early hours of that morning. It was even more gruelling given she had not heard from her darling brother Larry – Allan's best friend – since a raid on Munich five months before. Larry's absence had only drawn her and Allan even closer.

Over the days following the news that Ball was missing, Brenda captured her feelings in her diary. Almost eighty years on, they seem as raw now as the minute they were penned:

25 Wednesday: The worst day of my life – I am so unhappy – My poor darling Allan – I want him so very much.
26 Thursday: What a day – I feel almost ill because I am so unhappy – I did not know he meant everything to me – now I know – he must come back.

27 Friday: Took Mrs Sells to dinner because I cannot bear being alone
– I cannot help feeling so horribly lost without him – Please God bring
him back to me soon.
28 Saturday: Letter from 'drome – I was so upset – I miss him so I feel
I cannot go on without him. Daddy took us all to Hitchin – to the flics
so we would forget for a moment – but I couldn't, everything reminds
me of him.

Bomber Command's operation to Berlin on 23 August heralded the
start of many visits by the Pathfinders to the city over the autumn and
winter of 1943 – a sustained effort on Germany's capital that would
become one of the most intense and brutal air campaigns of the Second World War, known later as the Battle of Berlin.

The city was one of the most heavily defended in the world. By the
time the battle ended in the spring of 1944, Don Bennett had lost 198
crews on operations – leaving 650 of his young airmen dead – with 8
Group replacing itself in strength entirely one and half times.[2]

Whether Allan Ball would be amongst those lost, only time
would tell.

As the men in the skies prepared to do battle over Berlin, Bert Harris
was fighting his own battle with his bosses in the Air Ministry. Harris
was convinced that destroying Berlin using his bombers could end the
war and avoid a protracted and bloody land campaign following an
Allied invasion of Europe planned for 1944. 'We can wreck Berlin
from end to end if the USAAF will come in on it. It will cost us between
400–500 aircraft. It will cost Germany the war,' he told Winston
Churchill in a letter in November 1943.[3] Despite Harris's genuine
belief, the American Eighth Air Force that had been bombing Germany by day was in no shape to target Berlin in the way he was
suggesting, until its long-range Mustang fighters became available.
So, for now, Bomber Command would take on the job itself.

After the Pathfinder Force had successfully spearheaded operations against small-scale targets such as Peenemünde and delivered
crushing blows across the Ruhr, Harris now wanted Don Bennett's
men to help intensify and concentrate his favoured area-bombing

policy by using H2S radar, which had proved so effective against cities like Hamburg and Kassel.

Harris's strategy to attack Berlin, however, had widespread sceptics across the Allied services. Few in the army, navy or even in his own Air Ministry realistically believed bombing alone could deliver the *coup de grâce* and a German surrender. His decision to bomb Berlin was a loose interpretation of the Casablanca Directive produced after the meeting of Allied leaders in January 1943, which initially pushed for air attacks to break the German economy and morale, and to further divide Germany into a war on multiple fronts, as requested by the Soviets at the Casablanca Conference. This was modified in June 1943 under the codename Pointblank, with the emphasis on specifically targeting Germany's aircraft and ball-bearing industries ahead of the ground invasion of France planned for the summer of 1944.

Harris was instructed to launch operations against six key cities responsible for German fighter production. But he treated these directives with an attitude verging on contempt, classing them as 'panacea targets' which diverted him from his number-one priority. On one secret Air Ministry document that landed on his desk, which identified the strategic importance of bombing Schweinfurt – a small but nonetheless crucial city in the production of ball bearings – Harris simply scrawled 'sez you!' in the margin, before ignoring the brief to attack the town.[4] Despite the success of Peenemünde and the new-found navigational skills of the Pathfinders, he was still unconvinced Bomber Command possessed the capability to carry out precision attacks on small targets. Even if his bosses within the Air Ministry disagreed, there was no way they were going to sack Harris at such a crucial time in the bombing war.

Instead, undeterred, Harris continued with his focus on area bombing of cities, drawing up a list of urban areas to attack, with Berlin at the top. Crucially, he knew that Churchill in particular was also pressing for attacks on the capital, partly because he had been so impressed with the spectacular raids on targets such as Hamburg. Harris also believed that bombing the big towns and cities of Germany would bring such a state of devastation by the spring of 1944 that the Germans would have little choice but to surrender.

Berlin was a different proposition to any other target attacked before, however, and reducing it to a wasteland of rubble would be extraordinarily difficult. The city was the third largest in the world and its wide streets and solid blocks of flats were not conducive to firestorms in the same way Hamburg or Kassel had been. To reach Berlin meant a 1,200 mile round trip, which took eight hours for the heavy bombers. They would need to use the cover of darkness for the series of attacks, which given the distance was only possible when the nights were longer. For the aircrews, this translated into flying throughout the winter months in brutal conditions that were physically and psychologically demanding.

Quite apart from the threat from enemy fighters, flak or bad weather, airmen sat in a freezing, vibrating cabin knowing they would be dead within minutes without a constant supply of oxygen and layers of heavy clothing. It would also be damned hard work for the ground crews back in Britain servicing the aircraft in what would prove to be one of the bitterest winters for years.

And then there were the target's defences. Berlin was the most heavily defended city in Germany – and the most fortified capital in the world – protected by over 700 heavy flak guns, including three huge concrete flak towers, each 130 feet tall, on which perched twin-barrelled 128mm flak guns. The towers doubled up as air-raid shelters which could each hold up to 45,000 people. The flak belt of guns surrounding the capital was 40 miles wide, framed by a 60-mile searchlight belt.[5] Night fighters were rife in a Luftwaffe which was just reaching a peak in both numbers and experience. Its crews would defend the heart of the Reich to the death.

The Pathfinders' role in helping Harris 'wreck' Berlin came just as their cover had been blown. Since his force was founded the year before, Bennett had enjoyed relative anonymity with the wider public compared to the rest of Bomber Command. That's just how he liked it. It meant he could get on with the job without the distractions of journalists and public relations men wanting to find out more about this secret and elite unit. He specifically asked for no media attention.

But that changed in the autumn of 1943, when the Air Ministry decided to reveal the role of the Pathfinders to the world in a series of newspaper stories. After all, this was Bomber Command's secret weapon and letting the British public know about high-tech derring-do would cause no harm to morale. 'RAF PATHFINDERS GO INTO

ACTION' declared a headline in the *People* newspaper. 'ACE FLIERS RACE IN TO LIGHT UP GERMAN CITIES – AND NOT A BOMB IS WASTED', it added.[6] The *Daily Herald*, meanwhile, announced: 'THEY TURN ON LIGHTS FOR BOMBERS IN BIG RAIDS'.[7] Another boasted 'RAF REVEAL SECRET OF PATHFINDERS', while for the *Liverpool Daily Post*, the success of the RAF's night bombing was down to Bennett's 'energy, resourcefulness and thoughtful ingenuity'.[8] A fine compliment perhaps, but much to Bennett's horror, no doubt, the *Daily Mail* spared no detail with its headline: 'RAF REVEAL BIG SECRET OF NIGHT BOMBING'.

'The Air Ministry last night revealed one of the greatest secrets behind the night bombing offensive launched on Germany by Air Chief Marshal Harris,' the story opened.

> The newly revealed secret is the 'Target Indicator' – a super-type flare dropped by the Pathfinders, which can be seen at night from the sub-stratosphere through almost total cloud…The dramatic transformation of air raids into mass onslaughts, wiping out whole cities in a night, threatening the entire structure of Hitler's Germany, became possible with their use.[9]

In reality, the existence of 8 Group had been known by the Germans for some time. A secret publication was compiled by the Luftwaffenführungsstab – the German Air Staff intelligence section – and circulated to senior Luftwaffe commanders, containing a full summary of the Pathfinder tactics. Entitled 'British Pathfinder Operations', with a portrait of Don Bennett on its cover, the 12-page dossier outlined their tactics and methods, gleaned primarily from 8 Group airmen shot down and interrogated. The paper acknowledged the successes of the Pathfinders in improving Bomber Command's fortunes and reckoned Bennett was 'one of the most resourceful officers in the RAF'. But it couldn't resist claiming full credit as the originators of the pathfinding techniques first used by the Luftwaffe over London and Coventry in 1940.[10]

In fact, such was the knowledge German intelligence services felt they had about Bomber Command, it later emerged they even considered making a training film illustrating the planning and execution of an RAF night-bombing attack, right down to the finest detail, including auditioning actors in Germany who most resembled the leading RAF commanders – although it's not known if the actor playing Bennett was required to put on a fake Australian accent.[11]

A more serious concern for the Pathfinders was that, as Bomber Command ramped up its campaign against Berlin, the German air force was targeting Pathfinder aircraft directly with a range of new measures, realising if they could knock out the planes dropping the markers, they could sabotage an entire raid. At their disposal was a new piece of technology called Naxos, which allowed German night fighters to home in on the H2S radar transmissions primarily emitted from kit fitted to Pathfinder aircraft. More experienced German night-fighter crews were sent to a Naxos training school at an airfield in Werneuchen, north-east of Berlin, where they practised homing in on a captured American Liberator bomber and a Junkers Ju 86, both equipped with captured H2S sets. One night-fighter group fitted with Naxos became known as the *Schwerpunkt Gruppe*, meaning 'Precision Group' or 'Pinpoint Group'.[12] At the first warning of an Allied raid, its aircrew were scrambled to try and position themselves as near as possible to the expected route of the bomber stream and target the Pathfinders. Although eventually jammed by the Allies, Naxos was a useful tool and was used over the coming months to shoot down scores of British bombers and Pathfinders.

The afternoon before Brenda Bridger had received the bad news about Allan Ball, his squadron mates in 35 Squadron assembled in the briefing hut at RAF Graveley and groaned as the curtain was pulled aside to reveal that the target for that night was Berlin.

'I think everybody in the room expected a rough trip,' jotted John Christie in his diary. His crew was one of 23 aircraft from 35 Squadron detailed to attack Berlin. Christie's job was as one of five crews acting as 'backers up', dropping target markers over the target exactly four minutes after the raid started. Eight crews from the squadron were assigned blind-marker roles, six would act as recenterers – refreshing the marking as the raid developed – and the remaining four crews were to fly in the main force to gain experience.[13]

Ball himself was not listed to be on the Berlin operation that night. Instead, as a more experienced member of the squadron, he briefed the crews and would be on hand to interrogate them over coffee and rum on their return in the small hours of the following morning. But as the men rose from their seats in the cigarette-smoke-filled hut, a nervous-looking wireless operator quietly approached Ball and asked for a private word. The young airman admitted he was too scared to go on the operation. No one would make him fly. He was perhaps braver than many in admitting his fear.

But now they had a big problem. There were no spare wireless operators to replace the airman. Ball immediately relayed the news to Dixie Dean, his pilot and the group commanding officer, who also wasn't flying that night. Dean couldn't face telling Bennett they'd be a crew down for such a vital operation, so there was only one thing for it. 'Allan, will you fly with them?' Dean asked. 'What about debriefing?' Ball replied. 'Cut off a few corners on the way home and you'll be back in time!' answered Dean.[14] Both men grinned. In truth, Ball didn't need much persuading. This would be his fifty-eighth operation. Once he reached that magic 60 mark his current tour was finished and he could marry Brenda.

It was time to get ready.

At around 7.30pm, in the gorgeous late-August sunshine, 162 airmen of 35 Squadron were ferried by the noisy Bedford vans and dropped off at their Halifax bombers, roosting on the airfield. Among them was Alec Cranswick. This operation would be his eighty-eighth bombing mission. His crew had just been given a new plane – fresh off the production line. Before he climbed in, Cranswick looked up at the big black monster. Just below the cockpit window, on the side of the fuselage, one of the ground staff had daubed the Cranswick family crest in white paint: three herons above the motto *Thou Shalt Want Ere I*. Cranswick was proud of his family's motto. He just hoped as one of the blind-marker crews, and therefore amongst the first aircraft due to arrive over Berlin, no German fighter pilots would get close enough to read it.

At 20.11, the fat, spinning wheels of Cranswick's Halifax cleared the concrete runway and folded up neatly into the fuselage with a click. By

20.37, all 23 aircraft from 35 Squadron were headed east towards Berlin.[15]

Three hours later, the leading Pathfinder aircraft approached the German capital, spearheading an armada of 710 Lancasters, Halifaxes and Stirling bombers. The route – which took them across the Netherlands and northern Germany to Berlin before making its way back to Britain by swinging north over the Baltic Sea and Denmark – was marked along the way by seventeen Mosquito bombers.

Cranswick's aircraft was one of 30 Pathfinder crews from different squadrons tasked with using their H2S sets to find and then mark the target. The plan was for the blind markers to fly past Berlin and then cut back, dropping their target indicators and bombs on the northern edge of the city, which jutted out and – so it was hoped – would clearly appear on the radar screens of the H2S operators. The Pathfinders and main force following behind could then drop their bombs on these markers, and before long the bombing would creep back across the centre of the city, pulverizing the heart of Berlin. They would be directed by a master bomber – the first time one was being used over a German city.

At least that was the plan. But as they got over Berlin and the anti-aircraft guns and searchlights began to sweep the sky, it became clear that it was far trickier for the navigators trying to identify the target using the H2S set than anyone had imagined. Berlin appeared on the screen as a green welter of light, and echoes from other aircraft further confused the picture, while the northern suburb they were told would appear as a hook couldn't be identified from the block of green. Nevertheless, at around 11.40pm, the first red markers cascaded from the leading planes. They dropped further south than intended, but it would have to do.

Cranswick, flying his Halifax – codenamed L for Leather – at 19,000 feet, was one of the first over the target. At 23.43 exactly, four red markers and seven 500lb bombs tumbled out of the aircraft. Cranswick continued to fly straight and level for thirty seconds until the photoflash burst with the synchronised camera snap. Now the job was done it was time to get the hell out there. Cranswick put the Halifax into a steep dive, knowing this was the best way to escape the danger from enemy fighters and preserve the lives of his crew. But there was also a major risk he'd not be able to pull the plane out of the dive before it smashed into the ground. As the Halifax screamed and juddered through the sky, Cranswick bent down and grabbed a piece of rope he had at the ready. Quickly tying the rope to the control stick, he handed the other end to his flight engineer and with the shout of 'heave' the two men pulled back on the rope and the stick with all their might. 'If the wings don't drop off now they jolly well ought to!' Cranswick shouted over the noise, but to their relief the big bomber levelled out at 5,000 feet.[16] Cranswick was on his way to safely completing his eighty-eighth mission.

Cranswick's crew were the lucky ones. An estimated 230 German night fighters had risen up from bases across northern Europe to meet the British bombers. Around 150 Wild Boars were defending Berlin. For once, the weather over central Germany was reasonably clear, providing clear sightlines for the 5,000 or so young British and German airmen who were currently flying and fighting for their lives in the chaos above the capital.

In the melee, the master bomber was doing his best to keep the operation on track. Johnny Fauquier was a no-nonsense 34-year-old Canadian. He had commanded 405 Squadron – an all-Canadian squadron – since the previous spring, overseeing its successful transformation into one of Bennett's key Pathfinder squadrons. Now, as he orbited the raid in his Lancaster, he did his best to encourage the main force to bomb as accurately on the Pathfinders' markers as they could. 'Come on in fellows. The flak is nowhere near as bad as it looks,' he was heard to say over the radio, as if inviting them in for a dip in the chilly sea on a bank holiday. But there's no doubt a calm voice cutting through the havoc helped calm jittery nerves.[17]

Fifteen minutes after Cranswick had completed his bombing run, his squadron mate John Christie approached the target. Surrounded by the horseshoe-shaped glass canopy of the cockpit, the Norwegian pilot was presented with a fantastic, terrifying and awesome sight. He and his crew – on their twelfth Pathfinder operation – were now just 30 miles from the target, and he could see searchlights and flak ahead which 'looked worse than any other target I had ever seen,' Christie later wrote in his diary. 'Aircraft were falling left and right as we were running up . . . the whole place was light as daylight. One could hardly believe it was possible to get through and live.' Yellow balls of flak exploded all around and 'there were fighters everywhere and of course we could see hundreds of bombers in all directions.'

Dropping their load at one minute to midnight, Christie swung the big aircraft north and headed home. As he did so, he couldn't help noticing other bombers being picked off by German fighters. 'Every time they hit the ground they would cause a colossal explosion and a terrific fire lit up the area for miles around. I'm sure the German fighters used the lights from these burning aircraft to find and kill other victims.'

The German single-engine fighters were also using the blinding white fingers of the 200 searchlights to help identify their prey. 'The flak searchlights were splendid,' said one German pilot. 'When they caught a bomber they didn't let it go but offered it up for sacrifice.'[18] Many fighters got so close before they opened up with machine gun or cannon fire that their windscreens were splattered in oil and debris from the British bombers' fuselages. They nicknamed it 'Tommy oil'.

British crews feared being coned because it was so damned difficult to break free once the fingers of light had gripped their victim. A Pathfinder pilot watched in horror and fascination as a Lancaster nearby was caught by a bright-blue searchlight, before six or seven lights homed in on it, forming a cone of light. At the top of the cone 'a tiny speck, like a small moth', could be seen twisting and turning in a desperate attempt to escape. Flak streamed up the centre of the cone and the apex became a spatter of exploding shells. A red glow appeared, followed by a blinding red and orange flash. 'Flaming debris dribbled down the cone like melting red sealing wax. It happened in about two minutes. Seven men had died.'[19]

With flares and searchlights illuminating the sky, the German fighters were having a field day. But for them too it was an unbelievably dangerous place to fly. One young Luftwaffe airman recounted, 'the ghostly brilliant glare of Berlin's searchlights, exploding Flak shells in between, way up beyond our level. An ocean of Flak bursts! Coloured cascades dropped from the sky, yellow, green, red, the well-known ground markers! And the high explosives and incendiary bombs raged. But up here, in the brightness over the city, hell was let loose.'[20]

Another German pilot later recalled the scene:

Berlin was getting it! On the ground the big city was ablaze, first the detonations of the high-explosive bombs and then the phosphorus incendiaries amongst the lacerated houses. It was an unparalleled inferno. Hundreds of searchlights loomed towards us and moved across the sky like the fingers of corpses and ghostly hands, dazzling friend and foe alike. Many times I saw 30–40 aircraft all at once, cruising around. Everywhere were tracers, target indicators of all colours, night fighters' recognition flares when the flak opened up on one of them. Vast clouds of smoke that rose into the sky, luridly lit from within ... white vapour trails everywhere; and down below, the dreadful explosions . . . I had the impression everyone was shooting at everyone else. Me in the middle of it all – it was Hell – Dante's *Inferno*.[21]

A few minutes earlier, Hans-Joachim 'Hajo' Herrmann – an energetic and intelligent 30-year-old Luftwaffe bomber pilot – had jumped in his Focke-Wulf Fw 190 fighter and taken to the air. Although new to fighters, Herrmann was one of the most experienced German airforce pilots and a key figure in pioneering the new Wild Boar tactics now being used to try and stop the British bombers. He knew the bombers were coming and scanned the skies looking for the tell-tale target markers dropped by what he called the 'artful Pathfinders'.[22]

A few days before, the blond-haired, blue-eyed major had been one of those fighter pilots deceived by the Mosquito marking over Berlin as the rest of the British force headed to bomb Peenemünde. He was determined not to be spoofed again, and orbited in his fighter, watching and waiting. 'All we could do was rely on our sixth sense ... it was a matter of stalking them, of sensing them, of cunning and of feel,' he wrote later.

Herrmann heard over the radio the controllers tracking the bomber stream ... first Hanover, then Brunswick ... Despite his experience, he was nervous. He felt a knot in his stomach. His tongue was dry. And then he saw the city. 'The searchlights reached up to the sky and formed cones. Already one or two aircraft were glittering where they intersected. Damn! Two, three, four British bombers were heading from Potsdam in the direction of the city.'[23] Herrmann pulled his seatbelt tighter and reported over the radio 'Wild Boar 1 over Berlin.' 'To hell with radio silence,' he thought. 'Now it is a confrontation, eyeball to eyeball.'[24]

He dived towards the bomber stream and closed in on a single bomber trapped in the cone of searchlights, not letting himself be distracted by the exploding flak, swinging searchlights and tracer fire from other night fighters. Herrmann fired at the bomber from a range of 300 metres but missed. Just as he was about to fire again the bomber vanished into the darkness, released from the searchlights. 'I groaned with anger behind my oxygen mask,' he said. By now his radio was full of noise. Curses from the German crews were being flung about – against each other; against the flak or searchlights inadvertently targeting the fighters; against the enemy that refused to die or shot back; against their own stupidity and bad luck.

Moments later, Herrmann locked on to 'the next plump visitor', ignoring the cotton-wool puffs of bursting flak which he could smell through his oxygen mask. Lining up the Lancaster in his sights, he pressed the button and heard the dull hammering of his cannon fire. His aircraft vibrated, giving him 'a warm cleansing feeling of self-fulfilment'.[25] Herrmann's heart jumped as he saw the cannon fire rip into the bomber, which veered into a steep, flaming dive. As it did so, he spotted the hunched figure of the gunner in the Lancaster's rear turret, and at the same time the muzzles of its four guns briefly flashed. Surely destined to die in the next few seconds, the plucky rear gunner had perhaps had the last laugh. In an instant, Herrmann heard the rattle of bullets against his own aircraft. His engine cut and acrid fumes poured into the cockpit. He ripped his oxygen mask and head-set off, released the seatbelt and pressed the canopy release. Pushing the control column to the side so the plane rolled onto its back, he wriggled out and floated away from the Focke-Wulf, and found himself spinning through the 'metal-rich' airspace. He yanked the ripcord on his chest and, with a sharp jerk, the white silk canopy bloomed like a rose above his head. He had lived to fight another day.

*

Allan Ball's plane arrived over Berlin eight minutes ahead of schedule, and after orbiting around the city to ensure they dropped their markers on time, they began their run in to the target. The pilot battled with the control stick as exploding flak shook the airframe of the Halifax. This reception from the Germans was far hotter than on any operation Ball had been on – even over the Ruhr. Then it was 'bombs away' and time to escape. Ball couldn't resist peering out of the small observation blister for a quick peek at the mayhem outside.

Ball knew nothing of the first volley of cannon fire as it smashed through the airframe and into his skull, flinging him back against the side of the fuselage. Almost instantly there was another blinding flash and an explosion. Ball's torso quivered as hot metal tore through his head, chest, arms and legs, leaving him crumpled on the floor of the plane. He vaguely heard voices on the intercom shout, 'Fighters . . . our two starboard engines are on fire . . . abandon aircraft!' as the Halifax spun out of control. Bleeding and in pain, Ball somehow managed to crawl towards the middle of the fuselage to check on his crewmates before jumping. But when he tried to pull the emergency toggle on the escape hatch, the centrifugal force of the spinning plane was forcing it shut. Ball gave up. *Not long now. This is how it happens*, he thought. But Albert Arter, the young pilot, was having none of it. Badly wounded and seconds from death, he grappled with the controls to momentarily level out the plane, knowing it would give his crewmates the best chance of getting out. Ball had one more go at the door, which to his surprise just fell away. The icy night air swept into the smoking fuselage and Ball leant forward and dropped through the hole into the sky.

He took fourteen minutes to float down to earth. It was a terrifying experience for the 21-year-old. He watched as the Halifax from which he'd just leapt screamed into a dive, still tracked by the brilliant-white grip of the searchlights' cone. Looking down he could see Berlin burning between his swinging feet, while all around flak burst in ear-splitting crumps. In the last 2,000 feet he was illuminated by a searchlight, before quite suddenly he slammed into the ground in blessed darkness.

Ball's parachute had been taken by the wind and he floated down to the north-east of the city, where he crashed into a small copse. He was bleeding heavily from his wounds. His uniform was in tatters. But he had a choice. He could either bleed to death or fight on. Thinking of Brenda back home, he staggered to his feet and began to rip up the parachute silk. He made a sling for his left arm, bandaged his right leg, and stuffed a wad of silk into his gaping chest wound. It was almost impossible to dig a hole in the hard summer soil, so after putting some more parachute silk in his pocket and burying the rest as best he could, he waited for the all-clear to sound and limped out of the wood.

His plan was crude. Get to the Baltic coast and somehow board a boat to Sweden. He looked up at the North Star, which he could just make out through the orange haze as Berlin burnt. That was his guide. He started walking along a road, his right leg dragging behind. A lorry full of soldiers trundled by. Ball leapt into a ditch and froze. They were probably searching for him after seeing the plane go down. The truck drove on. He climbed from the ditch and continued walking north. He thought he'd lost the sight from his left eye, which was sticky and painful. Without a mirror he couldn't see that in fact a bullet or fragment of metal had pierced the left-hand side of his skull, travelled through the eyebrow and exited at the bridge of his nose. The 'blindness' was caused by overhanging skin, blocking his vision. When he put his hand to his face and realised, he used some of the parachute silk to make a head bandage, relieved to discover he could still see from both eyes.

By now he was weak through loss of blood. When the lorry looking for him passed yet again, Ball didn't hide. He needed help and decided to surrender, praying he'd not be lynched or beaten up. To their credit, when they saw how badly injured he was the German soldiers took him to hospital. But the first two medics refused to treat him, claiming his wounds were too serious. Finally, at a third hospital, he was stripped and taken straight into theatre. Someone produced a needle and plunged it into his arm. Then everything went black.

Allan Ball had 21 holes in him. A human colander. Yet he was still alive thanks to the skills of a German medical team in the heart of Berlin in the middle of a British air raid. When he woke from the operation the following morning, his arms and legs were strapped to an iron bed. He was guarded by a German soldier armed with a sub-machine gun – not that Ball was in any shape to leap out and make a dramatic escape. The surgeon spoke French, as did Ball, who was informed he'd been strapped to the bed after thrashing about so much in the night, probably reliving his ordeal. He was still very unwell, and stayed in the same room for two weeks. One night during that time, the RAF bombed Berlin again. Despite everything he'd just been through, Ball later described being on the end of that RAF bombing raid as the most frightening experience of his life. 'To listen to an aircraft coming down and then exploding on impact one mile away is impossible to describe,' he said. Ball was moved to a French POW hospital in the south of Berlin for his own safety following a third RAF raid. He was spat at by Berliners as the open-topped truck made its way through the city. Finally, 12 weeks later, he was taken to Stalag Luft III – the POW camp later made famous by *The Great Escape*.

On the morning of Friday, 15 October 1943, the post dropped through the letter box at Sunnyside in Hertfordshire. Amongst the usual letters and bills was a postcard for Miss Brenda Bridger. Brenda picked the card up. It was stamped 'Par Avion' and 'Mit Luftpost'. Her heart skipped a beat as she turned the card over and began to read. It was Allan's handwriting.

> Darling – Just got this post-card, after four weeks. I am feeling very fit at the moment, only longing to see you. I'm walking about, no hair on my head, just a wizard moustache. Please write every day if poss. Remember me to all your family. Hope to be with them all soon. Anyone can write as much as they like. Hope you've heard from Larry. I was hit by flack. I have 21 holes in me, a 3" scar on my left eye, also had a piece in my brain 1½". Left arm paralysed – soon be OK – otherwise I'm OK. All my love darling, Allan.

Later that day, Brenda wrote in her diary: 'What a day! Allan is safe – I have got a card from him. I thank God with all my heart for taking care of him.' A few days later, Ball followed up his initial card with a more heartfelt note: 'I love you with all my heart forever. I'll never leave you sweetheart, and I promise you when I come back I will never leave your side for a minute. I just want to sit and look at you, hold you in my arms and make love to you for <u>ever</u>.' Ball hoped that because of his injuries he might be repatriated before long, and he reassured

Brenda, 'we'll get married as soon as we can, and then all our worries will be finished.'

Despite his ordeal, Ball was one of the lucky ones from the 23 August raid on Berlin. The Pathfinders had been hit hard. 35 Squadron lost four aircraft – including the station commander at Graveley, who had decided to fly to inspire his men – almost a fifth of the squadron's total strength that night. 8 Group, meanwhile, saw 10 per cent of its total force obliterated, the worst raid of the war so far, with 48 Pathfinder aircrew killed, including a number of senior crews. Crucially, nine marker aircraft were shot down – valuable experience comprising years of training and operations, wiped out in a few violent hours.

Overall, Bomber Command lost 7.9 per cent of its heavy-bomber force – equating to 56 planes – its greatest single-night loss of aircraft in four years of war. Many had been pounced upon by German fighters after their bombing runs, as they wheeled away from Berlin to the north back across Germany. It was not all one-way traffic – nine German night fighters were lost, with at least two the victims of friendly fire.

The raid itself hadn't provided the opening blow Harris hoped for, as the majority of the bombs fell on the suburbs to the south and west and not the more vulnerable heart of Berlin. The Pathfinders' marking was not as accurate as planned and many main-force crews dumped their load on the first markers they set eyes on, rather than on the centre of the markers as ordered. But given the hot reception, who could blame them? Nevertheless, more than 850 Berliners were killed, many taken by surprise at the size of the raid. Until now, the raids over Berlin hadn't had a huge impact. It was a city far less damaged than London, for example. Goebbels was furious that more of those who perished hadn't taken shelter.

And it wouldn't get any easier for anyone. After all, this operation had been flown on a clear August night. As the Battle of Berlin gathered pace and the airmen returned again and again to the Big City, the Pathfinders would soon discover that despite their best efforts, the appalling winter weather, fierce defences and the sprawling size of Berlin would make the accurate marking of targets almost impossible. The biggest test of Don Bennett's men in the war so far had just begun.

CHAPTER NINETEEN

The Berlin Method

'WAKE UP, WAKE UP!' George Bennett whispered excitedly to his wife Celia in the bedroom of their Brisbane home at the beginning of another hot Australian midsummer's morning. 'Your son's been promoted again!' The news that Don Bennett was now an Air Vice-Marshal – aged just 33 – reached his proud parents via a local newspaper story in January 1944.[1] It was testament to his hard work and success that he had achieved with the Pathfinders in their eighteen-month existence. But 12,000 miles away in the depths of winter, their son was continuing to be absorbed by the increasingly grim battle over Berlin.

Following a break in September and October, in November 1943, Bert Harris had begun what was to become the main thrust of the Battle of Berlin over the next five months, with a series of new raids on Berlin and its neighbouring districts. In the early hours of 19 November, a force of over 400 Lancasters – spearheaded by the Pathfinders – attacked Berlin in an operation lasting just 16 minutes. Twenty-seven planes per minute rumbled over the streets of Germany's capital – more than double the rate achieved by Bomber Command in the thousand-bomber raids during the summer of 1942. It showed just what impact Bennett's men had made in squeezing the bomber stream up to intensify the bombing raids.

Three days later, on 22 November, Harris ordered a 'maximum effort' operation against the city. Practically every serviceable front-line aircraft in Bomber Command was called to action – an armada of over 750 machines. This was a huge gamble by Harris, given it would be months before he could assemble such a large force again. But his obsession with flattening Berlin made it, to him at least, a risk worth taking.

In attempting to tackle the specific challenge of the perpetual thick cloud over Berlin, and the difficulty in accurately forecasting the weather for a target so deep into Germany, Bennett had devised a new marking tactic called the 'Berlin Method'. Essentially a combination of the Parramatta and Wanganui techniques, Pathfinder crews dropped both sky markers and ground target indicators – whatever the weather – which were 'refreshed' throughout the raid by more target markers placed by Pathfinders using their own H2S radar sets. If the markers on the ground were obscured by cloud, main-force crews bombed the sky markers. A handful of Pathfinder aircraft were fitted with a new generation H2S set called the 'Mark III', a more accurate version of its older brother. Using this apparatus, 'special blind marker' Pathfinder crews would drop yellow flares on the aiming point for the rest of the Pathfinder planes and then the main force to follow. The pressure on these few crews was immense – over 5,000 airmen flying over the most fortified city in the world were relying on their ability to drop their markers accurately.

It worked. Over the course of 22 minutes on 22 November, 34 aircraft a minute dumped a total of 2,500 tons of bombs.[2] Down in the streets below, Berliners looked up and knew what was coming as the black clouds were transformed into a mesmerising, flickering sea of yellows, greens and reds by the falling target markers. Fifteen-year-old Gerda Kernchen had arrived home from her job sewing uniforms for Luftwaffe airmen. She lived with her parents and her nine-year-old sister Rena in a small cottage in Wittenau, on the north-west edge of Berlin. Whenever a raid was imminent, Gerda's neighbours – who had a radio they would tune into for the latest news – ran outside and banged their pots and pans. 'When the alarm sounded, you could already see the Christmas trees, the coloured flares being dropped by the Pathfinders to mark the target for the bombers. A bundle of flares would fall out of the aircraft and spread out into a cone shape as they fell, forming the shape of a Christmas tree, so that's what we called them. You could see the searchlights streaming up from the ground, searching for the aircraft. The city was surrounded by a ring of white light,' remembered Gerda.

The family rushed down to the root cellar under the house which they used as a shelter, just as bombs started dropping. 'We were in our cellar, and we heard a tremendous crash and the whole house shook. The biggest bomb, called an air mine, or blockbuster, had landed in our neighbourhood. The earth was soft peat, so most of the houses just moved on their foundations, but the houses closer to the blast were destroyed. When we left our cellar, we went to see where the bomb had landed. Then we saw one of the neighbours. He was dead. It was a really frightening sight, because the percussion had mutilated him, and his eyes were hanging out of his head.'[3]

Despite the brutal reality for those on the ground, the raid was a triumph. Bert Harris was buoyant. The RAF had scored their first really successful operation in the Battle of Berlin. Perhaps his strategy of bombing Berlin into submission would be successful?

And yet.

As the weeks dragged on, the reality of the massive task began to dawn on the crews. For every successful operation to the Big City, others failed to hit their mark. In 16 major raids on Berlin between November 1943 and March 1944, the city was only spotted by crews on two occasions. For most of the time all they saw below from their planes was thick soupy cloud. Technically it should not have mattered whether they could see the target. That, of course, was one of the key reasons for the Pathfinders. They had the very latest navigational technology, operated by some of the finest navigators Bomber Command could offer, working out complex calculations under combat conditions – when the brain was sluggish at high altitude and fuelled by bottled oxygen – to ensure they arrived as near as possible to the agreed time over the target. And indeed, time and time again, the Pathfinder aircraft arrived over Berlin and dropped their markers within a minute or less of their briefed time – a truly remarkable effort given they had flown almost 600 miles in the dark, buffeted by up to 100mph winds, thick cloud and driving rain, with every German flying over Europe trying to shoot them down.

But as the Pathfinders dropped their sky markers, they would watch them simply disappear into the cloud and smoke towering

18,000 feet above Berlin – or simply drift away from the target, carried by strong winds. This meant the crews of the main-force bombers were left groping about for an aiming point, or bombed on the very first target marker they saw rather than the centre of a cluster. This was made all the harder because – with justification – most Pathfinder crews refused to drop their markers unless they were convinced they were correctly over the target. Bennett would rather they came back with them unused than dump them on the wrong aiming point.

The new H2S Mark III radar, meanwhile, was not easy to operate and was prone to packing up completely mid-flight, forcing crews to rely on more traditional methods of navigation to locate the target.

'Any navigator who was rash enough to try and find out where he was by looking out of the window, would almost inevitably get hopelessly lost,' reckoned one veteran Pathfinder. There was another apocryphal tale of a navigator who, after several trips to the Big City, was persuaded to come out from underneath his blackout curtain and have a look at the action. Very cautiously, he pulled the curtain aside, peeped out at the scene below, exclaimed 'My God', hastily pulled the curtain to, and never looked out again.[4]

He could hardly be blamed. As the Battle of Berlin progressed, German night fighters had been advancing from their Wild Boar night-fighting tactics by adopting a new approach they christened *Zahme Sau*, or Tame Boar – an almost laughably misleading description given its devastating impact on Bomber Command. In short, it used legions of twin-engine night fighters to hunt down the bombers as they made their way to and from the target. This had only been made possible thanks to German boffins building their own clever high-tech antidote to Window – an airborne radar called SN-2 which could not be jammed by the millions of tiny foil strips. German scientists also developed a device called Kiel, which used infrared to home in on the heat emitted by a bomber's exhaust from as much as four miles away. It was perfect for individual interceptions and easy to use, although a full moon and burning ground targets sometimes impacted its effectiveness.[5]

Thankfully for the British, only a tiny number were made, so the German fighters mainly used SN-2 and their H2S-hunting Naxos radars to home in on the bomber streams rather than individual planes, which they knew they had found when their own planes were jolted by the slipstream from the giant sky-convoy. The bomber stream was then lit up by German fighters dropping flares from above, so their colleagues could visually attack single bombers, making up for the loss of illumination from the searchlights on the ground which were obscured by the thick cloud. The irony is that Bomber Command had spent three years trying to find a way to light up the dark and now they couldn't wait to escape back into it.

Many bombers were shot down by German night fighters armed with the upward-firing *Schräge Musik* cannon. None of Bomber Command's airmen – including the Pathfinders – were aware of *Schräge Musik* at the time. When they saw aircraft blow up in mid-air, some crews were convinced that they'd seen 'anti-morale' shells or missiles fired from the ground designed to give the impression that a Pathfinder aircraft had been hit. Others named them 'scarecrows'. Both were myths. Ironically, what they saw as the sky was lit up in a giant ball of orange most likely *was* a bomber 'brewing up' after taking a direct hit from a fighter. It was obvious when a Pathfinder plane blew up or crashed on the way to the target, because of the spray of colours fizzing out from unused target indicators. Main-force crews nicknamed them 'pretties' because of the colourful sight they made tumbling to the ground.[6]

While the heavy bombers were armed with .303 machine guns, even Harris later admitted these were about as much use against a modern fighter as using 'a pea-shooter against an elephant'.[7] But there is no doubt they acted as a deterrent, ensuring the fighter only attempted the briefest of attacks. The only real evasion once a fighter attacked was for the bomber pilot to plunge the bomber into the dramatic manoeuvre called the corkscrew. This required him to push the control column forward so the aircraft went into a steep, screaming dive, before pulling back again to climb, while simultaneously banking the aircraft from port to starboard – hence the name – in the hope it would shake off the chasing fighter. These aerobatics could last for up to fifteen minutes, with the pilot and flight engineer grappling with the controls as the rest of the crew grimly hung on for dear life.

In December 1943, on his first operation with 35 Squadron, to Leipzig – a city 90 miles south-west of Berlin – a Pathfinder bomb aimer was lying in the nose looking down at the twinkling green target indicators on which he had just dropped their bombs, when all hell was let loose by a shout of 'Corkscrew!' from the gunner over the intercom.

'We went into the most frightful heaves and pressures imaginable,' he later wrote.

> As we reached the top, down would go the port wing and the nose and the kite would drop away from me, leave me 'sticking' to the roof, and as we came to the bottom I would get my own weight back with a vengeance plus about three times its usual quantity into the bargain, and we would sweep up, up, up again; then over and down, down, down and round the corner with a groan and up, up, up to the stars with the kite hanging on the props. It may have been justifiable seeing as how the kite just behind got blown to bits by a fighter, but, heavens, my poor stomach!

He duly vomited in the nose of the Halifax – not a pleasant experience wearing an oxygen mask at 20,000 feet – before gingerly making his way back to his seat in front of the H2S set.

> When I had finished cleaning up in the nose, I crept back. I wanted to vomit. Oh I wanted to lie down! I wanted to rip off my oxygen mask! I was hot to the point of sweating! Above all I wanted to get out! Sitting down in my seat I leaned forward with my head resting on the instrument in front of me. I loosened my mask and gulped the cold air as my stomach threatened to come up my throat. I wanted badly to lie down or to stretch out but there wasn't room for that. I crushed back the desire to vomit successfully enough but if I had been warm before I was utterly freezing now. The wind whistled up through the crack in the floor and I began to shiver. I stood up in the cramped space and banged my head on the roof. I tried to start my instrument for something to do but it would not work. I sat down again and hugged the hot air pipe to my shivering body. Then I noticed I could not feel my feet. I put them on the hot air pipe. I stamped them up and down. My teeth

chattered, my hands shook and my whole body quivered. I was genuinely miserable.[8]

Despite its constant slog, the Battle of Berlin had its more lighthearted moments. Ernie Holmes began operating with 35 Squadron after volunteering his crew for the Pathfinders in the autumn of 1943. The crew were given a baptism of fire over Kassel in their first Pathfinder operation, and were forged into a close, happy team. One night, returning from an operation to Berlin, Holmes battled with the controls of the Halifax bomber in filthy weather. 'I'd never known anything like it. I had to fight the Halifax all the way. The weather was so bad,' he recalled. A voice suddenly piped up over the intercom: 'Ah shit!' Then the navigator started laughing and said: 'Old Derek's brought his ring up!' – a euphemism for being sick. 'So what! So have I,' another voice chipped in. 'So have I,' piped a third. 'Silence! Back to work!' said Holmes, keen to ensure his crew remained alert to enemy fighters. And then, one final voice came over the radio: 'It's alright for you buggers. Not only did I bring my ring up, but I brought my teeth up and I stood on them.'

'What a motley bloody crew I've got, bringing your rings up,' muttered Holmes. 'Well it's alright for you, you knew what you were doing. We didn't,' one replied. When they landed back at Graveley, Holmes taxied the bomber to the dispersal point, and one by one the men got off the aircraft. 'I switched off and came down and when I tried to walk I had difficulty with my legs,' remembered Holmes. 'As I jumped out of the aircraft onto the ground, my legs collapsed and I was sick as a dog.' Holmes's crew had the last laugh. 'What a bloody skipper we've got,' they joked, before checking their captain was OK.[9]

With the emergence of the Tame Boars, the four-hour journey back from Berlin was as dangerous as any other part of the operation. Even more so in some ways, because human instinct meant that once the bombs had been dropped and the initial drama of being over the target had receded, as they neared the North Sea, crews tended to drop their guard and relax a little. One estimate suggested losses were at times as high as two to one on the return leg.[10] The Tame Boars tracked the bombers on their route home before striking by attacking from underneath and breaking away. The German pilots called it the *Verfolgungsnachtjagd* –'Chase'.[11]

One night, Holmes and his crew were returning from an operation when suddenly there was an almighty thump, causing the Halifax to jolt. Holmes reckoned it was a German night fighter that had flashed past a few feet away – causing turbulence – the pilot, homing in on the bomber's H2S transmissions, having misjudged his final attack. 'Our closing speeds must have been 400mph,' said Holmes, who ordered the navigator to switch off the radar and they duly lost the German fighter.

Flak too remained a big menace for bombers trying to get home in one piece. Although crews were warned in preflight briefings which areas to avoid to bypass the heaviest flak, crosswinds and bad weather often meant planes blew off course and found themselves on the receiving end of a fierce barrage. One Pathfinder wireless operator was looking out of the astrodome in the top of a Lancaster when shells suddenly exploded all around, forcing the pilot into a dive. 'You could see all the bursts following us down,' he recalled. 'You know the feeling when you're the last one to go to bed? You go up the stairs thinking some bugger's behind you and that. When you're a kid . . . that's the feeling I got . . . that a split-second earlier they would have hit us.'[12] Being caught in searchlights and coned necessitated the same quick manoeuvre, although it didn't stop one wit suggesting that if the pilot flew the plane anticlockwise in tight circles instead, they would be closely followed by the Germans until all the bulbs in the enemy searchlights unscrewed.

Equally, return journeys could be without incident. With bombers lighter after shedding their load, if the plane hadn't been damaged and no one was injured, a flask of coffee might appear, and perhaps some chocolate bars and tinned orange juice, which tasted heavenly after chewing on a wad of tasteless gum for hours. Sealed off in their rear turrets, many rear gunners especially enjoyed smoking a blessed cigarette once the aircraft was low enough for their oxygen mask to be removed.

In these quieter moments, if he was really desperate to answer a call of nature, an airman might clamber to the Elsan loo at the rear of the fuselage carrying a portable oxygen bottle. There was an occupational hazard involved in doing so – if the pilot had to take evasive action, the Elsan's contents could end up swirling around the floor, sides and even the ceiling of the plane. To save themselves a laborious scramble down the aircraft, some crews grabbed empty jam jars from their station mess and kept them somewhere close by in case they had the urge on the long trips to Berlin.

Ernie Holmes was supplied with a specially made 'pee bag' – like a large condom with a spring-loaded aluminium cup – which involved a somewhat protracted effort to use, given the cramped confines of the flight deck and myriad layers of clothing, straps and buttons. In the Halifax, where the pilot sat above the wireless operator, it also meant added dangers. 'Is it raining outside?' the wireless operator asked Holmes over the intercom during one operation, noticing liquid dripping down onto his wireless set and assuming the cockpit window was open. Ever the fastidious Pathfinder, on this occasion Holmes had totally misjudged his aiming point and soaked his crewmate in the process. 'I don't think he ever forgave me,' he said.[13]

Often, after the drama of the bombing run, for many minutes on end nothing was heard on the return journey but the drone of the four engines. Each man would be occupied by his own thoughts – only for the peace to be instantly dissolved by the sudden rhythmic monologue of a clattering machine gun, as a fighter attacked and the bomber was plunged into a wild corkscrew. Despite such evasive moves and the habit of heavies 'weaving' from side to side to throw off flak, and although hundreds of bombers were packed together flying just a few hundred feet apart in streams – each with no more than about one cubic mile of airspace for wiggle room – collisions between heavy bombers were remarkably rare. The track of each bomber stream was planned in advance by group commanders, with each aircraft being given heights to fly. Crews used the onboard 'Gee' technology for the last 350 miles home to keep on this track.

Typically, the aircraft flew within three miles of the agreed 'track', spread in vertical heights of up to 4,000 feet, with an average of 300 planes per operation stretching out for up to 150 miles. The theory was that the closer they were, the safer they were from being picked off by German fighters. 'Don't be proud, stay with the crowd,' proclaimed the posters back on the bomber bases.[14] On the route home the stream tended to be more strung out after the drama of the bombing run, especially once they had flown clear of mainland Europe when the group planes began to disperse to land at their individual airfields. Yet one estimate suggested mid-air prangs destroyed just 42 aircraft in 60,000 sorties – a loss rate of 0.07 percent.[15]

But when collisions happened it made a lasting impression, and not just on those directly involved. Flying back from an operation one night, a rear gunner with 156 Squadron idly watched as two Lancasters flying very slightly below gently flew nearer and nearer each other. He was about to rotate his bin-sized, hydraulically powered turret away to continue his search for enemy fighters, when it dawned on him that the gap between the bombers was still narrowing and they weren't going to stop. 'Suddenly, I realised the truth, and shouted out a useless warning,' he wrote later. The two planes erupted together in one huge fountain of flame and debris, sending up shockwaves which almost turned the gunner's own aircraft on its back.

He banged his gloved fist on the gun mounting in sheer impotence. 'Why? Why?' he asked out loud, with only the continued roar of his own engines to answer him. 'Later, in that brief moment before exhaustion closed my mind in sleep, I watched again those two aircraft closing below, mentally to sound my useless warning, sickened and disgusted at the waste of war.'[16]

The reality is that the Pathfinders were only really safe once they had landed, which during the Battle of Berlin was often not until the blueish tinge of dawn appeared in the sky.

Even using navigation devices like H2S and Gee, actually getting back to base was still a tremendous challenge. Each airfield had its own radio beacon, which the crew focused on finding. Rather like today's system in civil airports, up to 15 bombers were 'stacked' in the skies in 500-foot height slots, circling around their home airfield before a WAAF or ground crewman spoke to each plane over the radio and – depending on how much fuel they had or how badly damaged the aircraft was – guided them down and ordered them to land on the runway lit with flares. To help the pilot in the final approach, he listened through headphones to an onboard radio aid which communicated with a beacon and sent out dots and dashes until a steady note was heard, meaning the aircraft was on track to land safely. Some runways also had an angle-of-glide indicator which shone amber or red lights if the plane was too high or low on its descent, and green if it was on the correct glide path. Even with such aids, bringing in 10 tons plus of Lancaster at 100mph in grim weather took great skill and bottle, especially when the pilot was tired or injured, fuel was running low and the plane was battle-damaged. Given such pressure, it is remarkable that Pathfinders often landed within a minute or two of their planned return times, after they'd been on eight, nine or even ten-hour missions to Berlin.

Low cloud or fog was a major headache, however, occasionally leading to more bomber-crew fatalities than German flak and fighters. Sometimes, it could even spell tragedy for men who thought they were finally safe and sound on British soil. Gwen Thomas was on duty at RAF Upwood in Cambridgeshire one foggy winter's evening as a Mosquito was attempting to land. After trying once, the pilot circled in the thick fog. 'He said: "We'll have one more go" and this time he crashed into a house. And in the house were five members of 156 Squadron who had just finished their last op and were going home on leave the next day,' recalled Thomas.[17]

Churchill himself attached 'great importance' to remedying the problem. In 1943, a team of scientists, engineers and meteorological experts was established to find a solution. Earl's Court ice rink in west London was requisitioned so the ice-making machinery could be used to make synthetic fog. Once the boffins thought they had a viable solution they needed an airman experienced – and brave – enough to test it. Step forward Don Bennett. Throughout 1943, Bennett conducted a series of experiments in foggy weather at the Pathfinders' airfield in Graveley, landing various aircraft, including a Lancaster, in an avenue of raging fires created by new technology called FIDO – which stood for 'Fog Investigation and Dispersal Operation'.

The system was simple but ingenious. Continuous lines of oil burners connected by a long pipe were laid either side of a runway. Petrol pumped through the pipe ignited the burners and the intense heat given off evaporated the water droplets causing the fog. (It also leaked, providing valuable fuel for airfield motorcars.) The equipment could create a clear space of 3,000 feet long and 150 feet wide to a height of

100 feet. While the surrounding area remained thick with fog, the pall of smoke and the ground glow helped crews locate the airfield, and the pilots then enjoyed a clear, fog-free run in.

FIDO was expensive to operate and not easy to land in. But it saved many lives. It didn't provide total immunisation against bad weather, however. This was brutally exposed after a raid on Berlin in the early hours of 17 December 1943 when 148 airmen were killed after 29 planes crashed in low cloud and fog which blanketed eastern England. With their fuel gauges nearing zero, some crews simply abandoned their giant lumbering bomber in the sky and bailed out, hoping it wouldn't wipe out a village when it finally crashed. Most who chose this option parachuted safely down to earth. Other crews took their chances and decided to try and land. For many, it was their biggest and last mistake.

Over the next hour, 8 Group was smashed to bits, leaving the bloody detritus of Don Bennett's finest crews scattered across the flat fenland of Pathfinder country. Forty-nine Pathfinder airmen lost their lives in accidents, joining a further 41 killed in action on the operation itself. The enemy and weather had combined to make it the deadliest night for the Pathfinders in the whole of the war. Little wonder it was named 'Black Thursday'. The heaviest hit was 97 Squadron, which lost 36 men. At its home on Bourn airfield in Cambridgeshire, the station sickbay was said to be 'overflowing with bodies'.[18] Two highly decorated squadron leaders with irreplaceable experience were amongst the dead. Over the space of around four hours the squadron had recorded about one-sixth of its total losses for the whole of 1943.[19] Its record book, written early the following morning, simply observed, 'the squadron had a disastrous night'.[20]

While the young airmen were being hammered by the Battle of Berlin, whether through enemy action or bad weather, the pressure was also mounting on the ground crews. Returned bombers damaged by flak and fighter cannon fire needed to be repaired. Engines had to be serviced. In one typical month during the Battle of Berlin, each Lancaster in the Pathfinders flew an average of five sorties, equating to about 50 hours flying time, yet there were only 15 technical failures for the entire month.[21] The seemingly menial work carried out on the barren, oil-stained concrete dispersal pans dotted around the windswept airfields in East Anglia had a massive impact on events over Berlin a few hours later.

The order that bombs and markers were loaded onto a Pathfinder aircraft was crucial. One mistake – one wrong-coloured flare in the wrong place – could spell disaster as the raid unfolded 600 miles away. The 'chop rate' for the armourers who loaded the ammunition and armed the bombs before the aircraft took off was second only to that of the aircrew. This rate increased in the Battle of Berlin as the stakes rose and the operations intensified, with more aircraft, more bombs and fuel more needed to be loaded in less time. One small miscalculation in handling a bomb could be deadly.

One afternoon before a raid to Berlin, Dick Raymond had just finished the preflight checks on his 83 Squadron Lancaster and strolled back to the ground crew Nissen hut for a cup of tea, when there was an almighty explosion and he found himself 'under a pile of rubbish'. Nothing was left of Raymond's plane but a pile of burning debris. The explosion killed three of Raymond's crew and twelve ground staff, including a WAAF lorry driver who had been dropping airmen off at their dispersals. 'It was caused by an armourer working on the photo-flash bomb, which accidently went off and detonated the other bombs. Poor chap never knew what hit him. Our navigator's body was never recovered. The plane was fully laden, fully fuelled, fully everything,' added Raymond, who was sent to an RAF hospital in Ely with head and leg injuries.

After a few days, Raymond was allowed a wheelchair but forbidden from leaving the hospital. But the 19-year-old had other ideas. 'The boys used to sneak me down in the lift. We'd chuck the wheelchair in some bushes and go into Ely. I had to wear this awful hospital blue which was like bloody pyjamas, but of course the publicans knew who we were and they opened the back doors for us.'[22] When Raymond was discharged from hospital a few weeks later and returned to Wyton, he found he was the only survivor from his original crew after the remaining members were all killed on ops with other crews. He was back in the air with a new crew that night.

As the Battle of Berlin moved into 1944, Harris turned the screw, ordering his Lancaster bombers to carry more bombs to pound Berlin. As a result, some main-force crews simply dumped their heaviest

4,000lb 'cookies' in the North Sea to increase their aircraft's manoeuverability over the target – and frankly, who could blame them? Night after night they were risking life and limb to drop their bombs through a sea of cloud – it's not like they could even appreciate the fruits of their bloody labour.

For every strong operation on Berlin, others failed to hit their mark. And still Harris sent his force to the city, despite repeated instructions from the Air Ministry urging him to 'adhere to the spirit' of the Pointblank directive by shifting his bombers' attentions to targets associated with the German aircraft and ball-bearing industries. This relentless drive on the German capital heaped the pressure on Bennett and his crews.

'Every time the crews came into the ops room, the route would be up on the map, and they'd look at the map and they'd say, "God! Berlin – again!"' remembered one Canadian Pathfinder. 'The old, usual chit-chat that had gone on had died. It was just not there. It was like walking into the jaws of death another night, because the losses on the Berlin raids were very heavy.'[23] Another airman recalled: 'When you were on the battle order it was like being hit between the eyes.'[24]

As the first shoots of green began to appear on the trees across Pathfinder country in the spring of 1944, it was time to take stock of what had been achieved in the bombing of Berlin. In reality, it was very difficult to know exactly. Bombing results were assessed by photographs from photo-reconnaissance planes. Yet Berlin was so often under a cloak of grey, damage was almost impossible to assess accurately. But while the accuracy and concentration of the bombing was never as good in thick cloud as it was when the weather was fine and ground markers were used, thanks to the Pathfinders' Berlin Method, it was still a damned useful way of hitting Berlin where it hurt, keeping up the pressure on the German defences and the morale of the civilian population.

Crucially, the Pathfinders had allowed Harris to sustain the momentum of his bombing offensive on a greater number of nights than would otherwise have been possible, something which was true for the entire campaign from early 1943 until the end of the war.

Over the duration of the Battle of Berlin, around 5,000 acres of Berlin – 27 per cent of its built-up area – had been destroyed by 33,000 tons of bombs. Many factories were hit, although few were put out of action for long. More damaging, perhaps, was the destruction to Berlin's railways and canals, which were so vital for transporting war materials. In defending Berlin with guns and personnel against the attacks of Bomber Command, the Luftwaffe used valuable military hardware which could otherwise have been deployed elsewhere.

And although the city remained standing, industrial production continued and the morale of its people had not been broken, the material and psychological damage sustained in the Battle of Berlin was still significant. Every German shell fired; every window in Berlin smashed; every military person killed – all needed to be replaced and in turn added to the burden on the German war machine. It was also a portent of things to come. Bomber Command had proved it could strike hard at the heart of Hitler's Third Reich.

While the Battle of Berlin had not been a total failure, neither was it the all-out victory Harris had hoped. The sprawling metropolis of Berlin was almost 30 times the size of Hamburg, yet when he set out Harris had wanted to destroy it with just four times the volume of raids. That was never a realistic option with the resources available. It was impossible to start a firestorm of any decent power like those that had wreaked such havoc on Hamburg and Kassel. Bennett, too, realised that there was only so much destruction that could be inflicted. 'Great damage was undoubtedly done to Berlin,' he said after the war, 'but the effect of each individual raid decreased as time went on.'[25]

The battle had also been bloody. Around 10,300 people – mainly civilians – were killed on the ground. Bomber Command, meanwhile, lost 2,690 airmen on operations and almost a thousand more were shot down and captured.

Nevertheless, Harris was convinced that his strategy regarding Berlin was the right one. 'I never doubted it,' he said years later. 'The only thing I doubted is whether we were ever going to be given more than a quarter or at most half of what we'd asked for originally to do the job with. As fast as we were given something it seemed to be taken away.'[26]

For Bennett, the Battle of Berlin had seen his force decimated as the losses mounted. In a horrifying four-week period in January 1944, three Pathfinder squadrons – 156, 83 and 97 – saw 227 men killed between them – the equivalent of 32 complete crews. The two heaviest-hit squadrons in Bomber Command in the Battle of Berlin – 7 and 156 Squadrons – were both from the Pathfinders.

A casualty rate of 5 per cent meant that the average Bomber Command crew could expect to be dead after 20 operations. At times during the Battle of Berlin, the loss rate amongst Pathfinders reached 13.5 per cent, including a high number of experienced crews and senior squadron commanders, who were difficult to replace quickly. During the battle, the Pathfinders had to recruit and train to marking standard 50 completely new crews each month.

Even the ever-unflappable Bennett had begun to feel the pressure as losses mounted and old friends perished. He was still only 33-years-old, with around 22,000 young men and women under his command. It's not surprising he felt the Battle of Berlin was the bitterest period of the whole war. 'The skies were teeming with fighters and the target itself was plastered with flak,' he later wrote.

'At one stage I thought the backbone of the Pathfinder Force was really broken.' Driving home from debriefing returning crews in the early hours of the morning, 'it was hard to avoid breaking down and shedding a few tears – which was probably a good safety valve in any case. To have this constant strain over such a long period, night after night and month after month, had its wearing effect, however tough one tried to make oneself superficially.'[27] Every morning after breakfast, Bennett anxiously called up headquarters to find out how many planes were lost from the previous night's operation, before personally speaking to the wives of the missing airmen if they lived nearby.

Part of Bennett's angst – apart from his clear personal pain at seeing so many young men die – was because these weren't just any old crews. The most successful Pathfinder crews were those with the most experience. Over the course of the Battle of Berlin, dozens of experienced crews were killed, while many others who finished their tours during the battle understandably decided to quit while they were ahead. This meant increasingly inexperienced crews, or those straight from training with no action under their belts whatsoever, were being thrown into front-line operations as soon as possible – so increasing their chances of being shot down. It was a vicious circle. Replacements came flooding in, yet Bennett was frustrated at the standard of crews the main-force group commanders were sending his way.

One secret report from 8 Group at the time summed up Bennett's conundrum. 'From the Battle of the Ruhr through to the end of 1943 there had been a marked improvement, but the Battle of Berlin caused many losses, also many of the old originals finishing a third or in some cases the fourth tour. A few excellent types had been kept on training, but many showed little inclination for the work. The general impression was that the "bottom of the barrel" was being reached.'[28]

This situation would be reversed to some extent into the spring and summer of 1944, when Bennett asked Hamish Mahaddie to step up his 'horse-thieving' skills to identify and persuade the best crews to join the Pathfinders. But the absence of Harris's support made it all the harder.

Bennett pleaded with Harris to let his crews have some breathing space. 'We have got to show the world we can go in the face of all they can throw at us and bomb Berlin,' Harris told him. 'We were wasting effort and getting nowhere and a little bit of an interruption would have made all the difference,' said Bennett after the war. 'I replaced my whole aircrew strength one and a half times during those raids,' he added, '. . . and this is the worst thing that could have happened to the command because these people were marking. I couldn't convince the Prime Minister through the channels I had.'[29]

The Battle of Berlin tested Bennett's professional relationship with Harris like never before. But in truth it had been deteriorating since the previous October, following a difficult raid over Hanover when the main attack went largely astray thanks to poor Pathfinder marking. Irritated at their performance, Harris sent a particularly stinging signal to Bennett, saying the attack had been 'a complete flop. The worst failure we have had yet.' He put the blame firmly at the door of the Pathfinders, telling Bennett to ensure in future his crews weren't simply 'blindly joining in' with inaccurate marking 'thus making confusion more confounded'.[30] Harris added: 'What happened at Hannover is a lesson which no doubt you will take to heart . . . Forget it. Pull your socks up, and make as sure as possible that no careless action of anyone of you individually can in future serve to lead the entire force astray as on this occasion.'

Bennett had replied to Harris two days later with a punchy five-page letter. While he agreed that the results had been 'extremely bad', he added that Bomber Command operations more generally were a 'paragon of success' compared to the 'farcical raids which I can assure you from personal experience were carried out before the PFF'.[31] However, Bennett conceded there needed to be a stocktaking of the state of the Pathfinder Force, and set out in detail the ways he felt his force was being let down by aspects beyond his control.

Crucially, he made the point – with some justification – that the 8 Group simply wasn't getting the best crews from other groups, as he'd been promised when the Pathfinders were established, and a third came straight from training units with no operational experience at all. Bennett told Harris the average experience of Pathfinder captains now stood at 20 sorties – 12 fewer than the previous winter. For the Pathfinders to work really efficiently, Bennett added, it needed the best crews, and ideally crews that had completed at least one tour with the main force. Yet they were often being sent the dregs.

Bennett also reminded Harris that the policy of increasingly using smaller 'spoof' raids as a feint to draw night fighters away from the main raid meant his squadrons sometimes had to be briefed on two or even three different operations per night. Pathfinder briefings were longer and complex enough as it was, only starting once Bennett had received news from Harris about the target earlier in the day. Each squadron had to be briefed on routes, timings of different waves, chosen target-marking patterns, bomb loads, use of different technology such as H2S, weather reports, likely flak and fighter strength on the way to and over the target, and so on. This just added to that the pressure.

Bennett set out a wish list for Harris. It included ensuring that the Pathfinders were sent more experienced crews, given greater periods of rest between operations so they could do more training, and given more priority in getting their hands on H2S Mark III kits, hooded flares and other specialist equipment.

Finally, Bennett pleaded with Harris to allow him to personally fly on operations over Germany, despite the fact it was technically against the rules because if he was shot down and caught it would be a huge security headache. 'I feel certain that I can never do this job as it should be done unless I am permitted to operate,' wrote Bennett.

Harris replied to Bennett's letter a few days later, dismissing or ignoring completely a number of his points. He promised to remind main-force group commanders about the need to send their best crews over – before adding the 'spirit of rivalry' between the Pathfinders and other groups was no bad thing – and agreed to look into the shortage of flares. Bennett wouldn't hold his breath.

As for Bennett's request to fly on operations, Harris delivered a rebuke worthy of a primary school teacher: 'I must repeat (as I have told you several times) that I cannot allow it. I have good reasons, not all of which can be made public to you personally.'[32] What Harris didn't realise was that Bennett had already started making unofficial and highly secretive flights over Germany in a bid to get a better idea of the challenges his crews faced. Usually this was in a high-flying Mosquito, in which Bennett would navigate to the target and take notes as the pilot circled the aircraft above the raid. After once being spotted by a Mosquito squadron commander in another group, Bennett warned him to, 'Keep your big mouth shut.'[33]

In spite of his offer to talk to group commanders again, Harris knew by and large they were unlikely to give up their best men to 8 Group. And besides, that suited him. Harris had always believed that the Pathfinders would operate more effectively remaining in their groups rather than as a single force.

In fact, little did Bennett realise that even as he was pleading for more experienced men, Harris was actively encouraging other bomber groups' commanders to create their own marking crews in the style of the Pathfinders. Still smarting that he had 'lost the battle' with the Air Ministry in founding the Pathfinder Force, 'I just went my own sweet way,' Harris admitted later.

'I let 'em [the Air Ministry] form the Pathfinder Force and let 'em take a number of the best volunteer pilots who wanted to go there . . . as soon as they got away with the insistence on just the one, I started behind their back on the others,' said Harris. While he saw that Bennett 'got a lot of absolutely first-class people' he also ensured 'they didn't get 'em all and they didn't bleed the Groups to death because the Groups, at my instigation, were busy forming their own ideas and their own surreptitious Pathfinders.'[34]

This was an astonishing move by Harris. When the Pathfinders had been formed in 1942 he had told the group commanders 'we must accept the decision loyally and do our best to make it a success.'[35] Yet from the very early days, by his own admission, he clearly had little intention of honouring that pledge.

By March 1944, with the nights getting shorter, operations to Berlin would soon have to be reduced. Harris's dream of crushing the German capital was over. All eyes were turning to the Second Front – D-Day – the invasion of France. But just as Bennett's Pathfinders were asked to play a crucial role in helping the Allies successfully invade mainland Europe, the Australian was about to find himself confronted with another new battle. The tensions that had been simmering between Bennett and Harris for the previous six months – and Harris's machinations going on behind the scenes – were about to boil over in a spectacular row, threatening to rip the heart out of the Pathfinders just when they would be needed most.

Don Bennett and his key staff in the operations room at the Pathfinder headquarters in Huntington. (Credit: *The Bennett family archive*)

Don Bennett and Queen Elizabeth on a Royal visit to RAF Wyton in May 1943. (Credit: *The Bennett family archive*)

Don Bennett testing FIDO in July 1943 flying in a 35 Squadron Lancaster at RAF Graveley, the first Pathfinder airfield to have the new system installed. (Credit: *The Howard Lees Collection via Chris Coverdale [8 Group Path Finder Force author and historian]*)

Ground crew pose in front of a 163 Squadron Mosquito.
(Credit: *Pathfinder Collection within the RAF Wyton Heritage Centre*)

Getting into the swing of things. The celebrations outside the officers' mess at Wyton for VE Day. (Credit: *Pathfinder Collection within the RAF Wyton Heritage Centre*)

Pathfinder airmen and WAAFs let their hair down in the officers' mess at Wyton. (Credit: *Pathfinder Collection within the RAF Wyton Heritage Centre*)

Heavy bombers of RAF Bomber Command en route to another target in mainland Europe. Despite hundreds of aircraft flying in close proximity, collisions were pretty rare. (Credit: *Pathfinder Collection within the RAF Wyton Heritage Centre*)

De Havilland Mosquito of 571 Squadron, in flight, 30 September 1944. (Credit: *RAF Museum*)

Handley Page Halifax of 35 Squadron, in flight, 1942. (Credit: *RAF Museum*)

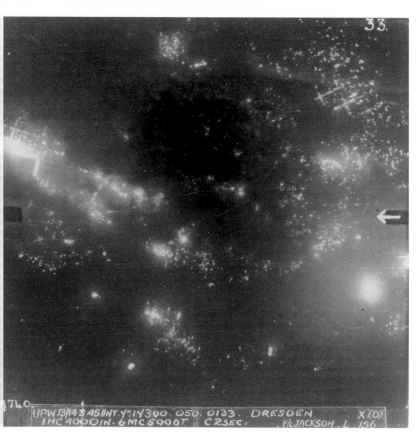

Dresden on the night of the raid on 13–14 February 1945. Original caption reads: 'This photograph of Dresden was taken by an aircraft of the Pathfinder Force using a day camera without flash in order to record the saturation of the target with incendiaries and without attempting to record ground detail. At this stage of the attack, incendiaries were still burning in the streets and on the bridges which enabled the photograph to be plotted. Later these incendiaries would burn out whilst the building fire would increase and the street pattern would then show as dark lines between the fires.'
(Credit: *RAF Museum*)

(*Left*) Avro Lancaster of 97 Squadron, in flight, 1945.
(Credit: *RAF Museum*)

Young Nachtjäger pilots take a break from taking on the British bombers to enjoy a smoke in the summer of 1943. The flying goggles were used in training during daylight hours to enhance the pilot's night vision. Four of these six men pictured would be killed in action within eight months, with only the two men on the far right at the front surviving the war. (Credit: *Theo Boiten*)

Junkers 88 in July 1944. (Credit: *Theo Boiten*)

(*Right*) Ulric Cross in 1945 after collecting his DFC for 'exceptional navigational ability' flying the Mosquito bomber. Cross made 22 sorties to Berlin alone and was one of the most decorated West Indians of the war. (Credit: *Imperial War Museum ref HU58315*)

(*Below*) Max Bryant (*left*) in his Lancaster with his flight engineer in 1943. 'Max just didn't make mistakes in the air,' recalled one colleague. (Credit: *Australian War Memorial*)

Max Bryant on his 21st birthday, in January 1942. 'We had a really good feed, topped by a birthday cake with 21 candles,' Bryant wrote home. 'I blew 'em all out in one breath too!' (Credit: *Australian War Memorial*)

PART FIVE

Relentless Skies

MARCH 1944 - MAY 1945

CHAPTER TWENTY

We Need to Talk About 5 Group

NINE AM, THURSDAY, 30 March 1944. After breakfast with Ly and the children, Don Bennett drove from his home at Wyton airfield four miles up the road to the Pathfinders' headquarters at Castle Hill House, the rather ugly Georgian townhouse in Huntingdon. A few minutes later, the Australian strolled from the main house, across the manicured lawn, past the cluster of shell cases which staff nicknamed 'The Folly' and through the door of a semicircular, corrugated-iron Nissen hut. From the outside, the dirty brown and green building seemed innocuous. Inside, however, was hidden the Pathfinder operations room – the brain of 8 Group.

The large room was dominated by a wall map of Europe and a blackboard on which details of operations were plotted. In the centre of the room, a large glass-topped planning table, surrounded by black chairs, showed another vast map of Europe with German defences marked in various colours. Small squares of plastic were also dotted around the tabletop. These weren't some vital operational prop, but drinks coasters on which the air staff could place their hot cups of tea, coffee and cocoa served punctually by a WAAF at 11am. It wouldn't do to mark the glass table with wet rings. Special coloured pencils designed to write on the glass lay on a little ledge around the edge of the table, and on various shelves surrounding it were black telephones on very long leads, which sometimes had a habit of getting tangled around ankles as people having conversations walked over to the wall map or the blackboard.[1]

It is here that daily operational orders were received from Bert Harris, who gathered with his team in the underground operations room in the grounds of Southdown – the codename for Bomber Command's headquarters in High Wycombe – to decide the target, or targets, for the night. They were then disseminated and sent to the Pathfinder squadrons.

On that particular morning, Harris and his senior officers, including his deputy, Air Marshal Sir Robert Saundby, and intelligence and meteorological experts, had taken 40 minutes to decide the target for the night. It would be Nuremberg – the 'Holy City' and spiritual epicentre of the Nazi Party, home to a huge SS barracks and an estimated 200,000 Germans working for the Third Reich's war effort. Harris then went back to his office and left the ten or so men to flesh out the details. These were sent by secure signal to the various group commanders, including Bennett.

But when the details clicked through the teleprinter at Castle Hill House and the route for the raid was plotted out on a map, Bennett was horrified. Operations to German targets were usually planned over various different legs with many jinks, partly to keep the Germans guessing as late as possible, but also to lessen the chance of night fighters locking onto the bomber stream. Bennett and his team – as navigation experts – nearly always had a decent say in this.

However, the route for that night proposed the stream would fly in a straight line for 265 miles, more or less starting south of Brussels, before turning south for the short run in to Nuremberg and back again to England. This 'straight in, straight out' route was more direct, with less time over enemy territory, fewer turning points and therefore less chance for navigational mistakes and collisions. But, coming right after the Battle of Berlin when German night fighters had shown just how effective they were in hacking down the British bombers, such a direct flight path seemed suicidal to Bennett.

Bennett called Saunby and objected, proposing an alternative route comprising various feints and dog-legs. But when the other group commanders were consulted over the phone, four out of the six supported the original plan. Despite the dangers, it was worth the gamble. Harris gave it his rubber stamp. Bennett was incensed at being overruled. For him, Harris's decision to press ahead was an 'awful, criminal' mistake.[2] But the operation was on.

The grave ramifications of this decision were played out 12 hours later, when 27-year-old pilot Günther Köberich and his two crewmates, flying in their Junkers Ju 88 at 16,000 feet, picked up an unusual echo on the plane's SN-2 radar. They had been directed by ground controllers towards the front of the huge bomber stream stretching out in a straight line across the Netherlands and Belgium. They soon made visual contact. 'I see four engines, it's a Lancaster,' said Köberich to his colleagues, who confirmed there were in fact two Lancasters flying side by side, almost in formation, their black silhouettes sharp against the bright moonlit sky.[3] The presence of two machines flying so close together explained the strange echo on the radar. 'We had already assumed that they must be Pathfinders,' remembered Köberich's crewmate Walter Heidenreich. He was right. The bombers belonged to 156 Squadron.

Köberich carefully steered his twin-engine night fighter below the left hand Lancaster until they were about 250 feet away. *THUD-THUD-THUD.* The upward-firing *Schräge Musik* cannons coughed out shells that smashed through the port wing of the first Lancaster. Köberich carefully shifted the Junkers a few feet to the right under the second bomber and the night fighter unloaded its cannon once again. Within one minute, the deaths of fourteen Pathfinder airmen were sealed. The night-fighter crew watched the two burning bombers peel away in symmetry and arc down through the sky. They hit the ground almost simultaneously with a tremendous explosion. The burning wrecks, observed Heidenreich with satisfaction, 'revealed the nature of our victims: cascades and Christmas trees, some in different colours, continued to burn for quite some time. They were indeed Pathfinders, so it was particularly satisfying to have shot them down.' One survivor, an air gunner, was flung clear as part of the plane exploded, and parachuted down to his eventual fate in a German POW camp. Alive yes, but with memories to haunt him for a lifetime.

The felling of the brace of Lancasters was a typical tale of the night. The German night fighters had a feast. Perched in the tiny gun turret of another 156 Squadron Lancaster, one Pathfinder rear gunner watched the horror unfold. 'I was aghast at the near daylight visibility provided by a brilliant moon,' he recalled. 'I could just look around and see for miles in all directions, and the patches of cloud below us made us like flies, crawling across a pure white tablecloth.'[4] He looked on as the Lancaster furthest away 'exploded in a welter of flames. Then the one nearer to us was also enveloped, though still flying straight and level, flames reaching back, three tiny figures only, clearly discernible, jumping out to fall away'. As an enemy fighter attacked, his Lancaster plunged into a desperate corkscrew, flinging him forward so he banged his head on his gun mountings. 'I regained my seat, swallowing the vomit in my throat, turning the turret hurriedly towards a flicker of flame close by, as another aircraft mortally hit cascaded down into the misty depths.'

The rear gunner's aircraft made it safely back to England. Thirty other airmen from 156 Squadron were not so lucky – killed or taken prisoner. Yet the Sod's Law of bombing operations meant other crews in the thick of it escaped completely. 'It was a pretty good prang and it didn't help the Blackshirt Mob either, for Nuremberg is their Holy City,' John Kelly excitedly wrote home after a successful mission with 83 Squadron. 'It's nice to think that I dropped five two-thousand pound HE's where it hurts most, but not as nice as dropping target indicators. Boy! You can really say you are giving the Hun a headache if you drop a cluster of those on a selected aiming point.'[5]

His squadron mate Dick Raymond also reached Britain unscathed, only to then narrowly avoid a sticky landing in bad weather. 'We didn't see a shot fired in anger on the way there or back. I think because we were in and out before the Germans realised what was going on,' he reckoned. But as the wheels of their Lancaster touched down on the runway at Wyton in a snowstorm, Raymond's pilot realised they would overshoot. 'I pushed the throttles through the gate and at the same time his ruddy seat collapsed,' recalled Raymond, and the Lancaster skimmed over the perimeter fence at the end of the runway and roared up into the sky. 'We should have stalled and how we got away with that we do not know. But we got away with it', proving what an important role a flight engineer played in supporting the pilot and, as on this occasion, saving the lives of his crew.[6]

Raymond was lucky, because the raid on Nuremberg was a bloody disaster, and Bomber Command's deadliest night of the whole war. Out of a force of 795 bombers, it lost 95 aircraft and almost 550 airmen – more men killed than Fighter Command lost in the entire Battle of Britain in 1940, and a 12.1 per cent loss rate. Bennett saw 11 of his aircraft chopped down, with 68 men dead and 11 taken prisoner. 'The Nuremberg raid was a gift. We simply did everything wrong,' Bennett later said. 'It was the nearest I ever had to mutiny. I had every squadron commander in Pathfinders come to me and say, "This is crazy, we can't go. My crews are refusing to fly", because it was a deliberate invitation to Germany, straight in on a moonlit night to a deep-penetration target and straight out again. You couldn't have asked for anything easier for the fighters.'[7] Bennett was clear the blame stood with Harris. 'We lost 97 aircraft simply because he sent them out to be lost. I told him beforehand [but] he wouldn't cancel. That was his biggest clanger.'[8]

Yet the losses at Nuremberg would soon prove to be the least of Bennett's problems. The attack was the final death rattle of the Battle of Berlin. For the next few months, the role of Bomber Command shifted from large-scale area bombing of cities towards smaller operations against precision targets.

Harris's vast air force was now temporarily under the command of the American general Dwight Eisenhower, the Supreme Commander of the Allied Expeditionary Force in Europe. No longer – for now at least – could Harris be dismissive of what he called panacea targets. Rather than using his aircraft to bomb cities, they would instead target the railways and transport systems across France and Germany, in the run-up to Operation Overlord – the cross-Channel invasion of northern France. Even with the Pathfinders' skills, Harris doubted whether Bomber Command could accurately hit such small targets, which were on average around half a mile long by a quarter of a mile wide. But the shift in strategy allowed him to accelerate the changes he'd been plotting for almost two years.

*

From early 1944, 5 Group – another group within Bomber Command but not technically a Pathfinder group – had begun experimenting with its own target-marking techniques, in a radical departure from those carefully established by Bennett and his team. Unlike Bennett's Pathfinder tactics, which generally favoured target marking from high altitude using Oboe and H2S navigation technology, 5 Group advocated low-level target marking from just a few hundred feet, which they believed was more accurate. These were then followed by a main force flying at more routine altitudes.

Such raids were dramatic and often very effective. 5 Group's 617 Squadron had carried out the famous Dam Buster raid in and around the Ruhr Valley the previous May, and in some ways that operation established the legitimacy of their tactics. And 5 Group was staffed by some hugely talented airmen, including the brilliant pilot Leonard Cheshire – a postwar household name for his humanitarian work with his wife Sue Ryder – who became one of the RAF's youngest commanding officers. Cheshire – who drove an Alfa Romeo and was suave and popular – had a legendary war career, including eight months leading 617 Squadron. He would become the most highly decorated bomber pilot when he was awarded the Victoria Cross in 1944. With some irony, he'd narrowly missed out on becoming a Pathfinder after Bennett insisted he be tested like everyone else, after which a miffed Cheshire – who had successfully completed three tours with Bomber Command – decided it wasn't for him. It was a costly judgement by Bennett, and his loss was 5 Group's gain.

Cheshire soon developed low-level marking techniques, spearheading tight formations of three Lancasters which would dive-bomb a target, aiming the aircraft like a gun, releasing the target indicator from as little as 15 yards away. His aircraft would often return from operations with branches or telegraph wires trailing from the bottom of the fuselage.

On 9 February 1944, Cheshire led 617 Squadron in a night-time strike against the Gnome & Rhône aero-engine factory in Limoges, central France. The factory was surrounded by houses and staffed by young French women. Accuracy was critical to avoid numerous innocent deaths and a political disaster. Flying at rooftop height, Cheshire buzzed the factory three times in his Lancaster to allow the factory workers time to escape. On his fourth run, his plane dropped a load of 30lb incendiaries from a height of 50–100 feet, which fizzed with intense brightness over the roof of the factory – an image dramatically photographed by his onboard camera. Eleven other Lancasters following up each then dropped a 12,000lb bomb – ten of which hit the factory plum. It was almost totally destroyed and there were no reported casualties. More importantly, the successful operation – albeit against a very lightly defended target – gave agency to 5 Group's low-level marking methods and allowed its boss, Sir Ralph Cochrane, to press Harris for a greater role.

Cochrane – a former First World War airship pilot – ensured his 5 Group missions often made their way into the newspapers. His whole approach was in sharp contrast to Bennett's preference that Pathfinders' work in 8 Group remained below the radar as much as possible.

There was a deep and often openly hostile rivalry between the two men – although they both insisted it was purely professional. Cochrane, an aristocratic Scotsman, was 15 years older than Bennett, and an experienced regular officer with undoubted tactical and strategic nous. But he'd not seen action in the current war, which marked him down in Bennett's eyes. Meanwhile, like many other senior RAF figures, Cochrane considered Bennett something of a young upstart. 'I'd made the mistake of becoming a civilian,' Bennett joshed after the war, referring to his decision to leave the RAF before rejoining.[9] It was certainly true that some RAF-types resented his rise through the ranks as a 'hostilities-only' airman.

Most importantly, though, Cochrane had the ear of Harris. A year before he had been instrumental in persuading a sceptical Harris to green-light the highly successful Dam Buster raids. The previous autumn, meanwhile, just as Bennett was pleading with Harris for better crews, Harris had been telling Cochrane to 'make sure that any tour-expired crews who would like to join 617 Squadron are given the opportunity of doing so. If you think it desirable I will have an official letter written to all AOCs bringing this to their notice.'[10] Bennett and Cochrane were in effect competing for the same crews, and Harris had made it clear where his loyalties lay.

In fact, Harris never hid his admiration for Cochrane, whom he considered his protégé, describing him as a 'genius' and declaring that 'nine out of ten times I would support Cochrane over anybody ... I had long experience of his abilities', while he reckoned Bennett was a 'brand new boy come up from "the wild and woollies" from Australia'.[11]

With Harris's plan to reshape the Pathfinders well under way, it was his relationship with Cochrane that threatened to hammer the final nail in the coffin for Bennett's 8 Group. In the spring of 1944, Cochrane suggested to his boss that 5 Group be allowed to try low-level marking of targets such as Berlin. Harris was enthused and called up Bennett on the phone proposing it. 'Cochrane says it would be a good idea to try very low-level marking on Berlin. What do you think?' Harris asked Bennett. Bennett immediately pooh-poohed the idea, believing it would be carnage for his crews given Berlin's defences, while map-reading and trying to identify landmarks and targets a few feet above a city, at high speed, at night, was nigh-on impossible. And besides, the perpetual cloud over Berlin meant the target markers wouldn't be seen.

'I don't think it would work,' Bennett replied. '... You just cannot map-read over a metropolitan area which has massive detail, at night, at low level. It wouldn't work.'

'Well, Cochrane thinks it would,' Harris replied.

Bennett stuck to his guns. 'I'm very sorry,' he told Harris, 'but I'm not going to waste anybody's neck.'

'Do you think it's dangerous?' Harris asked, getting more irritated.

'No, it isn't the danger at all, it is the question that it wouldn't work,' insisted Bennett.[12]

An hour later Bennett was summoned to see his commander personally. He borrowed a clapped-out Hurricane and flew it down to RAF Halton, from where he was then driven to High Wycombe and made his way to the corner office he knew so well. There, Harris dropped a bombshell, giving Bennett a 'frigid and formal' notification that he was immediately to be stripped of two Lancaster squadrons – 83 and 97 – which would return to their parent group, 5 Group. As if that wasn't bad enough, Bennett would also lose 627 Squadron, a Mosquito marker squadron, to Cochrane's command.

While all three squadrons technically remained Pathfinders, they were to be transferred to 5 Group bases at Woodhall Spa and Coningsby, in Lincolnshire. Harris framed the move as temporary, but to Bennett it was a 'tremendous slap in the face' to an elite unit which he believed had turned Bomber Command from a 'wasteful and ineffective force' into a 'mighty and successful' one.[13] Although Harris maintained that the idea was a temporary loan and could be revoked at 48 hours' notice, Bennett knew there was a real danger that if it proved successful, he'd be asked to return other 8 Group squadrons to their parent groups, which would lead to the break-up of his entire Pathfinder Force. Just as Bomber Command was expanding, the Pathfinders were being reduced in size. All that Bennett had worked for in building up the experience and reputation of his force seemed like it might soon be wiped out.

For the crews of 5 Group, it meant the upheaval of transferring to a new station and learning new tactics. Some old-timers were pleased to be returning to their spiritual home, others, not so much. The 83 Squadron logbook recorded how the move 'was a great blow to the squadron as they liked this camp and district very much indeed . . . everyone was sorry to see old Wyton for the last time'.[14]

After they'd arrived at their new home, the Pathfinder aircrew were given a terse talk by the base commander about shedding their habits learnt under Bennett. One airman piped up from the back of the room: 'We're fighting the Germans you know, sir, not 5 Group.'[15] For those left behind at 8 Group, there was a feeling that 5 Group was Harris's favourite. In a smoky mess bar on an 8 Group airfield, a group of airmen were taking bets on who might end up marrying the young Princess Elizabeth. One voice from a corner gloomily opined: 'I bet it will be someone from 5 Group.'[16]

Nevertheless, however much Bennett hated losing Pathfinder crews from his command, there was some merit in Harris's move. While the 5 Group tactics would, as it turned out, not be tested over Berlin – and surely would have been an utter failure given its massive defences and appalling weather – they were well suited to the smaller, more precise targets over France.

The squadrons of 5 Group quickly adapted and began to execute some hair-raising but accurate and successful operations. Unofficially – and most likely much to Bennett's irritation – they became known as 'Cochrane's Independent Airforce'. John Kelly wrote home to tell his parents about one particular mission to Paris. For someone who just a few months before had been living the high life with Hollywood's glamour set, his adventures over enemy territory were straight out of a blockbuster movie. 'It was almost like day and it was easy to see shops, houses, streets et cetera from the height we bombed,' scribbled Kelly.

> He [the Germans] had got it pretty well defended and a kitchen sink or something hit B/beer [the codename of Kelly's Lancaster] with a ter-rific wallop, but fortunately didn't do vital damage. There were plenty of Luftwaffe types about so I came home at zero feet all the way from Paris – quite easy in moonlight. Duggie was shaken to find a church steeple towering above him. We were hoping to come across a nice fat Army staff car so we could fill it up with .303 but no luck. One keen gun crew on an aerodrome had a squirt at us with a light flak squirter but I expect they had to duck and it spoilt their aim, they didn't get near us.[17]

There were also notable disappointments for 5 Group. In early May, 42 Lancasters were lost in an attack on a military camp near Mailly-Le-Camp after a radio failure meant Cheshire's order for the main force to bomb his markers wasn't heard, allowing German fighters to pounce in the confusion. In an attack on Brunswick – 5 Group's first real attack against a heavily defended German city – a thin layer of cloud obscured low markers dropped by 617 Squadron, and most bombs missed the city completely. It was becoming clear that 5 Group's low-level target marking could work brilliantly but only using smaller numbers of aircraft in clear weather conditions, while 8 Group could operate in any weather with a greater force – albeit sometimes less accurately.

Over the coming weeks, Bennett's men recovered well from haem-orrhaging crews, and as the spring operations gathered pace, they too proved they could hit more precise targets. An 8 Group-led attack on the small city of Friedrichshafen in late April was a smashing success. The target – a factory making tanks – was deep in southern Ger-many, the raid conducted on a moonlit night, and the memory of the

Nuremberg carnage was fresh in aircrews' minds. But thanks to clever use of diversions and feints by Bennett, the bulk of the German fighters were fooled into staying away, and 1,124 tons of bombs were dropped onto the target, destroying a tank gearbox factory and damaging several others. German officials later said it was the most damaging raid on tank production in the war.[18]

The Pathfinder master bombers were also playing an increasingly important role in the smaller operations, ensuring as much as possible that the bombs hit the targets and not French civilians. At 9.44pm on 25 April 1944, John Christie's Lancaster lifted off from the runway at Graveley to start his forty-eighth and final mission as a Pathfinder for 35 Squadron. His tour was almost over. The target was some railway marshalling yards at Villeneuve St George, near Paris, which would be directed by a master bomber. Christie was nervous. He and his crew had hoped to use their favourite Lancaster – codenamed S-Sugar – which had become their regular aircraft and they considered lucky. But an engine failure before take-off meant they had to use a different machine.

Nevertheless, before they took off, usual traditions for a crew on its last operation were observed. A pair of Wings was presented to the all-important ground crew, while their in-flight sweet rations were donated to the WAAFs in the section whose vital job it was to pack the parachutes. The ground crew also chalked the letters 'AGLA' on some of the bombs before they were loaded onto the aircraft. This custom supposedly stemmed from a visit to Graveley by a maharaja from the Indian province of Madras the year before. The region was donating money to 35 Squadron as part of a wider scheme allowing countries from across the Empire to support Bomber Command crews. The squadron became known as the 'Madras Presidency Squadron'. During his visit to the air station, the maharaja was reputed to have said, 'To you I say Agla, which means God be with you.' Since then, the whole base was 'Agla crazy'. One 35 Squadron crew member recalled:

No crew went on ops without Agla. Agla was everywhere. Agla was the magic word for any and every crew. Agla always went. The method was simple, Agla was just chalked on the sleeve of the flying overalls, or the front of the Mae West. It had to be freshly chalked each op, and while the crews were hanging about waiting for the crew buses, lots of pieces of chalk would be passed around, as the aircrew busily Agla'd each other.[19]

No doubt safely Agla'd too, Christie's journey over to the target was smooth, and five minutes before midnight, his plane swooped down over the railway sidings and released its brilliant white flares from 8,000 feet, illuminating the tracks, sheds and locos. But, unusually for the Mossies, they dropped their markers two miles away from the target, a mistake which would prove disastrous if the main force – now closing in fast – released the bombs and flattened the housing below. The master bomber – an experienced flight commander with 35 Squadron – immediately came on over the radio: 'Hawkins calling main force. Don't bomb yet. Stand by,' he said.[20] The pressure on the master bomber was huge. He had seconds to ensure the raid went to plan.

Christie picks up the action in a diary entry penned shortly afterwards:

> The master bomber then went around, and in the light of the flares, which gave an excellent illumination of the ground, he dropped just one white T.I. right in the right place. He then called up the main force again and told them to bomb this. As far as we could see not one bomb was dropped before the order was given. We dropped our bombs on the T.I. and the bomb aimer saw the bombs burst across the marshalling yards. The master bomber stayed over the target for 20 minutes and kept on directing the bombing in a masterly way . . . an example of how such a man can make a success out of a raid that would have otherwise been a failure with rather serious consequences; providing he knows his job and strict discipline is maintained by the force.

As the raid was coming to an end, the master bomber announced over the radio, 'Hawkins closing down, going home', to which someone else from another crew piped up: 'Three cheers for the master bomber! Hip! Hip! Hip! . . .'[21]

Just after 1am, Christie touched down at Graveley – the first plane home after his navigator had 'cut a few corners'. His crew had completed their Pathfinder tour and done more marking trips than any other crew in 35 Squadron. At the back of his diary Christie scribbled down some detailed analysis covering the operations he flew over the year from April 1943. It provides a fascinating snapshot into the survival odds of a Bomber Command crew which had served through the Battles of the Ruhr, Hamburg, Berlin and the early missions in the run-up to D-Day. Christie estimated that the average life expectancy of a Bomber Command airman on any squadron over this period was just 2.78 months, with a 6.2 per cent chance of surviving a whole tour. However, he concluded the effort was worth it. 'The offensive has hit the enemy industrially, and hit him hard just where it will hurt him most,' he wrote.

Harris's treatment of Bennett was arguably shoddy. He continued to favour Cochrane, giving him greater access to equipment such as the (much in demand but scarce) inflight VHF radio, much to Bennett's understandable frustration. Bennett reckoned Cochrane was getting his own way because 'it has always been his policy to shout the loudest in order to get what he wants'.[22] Harris had always advocated specialist target markers in each force, and his syphoning off to 5 Group was an erosion of the original Pathfinder Force Bennett had built. The move prompted the Australian to worry the Pathfinders had been a failure in the eyes of Bomber Command, which would affect his crews' morale. Only time would tell whether Harris removed any further squadrons or even got rid of Bennett's Pathfinders altogether. And while some RAF officers thought the Pathfinder Force was irrevocably damaged, others argued the splitting off of 5 Group made everyone raise their game, to the benefit of Bomber Command and the Allies. Bennett would have to draw on all his experience to keep his men motivated. As D-Day neared, their skill, courage and expertise would be tested more than ever.

CHAPTER TWENTY-ONE

Terrorflieger

MAY 1944. ACROSS SOUTHERN England, the huge Anglo-American and Canadian military build-up was underway in preparation for the cross-Channel invasion of France. Only a select few knew where exactly this would be, of course, but the sheer volume of men, women and machinery gearing up for the biggest invasion in history was awesome.

Meanwhile, Bomber Command and the USAAF continued to ramp up their supporting strikes, flying around the clock. In May alone, the RAF's Pathfinders carried out 2,271 sorties – a rise of 41 per cent on the previous month. After a slow start, the limitless resources of American aviation, and in particular the increasing use of Mustang long-range fighters escorting its bombers, began to nudge the odds in the Allies' favour. These co-ordinated attacks by the British and American air forces were extraordinarily effective, mainly targeting the transport systems of Germany and German-occupied territories in accordance with a directive known as the 'Transportation Plan'. And to be fair to Bert Harris, despite his reluctance to turn his bombers away from attacking cities towards precision targets, he increasingly pushed his bombers to implement the new strategy, and later admitted he had underestimated how accurate the bombing could be. Over the last week of May, Allied air attacks destroyed at least 500 German railway locomotives. Germany had precious little fuel and was heavily depend-ent on rail to transport almost everything, but especially tanks, guns and troops. Inhibiting the Germans' ability to supply northern France once the invasion started would be vital to its success. Rail traffic was reduced to 55 per cent capacity and then, once the bridges over the River Seine were destroyed at the very end of May, to just 30 per cent. 'The railway network is completely wrecked,' noted a German report. 'Paris has been systematically cut off from long-distance traffic and the most important bridges over the lower Seine have been destroyed.'[1]

Building on their success during 'Big Week' in February, the American B-17 bombers – increasingly escorted by hundreds of powerful P-47 Thunderbolts and P-51 Mustang fighters – continued their daylight bombing raids over northern Europe to grind down the German air force. These missions were costly for the Americans, but the overwhelming Allied firepower was even more devastating for the Luftwaffe. German fighter output actually reached a peak between the end of 1943 and the autumn of 1944. But more than 9,000 German aircraft were destroyed in transit in 1944 in Allied air attacks, before they could be used in anger.[2] By the end of May, the Luftwaffe had also lost over 2,260 fighters – almost 100 per cent of the number they started with – and as D-Day neared, there were fewer and fewer experienced and well-trained pilots left.

For both the American bombers and Bomber Command, this didn't mean the Luftwaffe had lost its sting just yet, however. And despite his commitment to these smaller, pre-invasion targets, Harris hadn't quite forgotten about Germany, either. In late May 1944 he sent his bombers, led by the Pathfinders, to strike cities along its western fringe, an area which would be crucial for supplies and reinforcements once the land battle had begun.

On Monday, 22 May, over 600 bombers took off from airfields around England in two separate raids to target Dortmund and Brunswick. Dick Raymond's 83 Squadron Lancaster had left the tarmac at Coningsby at 22.44 and was heading over the Netherlands en route to Brunswick when an almighty bang suddenly shook the plane. Raymond was next to the bomb bay throwing out strips of Window when 'the next minute the whole thing was ablaze'.[3] The plane had been targeted by a night fighter using its *Schräge Musik* cannon. The pilot gave the order to bail out. Raymond reached for his parachute and clipped it on, before opening the escape hatch.

'I did everything wrong,' he recalls. 'I didn't disconnect my inter-com, I didn't disconnect my oxygen, according to the books I should have been throttled but I wasn't. I got away with it.' Just as he jumped, the plane blew up. 'I could feel the bang as it exploded and Ken got blown straight through the roof.' Ken Lane, the pilot, was lucky; des-pite being blown out of his boots and propelled up through the Perspex cockpit, he was the only member of the crew to wear his parachute throughout the flight. Raymond usually left his parachute up near the front of the aircraft but on that operation he'd decided to carry it with him to the middle of the plane before he started throwing the Win-dow out. 'It was sheer bloody luck that I'd got it in the bomb bay with me because if it had been back at my station I couldn't have got there as the plane was burning. I was just damn lucky,' he said. 'People say to me "Cor weren't you brave?" Brave? What do you mean brave? I would have been bloody stupid to stay there and cook wouldn't I? You don't hesitate.'

Raymond pulled the cord on his chute and savoured the 'superb tranquillity' after the noise of the aircraft. As he floated down his big-gest worry was missing an important event. 'It sounds daft now, but I was to be best man at Ken's wedding on the following Saturday and the only thing I was worried about was that I'd miss the bloody wedding.'

Raymond landed in a field in the Netherlands. He was just 20 years old, alone and afraid. Like all aircrew, he had been given some instruc-tion in evasion techniques. Before each operation aircrew were also issued with some local currency, a small hacksaw, a compass, a silk escape map and an escape aid box. The box contained enough concen-trated food for a few days.

Raymond was picked up by some local farmers, who took him to their house and offered him some food. 'They gave me goat's milk and black bread and when you've just fallen out of the sky, with all due respect, you don't particularly want goat's milk and black bread,' said Raymond. He got out his escape map 'Where am I?' he asked them. 'I thought I was in France and I was talking schoolboy French to Dutch peasants and it didn't work.' The following morning a local doctor arrived and put Raymond on the back of his two-stroke motorbike. 'I enjoyed the ride across the dykes on the back of his bike. The sun was shining, it was a wonderful morning,' said Raymond.

The doctor took Raymond to his home and introduced his wife and two daughters. Then he said: 'I'm sorry, the Germans know you're here, there is nothing I can do about it.' 'If he tried to help me evade them, they'd have shot him and his family, just like that, no questions asked at all,' reckoned Raymond. 'They would have murdered them on the spot. So in came this goon and stuck a rifle in my ribs and said, "You are my prisoner, don't try to escape" and I thought, *Well you're a bloody fool. I'm not likely to run away with a rifle in my ribs, am I?*'

Raymond was reunited with Ken Lane and Don Cope, his bomb aimer, who had already been captured and were both shaken but otherwise well. They were taken by train across the countryside, narrowly escaping an American Thunderbolt fighter swooping in low with all guns blazing. When Cope asked if there was a loo on the train which he could use, the guard refused. 'Poor old Copey. In the end he peed himself all over the floor and the guard hit him over the head with his bloody rifle,' said Raymond.

Such casual violence was common treatment for Allied airmen shot down. Some were killed by the SS, the Gestapo or angry civilians. By contrast, if they ended up in the hands of the Luftwaffe, as fellow airmen, they tended to be treated more fairly. For Raymond, if it wasn't for the German guards, things could have been far worse. As they were taken through the Rhine Valley in a truck, 'we arrived at the wrong time, the boys had just bombed it. And we were in flying kit. The German guards had to form a ring around us and cock their rifles or the bloody civilians would have had us. They were calling us "baby killers, murderers, swines".' Finally, Raymond and his two crewmates arrived at Stalag Luft VII, a POW camp for Allied airmen, 250 miles south-east of Berlin.

Three of Raymond's crewmates had been killed when his plane blew up on the way to Brunswick. The attack was one of the first city raids by Cochrane's 5 Group, testing out its new low-level marking methods. It had mixed results, as Raymond's squadron mate John Kelly wrote home after the raid:

The C-in-C [Commander-in-Chief] promised that we could try our method over a strongly defended German target, and we certainly got one. On the outward journey I thought it would never get dark, in fact, on crossing the German coast it was possible to see the aircraft about a mile away. Most of all losses occurred there and as it got darker things became easier. The target had to be marked twice so altogether we were there for half an hour tearing round and round in circles. In the end we got the dump marked but most of main force had got cheesed and had jettisoned or dropped on our illuminating flares and gone off home. We only had one bomb to drop – a two thousand pounder but we did get it where it hurt him . . . In a way these Hun targets are much better than the French ones for no one worries much if you drop in the vicinity of the aiming point instead of on it, and after all, a tenement of munitions workers does as much good as a rolling mill or gasworks.[4]

On the same night, 8 Group had led a 370-plane attack on Dortmund. Three minutes after Raymond's plane took off from Coningsby, eighty miles to the south at Graveley, Ernie Holmes was pulling back on the control stick of his Lancaster. This was Holmes's twenty-second Pathfinder mission with 35 Squadron. That evening, the Lancaster carried eight men, with a second air bomber helping out on the H2S kit. As was often the case, some of the original crew had been replaced, meaning the aircraft was now manned by individuals with varying experience. The wireless operator and mid-upper gunner were on their forty-fifth and final Pathfinder sortie in their current tour. The flight engineer and the rear gunner were on their first operation.

Despite being experienced, Derrick Coleman, Holmes's air bomber, was unusually apprehensive before the operation. Before he took off he completed an inventory of his personal belongings – he'd never bothered before. The second air bomber also felt uneasy about the hours ahead, and decided to destroy most of his personal letters.

The weather closed in as the bombers gained altitude and headed east over the Netherlands. Flying through the thick clouds, ice began to form on the wings and engines. Holmes was struggling to maintain height so decided to shed two 1,000lb bombs over the North Sea to lighten the load, which seemed to work. They were still carrying their crucial target-indicator bombs. But a few minutes later, in a presage of things to come, a brick-sized block of ice which had formed on the wing detached and smashed through the cockpit window like a missile, smacking Holmes on the side of the head. He was dazed but otherwise OK, thanks mainly to a new type of American flying helmet which had extra-padded sides. The offending lump of ice was shoved down the Elsan loo by the flight engineer and Holmes flew the aircraft safely to Dortmund, where they dropped their target indicators and remaining bombs before heading back home.

At around 1.20am on 23 May 1944 – about the time Dick Raymond was walking through a dark Dutch field wondering how he'd get home – the four engines of Holmes's Lancaster purred reassuringly as his plane cruised at 16,000 feet on its way back over the Netherlands. Little did he realise that just a few hundred feet below, and closing fast, was Hans-Heinz Augenstein. The 22-year-old night-fighter ace manoeuvered his Junkers Ju 88 in for the kill.

Back in the Lancaster, suddenly there was a loud bang, the Lanc juddered violently and plunged into a dive. Holmes put both feet onto the instrument panel and yanked back on the stick to try and gain control. He looked out of the window and saw a fire starting in the port wing. Within a few seconds he had lost control. 'Bail out! Bail out! Walk south-west!' shouted Holmes, knowing the aircraft was over the Netherlands and that was the best chance of evasion.[5] Two of the crew leapt out. As Holmes began to unstrap himself to bail out, a huge explosion rocked the plane, knocking him unconscious. He came to a few seconds later to find himself being buffeted by high winds and pinned to the outside of the nose of the aircraft, which was plummeting through the sky. The cockpit canopy had disappeared and the starboard wing had been blown off. Holmes's left foot was still trapped under the instrument panel and his loose-fitting harness was snagged on something in the aircraft. He used all his strength to pull himself back through the gaping hole to free his foot and release the shoulder harness, before pushing hard away from the fuselage and free-falling. He immediately yanked on his parachute ripcord, floating down and landing with a hard splat in a muddy field. The flaming remains of the plane smashed into the ground just 50 feet away.

Astonishingly, apart from a few scratches caused by the shattered Perspex and a broken nose, Holmes was uninjured. In fact, the incidence of burns, gunshot and flak wounds to Allied airmen who bailed out after being shot down over Europe was low compared to injuries such as skull fractures and broken pelvises, arms and legs which they sustained in parachute landings. According to one study, the average airman abandoned his aircraft between 14,000 and 16,000 feet but often had little recollection of how he'd actually escaped the machine – with amnesia blocking out the most traumatic moments as the body's natural defence mechanism. He would find himself in the air, pulling on the ripcord, or on the ground with no clear idea of how he had arrived there.[6]

Holmes knew exactly how he'd arrived in the wet, dark field in the middle of the Netherlands. But he had less idea of how he might get out of it. He pushed the parachute into a bush and stumbled away from the light of the flaming aircraft. The sky was clear, so Holmes found the North Star and began walking south-west. The countryside was open, flat arable farmland. Holmes had been shot down a few miles west of Eindhoven, in the south of the Netherlands. His Lancaster had been seen plummeting to the ground for miles around and the Germans swiftly sent out search parties to hunt down survivors. Holmes heard dogs barking in the distance, so waded across a flooded field to shake them off his scent. Cold and wet, he walked through the night.

As the sun was rising at around 6am the following morning, Holmes was tired, hungry and hallucinating. Staggering through a corn field, he kept hearing a blacksmith hammering on his anvil in the distance and headed towards the sound, 'visualising him to have sandwiches in a white handkerchief with red dots'. In fact, it was a pretty 21-year-old brunette called Netje van der Heijden, who was cycling towards Holmes along a path, carrying two milk churns which clattered every time her bike hit a bump. As she passed, Holmes decided to risk it. He stood up and called out '*Goedemorgen*' and then slowly mouthed 'RAF'. The startled young woman didn't speak English but indicated for him to hide in the corn again and cycled off. Sometime later, Holmes heard voices. He gingerly peered up over the corn. Standing in front of him was a man in his forties. He had a strong, good-looking face and narrow eyes framed with laughter lines like a pair of crow's feet. A roll-up cigarette hung louchely from the corner of his mouth, and a battered trilby sat on his head. The man was Netje's father, Fons – a local farmer who quietly worked for the

Dutch Resistance, risking his life to hide Allied airmen on the run as part of a wider network which tried to smuggle the flyers back to Britain. Holmes was the twenty-third person Fons had sheltered. Those landing in occupied countries had a far better chance of evading capture than those landing in Germany, and as the war progressed, lines of courageous helpers who sheltered fugitive airmen were built up by MI9 – the British escape service – to get the men to neutral Spain or Switzerland, from where they could return home.

Holmes was taken to the family's farm, where he was gently helped out of his clothes, given a warm bath with water heated from a cauldron suspended over an outdoor fire, and fed. 'He's like a baby in a high chair,' joked Netje. Fons's wife Mina burnt Holmes's flying gear and gave him civilian clothes. Holmes was not alone. Apart from the Van der Heijdens, Dutch students avoiding the German military call-up also quietly worked on the farm. They spoke good English and translated conversations between Holmes and the Van der Heijdens. During daylight hours, Holmes remained out of sight in case he was spotted by a passing German patrol or a nosy neighbour. He spent hours separating seeds by hand, sorting them into those fit for human consumption and those for animal feed, realising later it was probably a form of therapy by the Van der Heijdens to help him recover from his ordeal. But there was also much laughing and smiles. The students would pull Netje's leg about bathing Holmes. She got her own back one day by cooking them all little pancakes. When they asked what the chewy bits were, she revelled in revealing she'd popped some pigs' nipples into the mixture.

Holmes soon settled in to life in hiding on the farm. In the warm evenings, he was taken to a local lake and swam with the students and the Van der Heijden children. As they sat on the lakeside afterwards, Holmes taught them about the stars and how to use the night sky to navigate. Jan, Fons van der Heijden's 21-year-old son, later wrote a folk tune he called 'The Baby in the High Chair'.

After almost three weeks on the farm, it was time to move on. There is no doubt that the kindness of Fons van der Heijden had saved Holmes from capture. But the farmer was also risking his own and his family's lives. If the Germans found out, they would probably be shot. Holmes said goodbye to his new friends – he'd never forget what they'd done for him – and was moved to hide with another family. He spent a few uncomfortable nights in a hay-lined hole in the ground, deep in a wood, being looked after by a gamekeeper and the Father of a local Roman Catholic monastery, and was reunited with his crewmate Derrick Coleman. After a few days, Holmes and Coleman were escorted on foot by a local Resistance member over the border, where they met a woman in her mid-twenties who took them in silence by bus to the Belgian city of Antwerp. At around 5pm on 17 June 1944, they were taken to a café. Coffees and pastries were ordered. A man aged about 35 approached the table. He was short and heavily built with dark eyes. He sat down and pulled out a piece of paper. The woman fished in her handbag and produced another piece of paper which she slid across the table. They slotted together like a jigsaw. Holmes looked on. Perhaps this was some sort of underground procedure to ensure no one would be betrayed? The man asked Holmes and Coleman some questions in French. What squadron were they in? Who had they got help from after being shot down? But the young airmen kept their lips sealed. Finally, the man said, 'Follow me', and they walked to a black saloon car waiting in the street. They climbed into the back, with two men in the front seats. The car pulled away from the kerb and drove for 70 yards, before swinging through an archway into a cobbled courtyard. A German sentry saluted. It was the Gestapo headquarters. 'Gentlemen, you're now in the hands of the German military police and we are handing you over to the Gestapo,' said one of the men. They had been betrayed by Belgian collaborators.

'The trick was very cleverly pulled,' said Holmes later. 'For, after four weeks of freedom, we didn't expect anything so simple to happen.'[7]

The men were separated. Holmes was pushed into a tiny room. He slumped to the floor, exhausted, and fell asleep, only to be woken by a hard kick in the back from a German soldier. 'I turned around in rage to retaliate and the next thing I know I got the muzzle of his rifle in my mouth,' said Holmes. The soldier started calling him *Schweinhund* and *Terrorflieger* before dumping him in another room with desks and a blackboard – probably a school – which overlooked a courtyard. Holmes looked out of the window and saw a man standing in civilian clothes. Scared he was about to be killed, Holmes started singing repeatedly at the top of his voice: 'My name is Holmes. I am a flight lieutenant in the Royal Air Force. My service number is 157389.' The man in the courtyard looked up and winked at him.

After a few hours, Holmes was stripped. They yanked off his dog tags and threw them across the room. They also spotted he was circumcised. 'You were caught in civilian clothes and you're a spy,' said the German interrogator. 'We shoot spies, but we have special treatment for Jews.' As it happens, Holmes wasn't Jewish, but that didn't really matter to his interrogators. Over the coming hours and days he wasn't beaten again, but instead subjected to a succession of psychological mind games by his captors, designed to ensure the spectre of execution hung over his head like a burning target indicator.

He was put on a train to Brussels, accompanied by a German armed guard. After getting a taste of freedom, Holmes hatched a plan. On a visit to the train lavatory, he spotted that the glass window was simply attached to its frame with two screws. He carefully unscrewed the first screw using his finger nail. Later, when it was dark outside, he would visit the cubicle again to repeat the process with the second. The odds seemed in his favour. With the train trundling through wooded countryside at a sedate 30mph, Holmes reckoned he had a chance of leaping out through the window and the embankment breaking his fall. He then planned to run into the forest before the guards could shoot.

But his plan was foiled when a guard used the loo and spotted the loose screw. Arriving in Brussels, Holmes was taken to a military prison, stripped again, and subjected to interrogation from one Gestapo officer who pretended to be a Rabbi, trying to use kindness to winkle out details about the Pathfinders from Holmes. 'He was an unusual shape – fat, small, squat, head and shoulders on a barrel,' remembers Holmes. But Holmes didn't crack and was reunited with Coleman after the Gestapo realised they were wasting their time. The two men were transported to Stalag Luft III, where they were welcomed by fellow inmates.

Holmes had survived the ordeal. He knew that at least four of his crewmates had been killed. Two more were now POWs and a third – initially on the run – was later captured too. Holmes was given a notepad by the Red Cross. Lying on his bed one day, he drew a cross with four black scrolls to enter the names of his dead colleagues. Under the cross, he wrote: 'In Memory, of those members of the crew flying Lancaster 'E' Edward who sacrificed their lives for their country on the night of the 22nd of May 1944'. Then, barely able to hold back the tears, he wrote:

> *When the sun sets and darkness falls. I will remember.*
> *When the sun rises and another day is born. I will remember.*
> *For remembrance is all that I possess of those I knew so well.*
> *Those who flew with me, into the silent night, to fight the foe.*
>
> *They asked not for bloodshed, nor did they start this fight.*
> *But when they heard this bugle call they fight, they jumped to fight for right.*
> *Often they prepared for missions, flying into the sleepy night.*
> *To bring death and destruction to those who called right, might.*
>
> *They did their job right, they did it well, but this couldn't last.*
> *For on the 23rd May we fell and became as the past.*
> *Four of the eight are missing. These we know are dead.*
> *Three more are accounted for, but the eighth man is still ahead.*
> *Making his way for his own homeland, Keep going my friend.*
>
> *Tommy, Johnny, Mack and Jock, have left this earth.*
> *But we who live, will remember. I with Derrick and Ron.*
> *From the setting of the sun, till the rising of the same,*
> *We will think of those, who kept up England's fame.*
> *Will you in England remember?*[8]

Later, Holmes discovered that a fifth crew member had died – 37-year-old 'Mac' McLaren, the air gunner and 'father of the crew'. He was the only one with children – twins.

Holmes and Raymond were two of almost 10,000 Bomber Command airmen to become prisoners of war in Germany. Conditions for POWs were harsh. Food was often scarce and of poor quality, camps were cold in winter, and overcrowded. Men were sustained by parcels of food, medicine and other comforts sent by the Red Cross. Many wrote to, and received letters from, friends and family in their respective countries. Allan Ball shared photos of his fiancée Brenda – much to the jealousy of his fellow prisoners – while his squadron mate Holmes wrote in his notepad some of the best vignettes contained in letters received from prisoners' wives, lovers, friends and families, often written sincerely, without a trace of irony or sarcasm. They included: 'I haven't heard from you in such a long time now, I suppose you are too interested in some nice German girl'; 'I'm glad you got shot down before flying became dangerous'; 'Try to get to Dresden and visit that art gallery. The Blue Madonna is really worth seeing'; and 'It's the same dull routine every day, work in the morning, come home, go to a dance or cinema. It's so monotonous. But still I suppose there are some things you have to do without too.'

Stimulated by such correspondence, the vast majority of POWs were content to sit out the war. Some tried to escape, of course, with hundreds more carrying out various jobs to aid escape attempts – the most famous in March 1944, when 76 men tunnelled out of Stalag Luft III.

But as most prisoners focused on helping people get out of the camps, one Pathfinder airman astonishingly set about doing the exact opposite. After his Halifax was shot down over Belgium following a raid on Frankfurt in late December 1943, Winston Barrington – a gunner in 35 Squadron – was sent to Stalag IVB, one of the largest POW camps in Germany, near the town of Mühlberg. Barrington had moved to Germany in 1935 after his father died and his mother Florence married a German man – a high-ranking Luftwaffe officer. Barrington was sent back to the UK to be schooled in 1938 and joined the RAF two years later, never planning to return to Germany.

When war broke out, Florence remained in Germany and Austria, keeping in touch with Barrington back in England through letters smuggled through Switzerland and Sweden. Learning that Barrington had been shot down and sent to Stalag IVB, the urge to be reunited after not seeing her only son for five years was too much. When working parties of prisoners leaving the camp brought news back that a woman called Florence was staying in a Mühlberg hotel and asking about her son, Winston Barrington and a few of his fellow prisoners hatched a secret plan to smuggle his mother into the camp.

One day, she met with a working party, swapping places with a real prisoner, who wanted to have a crack at escaping. 'I went down to meet them and changed into his clothes behind a building,' Florence recalled later.[9] 'I chopped off my hair, rubbed dirt into my chin to look like stubble and bound my bosom with strips of material. When we marched off I could hardly lift my feet in the heavy boots. By the time I had trudged the six miles to camp I was barely conscious.'[10] She memorised the escaped airman's service number, disguised her voice and practised talking like a man. She easily passed for a boyish airman in his late teens or early twenties – the German guards didn't bat an eyelid as the five foot five figure dressed in drab battle fatigues shuffled through the camp gates with the rest of the returning working party. 'They just counted us in at the gates, so I got in with the group,' said Florence. She later had an emotional reunion with Barrington.

Prisoners from the camp's 'escape committee' set up a 'petticoat patrol' protection squad to keep her presence secret, rigging up a camp bed in an office piled high with Red Cross parcels. Her 'boudoir' hideout also included a pallet for a table, a washing bowl and a bucket for a lavatory. In return, Florence – or 'Mrs B' as they knew her – did all their washing, mending of clothes and other little jobs. For the next five months, Florence remained in the camp, with most of the 20,000 Allied prisoners not realising that living amongst them was an RAF Pathfinder's middle-aged mum. Florence eventually returned to Britain with Barrington when the camp was liberated by the Russians at the end of the war.[11]

CHAPTER TWENTY-TWO

Master Bombers

A T DAWN ON 6 June 1944, 150,000 British, American and Canadian troops crossed the English Channel to storm the beaches of Normandy and gain a precious foothold in mainland Europe. D-Day – and the liberation of mainland Europe – had begun, and the Pathfinders were entering one of the most intense periods of the entire war. Operational strategy continued to shift from large-area bombardments to smaller-scale, low-level precision attacks. But that didn't lessen the danger, and over the coming months some of the Pathfinder's most experienced airmen would be hacked down from the skies.

Hours before D-Day, Don Bennett was ordered to ensure the gun emplacements fringing the beaches of Normandy were wiped out so the troops landing had the best chance of survival. Now more than ever, precision was key to achieving military objectives and preventing friendly fire casualties amongst Allied troops and French civilians. Crews were warned not to jettison any bombs in the English Channel in case they hit the invasion force. The mission to take out the gun batteries was codenamed Operation Flashlamp. The Pathfinders led more than a thousand bombers over the Channel to pound ten coastal gun batteries sunk into the sand dunes along the French coast, dropping over 5,200 tons of bombs – the greatest quantity in the war so far in one night – and more than three times the volume dumped on Cologne in the thousand-bomber raid two years previously.

Most of the targets were covered in cloud, so the raids were led by Mosquitos marking and bombing blind using Oboe technology. These were followed up by Pathfinder heavies. When Ian Bazalgette attacked a coastal battery in his 635 Squadron Lancaster, he later scribbled in his logbook: 'D-Day – Longues Coastal Battery – Supporter – Channel full of shipping – Sky black with Lancs.'[1] News of the landings was the only subject on everyone's lips back in Britain. Bazalgette's mother Marion wrote to her son, telling him 'My thoughts, prayers, hopes, and wishes are with you today . . . We have been listening at intervals to the news and getting on with work in between times, which is the best way to pass the time. On Sunday night, just at 10pm, a Lancaster went over here, very low, with a light on. I stood outside the drawing room door and waved, pretending to myself 'twas you, it was soon out of sight in the haze. We shall be anxious to hear from you as soon as it's possible. I can understand how you felt when you decided that NOTHING would keep you out of this.'[2]

Meanwhile, 5 Group attacked the battery at La Pernelle, one of only two gun emplacements that were not covered in cloud. 'Half an hour or so before the first troops went ashore, we pasted a large gun emplacement, only a thing about the size of an old redoubt but we had one hundred and eleven Lancasters on it – just one huge bomb crater left now,' John Kelly wrote in a letter home.[3] As the aircraft flew back over the English Channel, some glimpsed the vast armada below through the cloud or saw it as blips on their H2S screens. Everyone realised the tide of the war was turning.

Another pilot later wrote: 'When we broke cloud over the French coast the Channel was full of ships. The army had pulled its finger out at last and D-Day was on. We bombed at 0500 just as it was getting light, and had a grandstand view of the Americans running in on the beach . . . marvellous sight coming back as the sun came up.'[4]

The crucial attacks on the coastal batteries were largely successful – most were put out of action – and within hours the troops had secured a foothold. The following day, Don Bennett found himself walking up the steps at Chatham House in central London to give a long-arranged address to the Royal Institute of International Affairs on the subject of, ironically, World Peace. Hours later, he was back in the ops room at Huntingdon.

The following days were critical and tense, with Pathfinder operations continuing unabated, attacking airfields, radar stations, gun emplacements, ammo sites, fuel dumps, and railway and road junctions to prevent the Germans rushing troops to the coast. Some crews operated up to four nights consecutively. Bazalgette flew an operation targeting a group of enemy tanks which had pinned the Allied army down near Caen. The 25-year-old bombed 'a big forest with hundreds of tanks in it' from an altitude of only 800 feet with such accuracy that he earned a commendation from the army. When he returned to the airfield in Downham Market he opened the throttles of the giant Lancaster and 'buzzed' the control tower at rooftop height.

By 1 July 1944, the Allies had secured a tiny but important foothold in Normandy, landing over a million troops and more than 175,000 vehicles. The eight Lancaster and five Mosquito squadrons of 8 Group had flown more than 2,000 operations in June for the loss of 30 aircraft. 'It's been hard going,' the group monthly operations book recorded, 'but we now have the feeling that every effort is rolling the wheel faster and faster towards final victory.'[5]

It was crucial the momentum was maintained.

At around 11pm on Tuesday, 4 July, the Pathfinders took off from their airfields, leading 100 main-force bombers to attack marshalling yards at Villeneuve St George, near Paris. As part of the Pathfinders effort, Alec Cranswick was piloting one of 14 Lancasters from 35 Squadron. This was the 24-year-old's one hundred and seventh operation for Bomber Command. The previous April he had married Val Parr, a 21-year-old signals operator and former dancer who worked at the Pathfinders' headquarters in Huntingdon. Val had been in hospital for a month recovering from an operation, but Alec promised to pick her up the morning after the Villeneuve St George raid and take her home. There was much to look forward to. She was pregnant with their first child, and Cranswick was due to finish his wartime flying when he'd completed 110 operations. Neither Val nor Cranswick's mother had wanted him to carry on flying, and he could have easily never set foot in an aircraft again. After all, he had amassed possibly the greatest number of operations under his belt of any heavy-bomber captain in the RAF. Yet his desire to fly for Bennett's men saw him take to the skies again. In May, after Cranswick successfully completed his hundredth operation, he wrote the figure '100' and 'Whoo!! Whoo!!' in his logbook.[6]

As always, before he took off, Cranswick handed his beloved Alsatian Kluva over to one of the ground crew, reassuring him he'd see him again. Two hours later, as Cranswick's Lancaster swooped down to 8,000 feet and began its bombing run in the early hours of 5 July, the plane was hit by light flak. Fire quickly tore through the fuselage. Cranswick shouted 'Emergency! Jump!' to his crew as he battled with the controls. Seconds later, the machine split into two and spiralled to the ground. Only the wireless operator survived, thrown clear by sheer luck. When the Lancasters started to land back at Graveley, Kluva waited eagerly by the runway, ready to be let off his leash as usual when Cranswick's plane reached its dispersal point, so they could be reunited. After the final bomber touched down, Kluva continued his patient vigil, ears alert for the distant rumble of his master's plane that would never come.

The following morning, Val was dressed and waiting for Cranswick to pull into the hospital car park and take her home. Instead, she was greeted by an RAF padre, who broke the news. 'She was devastated and angry. She felt shattered,' recalled Gwen Thomas, who was a good friend of Val's. 'Alec needn't have gone on the mission. But these chaps felt they were immortal really. Why did they keep doing it? He didn't have to. He'd done a hundred and six ops.'[7] Later, Val wrote in her diary: 'I knew it could come. I must be brave for his sake. I loved him so much.'[8] She returned to Oxford, where a few months later she gave birth to a son, Alex.

Cranswick's death at the hands of a German shell was a stark reminder that operations over France could be just as dangerous as the big raids over Germany, however experienced the crews. There was simply no such thing as a soft target, especially since the Luftwaffe had reinforced its flak defences by moving 140 heavy and 50 light flak batteries from Germany to France. This was part of a long-established invasion contingency plan entitled 'Drohende Gefahr West' (Imminent Danger West), which detailed how the Luftwaffe would move flak formations from the Reich to France and the Low Countries to strengthen western air defences.[9] The formation of a Flak Corps III led to the transfer of some 3,500 light and medium flak guns to positions to cover the Channel coast, and to protect their V-weapon sites.

On 13 June, a V1 flying bomb exploded near Gravesend in Essex at 4am, the first of the 30,000 V-weapons which the Germans would use to bombard Britain over the following ten months. This was a last desperate throw of the dice from Hitler. But the threat was a major one, and V-weapon 'ski-ramp' launch sites and storage depots dotted across northern Europe were added to the long list of Bomber Command targets, under the codename 'Crossbow'. Both British and American bomber forces were ordered to eliminate as many sites as they could. From December 1943 to May 1944, Crossbow targets had taken 12 per cent of the bombing effort, but between June and August 1944 the proportion rose to 33 per cent.[10]

These targets required pinpoint marking and accurate bombing. In addition to their night-time operations, Pathfinders also started to lead bombing operations during daylight hours. This was both a novelty and a fearsome prospect for men who had been trained to operate under the cloak of darkness. One Canadian Pathfinder on mission to France looked back at the hundred or so Halifaxes following behind. 'It was by far the most beautiful sight I have ever seen,' he scribbled in his diary afterwards.[11]

After one raid on a V-1 storage site on 19 July 1944, a Pathfinder pilot on his first raid in a Mosquito after a tour on Lancasters wrote:

> First trip in Mossie and my first daylight op. Took off an hour after the Lancs and caught them up at the French coast, much to the joy of Don, who'd had enough of sitting behind the curtain in Lanc and twiddling knobs. France looked very peaceful in the afternoon sun, and I even caught a glimpse of Paris in the distance. Heavy flak at the target but the Lancs caught it while we watched. Left the Lancs at the coast and beetled back to base flat out. Arrived at dusk and beat up the mess, much to the consternation of gang at the bar. Decide that a Mossie is definitely a safer way of going to war.[12]

New bomb-marking techniques were devised, such as using Lancasters taking off every 15 seconds, flying in small formations of between 6 and 16, and releasing their bomb loads on a signal from the

Oboe-equipped leading Mosquito, which emitted a smoke puff or dropped its own bombs when it was nearing the target. Bearing in mind the pace of the operations as the campaign ramped up, there wasn't much time for pilots more used to flying in bomber streams at night to be taught the finer points of formation flying by day. As they bounced through the air in a stepped-down formation within a few feet of each other, it is a testament to their skill and flying ability that there weren't more accidents or collisions.

The master-bomber technique was also being deployed widely by all Pathfinders, where small targets would be marked by Oboe-equipped Mosquitos before the master bomber flying in a Lancaster quickly assessed their accuracy and directed the main force accordingly. Some Pathfinder Lancasters were also fitted with Oboe, where the plane was manned by its regular crew, but on the run in to the target, the 'guest' pilot and navigator also onboard – essentially experts in flying using Oboe – swapped places with the regular pilot and navigator to execute the attack.

Lightly defended at first, the Germans soon began to redirect what available fighters and flak batteries they had in an attempt to stop the Pathfinders marking and bombing the V-weapon sites.

Ian Bazalgette was all too aware of the need to knock the V-weapon sites out of action. Bazalgette, or 'Will' as his family called him so as to avoid confusion with his father of the same first name, saw first-hand the damage wrought by the V-1s as they landed near his parents' home in Malden, south-west London. Launched from a 160-foot-long ramp at sites across the Pas-de-Calais, the pilotless winged missiles navigated their way to the target using a preset guidance system. Each missile had a maximum range of 300 miles. They were soon nicknamed 'doodlebugs' or 'buzz bombs' on account of the distinctive sound they made. People across southern England listened alertly, knowing that as soon as the engine cut out and the sound stopped, almost 2,000lb of explosive would be coming their way any second.

At the end of June, Bazalgette took a few days leave from leading Pathfinder missions with 635 Squadron against V-1 flying bomb sites to spend some precious time at home. He was one of the most experienced Pathfinder pilots and loved the buzz and thrill of ops, yet some leave was always welcome. He helped his father build a small air-raid shelter, where his parents fled one night while he and his younger sister Ethel huddled under a mattress in the hallway as flying bombs crashed all around. Visits home by airmen to spend time with their families were essential for keeping up morale, and Don Bennett ensured his crews were allotted their fair share of leave. It mattered to the families too. Marion Bazalgette told her son that he was 'the link in the chain which keeps this family together' and seeing or receiving a letter from him 'will often restore the happy atmosphere to this household like the magic wave of a wand'.[13] After he'd finished his leave and headed back to work, she wrote:

Your leave seemed more than usually short and I am missing you, I hope the next weeks 'tween leaves go by quickly. I hope your journey was comfortable and went smoothly. We had a nice lull on Monday night, lasting all night. Yesterday began with one flying bomb coming down on a cottage in Traps Lane, our nearest yet. Houses on our opposite side had glass broken and ceilings down. We were lucky, only blackout blinds down. There were no casualties, one old lady crawled into the Morrison and was taken out unhurt; though considerably shocked. They came over at intervals all day, but only a few during last night, two were in Malden. The milk rounds woman left you a nice pint of milk yesterday. I wish you were here to enjoy it![14]

A few days later, Bazalgette replied to his mother:

My last leave was an amazing experience and you were all utterly delightful to me as usual. I do feel that I leave you in greater danger than I am called upon to undergo. A very sad thought – my fingers are permanently crossed for you all . . . Work has been very interesting since I returned, and in general we have had a grand time. One very good dance at Ely Hospital – bags of nice nurses with starched white jerkins. Tonight I am going to see 'Gone with the Wind' with a WAAF officer – my next victim. My crew are all happy and raising lots of hell. We seem to create more trouble than anyone else on the camp, but we do have fun.

Love to all, Will.[15]

Bazalgette was soon back in the action, and over the next month he flew 14 operations – an average of one every two days – as the Pathfinders upped the intensity of the campaign. Some operations were carried out in daylight, with RAF Spitfires providing fighter cover – a novelty and a welcome experience for the Bomber Boys – proving the tables had been well and truly turned from four years before when it was the Luftwaffe bombers boasting the fighter escorts as they attacked Britain.

By August, Bazalgette had been promoted to directing raids as a master bomber, in one case ordering the main force to follow him down to just 2,000 feet, which resulted in the target being bombed without any losses. Bazalgette told a friend: 'Barring the occasional sticky effort, I feel that the RAF fights very luxuriously. If ever I prayed sincerely, I did for the Army as we did our stuff on "D-Day". I am as happy as a bee with a bum full of honey these days. My crew are a grand bunch, and I am serving with a really grand Squadron.'[16]

On 4 August, Bazalgette and his crew were due to go on leave when another 635 Squadron crew dropped out of that morning's operation because their Lanc was fogged in at another airfield. The squadron was to lead a lunchtime attack against the V-1 storage facility hidden in caves at Trossy St Maximin, twenty miles north of Paris. Bazalgette and his crewmates conferred. They agreed to cancel their leave and fly. It wouldn't take long. It would be Bazalgette's fifty-eighth operational flight and he was close to completing his second tour of operations. He'd already planned to then do a third. The crew were driven out to their aircraft and sat around in the August sunshine munching iced buns and chatting until it was time to take off.

Two hours later, they were approaching Trossy St Maximin at 12,000 feet. Ten 635 Squadron Pathfinders were to mark the target for a main force of 61 Lancasters, all from 8 Group. But the V-1 storage facilities at Trossy St Maximin had been bombed on each of the two preceding days and the enemy air defences were ready. The sky was soon filled with black bursts of flak. There was no alternative but to fly straight and level through the tunnel of flak in order to mark the target accurately for the main-force bombers. This made the Pathfinder planes easy targets. First, the Lancaster of the deputy master bomber, flying half a mile ahead to drop the opening markers, was struck by a direct hit, blowing the tail clean off. It tumbled to the ground in flames, killing the eight crew. Watching the horror unfold, the master bomber dived in his Lancaster to take over the marking, but he too was put out of action when flak struck the length of his Lancaster's fuselage and the starboard elevator was damaged.

With both master bombers inoperative, the success of the attack now fell on Bazalgette's shoulders, flying the next Lancaster as 'primary visual marker'. He narrowed his eyes and focused on the job ahead, holding the plane steady at 8,000 feet as its metal frame was rocked by pressure waves from exploding flak. Then, in an instant, a ball of flak smashed through the starboard wing, igniting its petrol tanks and disabling the engines. Almost immediately more flak hit the nose. Ivan Hibbert, Bazalgette's bomb aimer, called out on the intercom, 'I've been hit.' His right arm had been almost completely blown off at the shoulder.

Bazalgette flew on with flames streaming from the starboard wing and only his port engines operating. With the bomb aimer out of action, as the plane approached the target, Bazalgette released the markers himself using controls in the cockpit. The flares fizzed down, allowing the main force behind to deliver their payloads bang on the money in a successful strike. He battled hard to keep the ailing plane from spinning as two other crew members dragged Hibbert to the rest bed near the rear of the plane and plunged a blessed needle of morphine into his shaking body.

It was now clear to Bazalgette they couldn't make it home. The situation was dire. So he decided instead to head in the direction where he knew Allied troops were pushing across France. Their best hope was to crash land behind the front lines. But aviation fuel from a ruptured tank was now sloshing about in the rear fuselage, and the starboard wing was dangerously close to folding. The rear gunner turned his turret towards the burning wing. 'I could not believe my eyes,' he said later. 'The starboard wing was like a herringbone after all the flesh has been eaten off it. I could hardly believe we were still flying. I knew we were a doomed aircraft.'[17]

It was now around 11 minutes since the plane had been hit, but time and options were running out. One crew member was prostrate on the bench and another had been overcome by fumes from the leaking petrol. As the port inner engine packed up too, the flight engineer George Turner shouted: 'You'll have to put her down, Baz.'[18]

Bazalgette asked Turner to fix his crash belt tightly around him and ordered the four uninjured crew to don their parachutes and bail out. He had no intention of following them and abandoning his remaining two injured crewmates, and set about seeing where he could put the plane down.

In the hot August sunshine, people living in the small village of Senantes had watched the drama unfold overhead and saw four white parachutes billow open below the flaming Lancaster. Now they braced for the worst as the Lancaster barrelled straight for them.

But then the pilot of the plane appeared to deliberately steer the bomber away from the village, completing a sweeping turn, before levelling out. The huge bulk of the smoking Lanc sank through the sky and skidded across a field, in what appeared to be a textbook crash-landing, only for it to hit a ditch and erupt into a huge fireball.

A few months later, Bazalgette's wireless operator Chuck Godfrey wrote to his mother:

> Dear Mrs. Bazalgette:
>
> No doubt you have been notified that Ian, your son and our skipper, was unfortunately killed when our plane crashed in northern France on August 4th. It's a very sad thought as he was a real good captain, and everyone in the crew really owe everything we have to him.
>
> Geoffrey Goddard, George Turner, Douglas Cameron, and myself were lucky enough to escape by parachute thanks to the excellent piloting of a helpless aircraft by Ian. After a month in hiding we managed to evade capture and returned to the UK last Sunday having been liberated by the army.
>
> The French people informed us after about a week that Ian had lost his life, but I'm afraid I've no further details as to where his body lies in peace. I do know that the Germans took F/L Hibbert and F/Sgt Leeder, the two remaining crew members, to Beauvais and I'm told that they were apparently buried in the military cemetery.
>
> If I can give you any further information I shall be very pleased to do so, but I think the other boys will be writing to you. Please accept my deepest sympathy. Our skipper was a grand fellow and I wish that

he could have been with us still and carry on with the work we have to do.

Yours Sincerely, C.R. Godfrey, F/O[19]

Ian Bazagette was the first of three Pathfinders in the war to receive the Victoria Cross. His citation opened by summarising the attack, and continued:

Squadron Leader Bazalgette fought bravely to bring his aircraft and crew to safety. The mid-upper gunner was overcome by fumes. Squadron Leader Bazalgette ordered those of his crew who were able to leave by parachute to do so. He remained at the controls and attempted the almost hopeless task of landing the crippled and blazing aircraft in a last effort to save the wounded bomb aimer and helpless air gunner. With superb skill and taking great care to avoid a small French village nearby, he brought the aircraft down safely. Unfortunately, it then exploded and this gallant officer and his two comrades perished. His heroic sacrifice marked the climax of a long career of operations against the enemy. He always chose the more dangerous and exacting roles. His courage and devotion to duty were beyond praise.[20]

The tragic death of Bazalgette and his fellow airmen highlighted the danger of attacking V-1 targets, which was made all the more frustrating because of their ephemeral nature. They were small and therefore hard to locate and destroy, but easy to repair. Only thanks to Oboe technology and the marking skills of the master bombers were the Pathfinders across both 5 and 8 Groups able to successfully hit as many as they did. Forty-one sites were attacked by the Pathfinders in July alone.[21] But Harris wasn't convinced that attacking V-weapon sites was the best use of his force, a view vindicated by the fact that the threat wouldn't really be snuffed out until the Allied land armies advanced through Europe and overran the launching sites on the ground.

Flak wasn't the only danger. By the summer of 1944, German air force monthly fighter losses were running at almost 50 per cent of its force strength.[22] One secret Allied intelligence report concluded, somewhat optimistically, that the Luftwaffe 'can no longer affect the military situation on any front'.[23] Yet while the German air force was being hit hard – despite the continued increase of its fighter production – this didn't mean it wasn't still a major threat to the Pathfinders.

At 9.08am on 6 August 1944, John Kelly was three and a half hours away from finding out just what devastating damage Luftwaffe fighters could inflict, as his Lancaster climbed into the sky above Coningsby on that gloriously sunny Sunday morning and headed towards the French coast for an operation near Paris. The 24-year-old had enjoyed a successful and busy period since 83 Squadron had transferred over to 5 Group the previous spring. 'We are up to our eyebrows in work, the trips do not take long, only about four hours or less, but this full moon makes things rather sticky as we are bombing from extremely low altitudes,' he wrote home in early June.[24]

His crew had marked the achievement of being promoted to blind markers by designing a crest to be painted on the front of their aircraft just below the pilot's cockpit. 'It is a very glamorous creature (heaps of geometry-curves etc) with a sort of transparent curtain affair over her shoulder and streaming behind, with a bandage around her eyes and a bomb held in her outstretched hand, to typify a blind marker,' Kelly told his parents. 'I have finished the sketching pencil on fabric, but now it remains to paint it and then stick it on the fuselage.'

Much of the squadron's operations since D-Day had been over France and the Low Countries, but Kelly shared a different perspective in a letter home in late July after a rare operation on a German city, in which he reckoned dropping 'cookies and two thousand high capacity bombs with bags of blast' was 'much more satisfying' than hitting French targets 'with the delay action stuff which we don't even see go off'.

'In a way it will be a pity if the show finishes soon,' Kelly wrote, 'because after next winter no one will have to worry about what we are going to do to those swine after the war, main problem will be damping down the ashes.' In late July, Kelly had painted a picture for his parents of life on an operational wartime airbase:

> It is a lovely sunny day here now, no aircraft are flying just now and one could almost forget there was a war on. Looking out the window soon

dispels all that though, for a couple of tractors are passing, driven by WAAFs, each towing a long string of bomb trolleys, each with its occupant nestling snuggly in place. Soon they will be hoisted in the bomb bays, and in not very many hours dropping down to pay yet another instalment of our debt to the 'poor misled German people'. Sorry if I am feeling a bit bitter in this letter, but writing certainly helps get it out of my system.

On the 26 July, Kelly wrote home, 'we are working tonight, I do not have any clues about the target yet, but I hope it is a German one because I have only 13 trips left and I want to deliver a few loads of HE etc on the old Hun before I finish, and the odd marker too.'

Now – exactly two months after D-Day – as he flew towards Paris, Kelly's desire to bomb Germany again would have to wait. He had more pressing matters to contend with. The flight from Coningsby hadn't exactly gone smoothly. Heavy cloud over France broke up the force of over a hundred heavy bombers, and while some crews turned around early after an order from the master bomber, many ploughed on. At around 12.30pm Kelly's Lancaster bombed the V-1 supply depot at Bois de Cassan, just outside Paris, after it had been marked by Oboe-fitted Mosquitos. He was focusing on keeping the aircraft straight and level at 14,000 feet so the onboard camera could get a clear shot of the bombs onto the target, when he spotted two miles dead ahead at least nine enemy fighters – either Messerschmitt 109s or Focke-Wulf 190s – closing fast. Almost simultaneously, seven more enemy fighters dived out of the sun on the port side, fizzing past Kelly's Lancaster like arrows. A further three FW 190s peeled off and attacked.

There were now at least 18 enemy fighters looking for a kill and the promised Spitfire fighter cover was nowhere to be seen. The odds were well and truly stacked against Kelly's Lancaster as the first German fighter zoomed in. 'Dive port!' shouted Kelly's rear gunner, a plucky little Australian called Gilbert Duggin, over the intercom. Kelly thrust the control stick forward, plunging the Lancaster into a steep dive to port, which threw the wireless operator into the side of the fuselage, snapping his ankle. Seconds later, enemy cannon fire from the attacking fighter punched a hole clean through the inner port engine with a loud bang. Duggin's four machine guns clattered in anger as a second fighter tore in and sprayed its cannon fire through the Lancaster's fuselage, pummelling Duggin's abdomen and legs and setting his turret alight. Despite his injuries, Duggin shouted a warning to Kelly that a third fighter was attacking from above. Kelly flung the bomber into another corkscrew in a desperate attempt to throw it off.

The German fighters were now targeting other Pathfinder bombers on the raid. At least 13 combats between the fighters and the bombers broke out in a vicious air battle. One Lancaster was shot down, killing its crew of eight, while the Spitfires, which had belatedly arrived, also managed to shoot down two German fighters, albeit after much of the damage had already been done.[25]

In the melee, Kelly had thrown off the fighters attacking his Lancaster thanks to some skilful flying, but black smoke was now pouring from the port wing and he was struggling to keep the plane under control. 'Put on your parachutes,' he ordered the crew. But there was little more he could do. 'Abandon aircraft!' he shouted. The mid-upper gunner obeyed his skipper's orders, opened the escape hatch and leapt out, his parachute blossoming open seconds later. He was never seen again. But the attack had damaged the aircraft's hydraulics and both Duggin in the rear turret and his crewmate manning the guns in the nose were trapped, desperately calling for help. Kelly managed to get the Lancaster back under control and cancelled the abandon aircraft order until his crewmates had been rescued. Malcolm MacNeil, a Canadian bomb aimer, climbed through to the nose and freed the trapped front gunner. He then went to the rear turret, released Duggin and dragged him to the rest bed where he gave first aid, before taking up the position at the gear guns himself. Kelly's wireless operator climbed up to vacated mid-upper turret, despite being in agony with a broken ankle, ready to fight off any further fighter attacks.

The fighters may have vanished, but the ordeal was far from over. Anti-aircraft flak batteries opened up and twice hit the Lancaster's bruised frame with yet more hot metal. Yet still the battered plane limped on, and Kelly nurtured it back over the Channel. Trying to reach their home base of Coningsby was out of the question. He decided instead to try to land at Ford, a nearby airfield in West Sussex. Controlling the Lancaster took huge skill. One engine was out, half

the tail was shot off. The steering, and the flaps – so crucial for landing – were almost totally ineffective. Worse still, the undercarriage
was jammed because the hydraulics had been ruptured. Kelly ordered
it to be lowered using compressed air from a bottle. Even then, only
the starboard wheel came down. That would have to do. If they stayed
in the air much longer, the aircraft would break up. Kelly was cleared
to land from the control tower at Ford and lined upon the runway
ahead. The plane roared over the perimeter fence, touching down
with a screech on one wheel and zooming along the tarmac until the
oleo strut collapsed. The plane skidded along on its belly in a shower
of sparks and shuddered to a halt. With some miraculous flying, Kelly
had safely got his crew home, despite the fuselage looking, he would
later tell his parents, 'like fair imitation of a colander'.

A few days later, Kelly and his crewmates flew down to see Duggin,
who was still recuperating in hospital. 'He is progressing very well
indeed there but it will be some time before he is out and about,' Kelly
told his parents. 'Altogether he has about eight bullet wounds, several
cannon splinter wounds, one very big, and of course the nose cap of a
cannon shell, complete with number, which was dug out of you know
where. He is quite cheerful, more so now as I was able to give him the
news that he has been awarded the DFC for his effort.' In addition to
Duggin, Kelly and MacNeil were also awarded Distinguished Flying
Crosses for their role in bringing the stricken bomber home. Back at
Coningsby, Kelly was treated as something of a hero for cheating
death. He was bought a beer by Guy Gibson, the Dam Buster-hero VC
winner and fellow 5 Group airman. Gibson would be killed over the
Netherlands just a few weeks later.

By the end of August 1944, Kelly had just six trips to complete
before his tour was over. 'Please do not worry unduly because what are
six trips when I have done nearly 40?' he reassured his parents in a
letter home. He admitted he was 'beginning to feel tired of flying on
ops, it really is a tremendous strain, particularly this sort of work, as it
entails so much extra training' but was encouraged that his luck had
taken a turn for the better. 'Heaven knows we need it,' added Kelly.
'Take care of yourself and don't worry about me . . .'

Kelly saw out his final missions safely and the news of his 'gong'
made the local paper, which reported it had been awarded for

'courage, fortitude and devotion to duty', adding he had successfully completed 46 missions over Germany and France.[26] 'So I have made the headlines again,' Kelly wrote to his parents when he saw the story in the paper. 'I can see that I shall have to wear my civvies when next I come home else I shall not be able to cope with all the free beer the various local bods will stand me.'

But their joy at knowing their Pathfinder hero had survived the war had a bitter aftertaste. A few weeks later another tiny story appeared in the same paper:

> Flying Officer James Kelly, RAF, who was reported missing from air operations on July 4, is now known to have been killed and buried near Calvados, France. He was 22 years old and the youngest son of Mr and Mrs R. Kelly, of the Brow, Purbrook.[27]

The airman, John's younger brother Jim, had been shot down in a dogfight and managed to ditch his Spitfire, only to be dragged out of his cockpit and, at the orders of the local German commander, executed in cold blood.

By September 1944, Allied armies were making their way steadily through France and into the Low Countries. Between 1 April and 30 September, 8 Group had flown 13,966 sorties – only 583 fewer than it launched in the previous 19 months. Over the same period, 884 Pathfinder airmen had been killed.[28] On 14 September, Eisenhower relinquished control of the air force strategy. For Bert Harris, it was now time to resume the full-scale bombing of Germany, after a five-month break. 'We should now get on and knock Germany finally flat,' Harris wrote to Churchill at the end of the month.

The end was in sight. But there was still so much bloodshed to come.

CHAPTER TWENTY-THREE

The Wooden Wonder

B Y THE AUTUMN OF 1944, Germany's night-fighter force was declining in potency and Bomber Command was suffering fewer casualties. But there was no let-up in the bombing effort by the Allies. Over the coming months, German cities which had thus far avoided the crosshairs of British and American bombers were targeted and destroyed – some controversially. The firepower deployed from the air was simply awesome – about 75 per cent of the total Allied wartime bomb load in Europe would be dropped by Bomber Command and the American Army Air Forces in the final eight months of the war. And despite the weakening of enemy airpower, the skies over Europe were still fraught with danger – over the same period, at least 456 airmen of 8 Group would lose their lives.[1]

Yet while bombing German cities had been a priority for the Allies since 1942, the sands were shifting. Some senior commanders believed that the swiftest end to the war would come from attacking transport and oil targets to stem Hitler's ability to fuel his tanks and planes and move weapons and troops quickly. Smashing towns and cities with bombs would bring eventual victory, but how quickly and at what cost? And when that victory came, the German industry and economy might potentially be in such dire straits that the cost of resurrecting the country in a post-Reich world could be overwhelming. The spoils of war would be piles of rubble, assuming the Russians advancing from the east hadn't got there first.

In late 1944, Harris was ordered by the Allied High Command to concentrate primarily on German oil and transport targets, but instead he persevered primarily with his attacks on cities. In this view, Harris was in step with the British public, where appetite for bombing German civilians had risen from less than half the population in 1940 to almost two thirds by 1944.[2] People wanted to end the war quickly and believed area bombing was key. Besides, Harris knew he had built his legend as the man who took Total War to the people of Germany. He also knew he had the personal support of Churchill, despite the Prime Minister's waning interest in the bombing campaign with so much else going on.

Harris's refusal to sway from his eagerness for area bombing created such friction with his commanding officers that at one stage he even offered his resignation to Sir Charles Portal, the Chief of the Air Staff. But Portal backed down, and Harris continued to direct the bulk of Bomber Command and the Pathfinders' efforts towards cities until the end of the war. He also encouraged his other group commanders to experiment with their own forms of target marking, albeit at a far smaller level than 8 Group. While he did increase raids on oil targets, it was rarely at the same intensity as his more favoured urban targets. Despite the directives from above, between October and December 1944, 53 per cent of Bomber Command attacks were on German cities, compared to 15 per cent against transport targets and 14 per cent against oil targets.[3]

As these internal conflicts rumbled on, Don Bennett cracked on with the job at hand, ensuring what targets he was given would be bombed as accurately as possible. From September 1944, 8 Group led attacks on Luftwaffe airfields, ports and coastal batteries, helping to winkle out stubborn pockets of German troops as the Allied forces advanced. Mindful of a friendly-fire incident when some Canadian troops were killed after using the same colour flares as the Pathfinder markers of the day, Bennett introduced a special marking crew called a 'long stop' whose job it was to drop a line of flares to halt the marking and bombing if it got too near Allied troops below.

On 10 September, the Pathfinders led Bomber Command in a huge raid on eight separate coastal batteries, each with its own aiming point. The operation required meticulous planning, with eight master bombers and eight deputy master bombers. Heavy bombers also pounded cities across the Ruhr, finishing a job they'd started 18 months before. After a relative lull over the summer, airmen were once again visiting familiar names – Dortmund, Essen, Cologne. The Pathfinders also helped Bomber Command support the Allied advance through the Low Countries as part of Operation Market Garden – the ambitious but ultimately unsuccessful plan to secure a way into Germany via the River Rhine.

On 19 September 1944 – the day after Eindhoven was liberated – Fons van der Heijden, who had put his life on the line to help shelter Ernie Holmes a few months before, burst into the kitchen of the family farm. 'We're about to be liberated!' the 48-year-old said excitedly, and busily set about distributing chocolate bars to his wife and six children, which he'd been given by Canadian troops four miles away. The farm was still in German-held territory, but its forces were retreating, driven back by Allied forces after bitter fighting. 'How lucky we have been! Soon the war will be over and our family will be safe,' Fons reassured his family. His 21-year-old daughter Netje quietly relayed the news to an injured American airmen they were hiding on the farm, who had been shot down a few days before. 'Keep quiet for a couple more days,' she whispered to him.[4]

The next morning, Fons went to church in the local village, where he sang in the choir, accompanied by his 14-year-old son Piet, who was training to be a priest. Netje went to milk the cows, as she always did. Things were looking up. But cycling back to the farm with her clanking milk churns, Netje looked on in horror as lorries swung into the farmyard and screeched to halt. Around 30 German troops leapt out and started searching the farm buildings, demanding to know where they were sheltering the airman. They soon discovered the flying jacket of the American, which had been hastily hidden in a bread oven. Word was sent back to the village. When Fons and Piet strolled out of the church after the service, they were surrounded by German troops and taken to the village café.

'Where is the Allied airman you are hiding on your farm?' Fons was asked. He knew nothing about the raid and guessed the Germans were bluffing. He denied knowing anything. The German officer gave him half an hour to rethink his answer. Assuming his cover had been blown, and desperate not to see his wife and young family harmed, Fons confessed: 'My wife and children know nothing about why you've come. I alone am involved,' he said. In front of Piet, who was sitting in the café with his father, Fons was sentenced to death. A friend stepped in and pleaded with the German officer to be lenient, but to no avail. A priest was permitted to enter the café to read Fons his last rites.

As the farmer was marched out of the café, he looked across to his eldest brother, who had gathered with some of the other villagers. 'You keep well, Sjef. See you!' Fons said to him, defiantly. Following him into a field, two German soldiers opened fire. Two bullets hit Fons in the back and head. The crack of the gunshots rang through the village. Netje, who had gone to her uncle's house nearby, sprinted to where her father lay sprawled in the mud and cradled his head in her arms, but he was already dead. The Van der Heijdens fled for their lives to friends on neighbouring farms, as the German troops ransacked the farm, looted belongings and shot the chickens in anger. Only later could the Van der Heijdens give Fons the proper burial he so deserved. He had saved the lives of scores of young airmen – including the young American, who was discovered by the Germans but miraculously spared.

As Bennett's force focused on providing tactical air support for the ground armies advancing through Europe and on area-bombing raids on cities, his use of Mosquito bombers to keep the Germans on their toes as the war in Europe came to a climax was as masterly as it was adventurous.

In 1943, Bennett had created the Light Night Striking Force (LNSF), an elite Mosquito force within 8 Group. From its embryonic single squadron, by early 1945 it comprised nine squadrons, each with around 20 aircraft, with 139 Squadron providing the marking. The LNSF was originally designed to act as a spoof force, drawing fighters away from separate, bigger raids. Soon it was carrying out 'nuisance' or 'siren' raids on those nights when the main force didn't operate. As it grew in strength, the LNSF became a major headache for the German people and their defenders, with as many as 120 Mosquitos barrelling through Third Reich airspace in a single night.

Many pilots and navigators who had completed tours on heavy bombers in the main force dreamt of flying Mossies. The missions were often exciting and exhilarating, with the aircraft getting up to speeds of 450mph – whether bombing Berlin from 30,000 feet, or as 'tunnel busters' chucking bombs into railway tunnel entrances at just 50 feet above the deck, or swooping down over canals under heavy gunfire to lay explosive mines. Attacks on Germany's waterways, crucial for transporting coal for the Reich's war industry, were often only possible through the nimble capabilities of the Mosquitos. Mine-laying was codenamed 'gardening'. Bombs were called 'veg'. In one attack, 16 Mosquitos swooped through heavy anti-aircraft fire to lay mines along the strategically important Dortmund–Ems Canal. One Mosquito pilot later wrote: 'We were able to get a good run up and dropped our veg about ½ way down the 6 miles stretch. All this stage we were about 50' above the canal. We climbed like —s, gaining 20,000' in about 2 mins.'[5]

Mosquitos of the LNSF were adapted to carry an oil drum-shaped 4,000lb 'cookie' bomb, so the two-engine bomber could be loaded with the same bomb load as that of the American B-17 Flying Fortress – the four-engine heavy bomber widely used by the USAAF, which had ten crew and was more than twice the weight. The comparison didn't escape the wit of the Mosquito airmen. After a few drinks in smoky pubs in Pathfinder country, they could sometimes be heard belting out a verse of the popular American patriotic anthem 'Mine Eyes Have Seen the Glory', with suitably adapted lyrics:

> *We fly our Flying Fortresses at 30,000 feet,*
> *We fly our Flying Fortresses at 30,000 feet,*
> *We fly our Flying Fortresses at 30,000 feet,*
> *But we only drop a teeny-weeny bomb!*

The Mosquito carried the same bomb load, of course. The difference was, however, that the Mosquito was more than twice as fast as the B-17, which had limited space to carry bombs because of all its armament. Rather than huge daylight raids, the Mossie's *raison d'être* was speed and stealth. In one three-minute early morning raid on Berlin, LNSF Mosquitos dropped more than 30 4,000lb bombs on the city, despite the heavy cloud. 'The defences seemed to have been caught napping,' said one of the pilots. 'But in a matter of seconds the flak became pretty severe. Our bombs fell smack on the markers. Although it was quite a heavy attack, the whole thing was over in a flash.'[6]

That was half the problem for the Germans. In 1945, the LNSF raided Berlin 170 times, including 36 consecutive nights – a feat which even prompted a rare signal of congratulations from Harris to Bennett. Sometimes a plane would fly to Berlin twice in one night, swapping crews in between operations while it was refuelled and rearmed on the tarmac. The trip to Berlin became so familiar its crews nicknamed the missions the 'Berlin Express' and the 'Milk Round'. Likewise the Germans – who heard these nicknames from captured Allied airmen – were so used to the three routes the Mosquitos took over the Big City, they christened them platforms one, two and three.[6] On other occasions, a single Mosquito loaded with four 500lb bombs attacked four different cities. The damage was relatively small compared to the huge raids by the heavy bombers, but the psychological impact of using the fast, nimble Mosquito against both civilians and the military was huge.

'During the night the cursed Englishmen return to Berlin with their Mosquitos and deprive one of the few hours' sleep which one needs more than ever these days,' Joseph Goebbels wrote in his diary on 27 February 1945.[7] A few days later, he scribbled: 'The air terror which rages uninterruptedly over German home territory makes people thoroughly despondent. One feels so impotent against it that no one can now see a way out of the dilemma.'[8] Goebbels became almost obsessed with the regular visits from the LNSF. 'In the evening we have the usual Mosquito alert,' he wrote in March 1945.

> This happens every evening with stereotyped regularity. The millions in the Reich capital are gradually becoming somewhat nervous and hysterical. This is understandable too when people have to spend every evening in the air-raid shelters under such primitive conditions. It is a torture which overstrains the nerves in the long run, particularly when people are firmly convinced that for the present no end to these nightly raids is in sight.[9]

Despite its success, Harris hated the name of the Mosquito and of the LNSF. 'The Mosquito carries to Berlin a bomb load equivalent to the Flying Fortress,' he told Bennett in a letter in February 1945.

> In consequence the use of such a term as 'Light Night Striking Force' discredits the weight of attack which these aircraft can impose on the enemy. The word 'Mosquito' itself has a similar effect, being connected in the minds of the public with an insect which produces an irritating but normally not particularly effective sting [sic]. For some time this Headquarters has endeavoured to impress upon the public generally that Mosquito raids are a most serious matter for the enemy, and as a consequence have attempted to have the word Mosquito omitted wherever possible from communiqués.[10]

Harris had perhaps missed the point of the LNSF. Its lightness was in comparison to the bludgeoning heavy-bomber raids he so adored. The airmen of the LNSF had to go through the same strict Pathfinder navigation training as the other crews, and before operating over enemy skies crews were sent to a Mosquito Training Unit at RAF Warboys. However, apart from 139 Squadron, which marked for the rest of the force, LNSF crews weren't technically Pathfinders in that they didn't get the badge. Nevertheless, their deployment and execution in harassing the Germans was largely down to Bennett – perhaps it was that which made Harris bristle, given the ongoing tensions between the two men.

Whatever Harris's objections to their names, it was too late to change them – the Mosquito had become baked in to the psyche of both the RAF and the public as an iconic aircraft, while the exploits of the LNSF were appearing regularly in the media. 'OH, WHAT A SURPRISE FOR THE FRITZIES! MOSQUITOS DROP 3,000 TONS ON BERLIN' screamed one headline in a British tabloid newspaper.[11] The Bomber Boys of the LNSF were becoming poster boys.

In late October 1944, one 22-year-old Mosquito pilot with 692 Squadron wrote to his girlfriend: 'Well since my last letter we have become a squadron of film stars! The newsreel bods are making a film of the "Light Night Striking Force" – that's us in case you don't happen to know. Take off, landing, formation, beat up and also briefing were filmed and we have all decided against Hollywood as the directors etc are a binding lot of BFs [bloody fools] – haven't the slightest glimmer of a clue.'[13] Others stood out through the simple virtue of their names. Ivor and Tommy Broom flew dozens of missions in their Mosquito. Naturally they became known as the 'Flying Brooms'. And then there was Deadman and Tombes, two Pathfinder crewmates whose names caused great mirth given the somewhat dicey life expectancy of their job.

As the role of the LNSF increased, so did the number of sorties they flew. Sometimes crews were asked to operate on three successive nights to Berlin – this was a strain, even in such a dynamic aircraft and 'definitely too much for the majority' of crews, observed one Pathfinder medical officer.[14] With the high pressure of operations, airmen let off steam whenever they could. On one occasion, crews from 692 Squadron started their evening in the officers' mess at Graveley, before relocating to the King's Head pub for a 'first class sing song with plenty of beer (in buckets!)'. After closing time, they returned to the officers' mess, 'throwing out all the members of the mess not in our squadron' before burning all the newspapers and having a pillow fight. 'Of course the whole time the beer was flowing very freely – too freely at times,' wrote one airman.

Yet despite their high rate of operations over some of the most fortified areas of Europe, the low casualties amongst the Mosquitos were one of the most remarkable aspects of Bomber Command's war. Of the 27,000 sorties flown by Mosquitos of the LNSF, just 108 ended in the loss of an aircraft.[15] Even Goebbels privately admitted 'the Mosquito is very difficult, in fact almost impossible, to shoot down.'[16]

Under increasing pressure from Hitler directly, the Luftwaffe looked for new ways to stop the Mossie menace. 'NAZI PILOTS CLAIM ONE MOSQUITO AS TWO' exclaimed the headline of one British newspaper in late 1944. 'So highly does the Luftwaffe regard our night attacking Mosquitos that when a Nazi pilot does shoot one down he is allowed to count this as two aircraft destroyed,' the story reported.[17]

All well and good, but for the German pilots just catching the damn things in the first place was proving a challenge. Some adapted their existing aircraft into specialist Mosquito hunters. Manfred Meurer, a

Junkers Ju 88 pilot, ordered as much armament and onboard equipment to be removed as possible to reduce weight and gain speed. He removed one of the *Schräge Musik* cannons and nitrous oxide was used to boost the engines for high-altitude flight. The modifications worked – Meurer successfully shot down a 139 Squadron Mosquito returning from Germany one night.[18]

But such interceptions were rare. Something special was needed. Hitler believed he had found the answer with the Messerschmitt Me 262 – a jet-powered fighter-bomber – which could reach speeds of 500mph or more and was capable of posing a serious threat to the dominance of the Mosquitos. In 1944, Luftwaffe ace Alfred Schreiber claimed a damaged Mosquito as the first aerial victory by a jet fighter in aviation history.

One night, Colin Bell and his navigator Doug Redmond were making their way back to their 608 Squadron base at Downham Market, in Norfolk, after their twelfth raid over Berlin. All seemed quiet, until – in the gloom of the cockpit – a white light on the instrument panel flicked on brightly. But for 24-year-old Bell, piloting his Mosquito through the inky night sky, this seemingly innocuous little dot spelt big trouble.

The Mosquito was equipped with airborne radar detection equipment. The light on Bell's instrument panel meant an enemy fighter was closing in using its own onboard radar equipment to establish visual identification before it attacked. Bell immediately tipped the Mosquito on its wing and into a power dive, plummeting more than 10,000 feet to try and shake the fighter off. Over the next few minutes the white light would disappear momentarily before always flicking on again seconds later, as the fighter locked on. 'We had been intercepted before but this attack was the most persistent and dangerous because we couldn't shake the German off,' remembered Bell. 'Once he got a visual on me, I was dead. A single accurate blast from a Me 262 cannon would turn your aircraft into confetti.'[19]

In a last desperate throw of the dice, Bell took his Mosquito down to the deck, flying at speeds of 400mph just a few feet above the trees. 'I knew that at ground level jets consume tremendous amounts of aviation fuel. And a Me 262 had only 45 minutes flying time from take-off to landing.' Sure enough, the white light soon vanished for good. Bell's gamble had worked. 'We were over an hour late getting back to base and suffering a lot of nervous twitch all the way,' he said later.

Despite claims by the Luftwaffe that the Me 262 shot down more than 300 Allied bombers, it was tricky to handle, beset by technical problems and came too late in the war to have any serious impact. 'We do not manage to shoot down many of the Mosquitos. With them the enemy has the upper hand one hundred per cent,' admitted Goebbels.[20]

Even for a Mosquito flying four miles up, bad weather and flak remained a bigger menace. Mosquito pilots were briefed to weave the aircraft, changing both direction and height, so as to outwit the predictive flak. As Bell approached Berlin on his fifth trip, when he was 'still a bit green' as an operational pilot, he didn't weave quite enough. A shell exploded right underneath the aircraft, flinging it up and disabling both engines. Bell was now over Berlin with no power. His navigator panicked, but Bell told him to sit tight. Lo and behold the Mosquito's engines restarted, and they returned to Downham Market, where they discovered that the tail of the Mosquito was shredded. 'If I had been a nano-second late the explosion would have ripped through the whole of the aircraft and brought us down,' said Bell. His riggers also found shrapnel in his parachute – if he'd tried to bail out, his blossoming parachute would have resembled a lace doily.

Despite these dangers, Bell was so confident that no fighter could catch up with his Mosquito – other than a jet fighter – that once he cleared the target he trimmed the aircraft up, which meant it would fly straight and level without any need to hold the controls. 'Wake me up when we get to Downham Market,' he told his navigator, shutting his eyes for a cat nap. By the end of the war, he'd completed 50 missions over Germany for the LNSF.[21]

When they weren't carrying out daredevil operations, the Pathfinder Mosquitos had other uses. One was requisitioned for an important humanitarian role – flying to Dublin to pick up barrels of Guinness, which slotted nicely in the bomb bay, for the officers' mess at Wyton. On another occasion, as part of the drive to provide entertainment for Pathfinder airmen, Mosquitos at Warboys were removed from their hangar to make space for a circus which had travelled from London. However, when it arrived, the circus master confessed that the young elephant and its keeper had gone AWOL on the journey. Hamish Mahaddie – who had organised for the circus to visit the airbase – hatched a plan. He immediately ordered a Mosquito crew of the LNSF to report to him for a briefing. 'You sent for me, sir,' said the young pilot, eagerly saluting. 'Yes, get in a Mossie and fly down the Great North Road, until you get to the Bedford turn-off, and see if you can find my elephant,' ordered Mahaddie.

'He did not turn a hair,' remembered Mahaddie later, '. . . and he looked at me straight in the eye and said: "Of course, sir. What colour is your elephant?" And I could only think it was elephant colour. So he gave me another rather weary salute and off he went.' A few minutes later, Mahaddie got a call on the station's radio. 'Zero One,' called the pilot circling in the Mosquito. 'I've found your elephant.'[22]

Not all Mosquitos in 8 Group belonged to the LNSF. Bennett retained two squadrons as Oboe-marker Pathfinders for the main force, while one very small and little known group of men performed perhaps the most important role of all – as weather hunters.

Throughout the Second World War the success of all bomber operations depended hugely on the weather, both over Britain and over targets in Europe. And for the Pathfinders and Bomber Command, the ability to bomb through bad weather was as important as the need to see in the dark. In the early years of the war, Bomber Command set out on missions over Europe with little idea of the weather they would encounter. Weather fronts came in from the Atlantic, crossed over Britain, and headed east over enemy territory, where observations and reports were erratic at best and totally unknown at worst.

Aviators relied on accurate forecasts to determine the route to and from the target. Flying through cloud for long periods – especially in winter – meant icing, which could give an aircraft the aerodynamics of a brick, either by affecting its lift or causing engine failure. Some squadrons used Kilfrost – a de-icing paste which was spread evenly over the aircraft on the edges of wings and control surfaces, the idea being that any ice forming on the paste would break away with some of the paste before any great weight of ice had built up. But it didn't always work, and if possible it was better for the bombers to avoid the worst of the weather. It fell to the Pathfinders to try and achieve this. From March 1943 until VE Day, Pathfinder Mosquitos of 1409

Meteorological Flight – codenamed 'Pampa' (an acronym for 'Photo-recce And Meteorological Photography Aircraft') – carried out some of the most vital aerial missions of the war, increasingly so as the war came to a head.

The accuracy and success of the Pathfinders, Bomber Command and the mighty United States Eighth Air Force – whose aircraft were bombing Germany by day – relied on these few individuals. Their job was to fly deep into enemy territory by day and night to record weather en route and over targets, so forecasters back in Britain could provide the most balanced and accurate assessment ahead of any planned raid.

The role of the Pathfinders' meteorological men grabbed the attention and imagination of the media. 'BAD WEATHER HUNTED BY THE RAF' said a headline in the *Daily Sketch*. Victor Lewis, the paper's Air Correspondent, wrote:

> Down on a RAF Bomber Command station two Mosquitos and their crews are standing-by, ready to take off to anywhere from the Arctic Circle to the Mediterranean. It doesn't matter if the weather is so bad that no other plane is flying: They will go. Their enemy is the weather, and for three years they have fought and beaten it. These are the men of the Meteorological Flight – a small body of experts who, in that long period, have challenged the weather at its worst and flown over Germany before every major attack launched by Bomber Command. The men of the Meteorological Flight have never yet refused a flight. That is their tradition. If they see an icing cloud which any other pilot would avoid, they go out of their way to fly through it. For that is their job; to hunt out bad weather . . .[23]

Despite the propaganda, improvements in the accuracy of bombing raids thanks to the met men didn't mean their forecasting was fool-proof. For Bennett, however, the met men 'flew high and fast, but the danger was extreme, and it was a most nerve-wracking job for the crews concerned'.[24]

The Pathfinders' Mosquitos were also continuing to prove a nerve-wracking prospect for Joseph Goebbels in Berlin. Had the Luftwaffe ever had anything like the Light Night Striking Force at its disposal

Goebbels would have surely revelled in its propaganda potential. Instead, he was forced to stew at their ever-increasing raids in his private diary jottings. His irritation at the Wooden Wonder could only have increased when Mosquitos bombed his own offices. The situation got so desperate that at one stage the use of Japanese-style Kamikaze pilots was even considered.[25]

Nothing came of the threat. And besides, even Goebbels now knew it was too little, too late. 'The air war has now turned into a crazy orgy. We are totally defenceless against it. The Reich will gradually be turned into a complete desert,' he wrote bitterly.[26]

In just a few months, his prophecy would prove correct.

CHAPTER TWENTY-FOUR

The Final Push

EIGHTEENTH OF NOVEMBER 1944. In one of the wettest autumns for years, Allied ground forces slowly inched north-east across mainland Europe amidst bitter fighting. Meanwhile, there was no let up from the air. The most intense period of aerial bombing in the history of warfare to date was about to begin, and Bomber Command and the Pathfinders would need to play a decisive role.

But Bert Harris was worried. Sitting in his office at Bomber Command's headquarters in High Wycombe, he began to draft a letter to Charles Portal, the Chief of the Air Staff. Harris had learnt that Portal was planning to transfer Ralph Cochrane from commanding 5 Group to head up Transport Command, an important unit which controlled all transport aircraft of the RAF.

Harris now had to do all he could to stop this move, because it threatened to derail his greatest plan yet for the Pathfinders. A few weeks before, Don Bennett had told Harris he would be looking to leave the RAF once victory over Germany was guaranteed, although no date for his departure had been agreed. With his forceful personality and strong views, Bennett was being courted by all three main political parties to stand as a Member of Parliament in the British general election, which was due to be held once hostilities in Europe had ended.

Bennett thought he was being transparent and honest with Harris. However, little did he realise that the sharing of his plans was music to

Harris's ears, because Harris would finally be able to have an elite force in Bomber Command headed up by the man he really wanted – Cochrane.

But Harris's plans were plunged into chaos following the news of Cochrane's impending transfer. Harris shot off the letter to Portal, objecting at the potential move, telling him, 'if he [Cochrane] is taken away at this particular juncture or during the next three or four months, it is my honest opinion that it will be a serious factor towards postponing the conclusion of the European War. As I have always told you, I always hoped that Cochrane would replace me.'[1]

Harris then revealed his other plan for Cochrane, reminding Portal that he 'was about to suggest closing up 8 and 5 Groups into one super PFF cum Main Force Group under Cochrane, and to ask for him to be promoted'.

It had been almost two and half years since Bennett was asked by Harris to form the Pathfinders, yet even now, with the war coming to its climax, Harris was pushing to make the changes he'd been pining for since the beginning. Harris used the letter to fire a robust personal broadside against Bennett, telling Portal: 'I then thought that Bennett was going – a loss which could be easier borne because Cochrane has now acquired most of Bennett's outstanding technical knowledge and, apart from that knowledge and his personal ability as an operational pilot, Bennett has serious shortcomings.'

Harris didn't detail what he thought Bennett's shortcomings were, but the two men didn't get on that well personally or professionally and these differences had come to a head with the removal of the three squadrons to 5 Group. It was no surprise Harris favoured Cochrane to head up his command's elite force. Harris was also increasingly encouraging other Bomber Command groups – in particular 1 Group and 3 Group – to experiment with their own forms of target marking.

How well Cochrane would have performed if he had taken the role can only be speculated about. Bennett had generated fierce loyalty amongst his airmen, but Cochrane was a formidable and talented group commander, who would have injected many of 5 group's pioneering tactics into the Pathfinders. But Portal didn't back down. Cochrane was transferred to his new post three months later, and Bennett remained in charge of the Pathfinders.

Which was perhaps just as well, because the Mosquitos and heavy bombers of his force would now play a key part in ensuring Bomber Command kept up the pressure over the closing months of the war. Between January and the end of the war in May 1945, British and American bombers dropped 180,994 tons of bombs on targets across Germany, France and the Low Countries – more than twice the weight of bombs Germany dropped on Britain in the entire war.

Bomber Command continuing to pound away at Germany might seem strange now, given the growing Allied supremacy, but the situation was far less clear at the time. Broadly speaking, the Allies had air superiority, but this might well be reversed if they didn't keep up the pressure. The last thing they wanted was for a German recovery to lead to a stalemate. German single-engine fighter production had rallied – even though there were fewer and fewer pilots and less fuel to get them in the air – and the Reich had produced powerful weapons such as the V-1 and V-2 bombs and the Me 262 jet fighter. What else might German scientists have up their sleeves to help Hitler recover his military fortunes? A gas weapon of mass destruction, or germ warfare, or even an atomic bomb? And although the Allied ground forces had made steady progress, they had endured a series of bloody counter-attacks from the German army. The fight hadn't quite left the Reich yet.

The Pathfinders – and Bomber Command – were now achieving levels of accuracy in their bombing which just a few years before could only have been dreamt about. In operations against long-range targets in Germany, an estimated 92 per cent of aircraft despatched bombed within three miles of the target.[2] On a raid to the Bavarian city of Ulm, deep in Germany, in December 1944, one former airman – who had not flown over enemy territory for three years – hitched a ride with a Lancaster to write about it for a national newspaper. He was astonished by the advances which had been made. As his plane approached the target, he observed how:

> . . . six or seven thousand feet below are the Lancasters of the Path-
> finder Force, like black specks outlined against a blazing cauldron. It is
> the most grim, the most terrible, the most beautiful thing I have ever
> seen in my life. This, remember, was my first raid for three years . . . I

was able to witness the vast changes which have revolutionised the whole technique of bombing. I was amazed. For one thing we should never have gone out on a night like this in the old days. There would have been too much cloud. But now the Pathfinder Force can pick out the target through ten-tenths cloud as a result of their secret navigational aids.[3]

Much of this increasing accuracy was thanks to the continuing evolution of the technology. Oboe stations were set up on mainland Europe, enabling aircraft to more accurately mark targets deep into Germany, including Berlin. Other, new blind-bombing devices – one called Loran and a new generation of Gee, christened 'Gee-H' – were unveiled by the boffins, while the American bombers increasingly used a version of H2S, called H2X, to assist their daylight bombing. Despite attempts by German scientists to block and jam the various apparatuses, the British boffins were emerging as victors in the scientific war of cat and mouse.

This didn't mean mistakes didn't happen. After all, the planes were still being flown by humans. One Lancaster was hit by shells after the pilot accidentally flicked on the landing-light switch over enemy territory, attracting the flak gunners below. He didn't realise his mistake because he had stuck some chewed gum over the warning light on the instrument display panel. On another operation, a Lancaster flight engineer opened the side window in the cockpit while holding an open flask of coffee. The change in air pressure sucked out the contents of the flask, splattering the Perspex turret of the mid-upper gunner. Within a few minutes, the liquid coffee had iced up all over the dome. 'For the whole of the trip the mid-upper gunner was inoperative because he couldn't see,' recalled the pilot.[4] At RAF Upwood, meanwhile, as a fully bombed-up and fuelled 156 Squadron Lancaster hurtled down the runway, the pilot, as he always did, encouraged it airborne with the words: 'Up, you bastard, up you bastard!' At which point the flight engineer – a new member of the crew – leant forward and raised the undercarriage, assuming the pilot was talking to him.[5] The Lancaster collapsed onto its belly, slid across the runway and came to a shuddering halt, miraculously intact.

Despite such mishaps, losses continued to drop. In the last six months of the war, a Lancaster bomber lasted on average for 60 combat sorties, up from 22 in 1943.[6] Between January and May 1945, 341 Pathfinder airmen were killed – less than a third the number of 8 Group men who perished over the same period the previous year.[7] Some of the more experienced Pathfinder airmen were now passing 100 sorties. But dangers still lurked on every mission. In the last months of the war, two Pathfinder airmen were awarded the Victoria Cross after being killed flying on operations within eight weeks of each other.

On the chilly winter's morning of 23 December 1944, 30 Pathfinder aircraft took to the skies for a daylight raid on marshalling yards near Cologne. The planes were due to attack in three formations, led by a Lancaster piloted by Robert Palmer, a 24-year-old on his one hundred and tenth mission. Palmer was actually a Mosquito pilot with 109 Squadron, but as an Oboe specialist he was needed to fly the Lancaster in the last critical moments to ensure the target was accurately bombed. Palmer and his navigator flew with the crew of a 582 Squadron Lancaster, swapping seats with the incumbents as they approached the target. The other aircraft following behind were ordered to drop their bombs as soon as Palmer's plane had done so. It was due to be cloudy over Cologne, but nearing the city at 17,000 feet the skies cleared to reveal a vivid blue sky, leaving the attacking aircraft vulnerable to fighters and flak – despite the accompanying fighter cover from RAF Mustangs. Palmer's plane was even more at risk because Oboe only worked accurately if it flew straight and level for about ten minutes towards the target.

Sure enough, as they approached the marshalling yards, the guns on the ground chucked up a maelstrom of metal. Two of the Lancaster's engines were hit and erupted into flames. Enemy fighters also attacked in force. But Palmer couldn't weave or take evasive action if he was to press home the attack. He skilfully nursed the two working engines, the uneven power meaning the Lancaster was almost impossible to keep straight and level, and only dropped the bombs when the Oboe signal confirmed they were over the marshalling yards. Almost as soon as he did so, the Lancaster lurched into a death spin, smashing into the ground and killing everyone on board except the tail gunner, who managed to parachute to safety. The attack was a success, but 31 Pathfinder airmen were killed, including both crews of two 35 Squadron Lancasters after they collided over the English Channel. Palmer was posthumously awarded a VC for displaying 'conspicuous bravery . . . His record of prolonged and heroic endeavour is beyond praise.'[8]

Eight weeks later, Ted Swales, a 29-year-old South African who was a good friend of Robert Palmer and had himself won a DFC on the Cologne operation in December, was asked to be the master bomber for a night operation to attack Pforzheim, a town in south-west Germany. Flying a Lancaster in 582 Squadron on his forty-third operational flight, Swales led a force of over 350 heavies to bomb the town from around 8,000 feet. Under Swales' orders, the Pathfinders' marking was accurate and soon numerous fires were burning in the town. Circling over the target, his Lancaster was attacked by a Messerschmitt Me 410, a twin-engine fighter-bomber, which made two passes, raking the Lanc with machine-gun fire. The plane was badly crippled: hard to steer and without any blind-flying instruments. Yet as he battled with the controls, Swales continued to remain over the target, calmly issuing orders on the radio to the main-force bombers, ensuring the raid maintained its intensity. Only when he was happy the job had been a success did he turn for home. Keen to save his crew, Swales fought with the Lancaster, skilfully flying between layers of cloud to try and avoid turbulence. When he knew they were safely over Allied-held territory, he ordered his crewmates to bail out. A few seconds later, just after the last man had jumped, the ailing bomber hit high-tension telegraph wires and crashed into the ground in northern France. Swales' body was found at the controls. His posthumous VC was awarded two months later. 'Intrepid in the attack, courageous in the face of danger, he did his duty to the last, giving his life that his comrades might live,' his citation read.[9]

Throughout the war, the *London Gazette* printed hundreds of such official citations for bravery awards to Pathfinder airmen. Yet while rousing tributes were of some comfort to the families, friends and colleagues of those airmen killed in action, it was by leafing through the normally benign pages of the newspaper classified columns that more heart-wrenching and personal tributes could often be found. This was an age before social media. Very often, the wish to tell the wider community about the dead or missing loved one was realised through the local paper. In a world of stiff upper lips and 'pressing on', such messages were all the more moving by their restrained brevity. Often, the tributes were printed months after the operation, when definitive news of a missing airman had finally reached home. At other times, when no news had been heard and a small hope still glimmered.

From the *Manchester Evening News*:

Shelmerdine – Treasured memories of our dear son and brother, Thomas. P. (Sergt. A/G., R.A.F.V.R. Pathfinders), on his 22nd birthday, missing from operations in August 1943. Out of the darkness comes the light. Mam, Dad and Harry.[10]

From the *Birmingham Mail*:

Hopcraft – Ernest. (Serg, Navigator, P.F.F.), missing, presumed killed, February 20 1944.
The Blow was hard, the shock severe. To lose a son we loved so dear. In thoughts of mum and pop.
A smiling face, a heart of gold. The dearest brother this world could hold. Will never be forgotten. Dennis.
You were my life, I loved you so, and now you've gone. But the precious memory is left. Renee.[11]

Deavin – Sergt. Frank Ernest (R.A.F., Pathfinder), presumed killed November 21 1943.
Till we meet, Frank dear, God bless you. You are never far away – Mother.
Still hoping and praying for your return. Fiancée Bette.[12]

From the *Newcastle Evening Chronicle*:

Nainby – In loving memory of our beloved son, Thomas. Sergt. RAF Pathfinder Force. Died from his injuries May 6, 1944.
To the world he was one of the many. To us he was all the world. Will always be remembered by his mam, dad and family.[13]

Death wasn't exclusive to the skies. The attack on Pforzheim, in which Ted Swales so tragically lost his life ensuring the military objective succeeded, was one of the most intense of the war. More than 17,000 people were killed and 83 per cent of the town was reduced to ashes – making it the third most deadly raid in Germany throughout the entire war.[14] The death toll was eye-watering, but also proved how far the accuracy and intensity of the Allied bombing had come.

Yet it was a seemingly innocuous raid ten days before, on the eastern German city of Dresden, which subsequently became one of the most controversial and talked about Bomber Command operations of the Second World War.

The bombing of Dresden was not a single event, but part of a wider series of operations under the codename Operation Thunderclap, which had originally called for devastating raids on Berlin, but had been modified to target other towns and cities in eastern Germany. Dresden was not high on Harris's list of urban areas to target, but with the Russians converging from the east, and the city thought to be a possible future strongpoint for a last stand by the German army, it became a legitimate target in supporting the ground war. It's likely the Allied High Command knew the city was packed with civilian refugees fleeing from the Russian advance. However, after five years of Total War – with Germany showing little sign of cracking – a large raid would create chaos and disorder, hamper movements of reinforcements from other fronts, and illustrate to the Russians the capability of Bomber Command.

The attack on Dresden on 13 and 14 February 1945 was divided into two waves – a tactic which had proved highly successful in other operations by Bomber Command in preceding months. Late in the evening, a flare force from the Pathfinders of 5 Group dropped their flares and red target indicators, which floated down over the green grass of the football stadium to the west of the city. More markers dropped by low-flying Mosquitos fizzed over the historic old town, before the master bomber observing was happy and called in the Lancasters of the main force.

One British Mosquito pilot with 627 Squadron was on just his second target-marking operation. Zooming low and dropping a 1,000lb red target indicator, he pulled back on the stick and only just missed smashing into Dresden Cathedral. He had been fractionally late over the target, and failed to hear the master bomber over the radio order in the Lancasters of the main force flying thousands of feet above. As 4,000lb cookies started exploding beneath him, the pilot felt his Mosquito jump 'like a small boat on a very rough sea being thrown about all over the place'. He pushed the throttles of the engines through the gate and got out of the area 'just as quick as I could jolly well could get out'.[15]

Bombers in the first raid dropped 800 tons of bombs, and fires in the city could soon be seen from a hundred miles away. Three hours later, the Pathfinders of 8 Group led the second force. Overseen by a master bomber from 635 Squadron, both the marking and bombing were highly accurate and concentrated. The old town of Dresden comprised combustible timbered buildings. In the debriefing a few hours later, one Pathfinder airman described it as a 'bird's nest target' – when asked by a WAAF to explain, he said 'well it was all shit and sticks'.[16] Within minutes, these buildings were in flames – 1,800 tons of bombs had been dropped, creating a firestorm so terrific it could be felt by the crews 18,000 feet above.

The raid on Dresden by Bomber Command was followed up by a huge daylight raid from the American Eighth Air Force. With over 4,000 tons of bombs dropped in 24 hours, the resulting firestorm was horrific, and the combined raids killed an estimated 25,000 people on the ground. Goebbels was quick to pounce on the raid and use it for propaganda, swiftly issuing a press release stating 250,000 civilians had been killed. Churchill winced at the devastation, reminding Portal to focus on oil and transport targets, rather than 'mere acts of terror and wanton destruction'.[17]

Despite the understandable controversy the raid created, for most of the airmen involved, Dresden was a legitimate target, and they had broken no law of war. Interviewed 40 years later, Don Bennett was clear in his mind: 'We have many people in this country who believe we were cruel horrible people bombing Dresden . . . it was a military target and it was vitally important to the Russian front, the eastern front, on that particular day.'[18] And at the time, for the Pathfinders and other Bomber Command airmen, the Dresden operation was just another chance to tick a sortie off their total and scribble the name of a new German city in red ink in their logbooks.

'As far as we were concerned it was just another raid, nothing special,' remembers John Ottewell, a 20-year-old Lancaster navigator from Burton, who was more worried about ensuring his 7 Squadron crew – on their twelfth Pathfinder mission and acting as the deputy master bomber – got back to England in one piece.[19]

In many ways, Ottewell and his fellow crewmates were typical of the new generation of Pathfinders who made up such a large part of the force in the final months of the war. Many of the more experienced airmen had been killed or had left the force, replaced by those who had still been at school when the war broke out, and were now still in their teens or early twenties. Young men, simply obeying orders. After 29 operations with 115 Squadron, Ottewell's crew were selected for 8 Group in November 1944. Ottewell was particularly friendly with the rear gunner, or 'tail end Charlie', a determined Welshman from the coal-mining town of Llanhilleth – appropriately called Charlie Sergeant. When not on ops, they would cycle to the nearest pub for nights out. The mid-upper gunner, Charlie Shepherd, a 20-year-old Londoner, would also join them. After every raid, Sheppard sent a postcard to his fiancée back in London so she knew he was safe. For the crew, it was an intense period of bombing. In February and March alone, they flew almost 65 hours on operations to 13 enemy targets and would complete 55 bombing operations by the end of the war.[20]

Over the final few weeks of the war, the Pathfinders continued to lead accurate and heavy attacks. Cities including Chemnitz, Leipzig and Hamburg were hit hard by massive raids. This was Total War at its most ruthless. A daring raid was even attempted to destroy Hitler's sumptuous 'Eagle's Nest' chalet overlooking the Bavarian Alps near Berchtesgaden, which he used as his country headquarters. The Führer wasn't home. On 18 April, Heligoland, the German island fortress, was attacked. An airfield and naval base were reduced to craters after individual Pathfinder master-bomber crews directed 900 bombers in six waves on three aiming points, in a daylight operation of such complexity it would have astonished Bomber Command airmen just a few years before.

Three days previously, Harris and his small team of decision-makers had ordered the Pathfinders to lead Bomber Command's last big city raid of the war, against Potsdam, a town bordering Berlin. The objective was to destroy an army barracks and marshalling yards. Overseen by the master bomber, a force of twelve Mosquitos and 500 Lancasters accurately marked and bombed the town centre and before long smoke was rising 14,000 feet. It was the first time four-engine bombers of Harris's force had entered Greater Berlin since the Battle of Berlin a year before. But so much had changed. Gone were the scores of enemy fighters and heavy flak. Just one Lancaster – a Pathfinder from 35 Squadron – was shot down, and the town was pulverised by the bombing, so much so that Churchill angrily asked one of his ministers: 'What was the point of going and blowing down Potsdam?'[21]

Yet despite Churchill's misgivings – perhaps he had one eye on the upcoming general election – if the public was becoming more squeamish at the idea of terror bombing, it didn't seem particularly obvious at the time. As the bombing over Germany reached its zenith in the last few months of the war, Londoners flocked to a new exhibition in the West End called 'Target Germany', which vividly reconstructed a Bomber Command raid on a German target. For six-pence a ticket – with money going to the RAF Benevolent Fund – excited parents and their children gathered in a hall off Regent Street, standing three-deep against rails on viewing galleries, looking down on a vast model of a German town 12 feet below. Lighting effects, the roar of aircraft engines and the sound of falling bombs added to the atmosphere.

'Most Londoners have either read descriptions or heard radio impressions of a Bomber Command raid on Germany. Many have now added to these impressions a vivid reconstruction of such an event,' reported the *Illustrated London News*. 'A running commentary accompanies the reconstruction, and outstanding scenes in the sequence are the approach of the Pathfinders and their ringing of the target with coloured flares, and the arrival of the main fleet of heavy bombers, who rain down their load of explosives and incendiaries, reducing the target to a blazing wreckage.'[22] The *Daily Herald*, mean-while, observed: 'Directly the voice of the announcer began, there was a rush to the rails surrounding the big contour map of the raided area below the gallery . . . There were gasps as the target was illuminated by the Pathfinders' flares, and the red glow of fires shone through the shell of buildings when the bombs of the master bomber and his followers crashed down'.[23]

On 30 April 1945, surrounded by Allied forces, Adolf Hitler blew his brains out in a sordid Berlin bunker. On 7 May, Germany surrendered. In the 8 Group operations book, members of the LNSF declared they had 'joined the heavies' in being 'all dressed up, but nowhere to go. Good things, and the need for them, come to an end.'[24] Yet it wasn't quite over for the Pathfinders.

Over the coming days, Don Bennett led a huge humanitarian effort. Almost 3,000 Allied POWs were repatriated by 8 Group from camps across Europe. 'I was the first aircraft to land, and we had machines coming and going every few minutes . . . the troops were cramped, but delighted to be taken home so quickly. The effect was magical,' he said.[25]

John Ottewell and his crew landed in Brussels to pick up two dozen POWs, who were each given large bars of Cadbury's chocolate. But despite months or years of surviving on little food, some refused to eat it. 'We said: "Well aren't you going to eat the chocolate?"' recalled Ottewell. 'And they replied: "Oh no, we are taking it back to England because England is starving." That was the propaganda pumped into them by the Germans. We had to keep telling them: "The war is over. England isn't starving,"' he added.

Repatriating POWs was not the only humanitarian operation for the Pathfinders. In the last days of the war, 3.5 million starving Dutch citizens were trapped in pockets of the northern Netherlands still occupied by German forces. Over 20,000 had already died. Some resorted to surviving by eating fried tulip bulbs. An audacious daylight plan was launched called Operation Manna, in which the Pathfinders and other Bomber Command groups airdropped food and medical supplies, flying over the rooftops at low level. Tacit agreement had been reached with the German High Command for German forces not to open fire on the planes, but there was still a big risk trigger-happy gunners might mow down the vulnerable bombers. The supply drops required careful marking by the Pathfinder planes, and explosive candles in their target-marker bombs had to be painstakingly removed by hand the night before.

'The operation had a different feeling than the others and it was wonderful to know we were doing something to help them,' said Ottewell. 'As we flew over we just prayed the Germans respected the truce.' Arie de Jong, a 17-year-old Dutch student, wrote in his diary: 'There are no words to describe the emotions experienced on that Sunday afternoon. More than 300 four-engine Lancasters flying exceptionally low suddenly filled the western horizon . . . One could see the gunners waving in their turrets – a marvellous sight.' One Canadian rear gunner remembered: 'People were everywhere. On the streets, on the roofs, leaning out of windows. They all had something to wave with – a handkerchief, a sheet. It was incredible.' Another airman recalled: 'I will always remember seeing "Thank you Tommy" written on one of the roofs.'[26] The trapped civilians were liberated soon after.

Eighth of May 1945, Victory in Europe Day. At RAF Wyton, officers and WAAFs gathered in front of the mess to celebrate. Effigies of Hitler, Mussolini and Emperor Hirohito were strung up. Noreen and Torix Bennett drew up their bicycles and looked on, squinting against the May sunshine. Somewhat bizarrely, the Pathfinders' celebrations were shared with two generals and six colonels from the Russian army, who had been given permission by Harris to visit 8 Group headquarters as a sort of inter-Allied goodwill gesture. Amongst the rather rictus smiles and formalities, the Russians kept a close eye on proceedings as they toured the air station. One grabbed a confidential note lying on the table in the operations room and slipped it into his pocket when he didn't think anyone was looking. It was quietly retrieved from his greatcoat later and no more was said about it. But it was a sign of things to come. Allies would soon be enemies.

Later that day, Don Bennett addressed the men and women under his command:

Great Britain and the Commonwealth have made a contribution to the civilised world so magnificent that history alone will be able to appreciate it fully. Through disaster and triumph, sometimes supported and sometimes alone, the British races have steadfastly and energetically over many long years flung their forces against the international criminals. They have fought the war from end to end without a moment's respite, in all theatres, and with all the arms – Land, Sea and Air.

Bomber Command's share in this great effort has been a major one. You, each one of you, have made that possible. The Pathfinder Force has shouldered a grave responsibility. It has led Bomber Command – the greatest striking force ever known. That we have been successful can be seen in the far-reaching results which the bomber offensive has achieved. That is the greatest reward the Pathfinder Force ever hopes to receive, for those results have benefitted all law-abiding peoples.

While you have been hard at work through these vital years I have not interrupted you, as I would like to have done, with messages of praise and congratulation. You were too busy; but now that your great contribution to the world has been made I want to thank each man and woman of you personally and to congratulate you on your unrelenting spirit and energy and on the results you have achieved.

Happiness to you all – always along the Path to Peace.[27]

As the party at Wyton and the other Pathfinder bases went on long into the night, down in central London crowds gathered in Trafalgar Square, singing and dancing. Bonfires were lit in Piccadilly and Cambridge Circus. Ulric Cross, who had completed his tour of 80 operations with 139 Squadron, decided to head into town and join them. But when he got there, it didn't seem right somehow, and he quietly made his way home.

'Everybody was overjoyed and I just didn't feel like taking any part in it,' Cross said later. 'I just felt that a lot of people had been killed. This was not a cause for celebration. The war did not stop people from being killed and a lot of my friends were killed . . . I was extremely glad the war was over.'[28]

He wasn't alone.

Epilogue

A T THE END OF the war in Europe, Bert Harris sent a signal to Don Bennett: 'The rubble that was Germany is the incontrovertible evidence that the path to the German cities was well and truly found. Your exacting task has been most magnificently accomplished. Congratulations and my warmest thanks'.[1] Despite the increasingly bitter clashes between the two men, the message from Harris seemed genuine and convivial. He had been a ruthless leader, but under his leadership Bomber Command had kept his promise that Hitler would reap the whirlwind.

Yet rubble alone was not enough to assess how important Bomber Command – and in particular the Pathfinders – was in contributing towards the final defeat of Nazi Germany. Bomber Command's war over northern Europe comprised over 336,000 individual sorties. Individually, they were often violent and confusing episodes of battle. Collectively, however, these sorties were statistics that could be analysed, like any others.

The Pathfinder Force was formed in August 1942 because Bomber Command could neither find nor accurately bomb targets in the dark. When Bennett launched the opening raids of his fledgling force, just 25 per cent of the aircraft despatched by Bomber Command on German cities bombed within three miles of the aiming point. By 1945, that figure had risen to 95 per cent.[2] And while Bomber Command never completely conquered the elements to deliver foolproof accuracy, the transformation in its bombing capabilities was nevertheless remarkable.

In the months prior to the Pathfinders' first real examination in the Battle of the Ruhr in 1943, one in ten aircraft sent by Bomber Command to the Ruhr region got within three miles of their target. Led by the Pathfinders using cutting-edge Oboe technology, this figure rose to 73 per cent in the Ruhr campaign in the spring and summer of 1943.[3] The cost was bloody – at least 774 Pathfinder airmen lost their lives between March and July 1943.[4] But some of the most important targets, which had been attacked many times in the past with little effect, were now being located and pounded with ruthless efficiency.

Some post-war critics sought to downplay the damage and impact Bomber Command achieved in the Ruhr, focusing instead on the much greater bombing effort in the last two years of the war. There is some merit in this. Yet contemporary evidence from within Germany suggests a different picture. The region was the most important cog in keeping the wheels of Hitler's war machine turning. It was Europe's biggest producer of steel and coal, which in turn were crucial for producing arms, tanks, planes and myriad military components. After Bomber Command's bombing campaign in 1943, steel production fell by 200,000 tons, forcing Hitler to cut his ammunition production and reduce aircraft manufacturing.[5] Whole production lines were affected. 'The Battle of the Ruhr marked a turning point in the history of the German war economy,' says the historian Adam Tooze. 'Disrupting production in the Ruhr had the capacity to halt assembly lines across Germany . . . Bomber Command had stopped Speer's armaments miracle in its tracks . . . The Ruhr was the choke point and in 1943 it was within the RAF's grip.'[6]

This would not have been possible without the Pathfinders' ability to lead Harris's bombers to their targets. And had Bomber Command's missions against the region been maintained, the disruption of production throughout the entire country could have been even more damaging. Yet Harris's decision to shift his bombers' attention away from the Ruhr to Berlin in the autumn of 1943 may have averted immediate disaster for Germany.

In contrast to its efforts against the Ruhr, the Battle of Berlin was the most challenging period of the war for both Bomber Command and 8 Group – and perhaps their biggest disappointment. Between August 1943 and March 1944 there were 19 major raids against the Big City. Over the same period, the Pathfinders lost 1,443 airmen.[7] Four of the top ten months for the most Pathfinder deaths in the war occurred during the Battle of Berlin. The damage on Berlin was still significant, but even with well-trained crews using the latest navigation technology, the distances, weather conditions and bristling enemy defences contrived to render the task impossible. Berlin was simply too big to be destroyed.

While Harris's dream of wrecking Berlin was always beyond his reach, his ability to wield a vast bomber force to crush towns and cities closer to Britain, including Hamburg and Kassel, became almost routine. Through better navigation and target marking, hundreds more planes were squeezed into bomber streams, passing over a target in less time, overwhelming defences, reducing bomber losses and wreaking havoc. This success was as much about the efficiency of the bombing as the accuracy of the bombs. The number of tons of bombs Bomber Command dropped over the target per square mile increased fivefold between 1943 and 1944, forcing Hitler to move equipment and manpower away from the fighting fronts to instead tackle the bombing threat.[8]

That the Pathfinders were able to transform the bombing effort was thanks partly to British ingenuity. The Lancaster and the Mosquito were the finest bombers to emerge from Britain during the war. H2S and Oboe – the most advanced navigation technology in the world at the time – was created by the eccentric brains at Malvern. The target-marker bombs – so often barely mentioned in accounts of the RAF's bombing war – greatly increased the ability of the Pathfinders to do their job, and transformed the overall effectiveness of Bomber Command. Pioneered by a former chemistry teacher with a penchant for chunky-knit cardigans, £6–7 million was spent on the manufacture of about 1.5 million target indicators – equivalent to about 175 new Lancaster bombers.[9] In the grand scheme of things, this was one of the most cost-effective expenditures of the war effort. Bennett reckoned the target indicator did 'more than any other single weapon' to concentrate the weight of the bomber offensive. 'Its effect in the attacks on heavily defended areas such as the Ruhr, Hamburg and Berlin has been of incalculable assistance,' he said in 1944.[10]

Given the turnaround in Bomber Command's fortunes, Harris's decision to break up 8 Group in the spring of 1944 must have been all the more infuriating to Bennett. Yet from the time he appointed the Australian as head of the Pathfinders in August 1942, Harris never gave up on his efforts to remould the force into the one he wanted. 'People are always saying that I was against the formation of the Pathfinder Force,' Harris said many years after the war. 'Well that is absolutely true . . . what I was hoping to get was a Pathfinder force in every group. And without in any way belittling the magnificent achievements of the Pathfinder Force as a whole, my idea of having a pathfinder apparatus of some sort in every group was eventually arrived at, and that is when we really got results.'[11]

Harris did Bennett something of a disservice, given the way Bomber Command performed in the Ruhr, the Battle of Hamburg and other cities such as Kassel, in 1943. Bennett and his Pathfinders were instrumental in raising the performance of Bomber Command despite, not because of, his boss. Nevertheless, it could equally be argued that Harris's decision to split off three squadrons to 5 Group in April 1944 made everyone raise their game, to the benefit of Bomber Command and the Allies as a whole.

Harris fully admitted that Bennett and Cochrane 'were rather at daggers drawn', which he didn't discourage 'because it made both of them do their damnedest'.[12] And the combined effort certainly bore fruit in the D-Day landings, when the Pathfinders of 8 Group and 5 Group played a vital role in smashing the coastal batteries behind the landing beaches hours before troops stormed ashore. Harris's underhand treatment of Bennett and favouritism towards Cochrane – a man whom he saw as his natural successor to lead Bomber Command – notwithstanding, 5 Group's arrival on the scene brought the likes of Leonard Cheshire into the fray as pathfinders, which only strengthened Harris's hand as the war came to its climax. Harris's decision to quietly allow some other Bomber groups – albeit on a much smaller level – to develop their own target-marking techniques in the closing months of the bombing offensive also undoubtedly gave his force greater tactical variety, whatever Bennett's misgivings.

With Normandy secured, all eyes turned once again to Germany. The weights of bombs dropped on German targets in the final months of the war are so dreadfully vast they're almost inconceivable. The RAF boasted over 1,500 heavy bombers which could each carry 20,000lb of bombs at a time – five times as many as in 1943. Between June 1944 and March 1945, the British and Americans dumped over a million tons of bombs. Even in these huge, devastating raids, success depended on navigation and accurate target marking. Target indicators dropped from Mosquitos at 24,000 feet fell within just 200 feet of their target, guiding the path for the heavies behind. The impact was huge. By 1945, Germany was producing 35 per cent fewer tanks than planned, 31 per cent fewer aircraft and 42 per cent fewer lorries as a result of the air bombing.[13] The Allied air campaign ensured the whole of Germany turned into a gigantic front, hindering its ability to fight a ground war against the Allied armies. German industry was pulverised and its factories silenced. The River Rhine ran clear for the first time in years.

One newspaper concluded:

> The Pathfinders are the aces of Bomber Command. Without them Bomber Command could never be the devastating force it is today. Without them the strategic long-range hammering of German cities could never have taken place during the last two years. Without them the softening-up of the enemy's communication lines, the smashing of railway centres in the occupied countries to produce the chaos that prepared the way for our invasion, could never have happened.[14]

There was no one means of winning the war, but the Pathfinders' contribution to the air offensive ensured that Bomber Command – alongside the American air force – played a significant role in the eventual Allied victory.

*

Yet statistics only tell half the story. While machines and technology played their part, the ability of the Pathfinder Force primarily lay with the young men and women from around the world within its ranks – what Bennett called its 'vital factor'. After the war, one rear gunner tried to characterise what he thought were the most essential attributes required:

> The highly complex task of taking a modern aircraft at night to find a distant target, so fanatically defended, and to return safely, needed a very special kind of person – and an element of luck . . . though never immune to fear, one became confident in one's fellow crew members when facing the most arduous and near-suicidal missions, with that inborn sense of unity, tinged with not a little arrogance and pride that provided the ingredients vital for survival: split-second reactions, almost faultless navigation, and a liaison between pilot and gunners resembling the uncanny.[15]

In three years, the Pathfinders grew from five to twenty-one squadrons. At least 3,712 Pathfinder airmen were killed in 50,940 sorties between August 1942 and May 1945, the final loss rate only marginally less than for Bomber Command's main force.[16] Every one of the 55,573 Bomber Command deaths was tragic, but for the supporters of the air war, their sacrifice prevented many greater times the number of Allied casualties on the ground.

The cost on the ground, too, was dreadful. Under the rubble lay an estimated 600,000 German dead. Many were directly involved in the Nazi war-making machine. But – like those caught up in the German bombing of Britain – the vast majority were the civilian victims of Total War. Most Allied airmen had little compunction over the rights or wrongs of their operations: they had a job to do and their main aim was to do that job and survive. While the operational policy of area bombing ended with the dropping of the atomic bombs on Japan in 1945, the controversy over its ethics still rumbles on today.

The men and women of the Pathfinder Force were not thinking of such matters when the war ended. The day after VE Day, 6,000 miles away in the Pacific Ocean, Japanese Kamikaze planes slammed into the decks of two Royal Navy aircraft carriers. While the war in Europe had finished, the conflict in the Far East raged on. Secret plans were being made for a vast US-Anglo invasion of Japan in the autumn of 1945. As part of that, many Pathfinder crews, weary from action over Germany, were scheduled to be deployed in a new long-range bomber force. Plans were only shelved when Japan surrendered on VJ Day in August 1945.

Others went on a goodwill tour of North America. Sixteen Lancasters of 35 Squadron were given a smart new livery of white paint and waved off from Graveley for the two-month trip. Meanwhile, F-Freddie, a Pathfinder Mosquito bomber which held the Bomber Command record of 213 combat operations over Germany, flew across the Atlantic and wowed crowds in the Canadian city of Calgary with its low-level flying. The next day, its crew were killed attempting another dramatic flyby when the aircraft hit a pole on an airfield control tower, shearing off its port wing and sending it crashing to the ground.

For most Pathfinders, however, the slide into peacetime was less fraught. Don Bennett was too restless to remain in the RAF. After a brief, unhappy dabble in politics, he returned to aviation, flying commercial airliners to South America and piloting the first passenger flight from Heathrow Airport in a converted Lancaster bomber. Ly and Noreen Bennett handed out sandwiches and drinks to passengers before the plane departed. In 1948, Bennett found himself over the skies of Germany once again during the Berlin Blockade, flying up to three sorties a night during perhaps the first major crisis of the Cold War. Bennett needed speed in his life. When he wasn't flying, he ran engineering firms building planes and sports cars, and entered the Monte Carlo Rally five times – often with his wife Ly as his co-driver. Age appeared not to diminish his attraction to danger. Nor did it pacify his strongly held opinions, which extended to some former RAF colleagues. While never one to be aware of his own shortcomings, his impatience with those whom he disagreed with during the war continued to burn brightly for years. 'He [Bennett] made a lot of enemies and really didn't get the rewards he should have got for his work during the war,' remembered one. 'He was one of those people you had to argue with. You could be steam-rollered otherwise.'[17]

Nonetheless, Bennett created genuine spirit amongst the men and women under his command, and devoted much of his post-war life to their welfare. In return, he was treated with affection by many. Along with Doc Macgown, he set up the Pathfinder Association and used his connections to help demobbed aviators find jobs. Its aim was also to allow members to keep in touch, and create 'a bond of friendship and esprit-de-corps firmly forged in the fires of war that must never be allowed to weaken'.[18] Differences were put aside at the annual dinner, where guests included German night-fighter aces, who just a few years before had been such a menace to the Pathfinders, and Harris, who – in one after-dinner speech – 'proved himself in a new role – that of a humorist. There was a merry twinkle in his eye as he rolled off anecdotes in droll fashion.' For all their battles, Bennett insisted after the war that while Harris had 'dropped a lot of clangers' he was nevertheless 'the best person' to lead Bomber Command:

> There was nobody with the press-on spirit of Bert Harris. He stood up for us against the politicians and all the niggling and so on and when people said 'Stop all bombing, you are killing women and children, how terrible', he was able to get up and say 'Yes and what did the Huns do to our women and children'? He had an answer all the time and generally speaking put them back in their boxes.[19]

Bennett and Harris were also united by the common goal of formal recognition of their forces' efforts in the war. While Harris pushed for a Bomber Command campaign medal, Bennett pursued his idea of a Pathfinder Star. Both were rejected. Harris refused a peerage in protest. The powers that be – including Churchill – washed their hands of Bomber Command because of the enduring controversy over the destruction caused by its bombing. 'We are not bitter, for we know in our own hearts just what we did – and that is our reward – the truest reward of all,' said Bennett in his autobiography.[20] But when Bennett died in 1986 aged 76, the lack of official recognition for the men and women who served him so loyally in the Pathfinders must have still hurt somewhat.[21]

For those Pathfinders who had found themselves in POW camps as the war came to an end, getting home was as much of an endurance test as the action that had led to their being imprisoned in the first place. Ernie Holmes and Dick Raymond had been shot down within hours of one another in May 1944 and found themselves in separate POW camps in Poland. In January 1945, with the Russians advancing from the east, Holmes and Raymond were two of around 80,000 Allied POWs in camps across Germany and Poland, forced to march westward by the Nazis in brutal winter weather wearing ill-fitting and unsuitable clothing. They could hear the distant booming gunfire of the Eastern Front. When bread rations ran out, men survived on sugar beet and potatoes, which froze even after being stuffed in pockets. Holmes and Raymond trudged for hundreds of miles over three weeks through ice, snow and temperatures of −30°C. 'The weather was so bad with snowstorms you just hoped that you could see the road you were following. If you went off into the snow, you were dead. Horses were dropping through sheer fatigue but they provided the next meal. The only reason I survived was because I was young,' said Raymond.[22] When they arrived at another POW camp thirty miles south of Berlin, a small party of men including Raymond decided to make a break for it under the cover of darkness and met up with advancing Americans. He was flown home via Brussels.

Holmes, meanwhile, struggling in bitter weather, slept in the snow. One night, he managed to get some shut-eye on the roof of a hearse in a barn. With little food, men caught chickens and plucked them as they walked, or milked cows and took it in turns carrying the bucket of milk on their heads. Someone found some hen's eggs, which were cracked into warm milk and eagerly devoured with ration biscuits – only to be vomited up because the mix was too rich for stomachs more used to meagre POW-camp food. As aircraft buzzed overhead, Holmes and a few men spread themselves out as they walked, so from above their bodies spelt the letters RAF in the hope they wouldn't be attacked by Allied or German fighters. Holmes ended up near Lübek on the Baltic coast, where he was liberated on VE Day by men from the Cheshire Regiment. In one of the British army trucks he recognised an old childhood friend he used to play football with. 'What are you doing here? You should have been here weeks ago!' said Holmes, grinning.

After the war, Raymond stayed in the RAF for three years before returning to Devon to run the family bakery. Holmes, awarded a DFC for his wartime service, also remained in the RAF, flying long-range transport aircraft to the Far East and taking part in the Berlin Blockade airlifts, before entering civvy street, training pilots in Britain and flying for airlines in East Africa. In his fifties, Holmes learnt he had a degenerative eye disease and would soon be blind. With two children at university, he couldn't afford to retire and had few qualifications. So he went back to college and got his A levels, before retraining as an assistant social worker, helping young offenders navigate their own paths through life.

Allan Ball – who had also become a POW after being shot down over Berlin and saved by German doctors – was repatriated back to Britain via Sweden, in September 1944, as part of a Red Cross scheme agreed with Germany to send home badly wounded airmen. Ball was operated on by Sir Archibald McIndoe, the pioneering plastic surgeon, and became one of 649 Allied aircrew who went through his operating theatre and formed the 'Guinea Pig Club'. Bone from Ball's right hip was shaved off and transplanted into his skull to fill up a hole left when the German doctors removed a three-inch circle to dig out a large piece of flak lodged in his brain. He returned to 35 Squadron before the end of the war, giving lectures to airmen about his experiences. Ball was awarded a DFC and married his sweetheart Brenda in August 1945 – providing her with much needed comfort after it was confirmed her missing brother Larry had been killed over Munich – before leaving the RAF the following year and beginning a successful career in the paper-milling industry.

After losing her own sweetheart Bruce after a raid on Berlin in late 1943, Gwen Thomas had not been looking to find love again, and got her head down keeping busy as a Pathfinder signals operator. But in July 1944 she met Nick Carter – a Pathfinder navigation instructor – and they fell in love. 'I still had the loss of Bruce in my heart. But gradually Nick and I became very close and I knew that I was in love with him.' They were soon engaged. When the war ended, like many ground crew, Thomas was given an opportunity to hitch a ride in a Lancaster over Germany as part of the so-called Cook's Tours – named after a travel agency – to see for herself just why thousands of young men like Bruce had sacrificed their lives. 'You were given a bag to be sick and you had to pay a half a crown if you used it,' recalled Thomas. 'We knew we had bombed the likes of Cologne, but it was astonishing to see the damage for oneself.'[23]

For some Pathfinder airmen, the lure of the skies remained too much. John Kelly was demobbed from 83 Squadron and joined BOAC, flying Comet jetliners around the world and ferrying Prime Minister Harold Macmillan to Moscow in 1959. John Ottewell, meanwhile, left 7 Squadron and carried on flying as a navigator until the mid-1970s. He took part in the Berlin airlifts, the partition of India, and flew in converted Lancaster bombers for BOAC on the London to Sydney route. After losing touch with his fellow crew members, Ottewell increasingly wondered what had happened to his closest friend in the crew, the rear gunner Charlie Sergeant, and presumed he was dead. But after the war Sergeant had returned to Wales, where he still lived, only a few miles away from Ottewell's Bristol home. Following a chance contact over social media, the two men were reunited in 2018. 'It was just like old times,' recalled Ottewell. 'We chatted away just as we had when we last saw one another seventy years ago. It was a very strange feeling.'[24] Both Ottewell and Sergeant were awarded Distinguished Flying Medals.

Colin Bell finished his Pathfinder service with 608 Squadron in the spring of 1945 and was awarded a DFC. He was transferred to ferry duties, bringing back newly built Mosquitos from Canada to the UK, and ended his full-time RAF service in 1946 flying out diplomatic mail to embassies in Europe and Africa. Bell qualified as a chartered surveyor and set up his own firm. Bell is proud of the role the Night Light Striking Force played in 8 Group. For him, 'Bomber Command's objective throughout the whole of the war was to destroy Germany's capability of waging war against us – purely that and nothing more.' For him 'it largely succeeded'.[25]

Bell's fellow Mosquito airman Ulric Cross read for the Bar in London and was called by the Middle Temple in 1949. He enjoyed a long legal career in London, East Africa and Trinidad and Tobago, becoming a high court judge and later appointed the Trinidad and Tobago High Commissioner in London. Cross was awarded the DSO and DFC, making him one of the most highly decorated West Indians in the RAF during the Second World War. He was the inspiration for a Ken Follett novel and, seven years after his death in 2013 aged 96, his life with his wife Ann was immortalised in a feature film. Despite his successes proving an inspiration to many, Cross wore his honours lightly. 'I don't give advice and I don't give a message and I don't pretend that I'm a role model. I don't say I have a legacy – none of it. I'm opposed to it,' he said years after the war. 'Treat people like people.'[26]

Perhaps Max Bryant would have approved of Cross's sentiments, had he survived the war. His best friend Don Charlwood arrived back in Australia in the spring of 1945 and oversaw the return of Bryant's diary and belongings to his parents. Charlwood was struck by the attitude of those who hadn't been in the thick of the action – a view shared by so many others when they went back to civilian life. He wrote to Bryant's mother:

> I hope by now that all Max's belongings have reached you safely. I would have sent them by post, but the weight of them prevented me . . .
>
> I can well imagine how you will feel when you open the case . . . For me it was the worst blow of the war.
>
> I feel appalled at times by the apathy of people here at home. I had never expected or wished a fuss to be made over men who returned; but this awful apathy makes me wonder sometimes if those other years were a dream. How can people eat and drink and sleep and take these things for granted? Only you families who have suffered so terribly realize what war means.
>
> I finished gleaning the pieces I wanted from Max's diaries. They are honest diaries indeed. Max's life was the life of most of us – except that most of us lived further from our ideals than Max ever did.[27]

Shortly before Bryant was killed, he had reflected on his own part in the war and on the future of the 19 other young Australians who had travelled with him to join Bomber Command:

What a long road there is to travel. I shall never believe the boys of the old flight have been killed, not till after the war and everything is cleared up. It is not possible that such real, vibrant personalities should suddenly cease to exist . . . In any case, their personalities live on with us in memory. If only one of our twenty survives, all his life he will have around him the laughing shades of nineteen other blokes of the most congenial bunch of lads ever to leave their homeland.

His words echo through the stories of almost every Pathfinder who didn't find their way home.

Acknowledgements

This book has only been possible thanks to the kindness, support and expertise of many people. Firstly, to the men and women who served in the Pathfinders, whose numbers have now dwindled to a small handful. They were patient and courteous answering my questions in person, on the phone and via email.

It was a pleasure to travel to Perth to meet Ernie Holmes and hear his remarkable story. My thanks to him, and to David and Lis Holmes for their generous time in making it happen. Ernie celebrated his hundredth birthday a few weeks before Colin Bell also turned 100. Colin is a tour de force of fascinating anecdotes and hair-raising tales. He gave up his time on numerous occasions and I owe him more than a few pints at the Running Horse. Many thanks to Dick Raymond for his very warm welcome and fascinating stories, and to John Ottewell, who provided valuable insight into the life of a Pathfinder navigator. It was great fun having lunch with John and his former tail gunner Charlie Sergeant – 80 years on from their adventures – and my thanks to Chris Ottewell and Helen Edwards for arranging this. I am grateful, too, for the time given by Charlie Shepherd's daughters Mellissa and Terressa. Wendy Carter (known as Gwen Thomas during the war) flew the flag for the WAAFs, telling me her moving stories. Thanks for the amazing sandwiches, Wendy.

I am in debt to the families and friends of those Pathfinder airmen no longer able to share their own stories. To Noreen Cooper, who was so welcoming and patient in answering all my questions about wartime life with her father Don Bennett, and happy to share with me their family photo album – I hope I've been able to paint the Pathfinder chief in a more three-dimensional picture than is often the case. My thanks to Ann and Nicola Cross, and Sue Hollick for their memories of Ulric Cross, and to Gabriel J. Christian for sharing with me his interviews. Juliet and Larry Stockford provided some super material about Allan Ball's astonishing war, while Clare Macgown was generous in helping me shed more light on Doc Macgown's part in making the Pathfinders so special. Special thanks as well to Marie-Louise van der Heijden, who took time to talk to me about her magnificent grandfather, Fons.

Many hours researching this book were spent in various archives and I've been lucky enough to use a large number of unpublished contemporary diaries, letters and other primary sources, thanks to the generous time of others. My thanks for Andrew Dennis of the RAF Museum in Hendon, John Clifford at Pathfinder Collection within the RAF Wyton Heritage Centre, and Dan Ellin and Peter Jones from the International Bomber Command Centre in Lincoln.

These archives are a wealth of material, and without them books like this couldn't be written. But in these challenging times, they welcome donations from the public more than ever. Thank you too to the staff at the Imperial War Museum in London and the National Archives in Kew. I also owe a mention to Charlotte Gray at the RAF Club in London, for offering to put a 'call to arms' out in the club's newsletter for former Pathfinders to get in touch, and to Graham Cowie of Project Propeller for opening his contacts book.

The Pathfinders were an international bunch and I've only been able to tell their full story due to the efforts of others around the world. Many thanks to Therese Lynch in Australia for her work at the Australian War Memorial in helping to dig out Max Bryant's extraordinary diary and to Don Charlwood's daughter Doreen Burge for sharing some of her father's recollections. Wing Commander Mary Anne Whiting of the Royal Australian Air Force in Canberra provided valuable guidance and Dave Birrell at the Bomber Command Museum of Canada gave some great accounts of Canada's significant contribution to the Pathfinders. Theo Boiten was always generous in sharing his expertise about the Nachtjagd.

Penning non-fiction is always something of a monumental research project, but it was made a little easier thanks to help with transcribing interviews and number crunching various stats – my thanks to Charlie and Lizzie Hennig, Josh Ferguson and George Iredale. Many thanks too to James Holland for sharing with me his Sydney Bufton material and permission to quote from his excellent *We Have Ways of Making you Talk* history podcast.

I am particularly grateful to the historian Victoria Taylor, who took time from her busy schedule to provide some much-needed expertise and sage advice on my first draft, and point out any glaring mistakes. Any errors that do remain are, of course, entirely my own. Thank you too to my old friend Keith Quilter and my father Martin for leafing through the manuscript and giving their honest feedback.

This book wouldn't have got off the ground without my agent Veronique Baxter at David Higham, and Jamie Joseph – my editor at Penguin Random House, who had faith in taking the project on. Jamie, and his colleague Hana Teraie-Wood – along with the editing skills of Fraser Crichton – helped turned a rough and ready first draft into a more polished effort.

Writing a book is a particularly selfish pastime, requiring hours of work often late into the evenings and at weekends. So my final thanks must go to my family and in particular my wife Jo, who remained patient and supportive and somehow kept her sense of humour. I promise I'll be around a bit more now, darling . . . well, until the next book.

Bibliography

In addition to the primary and secondary sources detailed in the Notes and References, I also referred to the following:

Anderson, William. *Pathfinders*. Jarrolds. 1946

Andre, Irving W. and Christian, Gabriel J. *For King and Country: The Service and Sacrifice of the British West Indian Military*. Pont Casse Press. 2009

Bennett, Air Vice-Marshal Donald. *Pathfinder*. Crecy Publishing. 2010

Birrell, Dave. *Baz: The Biography of Ian Bazalgette VC*. The Nanton Lancaster Society. 2018

Birrell, Dave. *Johnny: John Fauquier DSO and Two Bars DFC, Canada's Greatest Bomber Pilot*. Bomber Command Museum of Canada. 2018

Birrell, Dave. *People and Planes: Stories from the Bomber Command Museum of Canada*. The Nanton Lancaster Society. 2011

Bishop, Patrick. *Bomber Boys: Fighting Back 1940–1945*. Harper Press. 2007

Bishop, Patrick. *Target Tirpitz: X-Craft, Agents and Dambusters – The Epic Quest to Destroy Hitler's Mightiest Warship*. HarperPress. 2012

Boiten, Theo. *Nachtjagd Combat Archive: The Early Years. Part 3: 30 May–31 December 1942*. Red Kite Publishing. 2019

Boiten, Theo. *Nachtjagd Combat Archive: 1943. Part 1: 1 January–22 June*. Red Kite Publishing. 2018

Boiten, Theo. *Nachtjagd Combat Archive: 1943. Part 2: 23 June–22 September*. Red Kite Publishing. 2018

Boiten, Theo. *Nachtjagd Combat Archive: 1943. Part 3: 23 September–31 December*. Red Kite Publishing. 2018

Boiten, Theo. *Nachtjagd Combat Archive: 1944. Part 1: 1 January–15 March*. Red Kite Publishing. 2019

Boiten, Theo. *Nachtjagd Combat Archive: 1944. Part 2: 16 March–11 May.* Red Kite Publishing. 2020

Boiten, Theo. *Night Airwar: Personal Recollections of the Conflict Over Europe, 1939–1945.* Crowood Press. 1999

Bourne, Stephen. *The Motherland Calls: Britain's Black Servicemen and Women 1939–45.* The History Press. 2012

Bowman, Martin. *Nachtjagd, Defenders of the Reich 1940–1943.* Pen & Sword. 2015

Bowman, Martin. *Voices in Flight: The Path Finder Force.* Pen & Sword. 2016

Bramson, Alan. *Master Airman: The Biography of Air Vice Marshal Donald Bennett.* Airlife. 1985

Charlwood, Don. *Journeys Into Night.* Endeavour Media. 2018. Kindle Edition

Cheshire, Leonard. *Bomber Pilot.* Hutchinson & Co. 1943

Chorley, W.R. *Royal Air Force Bomber Command Losses of the Second World War. Volume Three: 1942.* Midland Counties Publications. 1994

Chorley, W.R. *Royal Air Force Bomber Command Losses of the Second World War. Volume Four: 1943.* Midland Counties Publications. 1996

Chorley, W.R. *Royal Air Force Bomber Command Losses of the Second World War. Volume Five: 1944.* Midland Counties Publications. 1997

Chorley, W.R. *Royal Air Force Bomber Command Losses of the Second World War. Volume Six: 1945.* Midland Counties Publications. 1998

Chorlton, Martyn. *The RAF Pathfinders, Bomber Command's Elite Squadrons.* Countryside Books. 2016

Churchill, Winston S. *The Second World War. Volume II.* Cassell & Co. 1951

Churchill, Winston S. *Their Finest Hour.* Houghton Mifflin Company. 1976

Cumming, Michael. *Pathfinder Cranswick.* Fighting High. 2008

Currie, Jack. *Lancaster Target.* Goodall. 2012

Currie, Jack. *Mosquito Victory.* Isis Publishing. 2008

Dyson, Freeman. *Disturbing the Universe.* Basic Books. 1979

Edgerton, David. *Britain's War Machine: Weapons, Resources and Experts in the Second World War.* Penguin. 2012

Edgerton, David. *England and the Aeroplane: Militarism, Modernity and Machines.* Penguin. 2013

Falconer, Jonathan. *Bomber Command Operations Manual 1939–45.* Haynes Publishing. 2018

Falconer, Jonathan. *RAF Bomber Crewman.* Shire Publications. 2010

Farrington, Karen. *The Blitzed City: The Destruction of Coventry, 1940.* Aurum. 2015. Kindle Edition

Feast, Sean. *The Pathfinder Companion.* Grub Street. 2012

Fitz Gibbon, Constantine. *The Blitz.* Allan Wingate. 1957

Freer, Paul George. 'Circumventing the law that humans cannot see in the dark: an assessment of the development of target marking techniques to the prosecution of the bombing offensive during the Second World War'. University of Exeter PhD thesis, 2017

Gardiner, Juliet. *Wartime Britain 1939–1945*. Headline. 2004

Gilbert, Martin. *Churchill: A Life*. Heinemann. 1991

Guinn, Gilbert S. and Bennett, G.H. *British Naval Aviation in World War Two. The US Navy and Anglo-American Relations*. Tauris. 2007

Hampton, James. *Selected for Aircrew*. Air Research Publications. 1993

Harris, Sir Arthur. *Bomber Offensive*. Collins Clear-Type Press. 1947

Hastings, Max. *Bomber Command*. Macmillan. 1999

Herrmann, Hajo. *Eagle's Wings: The Autobiography of a Luftwaffe Pilot*. Guild Publishing. 1991

Holland, James. *Big Week: The Biggest Air Battle of World War Two*. Bantam Press. 2018

Holland, James. *Dam Busters: The Race to Smash the Dams 1943*. Bantam Press. 2012

Holland, James. *Normandy '44: D-Day and the Battle for France*. Bantam Press. 2019

Holland, James. *The War in the West: A New History – The Allies Fight Back 1941–43*. Transworld. 2017

Jones, Reginald Victor. *Most Secret War: British Scientific Intelligence, 1939–1945*. Penguin. 1978

Overy, Richard. *The Bombing War: Europe 1939–1945*. Penguin. 2014

Overy, Richard. *Why the Allies Won*: Jonathan Cape. 1995

Melinsky, Hugh. *Forming the Pathfinders: The Career of Air Vice-Marshal Sydney Bufton*. The History Press. 2010

Middlebrook, Martin. *The Berlin Raids. The Bomber Battle, Winter 1943–44*. Pen & Sword. 2010

Middlebrook, Martin. *Firestorm Hamburg: The Facts Surrounding the Destruction of a German City*. Pen & Sword. 2012

Middlebrook, Martin. *The Nuremberg Raid: 30–31 March 1944*. Pen & Sword. 2009

Middlebrook, Martin. *The Peenemünde Raid*. Allen Lane. 1982

Middlebrook, Martin and Everitt, Chris. *The Bomber Command War Diaries: An Operational Reference Book 1939–1945*. Pen & Sword. 2014

Moorhouse, Roger. *Berlin at War: Life and Death in Hitler's Capital 1939–45*. The Bodley Head. 2010

Musgrove, Gordon. *Pathfinder Force: A History of 8 Group*. Macdonald and Jane's. 1976.

Nichol, John. *Lancaster: The Forging of a Very British Legend*. Simon & Shuster. 2020

Parfitt, Ken. *Those Were the Days*. Privately published. 2015

Pedan, Murray. *A Thousand Shall Fall*. Canada's Wings Inc. 1981

Price, Alfred. *Battle Over the Reich: The Strategic Bomber Offensive Over Germany. Volume One: 1939–1943*. Classic. 2005

Price, Alfred. *Instruments of Darkness: The History of Electronic Warfare 1939–45*. Frontline Books. 2017

Price, Alfred. *Luftwaffe Handbook: 1939–1945*. Ian Allen. 1977

Price, David. *The Crew: The Story of a Lancaster Bomber Crew*. Head of Zeus. 2020

Robinson, Bill. *A Pathfinder's Story: The Life & Death of Flight Lieutenant Jack Mossop DFC, DFM*. Pen & Sword. 2007

Saward, Dudley. *The Authorised Biography of 'Bomber' Harris*. Sphere Books. 1984

Smith, Albert and Ian. *Mosquito Pathfinder: A Navigator's 90 WWII Bomber Operations*. Goodall. 2011

Smith, Ron. *Rear Gunner Pathfinders*. Goodall Publications. 1987

Spooner, Tony. *Clean Sweep: The Life of Air Marshal Sir Ivor Broom*. Goodall. 2010

Sullivan, Chris. *Trials and Tribulations: The Story of RAF Gransden Lodge*. Matador. 2015

Trevor-Roper, Hugh (ed.). *The Goebbels Diaries: The Last Days*. Book Club Associates. 1978

Trotman, Flight Lieutenant P.J.P., DFC and Bar. *J for Johnnie*. Laundry Cottage Books. 2015

Wadsworth, Michael P. *They Led the Way: The Story of Pathfinder Squadron 156*. Highgate Publications. 2002

Wakefield, Kenneth. *The First Pathfinders*. William Kimber & Co. 1981

Wakefield, Ken. *Pfadfinder*. Tempus. 1999

Watkins, T.F., Cackett, J.C. and Hall, R.G. *Chemical Warfare, Pyrotechnics and the Fireworks Industry*. Pergamon Press. 1968

Webster, Charles and Frankland, Noble. *The Strategic Air Offensive Against Germany 1939–1945. Volume I: Preparation*. The Naval and Military Press. 2006

Webster, Charles and Frankland, Noble. *The Strategic Air Offensive Against Germany 1939–1945. Volume II: Endeavour*. The Naval and Military Press. 2006

Webster, Charles and Frankland, Noble. *The Strategic Air Offensive Against Germany 1939–1945. Volume III: Victory*. The Naval and Military Press. 2006

Webster, Charles and Frankland, Noble. *The Strategic Air Offensive Against Germany 1939–1945. Volume IV: Annexes and Appendices*. The Naval and Military Press. 2006

Westermann, Edward B. *Flak: German Anti-Aircraft Defenses, 1914–1945*. University Press of Kansas. 2001

Notes and References

Prologue

1   'The Cello and the Nightingale'. BBC News online. 25.03.16. https://www.bbc.co.uk/news/magazine-35861899. The recording can be heard in full online at the *Science Museum Group Journal*: 'The nightingales during the Second World War'. http://journal.sciencemuseum.org.uk/browse/issue-04/capturing-the-song-of-the-nightingale/the-nightingales-during-the-second-world-war/?textsize=normal.

2   The National Archives (TNA), Kew. AIR 27/99/10.

3   This and all subsequent quotes from or about Pilling are from: The RAF Museum (RAFM), Hendon. Correspondence and press articles relating to Flt Lt Hector Garrick Pilling MF10088/4.

4   *Royal Air Force Bomber Command Losses of the Second World War. Volume Three: 1942.* W.R. Chorley. Midland Counties Publications (1994), p.95.

5   *The Bomber Command War Diaries: An Operational Reference Book 1939–1945.* Martin Middlebrook and Chris Everitt. Pen & Sword (2014), p.267.

6   TNA, AIR 14/2788.

7   TNA, AIR 8/1356.

8   *The Strategic Air Offensive Against Germany 1939–1945. Volume I: Preparation.* Charles Webster and Noble Frankland. The Naval and Military Press (2006) [First published, HMSO, 1961], p.202.

9   TNA, AIR 20/2795.

Introduction

1   TNA, AIR 14/3410.

2   *The Strategic Air Offensive Against Germany 1939–1945. Volume II: Endeavour.* Charles Webster and Noble Frankland. The Naval and Military Press (2006), p.236.

3   *Liverpool Daily Post.* 9 December 1943, p.1.

4   *Selected for Aircrew.* James Hampton. Air Research Publications (1993), p.343.

5   As quoted by aviation historian Victoria Taylor: https://twitter.com/SpitfireFilly/status/1227872099047485442?s=19.

6   Joseph Patient. Imperial War Museum (IWM) Sound Archive 30267.

7   TNA, AIR 14/2693.

8   Private Papers of Flight Lieutenant G.P. Dawson. IWM 16764.

9   Author analysis of 8 Group deaths data held at RAFM.

10   *The Berlin Raids: The Bomber Battle Winter, 1943–44.* Martin Middlebrook. Pen & Sword (2010), p.311.

11   *Pathfinder.* Air Vice-Marshal Donald Bennett. Crecy Publishing (2010), p.252.

12   *The Pathfinder Companion.* Sean Feast. Grub Street (2012), p.14.

13   TNA, AIR 14/2831.

Chapter One – X Marks the Spot

1   TNA, HO 199/178.

2   *The Blitzed City: The Destruction of Coventry, 1940.* Karen Farrington. Aurum (2015), Kindle Edition, Location 3382.

3   Ibid. Locations 1297 and 1303.

4   Although, in one baffling case, a Kampfgruppe 100 commander who claimed to have flown almost a million miles as a pre-war Lufthansa pilot couldn't join on operations because he got airsick over 12,000 feet.

5   Unless otherwise stated, the detail about the Kampfgruppe 100 comes primarily from: *The First Pathfinders.* Kenneth Wakefield. William Kimber & Co (1981).

6   TNA, AIR 41/17.

7   Some of the Luftwaffe pilots actually thought Knickebein quite distracting, however, and found it could be more trouble than it was worth.

8   The entire X-Verfahren system is often incorrectly referred to as X-Gerät (Equipment X). In fact, X-Gerät is the X-Verfahren receiving kit on board an aircraft.

9   Unless otherwise stated, the detail about German navigation equipment and its use in the raid on Coventry comes from: *Instruments of Darkness: The History of Electronic Warfare 1939–45.* Alfred Price. Frontline Books (2017); and *Pfadfinder.* Ken Wakefield. Tempus (1999).

10   *Coventry Evening Telegraph*. 5 October 2009. https://www.coventry telegraph.net/news/coventry-news/horror-coventry-blitz-relived-tv-3074303.

11   *The Blitzed City*. Farrington. Location 1399.

12   TNA, HO 202/2.

13   *Instruments of Darkness*. Price. p.45.

14   Unless otherwise indicated, details of the raid are taken from reports in TNA, HO 199/178.

15   'Did Churchill annihilate Coventry? The controversial new play that claims the city could have been saved'. *Daily Mail*. 1 April 2008. https://www.dailymail.co.uk/news/article-552390/Did-Churchill-annihilate-Coventry-The-controversial-new-play-claims-city-saved.html.

16   TNA, HO 250/1.2.

17   *The Blitzed City*. Farrington. Location 102.

18   *Wartime: Britain 1939–1945*. Juliet Gardiner. Headline (2004), p.304.

19   TNA, AIR 41/17.

20   TNA, AIR 40/288.

21   TNA, HO 199/178.

22   *The First Pathfinders*. Wakefield. p.129.

23   *The Blitz*. Constantine Fitz Gibbon. Allan Wingate (1957), p.203.

24   'How St Paul's Cathedral Survived the Blitz'. BBC News. 29 December 2010. https://www.bbc.co.uk/news/magazine-12016916 (Retrieved 28. 02.2020).

Chapter Two – Ruffians

1   *Most Secret War: British Scientific Intelligence, 1939–1945*. Reginald Victor Jones. Penguin (1978), pp.156–7.

2   *The First Pathfinders*. Wakefield. p.15.

3   *Most Secret War*. Jones. p.101.

4   *Their Finest Hour*. Winston S. Churchill. Houghton Mifflin (1976), p.340.

5   *The Second World War. Volume II*. Winston S. Churchill. Cassell & Co., as cited in *The First Pathfinders*. Wakefield. p.15.

6   *Their Finest Hour*. Churchill. p.342.

7   *Churchill: A Life*. Martin Gilbert. Heinemann (1991), p.666.

8   *Their Finest Hour*. Churchill. p.337.

9 . TNA, AIR 41/17.

10   TNA, WO 208/3507.

11   TNA, WO 208/3507.

12   *The First Pathfinders*. Wakefield. p.111.

13   *The Bombing War*. Richard Overy. Penguin (2013), p.96.

14   *Most Secret War*. Jones. p.152.

15   *Their Finest Hour.* Churchill. p.337.
16   See 'Churchill Let Coventry Burn To Protect His Secret Intelligence'. The International Churchill Society. https://winstonchurchill.org/resources/myths/churchill-let-coventry-burn/.
17   *The Blitzed City.* Farrington. Location 1238.
18   *Churchill: A Life.* Gilbert. p.684.
19   Ibid. p.684.
20   Ibid. p.683.
21   TNA, HO 199/178.
22   *Bomber Boys: Fighting Back 1940–1945.* Patrick Bishop. Harper Press (2007), p.32.
23   'A History of Navigation in the Royal Air Force', RAF Historical Society Seminar at the RAF Museum, Hendon. 21 October 1996. *The RAFM*, p.17. https://www.rafmuseum.org.uk/documents/research/RAF-Historical-Society-Journals/Journal-17A-Air-Navigationin-the-RAF.pdf.
24   TNA, AIR 22/1.
25   *The Bombing War.* Overy. p.241.
26   12.1 per cent in 1939, compared to 4.6 per cent in 1942, the year with the next highest loss percentage. TNA, AIR 22/203.
27   Edgar Louis Graham Hall. IWM Sound Archive 6075.
28   *The Strategic Air Offensive Against Germany 1939–1945. Volume I: Preparation.* Webster and Frankland. p.203.
29   TNA, AIR 14/57.
30   TNA, AIR 20/4782.
31   TNA, AIR 14/2693.
32   *Battle Over the Reich: The Strategic Bomber Offensive Over Germany. Volume One: 1939–1943.* Alfred Price. Classic (2005). p.26.
33   *The Bombing War.* Overy. p.253.
34   *The Strategic Air Offensive Against Germany 1939–1945. Volume I: Preparation.* Webster and Frankland. p.202.
35   Ibid. p.144.
36   *England and the Aeroplane.* David Edgerton. Penguin (2013), p.99.
37   *Britain's War Machine.* David Edgerton. Penguin (2012), p.37; *England and the Aeroplane.* Edgerton. p.114.

Chapter Three – Flying like Icarus

1   Colin Bell. Interview with author, 2019. All subsequent quotes from Bell are from this interview.
2   *J for Johnnie. Flight Lieutenant P.J.P. Trotman DFC and Bar.* Laundry Cottage Books (2015), p.35.
3   Private Papers of Squadron Leader G.H.F. Carter DFC. IWM 5707.

4   *Pathfinder Cranswick*. Michael Cumming. Fighting High (2008), p.16.

5   Ibid. p.37.

6   Dick Raymond. Interview with author, 2019.

7   Ernie Holmes. Interview with author, 2019.

8   *Bomber Boys*. Bishop. p.44.

9   *For King and Country: The Service and Sacrifice of the British West Indian Military*. Irving W. Andre and Gabriel J. Christian. Pont Casse Press (2009), p.278.

10   Ulric Cross. IWM Sound Archive 31297. Further background provided by Ann and Nicola Cross, in interview with author in 2019.

11   *The Motherland Calls: Britain's Black Servicemen and Women 1939–45*. Stephen Bourne. The History Press (2012), p.62.

12   *For King and Country*. Andre and Christian. p.277.

13   'Obituary: Ulric Cross'. *The Times*. 11 October 2013; and Ulric Cross. IWM Sound Archive 31297.

14   IWM Sound Archive 31297.

15   Personal diary and letters by Robert Maxwell Bryant. The Australian War Memorial (AWM) PR00275. All subsequent quotes from Max Bryant's letters or diaries throughout the book are from this source.

16   Bryant family research carried out by Therese Lynch, www.your familygenealogist.com.

17   The Australian War Memorial https://www.awm.gov.au/articles/ encyclopedia/raaf/eats#:~:text=The%20scheme%20was%20known%20 in,factories%20and%20the%20war%20zone.

Chapter Four – The Most Expensive Education in the World

1   *Britain's War Machine*. Edgerton. p.216.

2   *RAF Wings Over Florida: Memories of World War II British Air Cadets*. Will Largent. Purdue University Press (2000). https://docs.lib. purdue.edu/purduepress_ebooks/9/.

3   From a speech by Ulric Cross in 2010, as part of Military History Week 2010 at Chaguaramas Military Museum in Trinidad. https://www.you tube.com/watch?v=SdSoTJ6VX7o.

4   Interview with Ulric Cross. IWM Sound Archive 31297.

5   From a speech by Ulric Cross in 2010, as part of Military History Week 2010 at Chaguaramas Military Museum in Trinidad.

6   Ibid.

7   Ulric Cross. IWM Sound Archive 31297.

8   From a speech by Ulric Cross in 2010, as part of Military History Week 2010 at Chaguaramas Military Museum in Trinidad.

9   Ibid.

10   *The Motherland Calls*. Bourne. p.59.
11   Ibid. p.11.
12   Ulric Cross. IWM Sound Archive 31297.
13   *British Naval Aviation in World War Two: The US Navy and Anglo-American Relations*. Gilbert S. Guinn and G.H. Bennett. Tauris (2007), p.37. Despite the title, this book also provides some excellent background on RAF cadets who went on to fly in Bomber Command.
14   Unpublished letters of John Kelly. RAFM X004-2500/001.
15   Unpublished letters of John Kelly. RAFM X004-2500/002.
16   Unpublished letters of John Kelly. RAFM X004-2500/001.
17   *Rear Gunner Pathfinders*. Ron Smith. Goodall Publications (1987), p.12.
18   *The Second World War. Volume III: The Grand Alliance*. W.S. Churchill, Reprint Society (1952), p.595, as cited in *British Naval Aviation in World War Two*. Guinn and Bennett. p.18.
19   *British Naval Aviation in World War Two*. Guinn and Bennett. pp.17–18.

Chapter Five – Hooray for Hollywood!

1   Unpublished letters of John Kelly. RAFM X004-2500/004.
2   Unpublished letters of John Kelly. RAFM X004-2500/002.
3   Colin Bell. Interview with author, 2018.
4   Unpublished letters of John Kelly. RAFM X004-2500/004.
5   Unpublished letters of John Kelly. RAFM X004-2500/005.
6   Unpublished letters of John Kelly. RAFM X004-2500/004.
7   Colin Bell. Interview with author, 2018.
8   Unpublished letters of John Kelly. RAFM X004-2500/004.
9   Unpublished letters of John Kelly. RAFM X004-2500/005.
10   Little wonder Hollywood stars liked visits from RAF cadets – Garson was in fact 38 years old.
11   Unpublished letters of John Kelly. RAFM X004-2500/005.
12   Don Charlwood, unpublished account, kindly shared with the author by Charlwood's daughter, Doreen Burge.

Chapter Six – We Guide to Strike

1   *The Bombing War*. Overy. p.292; *The Bomber Command War Diaries*. Middlebrook and Everitt. pp.272–3; *The Strategic Air Offensive Against Germany 1939–1945. Volume I: Preparation*. Webster and Frankland. pp.408–9.
2   *Daily Mirror*. 1 June 1942. p.1; *Daily Express*. 1 June 1942. p.1.
3   Unpublished letters of John Kelly. RAFM X004-2500/004.

4   Interview with Sir Arthur Harris. RAF Centre for Air and Space Power Studies. 1977. https://www.youtube.com/watch?v=UCWK-O7cKvc.

5   W.R. Freeman to Harris in a letter dated 3 June 1942. TNA, AIR 20/2795.

6   Interview with Harris. RAF Centre for Air and Space Power Studies. 1977.

7   TNA, AIR 20/4768.

8   From the 'De-housing' paper by Lord Cherwell, as cited in *The RAF Pathfinders: Bomber Command's Elite Squadrons*. Martyn Chorlton. Countryside Books (2016). p.11.

9   Bufton Papers, 3/11, Churchill College, Cambridge, as cited in 'The Other Bomber Battle: An Examination of the Problems that arose between the Air Staff and the AOC Bomber Command between 1942 and 1945 and their Effects on the Strategic Bomber Offensive'. Rex F. Cording. University of Canterbury PhD thesis (2006), p.86.

10   'The "Whirlwind" of Bomber Harris'. *Air Force Magazine*. 1 September 2001. https://www.airforcemag.com/article/0911keeperfile/ and British Pathe. 'On The Chin!' (1942). https://www.youtube.com/watch?v=to4djmDqJRI.

11   *The Bomber Command War Diaries*. Middlebrook and Everitt. p.274.

12   Interview with John Toombes. IWM Sound Archive 28633.

13   'David Bensusan-Butt, 1914–1994'. H. W. Arndt and R. M. Sundrum. *The Economic Journal*, Vol. 105, No. 430 (May 1995), pp.669–75.

14   *The Strategic Air Offensive Against Germany 1939–1945. Volume I: Preparation*. Webster and Frankland. pp.178–81 TNA AIR 8/1356 and *The Bombing War*. Overy. p.267.

15   Ibid. p.179; TNA, AIR 20/869.

16   TNA, AIR 41/41.

17   *The Second World War. Volume IV: The Hinge of Fate*. Winston S. Churchill. Cassell & Co. (1951), p.250.

18   TNA, AIR 14/1939.

19   Ibid.

20   TNA, AIR14/516.

21   TNA, AIR 20/4809.

22   TNA, AIR 20/4782.

23   TNA, AIR 20/4809.

24   *Proceedings of the Royal Air Force Historical Society*, Issue No. 6 (September 1989). p.22.

25   TNA, AIR 20/3527.

26   TNA, AIR 20/4782.

27   Ibid.

28   Ibid.

29   TNA, AIR 20/3802.

30   *Proceedings of the Royal Air Force Historical Society*, Issue No. 6 (September 1989). p.23.

31   *Bomber Command*. Max Hastings. Macmillan (1999), p.239.

32   *Forming the Pathfinders: The Career of Air Vice-Marshal Sydney Bufton*. Hugh Melinsky. The History Press (2010), p.77.

33   TNA, AIR 14/2058.

34   TNA, AIR 20/778.

35   Harris Papers RAFM.

36   TNA, AIR 20/778.

37   *Bomber Offensive*. Sir Arthur Harris. Collins Clear-Type Press (1947), p.25.

38   From a taped interview between Harris and Dudley Saward (Harris's biographer) in 1972, held by the Bomber Command Association at Hendon, cited in 'The Other Bomber Battle' Cording. p.136.

Chapter Seven – The Don

1   This conversation is taken from Bennett's account in his autobiography (Pathfinder. Bennett. p.155). He says it was 'roughly the gist' of the conversation. I have taken the liberty of putting the exchange into quotes to aid the narrative, and certainly Harris went on the record on a number of occasions post-war to voice his objection to the PFF in this form, but still saying that he supported Bennett.

2   *Pathfinder*. Bennett. p.156.

3   Ibid. pp.13–19.

4   *Courier Mail*. 24 January 1944.

5   *Sunday Mail*. 11 June 1944. Clipping from the Bennett family's private collection, courtesy of Noreen Cooper.

6   *Everybody's Weekly*. 29 January 1944.

7   *Bomber Offensive*. Harris. p.130.

8   *The Crew: The Story of a Lancaster Bomber Crew*. David Price. Head of Zeus (2020), p.192.

9   From an unnamed newspaper clipping in the Bennett family's private collection.

10   From an unnamed newspaper clipping in the Bennett family's private collection.

11   *Daily Telegraph*. 16 June 1942; *Northern Echo*. 19 August 1939.

12   Pathfinder. Bennett. p.137.

13   Ibid. p.138.

14   Ibid. p.139.

15   From an article in an unnamed Brisbane newspaper from June 1942. Clipping held in the Bennett family's private collection.

16 *The Nuremberg Raid*. Martin Middlebrook. Pen & Sword Aviation (2009), p.43.
17 TNA, AIR 20/778.

Chapter Eight – Blooded

1   Harris Papers RAFM.
2   Thomas Gilbert Mahaddie. IWM Sound Archive 10596.
3   Ibid.
4   *Battle Over the Reich*. Price. p.49.
5   *News Chronicle*. 29 February 1944.
6   From Part V of 'Enemy Coast Ahead', an unpublished draft manuscript written in 1944 by Guy Gibson. RAFM DC71/8/122.
7   Ibid.
8   Ibid.
9   *The Bomber Command War Diaries*. Middlebrook and Everitt. p.305.
10 John Ottewell. Interview with author, 2019.
11 Aircraft statistics are taken from a variety of sources. All casualty and bomb figures are from TNA, AIR 22/203: 'Bomber Command War Room Total Wastage'. Statistics on aircraft size, bomb capacity etc. from: *The Bombing War*. Overy; *Bomber Command Operations Manual 1939–45*. Jonathan Falconer. Haynes Publishing (2018).
12 'The Wartime Memoirs of Geoffrey P. Dawson DFC 1942–1944'. IWM 16764.
13 It took 1,100 man hours to produce one Lancaster aircraft per month, including spare parts, as opposed to 1,800 for the Stirling and 1,350 for the Halifax. TNA, AVIA 10/269. The Lancaster dropped 107.2 tons of bombs per aircraft missing compared to 48 tons for the Halifax. Stirling figures are unavailable but the bomb tonnage will be lower per aircraft lost than the Lancaster. TNA, AIR 19/352.
14 *Bomber Offensive*. Harris. p.103.
15 Unpublished letters of John Kelly. RAFM X004-2500/009. All subsequent Kelly quotes in this chapter are from this source.
16 Ernie Holmes. Interview with author, 2019.
17 TNA, AIR 22/203.
18 Interview with Donald Bennett. IWM Sound Archive 9378.
19 Interview with John Eric Tipton. IWM Sound Archive 15105.
20 Colin Bell. Interview with author, 2019.

Chapter Nine – Boffins

1   Interview with Jack Brown Franklin. IBCC Digital Archive. https://ibccdigitalarchive.lincoln.ac.uk/omeka/collections/document/8743.

2   Ibid.

3   Operation details and results are from the following sources: TNA, AIR 27/853-37; TNA, AIR 27/853-38; *The Bomber Command War Diaries*. Middlebrook and Everitt. p.338; and *The Pathfinder Companion*. Feast. p.23.

4   *Most Secret War*. Jones. pp.276–7.

5   *Pathfinder*. Bennett. p.176.

6   I'm indebted to technology writer David Robertson for his background information about Alec Reeves and Oboe, and for sharing with me the manuscript of a lecture he gave on the subject at Imperial College London.

7   Detail on Oboe from a variety of sources, including: TNA, AVIA 7/917; TNA, AIR 20/1471; TNA, AIR 20/871; TNA, AIR 20/878.

8   TNA, AIR 49/78.

9   TNA, AIR 14/2687.

10   Interview with Harris. RAF Centre for Air and Space Power Studies. 1977.

11   'People I remember at Defford'. Neil Ramsey. IBCC Digital Archive. https://ibccdigitalarchive.lincoln.ac.uk/omeka/collections/document/19915.

12   *Operational Research in Bomber Command*. Air Historical Branch. p.66

13   Ibid. p.64.

14   *Nottingham Journal*. 28 November 1944.

15   According to a newspaper cutting in the private papers of Dr B.J. O'Kane. IWM 5979.

16   Private papers of Dr B.J. O'Kane. IWM 5979.

17   Interview with Donald Bennett. IWM Sound Archive 9378.

Chapter Ten – Fireworks

1   *Daily Express*. 31 January 1944.

2   'Hitting the Mark, but Missing the Target: Luftwaffe Deception Operations, 1939–1945'. Edward Westermann. *War in History*, Vol. 10, No. 2 (April 2003), pp.206–21.

3   Ibid.

4   Ibid.

5   The idea of marking a target was not new. Both the German air force in the Spanish Civil War and the RAF in pre-war Iraq had used primitive forms of markers, but they were small and not particularly bright. Marker bombs had also been developed early in the war, including those released through the flare chute of an aircraft.

6   Background on Coxon taken from a number of sources: RAFM X005-4810/025; *Daily Express.* 20 March 1945 (TNA, AVIA 15/1379); *Manchester Evening News.* 6 September 1948; *Birmingham Gazette.* 14 October 1948; *Birmingham Mail.* 19 March 1945.

7   RAFM X005-4810/025.

8   Unless otherwise noted, the information about the target indicators and flares in this chapter comes from the following TNA files: AIR 14/1884; AIR 14/2715; AIR 20/5753; AIR 14/990; AIR 14/4140; AIR 14/1759; AIR 14/2028; FD 1/6475; AIR 14/2710; AVIA 15/1379.

9   The account of Coxon's challenges in getting his markers approved is taken from an interview he gave with the *Guardian* on 13 July 1985.

10   Although Coxon is credited as the main driving force behind the creation of the target indicators used by the Pathfinders, post-war, Arthur Morley, an RAF wing commander who worked for Sydney Bufton, claimed to have come up with the idea. The dispute ended up in court, where the likes of Don Bennett wrote strong letters of support for Coxon. Morley was eventually awarded £500 by the Royal Commission for his contribution. Coxon was awarded £1,500.

11   RAFM X005-4810/025.

12   'The War Memoirs of 1096366 Cpl T Waller'. Thomas Waller. IBCC Digital Archive. https://ibccdigitalarchive.lincoln.ac.uk/omeka/collections/document/36.

13   My thanks to Dr Kit Cuttle, lecturer in Advanced Lighting Design at the Queensland University of Technology in Brisbane, who was kind enough to convert candlepower into something today's reader can relate to.

14   Private Papers of Flight Lieutenant G.P. Dawson. IWM 16764.

15   *Flak: German Anti-Aircraft Defenses, 1914–1945.* Edward B. Westermann. University Press of Kansas (2001), p.198.

16   'Interview with Charly Pfeifer'. Peter Schulze. IBCC Digital Archive. https://ibccdigitalarchive.lincoln.ac.uk/omeka/collections/document/16.

17   TNA, AVIA 15/1379.

18   RAFM X004-2500/012.

19   Stephen Dawson's memoir notebook. IBCC Digital Archive (2021). https://ibccdigitalarchive.lincoln.ac.uk/omeka/collections/document/6708.

20   Basil Oxtaby. IWM Sound Archive 12613.

21   *News Chronicle.* 29 February 1944.

22   *Pathfinder.* Bennett. p.179.

23   TNA, AIR 25/155.

24   *Bomber Offensive.* Harris. p.144.

Chapter Eleven – Essenised

1 Information about Allan Ball from interviews with, and details supplied by, his daughter Juliet Stockford and his grandson Larry, and TNA, AIR 27/380-6.
2 '35 Squadron Pathfinder motto'. IBCC Digital Archive. https://ibccdigitalarchive.lincoln.ac.uk/omeka/collections/document/8257.
3 *Pathfinder Cranswick*. Cumming. pp.92–4.
4 *The Strategic Air Offensive Against Germany. Volume II: Endeavour*. Webster and Frankland. p.115.
5 *Flak*. Westermann. pp.190–91.
6 Ibid. p.186.
7 Ibid. p.220.
8 *Firestorm Hamburg*. Martin Middlebrook. Pen & Sword (2012), p.61.
9 *Flak*. Westermann. p.220.
10 TNA, AIR 14/1761.
11 Interview with Harry Irons. IWM Sound Archive 27796.
12 Interview with Frank Tudor. IWM Sound Archive 17733.
13 *Night Airwar: Personal Recollections of the Conflict over Europe, 1939–1945*. Theo Boiten. Crowood Press (1999), p.72.
14 *Journeys into Night*. Don Charlwood. Endeavour Media (2018). Kindle Edition.
15 *The Strategic Air Offensive Against Germany. Volume II: Endeavour*. Webster and Frankland. p.118.
16 *The Everlasting Arms: The War Memoirs of Air Commodore John Searby*. Martin Middlebrook (ed.). William Kimber (1988), p.95.
17 This uncorroborated story was told to Edward Fennessy, a British wartime radar expert, by General Wolfgang Martini after the war, and was relayed in an interview Fennessy gave to the IWM in 1992 (IWM Sound Archive 12777). In his autobiography, Don Bennett claims Hitler was told days after the Essen raid by other experts that the RAF had such technology, but refused to believe it.
18 'Book review: *Berlin at War: Life and Death in Hitler's Capital, 1939–45* by Roger Moorhouse'. *Independent*. 22 October 2011. https://www.independent.co.uk/arts-entertainment/books/reviews/berlin-at-war-life-and-death-in-hitlers-capital-1939-45-by-roger-moorhouse-2056860.html.
19 Edward Fennessy. IWM Sound Archive 12777.

Chapter Twelve – The Horse Thief

1 *Journeys into Night*. Charlwood. p.219.
2 Dick Raymond. Interview with author, 2018.
3 Interview with Ronald Curtis. IWM Sound Archive 17743.

4   Interview with Hugh Parrott. IWM Sound Archive 16279.
5   A letter from Albert Arter to his parents published in the 77 Squadron
       Association magazine, winter 2019.
6   *Essex Chronicle*. 4 June 1943.
7   *Lancashire Daily Post*. 4 February 1944.
8   *Gloucestershire Echo*. 3 July 1945.
9   *Birmingham Mail*. 14 February 1944.
10   Interview with Ian Hewett. IWM Sound Archive 10310.
11   TNA, AIR 49/78.
12   TNA, AIR 20/909.
13   Harris Papers RAFM.
14   RAFM X004-2500/011.
15   *News Chronicle*. 29 February 1944.
16   Interview with Ronald Curtis. IWM Sound Archive 17743.
17   *Baz: The Biography of Ian Bazalgette VC*. Dave Birrell. Bomber Com-
       mand Museum of Canada (2014), pp.93–4.
18   Interview with Thomas Gilbert Mahaddie. IWM Sound Archive 10596.

Chapter Thirteen – Happy Valley

1   TNA, AIR 20/909.
2   Casualty stats based on the author's own analysis of 8 Group roll of
       honour (1942–5) held by the RAF Museum archives.
3   Private Papers of Flight Lieutenant G.P. Dawson. IWM 16764.
4   Personal diary of Maj. J.K. Christie, 1943–1944. RAFM MF10016/5.
5   RAFM X001-3517/002.
6   TNA, AIR 14/1773.
7   Unpublished memoirs of Mr Holman's service as a ground mechanic
       with 35 Squadron. RAFM B4264.
8   TNA, AIR 50/185/134; *Argus*. 4 September 1943; 'Obituary'. *Sydney
       Morning Herald*. https://www.smh.com.au/national/shot-down-nazis-
       shared-a-beer-with-king-george-20070911-gdr2s5.html?page=fullpage
       #contentSwap1. Williams died in 2007.
9   Robert Maxwell Bryant was, in fact, a pilot officer; this telegram is
       reproduced verbatim.
10   *Journeys into Night*. Charlwood. p.263.
11   Although this is not absolutely certain, Bryant's aircraft crashed in the
       vicinity of two possible downed aircraft claimed by German flak teams,
       according to research by Theo Boiten.
12   TNA, AIR 25/155.
13   TNA, AIR 14/2830.
14   Author analysis of 8 Group deaths data held at RAFM.
15   *The Bombing War*. Overy. p.326.

390 NOTES AND REFERENCES

Chapter Fourteen – In Sickness and in Health

1   Author interview with Noreen Cooper, 2019.
2   Ibid.
3   Ibid.
4   *Disturbing the Universe*. Freeman Dyson. Basic Books (1979), p.19.
5   Author interview with Noreen Cooper, 2019.
6   Letter from Macgown family papers.
7   TNA, AIR 25/157.
8   TNA, ADM 204/569.
9   TNA, AIR 49/78.
10   TNA, AIR 25/155.
11   Christie diary. RAFM MF10016.
12   Interview with John Toombes. IWM Sound Archive 28633.
13   TNA, AIR 14/2831.
14   TNA, AIR 14/2832.
15   RAFM X004-2500/012.
16   The NTU moved to Upwood in June 1943 and Warboys in March 1944.
17   *News Chronicle*. 29 February 1944.
18   Interview with Gordon Webb. *The Memory Project*. http://www.
     thememoryproject.com/stories/2687:gordon-webb/.
19   Interview with Air Vice-Marshal Don Bennett. RAF Centre for Air and
     Space Power Studies. 1980. https://www.youtube.com/watch?v=UjH0U
     wNJ6O4.
20   *Birmingham Gazette*. 31 January 1944.
21   RAFM X004-2500/012.
22   *News Chronicle*. 29 February 1944.
23   Macgown family papers.
24   'The Many Behind the Few: The Lives and Emotions of Erks and WAAFs
     of RAF Bomber Command 1939–1945'. Dan Ellin. Warwick University
     PhD thesis (2015), p.315.
25   'Interview with Sinclair Nutting'. Jean Macartney. IBCC Digital
     Archive.   https://ibccdigitalarchive.lincoln.ac.uk/omeka/collections/
     document/3468.
26   *Disturbing the Universe*. Dyson. pp.22–4.
27   Ibid. p.24.
28   *Oban Times*. November 1979.
29   Macgown family papers.
30   Colin Bell. Interview with author, 2019.
31   *Rear Gunner Pathfinders*. Smith. p.93.
32   Herbert Edward Dunford. IWM Oral Interview 15744.
33   TNA, AIR 49/78.

34   Ibid.
35   Air Ministry, Royal Air Force Personnel Statistics for the period 3rd September 1939 to 1st September 1945 (Air Ministry, 1946), pp. 1–5, 6–31, as cited in 'The Many Behind the Few'. Ellin. p.15.
36   TNA, AIR 14/2830.
37   Brian Frow – Memoirs of a bomber baron. RAFM X002-5619.
38   'Interview with Sinclair Nutting'. Jean Macartney. IBCC Digital Archive. https://ibccdigitalarchive.lincoln.ac.uk/omeka/collections/document/3468.
39   TNA, AIR 25/176.
40   *Baz*. Birrell. p.81.
41   TNA. AIR 14/2833.
42   Wendy Carter (née Thomas, who during the war was known as Gwen). Interview with author, 2019. All subsequent quotes from Carter in this chapter are from the same source.
43   TNA, AIR 14/2831.
44   Ibid.
45   Macgown family papers.

Chapter Fifteen – Firestorm

1   TNA, AIR 24/257.
2   Personal diary of Maj. J.K. Christie, 1943–1944. RAFM MF10016/5.
3   *Nachtjagd Combat Archive: 1943. Part 2: 23 June–22 September.* Theo Boiten. Red Kite Publishing (2018), p.31.
4   *Firestorm Hamburg*. Middlebrook. p.136.
5   Ibid. p.147.
6   *The Strategic Air Offensive Against Germany 1939–1945. Volume II: Endeavour.* Webster and Frankland. p.156.
7   *Toronto Daily Star*. 28 July 1943.
8   *Firestorm Hamburg*. Middlebrook. p.276.
9   'Interview with Philip Bates'. Brian Wright. IBCC Digital Archive. https://ibccdigitalarchive.lincoln.ac.uk/omeka/collections/document/3340.
10   *Firestorm Hamburg*. Middlebrook. p.284.
11   Ibid. p.286.
12   Ernie Holmes. Interview with author, 2018.
13   Personal diary of Maj. J.K. Christie, 1943–1944. RAFM MF10016/5.
14   Interview with Donald Bennett. IWM 9378.
15   TNA, AIR 25/155.
16   *Berlin at War*. Roger Moorhouse. Bodley Head (2010), p.319.

Chapter Sixteen – The Boffin Bashers

1   *Press and Journal.* 27 February 1978. p.6.
2   Much of the background detail about the raid comes from TNA, AIR 14/3410 and *The Peenemünde Raid*. Martin Middlebrook. Allen Lane (1982).
3   *The Everlasting Arms.* Searby. p.150.
4   TNA AIR 27/767-15.
5   *The Everlasting Arms.* Searby. p.153.
6   'An interesting war'. Arthur Spencer. IBCC Digital Archive. https://ibccdigitalarchive.lincoln.ac.uk/omeka/collections/document/3606.
7   'Interview with Harry Inkpen'. Anne Brodie. IBCC Digital Archive. https://ibccdigitalarchive.lincoln.ac.uk/omeka/collections/document/11136.
8   *The Peenemünde Raid.* Middlebrook. p.79.
9   *Nachtjagd Combat Archive: 1943. Part 2.* Boiten. p.69.
10   Wendy Carter (née Thomas, who during the war was known as Gwen). Interview with author, 2019.
11   Interview with James Ronald 'Jock' Cassels. IWM Sound Archive 14615.
12   'Black History Month Royal Air Force Heroes'. 1 October 2019. https://www.raf.mod.uk/news/articles/black-history-month-royal-air-force-heroes/.
13   *The Motherland Calls.* Bourne. pp.60–61.
14   Ulric Cross. Unpublished interview with Gabriel Christian.
15   'An interesting war'. Arthur Spencer. IBCC Digital Archive. https://ibccdigitalarchive.lincoln.ac.uk/omeka/collections/document/3606.
16   *The Peenemünde Raid.* Middlebrook. p.117.
17   Interview with Bill Griffiths. IWM Sound Archive 25267.
18   *Johnny: John Fauquier DSO and Two Bars DFC, Canada's Greatest Bomber Pilot.* Dave Birrell. Bomber Command Museum of Canada (2018), p.124.
19   *The Everlasting Arms.* Searby. p.157.
20   *The Peenemünde Raid.* Middlebrook. p.167.
21   *Schräge Musik* translates as 'Offbeat Music' or, more literally, 'Slanted/Oblique Music'.
22   *Nachtjagd Combat Archive: 1943. Part 2.* Boiten. p.70.
23   *Scotsman.* 19 August 1943.
24   *The Everlasting Arms.* Searby. pp.158–9.
25   From a speech by Ulric Cross in 2010, as part of Military History Week 2010 at Chaguaramas Military Museum in Trinidad. https://www.youtube.com/watch?v=SdSoTJ6VX7o; and from *The Motherland Calls.* Bourne. p.61.

26   'Interview with Arthur Spencer'. Pam Locker. IBCC Digital Archive. https://ibccdigitalarchive.lincoln.ac.uk/omeka/collections/document/3604.

27   Letter from Peter Lamprey to W. Gunton. IBCC Digital Archive. https://ibccdigitalarchive.lincoln.ac.uk/omeka/collections/document/6538.

28   TNA, AIR 25/155.

29   From a speech by Ulric Cross in 2010, as part of Military History Week 2010 at Chaguaramas Military Museum in Trinidad.

Chapter Seventeen – Oh Tannenbaum! Oh Tannenbaum!

1   Unless otherwise stated, the operational background and raid statistics used in this chapter have been assembled from the following TNA files: AIR 14/3770; AIR 20/5972; AIR 40/345; AIR 14/4130; AIR 14/1879.

2   Details of the German night-fighter reaction are taken from *Nachtjagd Combat Archive: 1943. Part 3: 23 September–31 December*. Theo Boiten. Red Kite Publishing (2018), pp.52–6.

3   Christie diary. RAFM MF10016.

4   Private Papers of Flight Lieutenant G.P. Dawson. IWM 16764.

5   TNA AIR 40/345.

6   All first-hand accounts are from the translations of statements held by Stadtarchiv Kassel, recorded by the Vermisstensuchstelle des Oberbürgermeisters der Stadt Kassel (VOSK) (the town's mayoral office) about the bombing of Kassel on 22–23 October 1943. The collection was catalogued by IBCC Digital Archive staff. 'Anton Sch and anonymous'. VOSK. IBCC Digital Archive. https://ibccdigitalarchive.lincoln.ac.uk/omeka/collections/document/8736.

7   'Oskar W'. VOSK. IBCC Digital Archive. https://ibccdigitalarchive.lincoln.ac.uk/omeka/collections/document/8717.

8   'Heinrich O'. VOSK. IBCC Digital Archive. https://ibccdigitalarchive.lincoln.ac.uk/omeka/collections/document/8940.

9   'Clara H'. VOSK. IBCC Digital Archive. https://ibccdigitalarchive.lincoln.ac.uk/omeka/collections/document/8940.

10   'Anton Sch and anonymous.' VOSK. IBCC Digital Archive. https://ibccdigitalarchive.lincoln.ac.uk/omeka/collections/document/8736.

11   'Anna D'. VOSK. IBCC Digital Archive. https://ibccdigitalarchive.lincoln.ac.uk/omeka/collections/document/8738.

12   'Kitty Michel', VOSK. IBCC Digital Archive. https://ibccdigitalarchive.lincoln.ac.uk/omeka/collections/document/8942.

13   'Gretel S'. VOSK. IBCC Digital Archive. https://ibccdigitalarchive.lincoln.ac.uk/omeka/collections/document/8734.

14 'Grete G'. VOSK. IBCC Digital Archive. https://ibccdigitalarchive. lincoln.ac.uk/omeka/collections/document/8934.

15 'Wilhelmine K'. VOSK. IBCC Digital Archive. https://ibccdigitalarchive. lincoln.ac.uk/omeka/collections/document/8726.

16 *Nachtjagd Combat Archive 1943. Part 3* Boiten. p.53.

17 *The Strategic Air Offensive Against Germany 1939–1945. Volume IV: Annexes and Appendices*. The Naval and Military Press Ltd (2006), Charles Webster and Noble Frankland. p.23.

18 *Nachtjagd Combat Archive, 1943. Part 3*. Boiten. pp.53–5.

19 'The Hell That Was Kassel'. *News of the World*. Undated. Included in the diary of Doug Renton. Bomber Command Museum Archives, Canada. https://www.bombercommandmuseumarchives.ca/s,rentondiary.pdf.

20 Wilfred Hart. IWM Sound Archive 15113.

21 TNA AIR 14/3770.

22 'Staff Sergeant Otto St'. VOSK. IBCC Digital Archive. https:// ibccdigitalarchive.lincoln.ac.uk/omeka/collections/document/8950.

23 'Andreas H and Emma H'. VOSK. IBCC Digital Archive. https:// ibccdigitalarchive.lincoln.ac.uk/omeka/collections/document/8956.

24 'Ludwig Heinemann and Karl M'. VOSK. IBCC Digital Archive. https:// ibccdigitalarchive.lincoln.ac.uk/omeka/collections/document/8804.

25 'Anton Sch and anonymous'. VOSK. IBCC Digital Archive. https://ibc cdigitalarchive.lincoln.ac.uk/omeka/collections/document/8736.

26 'Andreas H and Emma H'. VOSK. IBCC Digital Archive. https:// ibccdigitalarchive.lincoln.ac.uk/omeka/collections/document/8956.

27 TNA AIR 14/3770.

28 'Emil E'. VOSK. IBCC Digital Archive. https://ibccdigitalarchive. lincoln.ac.uk/omeka/collections/document/8952.

29 'Oskar Spieß'. VOSK. IBCC Digital Archive. https://ibccdigitalarchive. lincoln.ac.uk/omeka/collections/document/8951.

30 'Franz N and Elisabeth N'. VOSK. IBCC Digital Archive. https:// ibccdigitalarchive.lincoln.ac.uk/omeka/collections/document/7483.

31 'Minna G and Albrecht von E'. VOSK. IBCC Digital Archive.https:// ibccdigitalarchive.lincoln.ac.uk/omeka/collections/document/8741.

32 'Ludwig Heinemann and Karl M'. VOSK. IBCC Digital Archive. https:// ibccdigitalarchive.lincoln.ac.uk/omeka/collections/document/8804.

33 'Fritz Köhler'. VOSK. IBCC Digital Archive. https://ibccdigitalarchive. lincoln.ac.uk/omeka/collections/document/8708.

34 TNA AIR 40/345.

35 *Nachtjagd Combat Archive, 1943. Part 3*. Boiten. p.56.

36 'Interview with Jim Penny. One'. Mick Jeffery. IBCC Digital Archive. https://ibccdigitalarchive.lincoln.ac.uk/omeka/collections/ document/8822.

37 *Bomber Offensive*. Harris. p.185.

Chapter Eighteen – Tommy Oil

1   Brenda Bridger diary excerpts from the Allan Ball family archive, published with kind permission of Juliet Stockford.
2   Interview with Bennett. RAF Centre for Air and Space Power Studies. 1980.
3   *The Strategic Air Offensive Against Germany 1939–1945. Volume II: Endeavour.* Webster and Frankland. p.190.
4   *The Bombing War.* Overy. p.343.
5   *Flak.* Westermann. pp.230–31.
6   *People.* 30 August 1943.
7   *Daily Herald.* 29 August 1943.
8   *Liverpool Daily Post.* 9 November 1943.
9   *Daily Mail* cutting. Exact date unknown but approx. November 1943, as the Düsseldorf raid it refers to was on 3–4 November. Included in the diary of Doug Renton. https://www.bombercommandmuseumarchives.ca/s,rentondiary.pdf.
10   TNA, AIR 20/778.
11   TNA, AIR 14/1802.
12   *Nachtjagd Combat Archive: 1944. Part 2: 16 March–11 May.* Theo Boiten. Red Kite Publishing (2020), pp.14–15.
13   TNA, AIR 27-380-15; TNA, AIR 27-380-16.
14   Ball's story in this chapter is taken from his own account, held in his family's archive.
15   Although four turned back early because of mechanical faults.
16   *Pathfinder Cranswick.* Cumming. pp.148–9.
17   *The Berlin Raids.* Middlebrook. p.65.
18   *Eagle's Wings: The Autobiography of a Luftwaffe Pilot.* Hajo Herrmann. Guild Publishing (1991), p.186.
19   Private Papers of Flight Lieutenant G.P. Dawson. IWM 16764.
20   *Nachtjagd Combat Archive: 1943. Part 2.* Boiten. p.81.
21   Ibid. p.77.
22   *Eagle's Wings.* Herrmann. p.183.
23   Ibid. p.186.
24   Ibid. p.187.
25   Ibid. p.189.

Chapter Nineteen – The Berlin Method

1   *Courier Mail.* 24 January 1944.
2   Bomb load dropped, damage to Berlin and overall casualty stats for this chapter are taken from a variety of sources: author's own analysis of the

8 Group roll of honour from the RAFM; Webster and Frankland's official history; and *The Berlin Raids* by Martin Middlebrook.

3 Reprinted with permission of author and journalist Elinor Florence, who interviewed and wrote the stories of many veterans during the research for her bestselling novel *Bird's Eye View*, about a Canadian woman who joins the Women's Auxiliary Air Force and serves as an aerial photographic interpreter during the Second World War. You can read more at www.elinorflorence.com.

4 *Pathfinders*. William Anderson. Jarrolds (1946), p.77.

5 TNA, AIR 14/1802.

6 'Interview with Arthur Loudon'. Rob Gray and Lucy Davidson. IBCC Digital Archive. https://ibccdigitalarchive.lincoln.ac.uk/omeka/collections/document/2337.

7 Interview with Harris. RAF Centre for Air and Space Power Studies. 1977.

8 Private Papers of Flight Lieutenant G.P. Dawson. IWM 16764.

9 Ernie Holmes interview with Richard Buckley, 2010. Holmes family archive.

10 TNA, AIR 14/1761.

11 TNA, AIR 14/1802.

12 'Interview with Ernie Patterson. One'. Annie Moody. IBCC Digital Archive. https://ibccdigitalarchive.lincoln.ac.uk/omeka/collections/document/8821.

13 Ernie Holmes interview with Richard Buckley, 2010. Holmes family archive.

14 *Rear Gunner Pathfinders*. Smith. p.46.

15 'A Failure of Intelligence: Part I'. Freeman Dyson. *MIT Technology Review*. 1 November 2006. https://www.technologyreview.com/2006/11/01/227625/a-failure-of-intelligence/.

16 *Rear Gunner Pathfinders*. Smith. p.70.

17 Wendy Carter (née Thomas, who during the war was known as Gwen). Interview with author, 2019.

18 *The Pathfinder Companion*. Feast. p.89.

19 All losses figures from *Royal Air Force Bomber Command Losses of the Second World War. Volume Four: 1943*. W.R. Chorley. Midland Counties Publications (1996), pp.419–29.

20 TNA, AIR 20-767-23.

21 For March 1944: TNA, AIR 25/156.

22 Dick Raymond. Interview with author, 2018.

23 *Johnny*. Birrell. p.140.

24 Stephen Masters. IWM Sound Archive 10597.

25 *The Strategic Air Offensive Against Germany 1939–1945. Volume II: Endeavour*. Webster and Frankland. p.196.

26   Interview with Harris. RAF Centre for Air and Space Power Studies. 1977.
27   *Pathfinder*. Bennett. pp. 190, 202, 205.
28   TNA, AIR 14/2821.
29   Interview with Bennett. RAF Centre for Air and Space Power Studies. 1980.
30   Harris Papers RAFM.
31   Ibid.
32   Ibid.
33   *Master Airman: The Biography of Air Vice Marshal Donald Bennett*. Alan Bramson. Airlife (1985) p.92.
34   From a taped interview between Harris and Dudley Saward (Harris's biographer) in 1972, held by the Bomber Command Association at Hendon, cited in 'The Other Bomber Battle'. Cording. p.136.
35   TNA, AIR 14/2058.

Chapter Twenty – We Need to Talk About 5 Group

1   *Pathfinders*. Anderson. pp.82–3.
2   Interview with Donald Bennett. IWM Sound Archive 9378. While Bennett recalls 97 aircraft were shot down, most accounts conclude it was 95.
3   *Nachtjagd Combat Archive: 1944. Part 2*: Boiten. pp.36–7.
4   *Rear Gunner Pathfinders*. Smith. p.80.
5   Unpublished letters of John Kelly. RAFM X004-2500/012.
6   Dick Raymond. Interview with author, 2018.
7   Interview with Bennett. RAF Centre for Air and Space Power Studies. 1980.
8   Interview with Donald Bennett. IWM Sound Archive 9378.
9   Ibid.
10   TNA, AIR 14/2062.
11   *Master Airman*. Bramson. p.91.
12   Interview with Bennett. RAF Centre for Air and Space Power Studies. 1980.
13   *Pathfinder*. Bennett. pp.206–7.
14   TNA, AIR 27-688-7.
15   *Bomber Command*. Hastings. p.365.
16   As recorded by a medical officer: TNA, AIR 49/78.
17   Unpublished letters of John Kelly. RAFM X004-2500/012.
18   *The Bomber Command War Diaries*. Middlebrook and Everitt. pp.500–501.
19   From an undated copy of *Marker Magazine*, the post-war magazine of the Pathfinder Association.
20   Personal diary and record of operations with no. 35 Squadron. Captain J.K. Christie. RAFM MF10016.

21 Hawkins was the codename used – the master bomber for this raid was Edmund Keith Creswell, a highly regarded pilot with 35 Squadron who went on to be an accomplished master bomber.

22 Harris Papers RAFM.

Chapter Twenty-One – *Terrorflieger*

1 These statistics and the quote are from a blog written by the historian James Holland, 'Air Power Over Normandy', posted on 26 May 2014. http://www.griffonmerlin.com/2014/05/26/air-power-over-normandy/. For more on the Normandy campaign see also James Holland's book *Normandy '44: D-Day and the Battle for France.*

2 *The Bombing War.* Overy. p.375.

3 Dick Raymond. Interview with author, 2018.

4 RAFM X004-2500/012.

5 Ernie Holmes interview with Richard Buckley, 2010. Holmes family archive.

6 Based on a report from a British major who was a medical officer for four years at Obermassfeld Prisoner of War Hospital, an aircrew hospital, who outlined his observations and impressions of aircrew who had passed under his treatment. TNA, AIR 14/2831.

7 Holmes's escape account taken from interrogation by the RAF on his return to the UK in May 1945, held in the Holmes family archive.

8 From Holmes's POW notepad, held in the Holmes family archive.

9 'My Life In Stalag IV B'. *Newcastle Journal.* 18 April 1973. p.7.

10 'The Woman who broke INTO Stalag IVB'. *Newcastle Evening Chronicle.* 28 August 1980.

11 This astonishing story was first revealed by the *Daily Mirror* in June 1945 under the headline 'Mother Hid Five Months in Son's Gaol Camp', after Florence Barrington gave the paper an exclusive interview. Apart from a handful of local newspaper stories when she was reunited with some of the POWs many years later, and after her death in 1979, it has remained largely unknown for 80 years. While I've not been able to find official evidence of its veracity – and some of the details seem a little conflicted in the various press reports – a number of other POWs in the camp at the same time later confirmed it did happen, including Andrew Grainger, who was part of the camp's escape committee. Florence's story – with a big dollop of poetic licence – was made into a 1980s TV series and a 1992 film starring Hugh Grant. Both, according to critics, were largely forgettable.

Chapter Twenty-Two – Master Bombers

1 *Baz.* Birrell. p.110.

2   Ibid.
3   Unpublished letters of John Kelly. RAFM X004-2500/012. Unless other-
     wise indicated, all further quotes from Kelly's letters in this chapter are
     from this source.
4   'Pathfinder and Master Bomber'. *We Have Ways of Making You Talk*
     podcast. Episode 218. December 2020; Private Papers of Group Captain
     C.B. Owen DSO DFC. IWM 3754.
5   TNA, AIR 25/163.
6   *Pathfinder Cranswick*. Cumming. p.176.
7   Wendy Carter (née Thomas, who during the war was known as Gwen).
     Interview with author, 2019.
8   *Pathfinder Cranswick*. Cumming. p.187.
9   *Flak*. Westermann. pp.259–60.
10   *The Bombing War*. Overy. p.577.
11   Doug Renton diary. Bomber Command Museum of Canada. https://
     www.bombercommandmuseumarchives.ca/s,rentonstory.html.
12   'Pathfinder and Master Bomber'. *We Have Ways of Making You Talk*
     podcast. Episode 218. 15 December 2020; Private Papers of Group Cap-
     tain C.B. Owen DSO DFC. IWM 3754.
13   *Baz*. Birrell. p.126.
14   Ibid. p.119.
15   Ibid. p.122.
16   Ibid. p.129.
17   Ibid. p.137.
18   Ibid. p.138.
19   Ibid. p.146.
20   Ibid. p.202.
21   TNA, AIR 25/165.
22   *The Bombing War*. Overy. p.376.
23   Ibid. p.374.
24   RAFM X004-2500/012.
25   'V Group News, August 1944'. IBCC Digital Archive. https://
     ibccdigitalarchive.lincoln.ac.uk/omeka/collections/document/18150.
26   *Hampshire Telegraph and Post*. 3 November 1944.
27   *Hampshire Telegraph and Post*. 9 February 1945.
28   Author analysis of 8 Group deaths data held at RAFM and *Royal Air
     Force Bomber Command Losses of the Second World War. Volume Five:
     1944*. W.R. Chorley. Midland Counties Publications (1997), p.000.

Chapter Twenty-Three – The Wooden Wonder

1   Author analysis of 8 Group deaths data held at RAFM.

2   *The Bombing War.* Overy. p.378.
3   *Pathfinder Force: A History of 8 Group.* Gordon Musgrove. Macdonald and Jane's (1976), p.155.
4   From an interview with Netje van der Heijden, *The Saginaw News*, 1965. Holmes family archive.
5   H.A. Hooper DFC Line Book. Pathfinder Collection within the RAF Wyton Heritage Centre.
6   British newspaper report included in H.A. Hooper DFC Line Book. Pathfinder Collection within the RAF Wyton Heritage Centre.
7   TNA, AIR 14/1802.
8   *The Goebbels Diaries: The Last Days.* Hugh Trevor-Roper (ed.). Book Club Associates (1978), p.3.
9   Ibid. p.113.
10   Ibid. p.146.
11   Harris Papers RAFM.
12   *People.* 4 March 1945.
13   Private Papers of Flight Lieutenant S.P. Brunt. IWM 8545.
14   TNA, AIR 49/78.
15   *Journey's End: Bomber Command's Battle from Arnhem to Dresden and Beyond.* Kevin Wilson. Orion (2010), p.226.
16   *The Goebbels Diaries.* p.106.
17   *Dundee Courier.* 21 August 1944.
18   *Nachtjagd Combat Archive: 1943: Part 2.* Boiten. p.43.
19   Colin Bell. Interview with author, 2018.
20   *The Goebbels Diaries.* p.161.
21   'Mosquito Missions'. *We Have Ways of Making You Talk* podcast. Episode 154. 18 June 2020. https://play.acast.com/s/wehaveways/mosquitomissions.
22   T.G. Mahaddie, *Hamish: The Memoirs of Group Captain T.G. Mahaddie.* Ian Allen (1989). pp.101, 102.
23   *Daily Sketch*, undated. Pathfinder Collection within the RAF Wyton Heritage Centre.
24   *Pathfinder.* Bennett. p.210.
25   *The Goebbels Diaries.* p.136.
26   Ibid. p.18.

Chapter Twenty-Four – The Final Push

1   Letter from Harris to Portal. 18 November 1944. Cited in: 'The Other Bomber Battle'. Cording. pp.143–4.
2   TNA, AIR 14/2693.

3   'He flew with the R.A.F. to Ulm. Ex-pilot amazed by our new bombing technique'. IBCC Digital Archive. https://ibccdigitalarchive.lincoln.ac.uk/omeka/collections/document/2452.

4   Ronald Olsen. IWM Sound Archive 15743.

5   *They Led the Way: The Story of Pathfinder Squadron 156*. Michael P. Wadsworth. Highgate Publications (2002), p.118.

6   *The Bombing War*. Overy. p.388.

7   Author's own analysis of 8 Group Roll of Honour held by RAFM.

8   *London Gazette*. 23 March 1945.

9   *London Gazette*. 24 April 1945.

10 *Manchester Evening News*. 18 November 1944.

11 *Birmingham Mail*. 20 February 1945.

12 *Birmingham Mail*. 21 November 1944.

13 *Newcastle Evening Chronicle*. 5 May 1945.

14 Behind Hamburg and Dresden. TNA, AIR 14/3411.

15 Ronald Olsen. IWM Sound Archive 15743.

16 Interview with Thomas Mahaddie. IWM Sound Archive 10596.

17 *The Bombing War*. Overy. p.396.

18 Interview with Donald Bennett. IWM Sound Archive 9378.

19 John Ottewell. Interview with author, 2018.

20 Charlie Shepherd logbook. Shepherd family archive.

21 *The Bombing War*. Overy. p.397.

22 *Illustrated London News*. 21 April 1945.

23 *Daily Herald*. 29 March 1945.

24 TNA, AIR 25/173.

25 *Pathfinder*. Bennett. p.251.

26 *People and Planes: Stories from the Bomber Command Museum of Canada*. Dave Birrell. The Nanton Lancaster Society (2011), p.99.

27 TNA, AIR 25/173.

28 *The Motherland Calls*. Bourne. p.61.

Epilogue

1   Harris Papers RAFM.

2   TNA, AIR 14/2693. The 95 per cent statistic excludes Berlin.

3   Ibid.

4   Figure based on analysis of the 8 Group Roll of Honour book from Ely Cathedral. RAFM.

5   *The Wages of Destruction*. Adam Tooze. Penguin (2006), p.598.

6   Ibid. pp.597–602.

7   Figure based on analysis of the 8 Group Roll of Honour book from Ely Cathedral. RAFM.

8   'Operational Research in Bomber Command'. Basil Dickins. 1945. Lady Margaret Hall Archives.

9   TNA, AVIA 15/1379; RAFM X005-4810/025.

10   TNA, AVIA 15/1379.

11   Interview with Harris. RAF Centre for Air and Space Power Studies. 1977.

12   Harris Papers RAFM, as cited in 'The Other Bomber Battle'. Cording. p.145.

13   *Why the Allies Won*. Richard Overy. Jonathan Cape (1995), p.131.

14   *Buenos Aires Herald*. 18 July 1944.

15   *Rear Gunner Pathfinders*. Smith. p.42.

16   Figure based on analysis of the 8 Group Roll of Honour book from Ely Cathedral. RAFM.

17   Interview with Bernard O'Kane. IWM Sound Archive 11065.

18   From an issue of *Marker Magazine*. Macgown family archive.

19   Interview with Donald Bennett. IWM Sound Archive 9378.

20   *Pathfinder*. Bennett. p.252.

21   Bennett was responsible for 8 Group Pathfinders in Northern Europe. However, there was also a separate RAF Pathfinder squadron operating over the Balkans – 614 Squadron – which carried out some hair-raising missions of its own.

22   Dick Raymond. Interview with author, 2018.

23   Wendy Carter (née Thomas, who during the war was known as Gwen). Interview with author, 2019.

24   John Ottewell. Interview with author, 2018.

25   Colin Bell. Interview with author, 2019.

26   Ulric Cross. Unpublished interview with Gabriel Christian, 2011.

27   Personal diary and letters by Robert Maxwell Bryant. AWM PR00275.

Index